Trends in Latin American Psychology

Wilson López-López
Hernán Camilo Pulido-Martínez
Irene Giovanni-Aguilar
Editors

# Trends in Latin American Psychology

## Research Published in Universitas Psychologica

Springer

Pontificia Universidad JAVERIANA Bogotá | Facultad de Psicología

*Editors*
Wilson López-López
Faculty of Psychology
Pontificia Universidad Javeriana
Bogota, Colombia

Hernán Camilo Pulido-Martínez
Faculty of Psychology
Pontificia Universidad Javeriana
Bogota, Colombia

Irene Giovanni-Aguilar
Faculty of Psychology
Pontificia Universidad Javeriana
Bogota, Colombia

ISBN 978-3-031-87556-4 ISBN 978-3-031-87554-0 (eBook)
https://doi.org/10.1007/978-3-031-87554-0



The original submitted manuscript has been translated into English. The translation was done using artificial intelligence. A subsequent revision was performed by the author(s) to further refine the work and to ensure that the translation is appropriate concerning content and scientific correctness. It may, however, read stylistically different from a conventional translation.



This Springer imprint is published by the registered company Springer Nature Switzerland AG
The registered company address is: Gewerbestrasse 11, 6330 Cham, Switzerland

# Preface

The book *Trends in Latin America Psychology* emerges as an initiative by the academic publisher Springer Nature in collaboration with the journal *Universitas Psychologica*, published by the Faculty of Psychology at Pontificia Universidad Javeriana. This invitation acknowledges the journal's trajectory and academic impact, consolidated over more than two decades.

Since its founding, *Universitas Psychologica* has established itself as a key channel for disseminating scientific knowledge in Latin America. Over its 23-year history, it has published more than seven thousand articles, written by thousands of authors and reviewed by scholars from all five continents. The journal has served as a privileged space for academic dialogue, fostering the exchange of ideas, critical discussion, and the advancement of psychology as a discipline in the Spanish-speaking world. This international recognition reflects its position as one of the most prominent references in the region—one of its major achievements. In acknowledgment of this academic standing and its impact on Ibero-America, Springer Nature saw an opportunity to bring high-quality research from the region to geographically distant scientific communities, thus giving rise to this project.

A commitment to editorial excellence has been crucial in achieving this impact. From its early inclusion in regional databases such as Redalyc and SciELO to its positioning in international indexes like PsycInfo, Scopus, and the Web of Science Core Collection, *Universitas Psychologica* has solidified itself as a reliable source of knowledge. These achievements have been made possible through the implementation of rigorous editorial processes, spanning from content evaluation to effective visibility and dissemination strategies, all supported by a robust administrative and financial management framework.

Editorial challenges have been guided by the pursuit of excellence, requiring swift adaptation to technological advancements in information and communication. One of the most significant milestones in the journal's history was its transition to a fully digital format, completely moving away from print. This change not only modernized its editorial management through online platforms but also enhanced the reader experience. For instance, users can now interact with different sections of articles, directly download tables and figures, and monitor real-time usage metrics such as downloads, citations, and altmetrics that measure impact on social media. Today, the journal aligns with international principles, such as those established in the DORA Declaration, which advocates for a shift in evaluation systems—moving away from assessing journals as a whole toward focusing on the impact of individual articles.

Furthermore, the quality of published content has been upheld through a double-blind peer review system and the development of standardized evaluation formats. Over the years, more than a thousand reviewers have contributed to a process characterized by theoretical and methodological rigor, while also adopting a constructive and pedagogical approach that has positively influenced authors' work. These evaluation processes have evolved over time, reflecting broader changes within Latin American academic communities. The growth of doctoral training in the region has played a key role in enhancing both the quality of submitted articles and the peer review process.

The journal's strategic management has also prioritized visibility and dissemination. Visibility is understood as a process that fosters academic engagement and, ultimately, knowledge transfer—strengthening the connection between researchers and their scholarly outputs across diverse academic communities. This engagement extends to professors, researchers, students, and specialized users or professionals from various disciplines who find practical applications for the published research.

Dissemination, as a process, involves the social appropriation of knowledge—ensuring that published findings reach broader society. In this regard, the journal has maintained a consistent presence in media outlets, and many of its articles have contributed to public policy discussions. Additionally, the journal's digital platform facilitates content sharing on social media while enabling engagement through comments and discussions arising from the published research.

None of these achievements would have been possible without the dedicated editorial and administrative teams, including faculty members who have guided the journal's editorial coordination and administrators who have secured resources and enhanced management processes.

Knowledge ecosystems linked to scientific communication illustrate how academic actors continuously redefine their thematic, theoretical, and methodological interests, thereby constructing interconnected networks of knowledge (López-López & Rooryck, 2022). The articles published in *Universitas Psychologica* across various platforms underscore its relevance in regional psychology, enabling an understanding of how published research maps the discipline's ecosystem in Latin America. This includes identifying trends in research incentives, investments in science and technology, and priority topics on national and international social and political agendas (López-López et al., 2023).

This book is received by the Faculty of Psychology at Pontificia Universidad Javeriana as a commemoration of the 22nd anniversary of *Universitas Psychologica*. Through this prestigious publication by Springer Nature, the journal once again pushes boundaries, aiming for greater visibility in new regions of the world while pioneering the use of machine translation software to expand its reach. This support reinforces our commitment to sustaining editorial excellence, ensuring that

*Universitas Psychologica*, as an infinite network of knowledge, continues to transcend time—an endeavor that remains a core mission of our Faculty.

Bogota, Colombia Wilson López-López

## References

López-López, W., Lucio-Arias, D., Díaz-Nova, A. M., & Silva, L. M. (2023). International collaboration in Latin American psychology through the analysis of co-authorship networks. *Trends in Psychology, 31*, 503–519. https://doi.org/10.1007/s43076-023-00266-y

López-López, W., & Rooryck, J. (2022). La coalición S en el contexto del ecosistema de conocimiento científico de América Latina: Asimetrías e implicaciones. In E. Príncipe, E. Rode, & S. de Mello (org.) *Comunicação científica aberta* (pp. 229–240).

# Contents

# Part I
# Social and Community Psychology

# Introduction to Part I: Social and Community Psychology

**Hernán Camilo Pulido Martínez**

## A Small Mosaic Depicting the Application of Social Psychology in Latin America

In the context of the diversity of ways of producing knowledge that fall under the label of social psychology, this section considers five chapters that constitute a sample of this field in Latin America. To contextualize and discuss these chapters within the production that takes place at the regional and global level, it is argued that the diversity of ways of conceiving what, at a historical moment, can be considered social psychology leads to de-essentializing it, as well as considering that the delimitations of social psychology focused on the practices carried out by psychologists show a greater breadth to include what is done in the peripheral worlds of psychology.

## The Diversity of Social Psychologies

In social psychology, as in other areas of the discipline, it is not easy to establish clear boundaries between the different branches that may comprise it. Clearly, this fact is demonstrated in the specialized literature, where in books and articles it is possible to find a wide range of proposals referring to different ways of composing the field known as social psychology (Muchinik, 2002; Munne, 2008).

This situation of constant mobility in the demarcation is caused by the very nature of the ways in which divisions are established in academic knowledge. As social studies of science have shown, researchers, when proposing divisions or boundaries, do more than just confirm the state of a field; they constitute it

H. C. Pulido Martínez (✉)
Pontificia Universidad Javeriana, Bogotá, Colombia
e-mail: cpulido@javeriana.edu.co



W. López-López et al. (eds.), *Trends in Latin American Psychology*,
https://doi.org/10.1007/978-3-031-87554-0_1

(Restrepo-Forero, 2003). Particularly for social psychology, the proposals that have been constructed by those interested in establishing what social psychology is, have done more than just confirm how it is configured; they have constructed it in very diverse ways.

In this context, it's not surprising that there are so many ways to define what can be understood as social psychology. For illustration, one can refer to the proposal by Blanco and De la Corte (2002), who consider that social psychology comprises fields such as work and organizational psychology, social health psychology, community and social services psychology, environmental research, legal and political psychology, psycho-social theory and metatheory, social psychology of language, research on emotion, as well as studies on group processes and social identity. Similarly, it's relatively common for other researchers to focus on the controversies and subsequent crises that have arisen to denote demarcations in which social psychology can be considered as composed in terms of its psychological and sociological variants (Garrido & Álvarez, 2007; Quiroz-Palacios, 2011). It is also common to distinguish two branches of social psychology: one, the experimental approach, which is currently reflected in fields such as social neuroscience; and the other, the constructionist approach, which emphasises language as a tool for constructing relationships and understanding the world through a socially discursive perspective (Cruz, 2004; Garay et al., 2005; Milagres-Boechat & Teixeira-Portugal, 2010; Sisto-Campos, 2012).

In terms of what the field of social psychology should be, there are also ways of proposing distinctions that have been particularly relevant for countries located on the periphery of the "worlds of psychology" (Moghaddam, 1987). These "other" proposals for describing social psychology emphasize the geographical location where knowledge is produced. In response to narratives that legitimize the universal enterprise of psychology as that produced by North Atlantic countries, these versions about what social psychology constructed from the global south is, opt to assert a different geopolitical position. For this purpose, these forms of asserting what social psychology is affirm that it has national characteristics.

This demarcation strategy highlights that the versions presented as the official understanding of social psychology are essentially the national psychologies of countries that have developed psychological concepts, such as the United States and some European countries like the United Kingdom, France, and Germany (Pulido-Martínez & Urbina-Barón, 2019). Therefore, they do not represent the factual global reality of the psychological enterprise. In this context, a common method of establishing boundaries points out that there are psychologies presented as universal, and other psychologies that are developed in countries that receive, replicate, adapt, hybridize, and reinvent this knowledge in the global south.

These latter demarcations aim to indicate, on one hand, that the "official" social psychology is just one of the many indigenous psychologies, since it is the product of a specific geographical location, shaped by the issues of that particular context. However, researchers note that even though it is an indigenous psychology, it is often presented with a universalist character, seeking validation around the world (Kalampalikis et al., 2006; Molinari, 2004). On the other hand, these alternative types of demarcations claim a certain place by adding what has been termed a "surname" to the social psychological knowledge. This results in national social psychologies, for example, Spanish (Blanco & De la Corte, 2002) or Brazilian (Prioli-Cordeiro & Spink, 2018), as well as the distinction of "regional" social psychologies such as those with a Latin American (Arias-Gallegos, 2011; Montero, 2010; Rodríguez-Villegas, 2017) or Ibero-American nuance (Paez et al., 2021).

For peripheral locations (Colussi, 2022), perhaps the most intriguing approach to shaping social psychology is represented by what can be termed "counter-psychological" proposals (Parker, 2007). In this regard, researchers, for example, claim a place for the psychology practiced in the Latin American region by contrasting it with a distinct psychological knowledge that generates more suitable practices for solving local problems. In contrast, these alternative forms of social psychology are more fitting than the hegemonic psychology produced in North Atlantic societies, which seeks to present itself as official and, therefore, universal. A prime example of this type of proposal is described by Maritza Montero, who points out that community psychology, critical social psychology, and liberation psychology, as practiced in the region, differ from the rest of the world in epistemological, theoretical, and methodological aspects (Montero, 2004).

Indeed, this variability in defining social psychology is a phenomenon that also extends to other related disciplines (Restrepo, 2017). Following this author proposition, it can be stated that the variety of demarcations, rather than being a matter of imprecision, is a characteristic aspect of the social sciences, which in practice do not conform to a defining essence. In this regard, as established in the literature, the boundaries within and between different approaches to psychology are influenced by factors such as the social context, the state of development in the field, and the diverse criteria held by members of the discipline. These criteria concern perspectives, themes, research methods, geographical regions, and academic communities that should be included to define what is considered social psychology at a particular historical moment (Kruglanski & Stroebe, 2012; Lubek, 1992; Jaraba-Barros, 2015; Richards, 2002).

Therefore, it's important to note that acknowledging the flexibility present in the ways social psychology is defined opens up space to consider that it can be delineated based on the idea that social psychology is what those who consider themselves part of social psychology in any of its variants do (Pulido Martinez & Jaraba Barrios, 2017). This broad proposal for studying social disciplines, which suspends essentiality and emphasizes practice (Restrepo, 2012), makes it feasible to view social psychology in particular by increasing coverage and understanding about both the diversity of manifestations that can fall under the label of social psychology and the role it plays in contemporary societies where it arrives as a foreign product that is appropriated.

In considering the role and operations of psychology in societies that do not produce psychological objects, two central aspects emerge. Firstly, it can be thought that local problems have a differential relationship with those for which psychological concepts were created and strategies developed, as provided by the psychological discipline. In this context, the process of making concepts and strategies relevant demands, in the best of cases, adaptations of psychological proposals to the changing cultural conditions, among other factors.

Secondly, as Castaño and Sanchez (1978) pointed out, local problems may become subordinate to the science that presents itself as universal. In this case, the tendency to act "as if" local problems were similar to those for which psychological concepts and strategies were formulated regularly emerges. In any case, this division between producers of psychological objects and consumers of the same establishes a geopolitics of psychology. This geopolitics reveals a clear division of psychological labor between those who produce psychological objects and others who disseminate them around the world.

## Local Contributions as Inputs to Social Psychology

The five chapters presented below serve as examples of the diverse approaches to practicing psychology in the region. As such, each of these works highlights central issues that are currently impacting Latin American countries.

Firstly, Muñoz et al. (2020) in their chapter analyze the particular situation Chile went through with the social protests that took place during the pandemic. While it is an analysis of the specific situation that this country experienced, it can also be a useful analysis for other places in the region where, even under the emergency health conditions caused by the pandemic, citizens took to the streets in political protest. Unlike other works in social psychology that ignore social class as a central category, in this work, it is considered a mediating variable of social action. As the authors point out, social class has been relegated in social studies, an issue that represents a real deficiency because, as the study shows, when social class is introduced as a conceptual and methodological instance, a series of data emerge that reflect, contrary to what would be expected, that those who participated most in the marches were not the subjects in the most precarious or vulnerable conditions, but rather those belonging to the middle and upper strata who participated in these social movements. This point is central to discussing the problems of participation and social criticism, since, according to this study, it is those who have certain privileges who are in a position to promote and join the protests.

Also, in relation to national problems that are connected with the historical, social, and cultural processes of a particular country, Giovanni et al. (2020) study the reintegration of former combatants in Colombia. Based on the contribution of studies indicating that a successful reintegration process should involve support not solely focused on the individual, but also considering the group of former combatants and their families. Contrary to many psychological interventions carried out with former combatants, the systemic perspective adopted by the researchers to identify the factors that facilitate or hinder reintegration reaffirms the role of the family, relationships, and communication within it. This approach ensures more relevant interventions for the better reintegration of this population.

In the third chapter, Reyes-Valenzuela et al. (2017) present a research involving three Latin American countries in the complex phenomenon of contemporary migration. The social integration of Colombian and Cuban migrant populations in Ecuadorian society is the focus of this study. These two populations migrate for different reasons, the first due to political violence, the second due to economic limitations, and they show differences in their degree of integration. Conceptually, this chapter places the relationship between social integration within a sociological and psychosocial framework, which, the authors point out, has not been sufficiently considered by researchers in studying such phenomena. The results highlight the importance of job market integration, differences in group adaptation, and some recommendations for the formulation and implementation of public policies. As demonstrated by this study, even in cases of cultural proximity, populations differ, necessitating scientific approaches that identify the specific processes involving migrants from each country. The studies contribute differences in terms of aspects that hinder or facilitate integration. In general terms, the authors emphasize that interventions to achieve better social integration should not only encompass migrant populations but also consider the members of the receiving society, who welcome people in search of better well-being.

The study by Jimenez-Bustos et al. (2017a) examined the relationship between ethnic identity and social behaviors in the adolescent population of the Mapuche community in southern Chile. Utilizing various instruments, the researchers found that a stronger development of ethnic identity correlates with a decrease in antisocial behaviors in the population under study. However, they also discovered no significant relationship between ethnic identity and the presence of prosocial behaviors. Given the importance of these findings, the study's recommendations emphasize the need for separate considerations when intervening in these populations.

In the final chapter, central aspects are discussed that are crucial for some approaches to psychology present in the Latin American region. The debate between constructivist and realist approaches in social psychology forms the core of the arguments presented by XXX. This represents a regional interpretation of the ongoing discussion about social psychology. Advocating for the integrative advantages of the psychosocial perspective, the chapter analyzes various aspects of both constructivist and realist social psychology from the perspectives of European and Latin American authors. The psychosocial perspective and critical realism, involving representatives of integrative work such as Ignacio Martin-Baro, hold a central position to reaffirm the repeatedly expressed intention to value forms of psychology that consider situations of injustice and social vulnerability. The aim is to transform these situations with interventions that go beyond those traditionally prescribed within the discipline.

## Various Manifestations of Practicing Social Psychology: A Single Region

These five chapters compose a small mosaic that illustrates the variety of perspectives and issues considered within the boundaries of the field of social psychology in the Latin American region. The journal *Universitas Psychologica* has contributed to the construction of this type of mosaic by being a forum where researchers with diverse conceptual perspectives can present their research and contribute to what is called social psychology.

In this context, by being included in this mosaic, the social protest introducing an analysis related to social class, the reintegration of ex-combatants emphasizing the importance of involving their families, the differences in migration between countries in the region, the ethnic identity and the reduction of antisocial behaviors, as well as the variations that psychology assumes when it aims to be non-constructivist in the region, demonstrate how local issues are at the heart of indigenous production. So that, this production, as it should be, can be termed critical, in terms of finding unique solutions to local problems by using, adapting, and appropriating the tools provided by the discipline. These chapters, therefore, are contributions that enhance what has been called the ongoing and universal improvement program of the discipline and to the welfare of those who are under study (Rose, 1996).

## References

Arias-Gallegos, W. L. (2011). Líneas comunes en la historia de la psicología latinoamericana. *Revista de Psicología Arequipa, 1*(1), 27–47.

Blanco, A., & De la Corte, L. (2002). La década 1989-1998 en la psicología española: Un análisis de la investigación en psicología social. *Papeles del Psicólogo, 82*, 25–43. https://www.redalyc.org/pdf/778/77808203.pdf

Castaño, D., & Sanchez, G. (1978). Problemas de la importacion de la tecnologiapsicolaboral en los paises en desarrollo. *Revista Latinoamericana de Psicologia, 10*(1), 71–82.

Colussi, M. (2022). ¡Psicología Latinoamericana? *Revista de Investigación. Escuela de Ciencias Psicológicas, 5*, 79–95. https://doi.org/10.57247/riec.vi5.87

Cruz, J. E. (2004). Apuntes sobre una historia del paradigma dominante en psicología social. *Revista de Estudios Sociales, 18*, 77–88. http://www.scielo.org.co/pdf/res/n18/n18a09.pdf

Garay, A., Iñiguez, L., & Martínez, L. M. (2005). La perspectiva discursiva en la psicología social. *Subjetividad y Procesos Cognitivos, 7*, 105-130.https://www.redalyc.org/pdf/3396/339630246006.pdf.

Garrido, A., & Álvarez, J. L. (2007). *Psicología social: Perspectivas psicológicas y sociológicas*. McGraw-Hill/Interamericana de España.

Giovanni, I., Duran, A. D., Aponte, D. M., & Laverde, D. J. (2020). Factores que facilitan y dificultan los procesos de integración de excombatientes y sus familias. *Universitas Psychologica, 19*. https://doi.org/10.11144/Javeriana.upsy19.ffdp

Jaraba-Barros, B. A. (2015). Saberes y prácticas psicológicos desde los estudios sociales de la ciencia y la tecnología. *Summa Psicológica UST, 12*(1), 5–7. https://doi.org/10.18774/summa-vol12.num1-248

Jimenez-Bustos, R. A., Perez-Luco-Arenas, R. X., & Bustamante-Rivera, G. E. (2017a). Identidad etnica y conductas sociales en adolescentes indigenas mapuche sancionados por la ley de responsabilidad penal adolescente en regionies del sur de Chile. *Universitas Psychologica, 16*(1), 1–22. https://doi.org/10.11144/Javeriana.upsy16-1.iecs

Kalampalikis, N., Delouvée, S., & Pétard, J.-P. (2006). Historical spaces of social psychology. *History of the Human Sciences, 19*(2), 23–43. https://doi.org/10.1177/0952695106065127

Kruglanski, A. W., & Stroebe, W. (2012). The making of social psychology. En A. W. Kruglanski, & W. Stroebe, Handbook of the history of social psychology. 3–18. : Taylor & Francis Group.

Lubek, I. (1992). The histor(y/es) of social psycholog(y/es). *Canadian Psychology, 33*(3), 657–661. https://doi.org/10.1037/h0084671

Milagres-Boechat, F., & Teixeira-Portugal, F. (2010). Pós-construcionismo e neo-experimentalismo em Psicologia Social. *Estuidos e Pesquisas en Psicologia, 10*(3), 930–945. https://www.redalyc.org/pdf/4518/451844633018.pdf

Moghaddam, F. (1987). Psychology in the three worlds: As reflected by the crisis in social psychology and the move toward indigenous psychology. *American Psychologist, 42*(10), 912–920. https://doi.org/10.1037/0003-066X.42.10.912

Molinari, J. M. (2004). Hacia una nueva geopolítica de la psicología: Prospectiva, conceptos y tendencias. *Acta Psiquiátrica y Psicológica de América Latina, 50*(1), 25–33.

Montero, M. (2004). Relaciones Entre Psicología Social Comunitaria, Psicología Crítica yPsicología de la Liberación: Una Respuesta Latinoamericana. *Psicoperspectivas, 13*(2), 17–28. Obtenido de https://www.scielo.cl/scielo.php?script=sci_arttext&pid=S0718-22282004000200002

Montero, M. (2010). Crítica, autocrítica y construcción de teoría en la psicología social latinoamericana. *Revista Colombiana de Psicología, 19*(2), 177–191. http://www.scielo.org.co/pdf/rcps/v19n2/v19n2a03.pdf

Muchinik, E. (2002). Psicología social. Aspectos históricos. In J. F. Morales-Domínguez, A. Kornblit, D. Páez-Rovira, & D. Asún (Eds.), *Psicología social* (pp. 15–29). Pearson Education.

Munne, F. (2008). *La psicología social como ciencia teórica*. Universitat de Barcelona.

Muñoz, N., Asún, R., & Zúñiga, C. (2020). Recuperando la clase social en el estudio de la acción colectiva. El caso de un movimiento socioambiental chileno. *Universitas Psychologica, 19*(1), 1–15. https://doi.org/10.11144/Javeriana.upsy19.rcse

Paez, D., Sonia, P., Gracia, M. C., Pinto, I., Elena, Z. E., Lopez-Lopez, W., et al. (2021). ¿Por qué es necesaria una red virtual que potencie la producción cientítica Iberoamericana? *SOCIOTAM Revista Multidisciplinaria de Investigaciones sobre la Sociedad, la Política y la Cultura, 21*(2), 61–88. Obtenido de https://sociotam.uat.edu.mx/index.php/SOCIOTAM/article/view/187/150

Parker, I. (2007). *Revolution in psychology: Alienation to emancipation*. Pluto Press.

Prioli-Cordeiro, M., & Spink, M. J. (2018). Apontamentos sobre a História da Psicologia Social no Brasil. *Estudos e Pesquisas em Psicologia, 18*(4), 1068–1086. http://pepsic.bvsalud.org/pdf/epp/v18nspe/v18nspea03.pdf.

Pulido Martinez, H. C., & Jaraba Barrios, B. A. (2017). Entre psicologias, practicas y descentramientos: o de la constitucion de la subjetividad de los psicólogos. *Psicoperspectivas, 16*(3), 99–109. https://doi.org/10.5027/psicoperspectivas-Vol16-Issue3-fulltext-1078

Pulido-Martínez, H. C., & Urbina-Barón, A. M. (2019). Geopolíticas del Conocimiento Psicológico y Riesgos Psicosociales: Reproduciendo la Subordinación por Medio de las Tesis de Grado y Postgrado. *Psykhe, 28*(1). https://doi.org/10.7764/psykhe.27.2.1198

Quiroz-Palacios, A. (2011). Historia, desarrollo y perspectivas de la psicología social. *Katharsis, 12*, 9–36. https://bibliotecadigital.iue.edu.co/bitstream/20.500.12717/2178/1/152-Texto%20del%20artículo-5002-1-10-20200913.pdf

Restrepo, E. (2012). Antropologiasdiscidentes. *Cuadernos de Antropología Social, 35*, 55–69. Obtenido de https://www.aacademica.org/eduardo.restrepo/67

Restrepo, E. (2017). Antropologías del mundo. Perspectiva analítica y política. In A. Mejias (Ed.), *Antroologías del sur. Cinco miradas* (pp. 99–126). Biblioteca Digital Latinoamericana de Antropología.

Restrepo-Forero, O. (2003). *On writing review articles and constructing fields of study*. [Master's thesis, York University]. York.

Reyes-Valenzuela, C., Jaramillo-Tejada, F. J.-S.-S.-F., & Martos-Méndez, M. J. (2017). Dimensiones de integración social en población colombiana y cubana que vive en que vive en Quito, Ecuador. *Universitas Psychologica, 16*(5). https://doi.org/10.11144/Javeriana.upsy16-5.disp

Richards, G. (2002). The psychology of psychology. A historically grounded sketch. *Theory and Psychology, 12*(1), 7–36.

Rodríguez-Villegas, E. (2017). Reflexiones en torno a la tradición crítica en la psicología social de América Latina. *Quaderns de Psicologia, 19*(3), 209–315. https://doi.org/10.5565/rev/qpsicologia.1403

Rose, N. (1996). *Inventing ourselves. Psychology, power and regulation*. Sage.

Sisto-Campos, V. (2012). Análisis del discurso y psicología: A veinte años de la revolución discursiva. *Revista de Psicología de la Universidad de Chile, 21*(1), 185–208.

# For a Non-constructionist Critical Social Psychology: Reflections from the Critical Realism of Ignacio Martín-Baró

**Amalio Blanco, Luis de la Corte, and José Manuel Sabucedo**

At this stage in the development of social sciences, it is widely accepted that our understanding of the world is shaped not by nature but by social constructions or 'social artifacts.' These constructs emerge from active and cooperative exchanges between people, as described by Gergen's second principle of social constructionism (1985, 1996, 2015). Concurrently, Lewin's principle of irreducibility reminds us that these social constructions exist at an onto-epistemic level that is distinct from and irreducible to the interpersonal and individual levels (Jiménez Burillo, 2005). This level of reality coexists with three others: the physicochemical (the most basic), the biological, and the cultural. These levels are not separated by ontological breaks but are characterized by continuity, exchange, interdependence, and mutual influence. These processes form the core of the psychosocial perspective, which is primarily concerned with the 'third level' encompassing intelligent life, mental processes, and social interactions. However, this perspective does not exclude the foundational levels but rather depends on their presence, thus moving away from traditional dualisms famously critiqued by Kant in his *Critique of Pure Reason*. Our main concern is the social level and its interactions with mental processes (subjectivity). It is essential to consider how these interactions manifest in culture and

*This chapter is the English translation of an article originally published in Spanish as*: Blanco, A., Corte, L. de la, & Sabucedo, J. M. (2018). Para una psicología social crítica no construccionista: reflexiones a partir del realismo crítico de Ignacio Martín-Baró. *Universitas Psychologica, 17*(1), 1–25. https://doi.org/10.11144/Javeriana.upsy17-1.pscc. *Please cite the original version of the article in Spanish.*

A. Blanco (✉) · L. de la Corte
Universidad Autónoma de Madrid, Madrid, Spain
e-mail: amalio.blanco@uam.es

J. M. Sabucedo
Universidad de Santiago de Compostela, A Coruña, Spain



W. López-López et al. (eds.), *Trends in Latin American Psychology*,
https://doi.org/10.1007/978-3-031-87554-0_2

within the macro- and microsocial structures that shape people's lives. These structures are influenced by cultural values and beliefs, socialization patterns, and models of interpersonal and intergroup relationships. This chapter aims to explore the necessary interdependence between objective and subjective levels of reality and the implications of their interactions. We will also address the consequences of these interactions and advocate for a critical examination of their permanence or change. Throughout this discussion, the epistemological stance of Ignacio Martín-Baró will serve as a crucial reference point.

## The Necessary Dialogue Between Sensitivity and Understanding

In a short essay on the theory of knowledge of dialectical materialism written in 1963, Martín-Baró sets forth two proposals that we will find again, more elaborated, in his mature theoretical formulations. In the first of them, and in open opposition to the main thesis of materialism, he affirms the existence of "real beings that are not matter" (Martín-Baró, 2016, p. 85). The social psychologist who will become later will group them around ideology and will surprise both his own and strangers with that heterodox definition of social psychology as "the scientific study of action as ideological" (Martín-Baró, 1983, p. 17). By defending the real existence of entities that lack a material substrate, the philosophy student believes he has become immune to idealism: "we are far from any shadow of idealism," he affirms categorically (Martín-Baró, 2016, p. 86).

Following the trail of Saint Thomas, who asserted that every being is 'potentially intelligible,' Martín-Baró in his second proposal maintains that the knowable nature of every being does not imply that its existence is encapsulated by its knowability. Instead, he argues that "its reality, its existence is indifferent to whether we know it or not" (Martín-Baró, 2016, p. 88). The existence of a reality that goes unnoticed by our consciousness but becomes visible through its consequences at different levels of interpersonal and intergroup behavior is now central to a long-standing research tradition in the field of automatic and unconscious information processing (Dijksterhuis, 2010). This challenges the notion that meaningful action between interlocutors requires language and conversation and, consequently, dismisses the idea that such interactions lack significance and impact.

We are faced with two far-reaching arguments that distance their author from social constructionism[1] and reveal a clear lack of enthusiasm from the 21-year-old student for the exclusive dualisms of naturalism and idealism. Instead, Martín-Baró

[1] In a passionate article, Carl Ratner maintains the idea that the "New Psychology of Liberation" that interprets Martín-Baró from social constructionism, contradicts this author's Psychology of Liberation in the following aspects: (a) it articulates concepts that contradict Martín-Baró's words; (b) they omit (ignore) important concepts handled by the author; (c) they distort his ideas by quoting them incorrectly and presenting them in an incomplete and decontextualized way, and (d) they turn concrete psychosocial issues into undefined and bland abstractions (Ratner, 2015, p. 60).

suggests a continuous flow between subjectivity and objectivity in a dialectical synthesis, postulating the principle of mutually constitutive interaction between the human being (subjectivity) and society (Martín-Baró, 2016, p. 191). His initial, somewhat timid steps are evident in his youth essay "Suffer and Be" (Martín-Baró, 2016). A more systematic and informed development of these ideas would come years later, during his mature years, following a simple argument: the objective conditions of subjectivity cannot be ignored. Although subjectivity "is not visible and often results in difficult or questionable measurement," it nonetheless "constitutes an objective reality, known or not" (Martín-Baró, 2016, p. 206).

These conditions refer us to the "structural and historical character of realities and human acts [and] move us away from all type of idealistic ethical reflection that does not take this character into account in a direct and immediate way," he would write in another youth essay (Martín-Baró, 2016, p. 198). Along with the historical, which social constructionism prioritizes and which over a hundred years ago no one questions, the structural, where the social finds regularity and constancy, something that constructionism rejects by principle. From his point of view, and to summarize it with a broad brushstroke, things would go, alternatively and indistinctly, from heaven (epistemological priority of the products of reason: the primary is the spirit; reality is reduced to the idea) to the earth (the primary is matter, facts susceptible to observation through the senses), and from the earth (explanations based on empirically proven facts that give rise to universal laws) to heaven (descriptions based on perceptions and subjective interpretations of reality supported by linguistic conventions), to recall the well-known metaphor of Marx and Engels in *Feuerbach. Opposition between materialist and idealistic conceptions*.

In the epistemological framework of social psychology, this position does not represent any novelty. That was the path followed, for example, by Kurt Lewin in his *Comparative Epistemology* (Lewin, 1991), Lev Vygotsky in his "dialectical synthesis" (Vygotski, 1931/1995) and George H. Mead in his successive and never well-considered approaches to the study of the consciousness of meaning and of the main one of all, the "*self*" (Mead, 1964, 1972). They are not the only ones who bet decisively on overcoming that one-way epistemology to which empiricist materialism and idealist rationalism succumbed and which social constructionism now worships. Max Horkheimer also did. His position interests us especially not only because he is one of the most distinguished figures of philosophical thought of the last century, but for being the most qualified representative of critical theory: in reality, naturalism is not radically wrong, because "the spirit is indissolubly united with its object, nature" (there is no ontological rupture between the levels of reality), so that every psychic process ("spiritual act" is the expression he uses) "implies some kind of matter or nature." Presented as an absolute, the spirit and its products (the ideas, the meanings, the narratives, the language, and the interpretive repertoires) become pure myth, he wrote in *The critique of instrumental reason* (1947), one of the most emblematic works of the past century (Horkheimer, 2002, p. 176). Let's remember that this was precisely Marx's argument against the "mystification" that dialectics suffers at the hands of Hegel: the idea turned into the demiurge of the real.

All of this is true, but it would be unfair not to remember, and acknowledge, that at its origin, the relationship of interdependence and mutual influence between the self and the world, nature and history, biology and culture, etc., has as its indisputable reference the synthesis between rationalism and empiricism with which, in a lapidary way, begins the *Critique of Pure Reason*, whose first edition dates from 1781. In it, Kant tries to reconcile the two apparently antagonistic tendencies that had debated until that moment the theory of knowledge: the metaphysical rationalism of Descartes and the realism of the English empiricists, with Bacon at the head. Kant writes, "There can be no doubt that all our knowledge begins with experience," with the activation of our senses in the face of the stimulation of a certain object; but not all of it comes from that experience, "for it could well happen that our empirical knowledge was a composition of what we receive from impressions and what we apply from our own faculty of knowing" (Kant, 1994, p. 98, italics ours), of what the subject properly contributes from himself (his way of perceiving and interpreting reality).

Knowledge is at the same time the fruit of experience (facts, data, and sensory impressions arising from contact with objects of reality: empirical thought) and of the thoughts and ideas that, apart from it, the subject contributes ('applies'). There are a priori elements (pure knowledge) that are 'absolutely' independent of experience. Alongside knowledge 'ruled by objects,' Kant admits the possibility that experience can be regulated by concepts (the possibility of a priori knowledge apart from objects). Both sensitivity (the capacity to receive representations of objects) and understanding (the capacity to produce representations and think about objects) are indispensable in the task of knowledge: "understanding cannot perceive and senses cannot think anything. Only when they unite does knowledge result," so that "thoughts without content are empty; intuitions without concepts are blind," he writes in the Introduction to the chapter on transcendental logic (Kant, 1994, p. 132). Applied to psychology, Vygotsky himself had postulated something very similar in the 1930s: a psychology subjected to the tyranny of reason, which dispenses with the mind, consciousness, and meaning, is as flawed as a psychology tyrannized by subjectivity, which defends the existence of a psyche (consciousness) in a pure state, weightless and alien to everything happening around it. A dialectical synthesis is necessary.

It could be said, then, that Kant was the first critic of the causal-mechanistic model of human knowledge; he was really the one who put the objective bases of conventional knowledge (Baconian realism) on the ropes, and not the constructionist movement as Gergen (1985, p. 267) claims. The question at issue, as stated in the Preface to the first edition of the *Critique of Pure Reason*, is nothing less than the existence of knowledge "without resorting to experience"; the possibility of an "extra-empirical reason," so that when Kenneth Gergen affirms in the first of the assumptions of social constructionism, that it is not experience that defines the terms of our understanding of the world (Gergen, 1985, p. 266), we literally return to Kant. Despite the scant prominence that Gergen gives him, the true champion of the critique of the antinomy between "exogenous" and "endogenous" perspectives is the philosopher from Könignsberg. However, contrary to what the author himself maintains (Gergen, 1985, p. 271), in the course of its development, constructionism has not transcended this antinomy, but has insistently deepened it by positioning itself on the side of the endogenous perspective and has ended up opening a practically insurmountable gap between both positions. First, by reducing reality to knowability and encapsulating it in linguistic conventions and then questioning sensible experience (Gergen, 1985, p. 272).

## The Epistemological Turn

The socio-historically constructed and shared nature of knowledge and human subjectivity has had high-profile supporters at least since *The Poverty of Philosophy* by Marx, written in 1846, the *Introduction to the Dialectics of Nature* by Engels, dating from 1875, and, above all, since Dilthey published the *Introduction to the Sciences of the Spirit* in 1883. If Kant was responsible for turning knowledge theory upside down, Dilthey was in charge of giving it an epistemological turn, paving the way for the differentiation between natural sciences and social sciences (an aberration by Kant's standards) and granting epistemological status to the autonomy of the latter ("the sciences of the spirit form an autonomous system in itself," he writes in the Prologue to the first volume of the *Introduction to the Sciences of the Spirit*). The so-called sciences of the spirit are not 'opposite' but 'next to the sciences of nature,' and they do so in a key that is well worth quoting in its entirety: "the material of these sciences is constituted by the historical-social reality to the extent that it has been preserved as historical news in the consciousness of humanity and to the extent that it has become accessible to science as news about the current state of society" (Dilthey, 1985, p. 57).

This key concept is today taken for granted as solidly established in the field of social sciences as a reaction to the biologicist and mechanistic reductionism in explanations of social life, behavior, and the human psyche (subjectivity). Although the receptacle of this trace can only be individual consciousness, it does not cease to be, at the same time, a trace that affects people in one of their most psychosocially relevant dimensions: their group membership (in macro or microsocial terms) and categorical identity. This shared trace endures, thanks to the (relative) constancy and regularity (stability) of the order and structure that characterize any supra-individual entity in the form of norms, precepts, laws, values, customs, traditions, beliefs, etc. The old hypotheses of a 'Volkgeist' in the German style of Wundt's 'Psychology of Peoples' or of a 'group mind' in the style of William McDougall or Charles Ellwood have been overcome. In current social psychology, we have ample evidence of this trace through the contents of socially situated cognition (Semin & Smith, 2013) and socially shared cognition (Thomson & Fine, 1999), examples of a priori knowledge and extra-empirical reason in the Kantian sense, which address problems of significant social relevance such as racism, xenophobia, anti-Semitism, homophobia, sexism, and a long and worrying etcetera.

This elementary and incontrovertible fact turns a part of the subjective reality into a partially objective reality, which certainly poses serious problems to the method used by the natural sciences.[2] Ortega y Gasset, for example, found them so serious that he identified them with the crisis of modernity that was already beginning to be discussed in his time. Having lost faith in enlightened reason, the path is open for the enhancement of historical rationality: "the time has come for reason, which was only physical, to free itself from this limitation and for man to believe in historical reason" (Ortega y Gasset, 1983, p. 329). This same model of reason is the central argument in the Sociology of Knowledge by Karl Mannheim, first, and later by Robert Merton. Their main thesis, formulated in another of the emblematic works of social thought of the past century, *Ideology and Utopia*, has a very psychosocial air: the forms and products of knowledge "cannot be properly understood while their social origins remain obscure" (Mannheim, 2004, p. 34). Formulated in such clear terms, this thesis, so friendly to social constructionism, unfolds in no less than three powerful assumptions that, however, end up distancing themselves from its main arguments.

The first of them refers to the collective nature in the genesis of ideas, of synthetic judgments a priori. If we follow the path traced by Kant, it is a mistake to believe that the thoughts and emotions that move to action originate in the individual and "that they can be adequately explained based solely on the experience of their own life." This hypothesis is based on the weak "fiction of the isolated individual capable of fending for himself," in the words of Max Horkheimer; it features a human being incapable of being conceived "within a sphere of static interiority," in the emblematic expression of Berger and Luckman, and contradicts the absoluteness of the self as the sovereign subject of knowledge in which social constructionism has settled, which will end up diminishing in the absoluteness of language as the only source of knowledge, as the only reality, and as the only line of action.

In reality, those who think are not solitary individuals but, according to Mannheim (2004, p. 35), are people "who belong to certain groups and who have developed a particular style of thought in an endless series of responses to certain typical situations that characterize their common position," which is not reduced to sharing mere "rules of interpretation" (Gergen, 1996, p. 316), but translates into rules that define feelings and actions (e.g., intergroup norms and emotions) that leave a perfectly objectifiable trace in people's lives (just think of the trail left by collective violence in Latin America). This position is irreducible to the stance that individuals belonging to these groups may adopt on an individual basis, following one of the most basic principles of Gestalt theory, which had such an influence on Lewinian theory to which Gergen (1985, p. 269) grants a leading role in the implementation of an "endogenous" perspective, through the emphasis that some of his disciples

[2] Professor Jiménez Burillo, who knows the epistemological secrets of social psychology like few others, summarized it in very concise terms: "what was at stake [already at the end of the nineteenth century!] was whether the new knowledge about the individual and society should be developed by the safe path of Natural Science or, on the contrary, should rather use different forms of knowledge, more appropriate for their human subjects" (Jiménez Burillo, 1997, p. 30).

(Festinger and Schachter) placed on the importance of cognition, but seems to do so without paying due attention to the visible, measurable, and quantifiable consequences of socially shared cognition (the example of collective violence remains valid).

All the contents and forms that our knowledge takes, secondly, have a historical reference; they are inevitably situated "within the framework of a historical-social situation from which individual differentiated thought gradually emerges" (Mannheim, 2004, p. 35), giving a clear account of the "rooting of knowledge in the social texture" or, in other words, of the prevalence of being overthinking, which will be one of the main lines of critical theory (Horkheimer, 1974) and of the inescapable relations between knowledge and its existential (founding) factors to which Robert Merton, with Marx in the background, will pay special attention. The existential basis of mental productions originates in social dimensions (the structure: social position, class, generation, occupational role, mode of production, group structures, historical situation, power structure, etc.) and cultural (values, *ethos*, climate of opinion, type of culture, worldview, etc.) (Merton, 1977, p. 52). Among them, "scholars of intellectual life have highlighted the corrupting influence of group loyalties" (Merton, 1977, p. 184), always present in the construction of knowledge and human action, of which constructionism is no exception.

Thirdly, and as a consequence (or as an inevitable foundation) of all this, the constructed nature of social order (Berger & Luckman, 1968) or of ordered disorder (Martín-Baró, 1989a, pp. 13–90) makes its presence known. Although well known and repeatedly commented upon, it is worth recalling the terms of Berger and Luckman's argument: (a) social order is not given or derived from biological data or laws of nature; it only exists as a result of human activity. At the same time, and due to the interdependence and mutual influence between different levels of reality, "the need for social order as such arises from man's biological equipment." In his psychosocial history of violence, Martín-Baró himself (1983), hardly suspected of biological whims, refers to the human being as "a being open to violence and aggression as behavioral possibilities that are based on the configuration of the organism itself" (p. 405); (b) typically human phenomena do not take place in the static interiority of the subject, but in the domain of the social: "the *homo sapiens* is always, and to the same extent, a *homo socius*"; (c) individual development (subjectivity) is preceded by a social order; when this is institutionalized, it is experienced as something that exists "above and beyond the individuals who happen to" embody the institutions at different moments in history (Berger & Luckman, 1968, pp. 72–80). The active and cooperative exchange that gives rise to the ideas and theories with which we know and interpret reality (Gergen, 1985) is the result of a "reciprocal typification of actions," whose most outstanding characteristics are habituation, regularity, and stability; in a word, institutionalization (Berger & Luckman, 1968, p. 76).

When we speak from social science about the collective genesis of ideas, the historical-social framework of the contents and forms of knowledge (Mannheim) and consciousness (Dilthey), the "created" nature of social order and its ideological base (culture), the brilliant figure of Lev Vygotsky inevitably emerges. The historical reason, or, if you prefer, the historical-social or historical-cultural reason, which in the fallacy of the isolated, solitary, and self-sufficient individual (in the absoluteness of the self-characteristic of social constructionism) of Horkheimer, Mannheim, Elias, Berger, and Luckman, etc., its most finished example, finds in Lev Vygotsky a solid epistemological support and an original backing in the field of research, now within psychology itself. This support is particularly critical of mechanistic biologism, which, in his view, is incapable of considering the development of higher psychic functions "as facts of historical development" by conceiving them "as natural processes and formations, confusing the natural and the cultural, the natural and the historical, the biological and the social in the psychic development of the child"; all these confusions pave the way for "a radically erroneous understanding of the nature of the phenomena it studies" (Vygotski, 1995, p. 12). The solution does not precisely pass through comprehensive psychology, represented today by constructionism, because it replaces the universal laws of nature with the universal laws of the spirit, ignores the differences between the natural and the cultural, and is asocial. It talks a lot about history, but "refuses to recognize the simple truth that historical development is the development of human society and not of pure human spirit, that the spirit has developed as society has developed." In a word, rather than framing the psychic development of the person in a historical context, idealistic psychology "declares that history is the realm of the 'spirit'" (Vygotski, 1995, p. 27).

The "postulate about development without changes in the biological type" and the "genetic law of cultural development," which pave the way for the thesis par excellence of sociocultural theory (the "sociogenesis of higher forms of behavior"), are epistemologically indebted to historical reason: the mechanism underlying higher psychological functions is a copy of the social (Vygotski, 1995, p. 151), that is, of historical development, because it is in history as praxis where the development of human society originates. For several reasons: first, because, contrary to what happens with higher psychological functions, elementary psychophysiological functions hardly change in the course of historical becoming (Vygotski, 1995, p. 27); then, because when we talk about the cultural development of the person we refer to the psychic development that occurs over a certain moment of historical development (Vygotski, 1995, p. 35), and, finally, because in their ontogeny, psychological functions (subjectivity) refer us first to the social plane and only later consolidate as a properly intrapsychic category, according to the well-known genetic law of cultural development, that is, of psychic development: "every function in the cultural development of the child appears on stage twice, on two planes; first, on the social plane, and then on the psychological one, at first among men as an interpsychic category and then inside the child as an intrapsychic category" (Vygotski, 1995, p. 150).

Really, without intending it explicitly, in addition to a severe critique of idealistic positions, Vygotsky has provided us with some arguments to establish a correspondence between positivist mechanicism and constructionist idealism: both start from exclusive and excluding positions, thus maintaining an "ontological rupture" between different levels of reality and disregarding psychosocial processes such as interaction, interdependence, and mutual influence between them. Both constantly appeal to universal categories. In some way, the natural reason of positivism and the subjectivization of reason that constructionism promotes is the same universal, necessary, and substantialist reason. Where the positivist sees exclusively facts and things, the constructionist only sees meanings, and, in the end, in both cases access to reality is limited and partially obscured. The data (positivism) and the meaning (constructionism) become fetish. If respect for the given is the fetishistic religion of positivism, reverential respect for what is thought in the interiority of the knowing subject becomes the new fetish of constructivism.

Both perspectives disregard the influence of social structure and its effects on people's lives and experiences. In both cases, especially within social constructionism, there is an unjustified split between the historical-cultural and the structural. From these positions, the person becomes the only unit of analysis, thus contravening one of the guiding principles of the psychosocial perspective: the importance of context and situation. Consequently, the psychologistic individualism that defines them reinforces social structures regardless of how unjust, violent, dehumanizing, or oppressive they may be. When the dialectic of interpersonal relationships is reduced to individuality, "individualism ends up reinforcing existing structures by ignoring the reality of social structures and reducing structural problems to personal problems" (Martín-Baró, 1998, p. 291). Additionally, positivism puts knowledge at the service of calculation, utility, and results (instrumental reason), while constructionism puts it at the service of any particular endeavor. Subjective reason ends up becoming instrumental reason at the service of personal interests, a kind of individualistic pragmatism: "subjective reason accommodates everything. It offers its services to both opponents and defenders of traditional humanitarian values" (Horkheimer, 2002, p. 62). Selfish interest thus becomes a common identity mark, and utility, or the satisfaction of the subject, becomes the criterion of truth (Horkheimer, 2002, p. 83).

## Some Spurious Conclusions from Social Psychology as a Historical Enterprise

It is within this framework that Kenneth Gergen's proposal from the early seventies to define social psychology as a form of history fits. Although it was a bold proposition, it was not particularly original. Gergen's main argument—that social psychology is a historical endeavor due to the open and unstable nature of the facts it deals with and their fluctuation and change over the course of historical development (Gergen, 1973, p. 310)—refers us, as we have just seen, to the core ideas of dialectical materialism, Dilthey's comprehensive philosophy, the critical theory of the Frankfurt School, the sociology of knowledge, and sociocultural theory.

All these proposals, each in its own way, question the possibility of developing laws of transhistorical and universal validity, when addressing issues related to social life or human behavior; all distance themselves from the accumulation of knowledge in the sense that this principle has been given in natural science and accept the assumption that science is more than mere accumulation of data; they are equally critical of the model of individualistic, hedonistic, and ahistorical subjects that has been (mis)represented by positivism and admit the constructed nature of social reality as a result of historically situated human practices and transactions; all would also agree on the transitive nature of the facts dealt with by social science, i.e., their dependence on the meaning that people attribute to them and the possibility of modifying them as a result of changes in the attributed meanings; all also open the door to alternative research methods, understanding that experimental and laboratory methods aim to "close" artificially a reality that is "open" by nature; in all of them, implicitly or explicitly, there is a critique of the possibility of a value-free science; in addition, they do not doubt that scientific knowledge generates theoretical perspectives of only partial validity due to the cognitive limitations of our mind, which make it impossible to apprehend in a single attempt (or in a finite number of them) all the causal variables that contribute to the production of the phenomena they try to explain. Finally, it is important to note that all of them, clearly distancing themselves from constructionism, take for granted the utility of knowledge, a sort of scientific rationality, which comes to our aid when responding to social problems.

The issue with social constructionism is not its arguments, which are not novel, but the apodictic nature of its formulation. Social constructionism asserts that the facts dealt with by social psychology lack regularity; that the concepts and theories we use are prescriptive and politically motivated, indicating what is preferable or socially desirable; that psychosocial theories are tools for power and social control; that human behavior is unpredictable, and attempts to predict it place people in vulnerable situations; that human subjectivity is the only reliable source of knowledge; that developing general laws on social behavior is impossible; that empirical observation does not lead to theoretical understanding of psychosocial phenomena; that current psychology will be irrelevant in the future; that academics are biased against application; that theory is limited only by language conventions; that psychology and social psychology cannot be positive sciences; that sensory experience and data are not part of subjectivity; and that experimental studies are socially empty and have only served to empower oppressive forces, and so on.

Since experience is not the only source of knowledge, it is reduced to mere linguistic conventions; as reality presents itself to us in a deceptive way, reality does not exist beyond the ideas we have about it; since there is no universal truth, truth does not exist. The supposed ontological muteness (reason purified to the extent of "even renouncing the task of judging actions and ways of life of human beings," in the words of Horkheimer, 2002, p. 50) and the renunciation of all criteria of truth, two of the most outstanding assumptions of constructivism, do not come out particularly strengthened from these emphatic statements with a vocation for eternity: "truth does not exist; behold the truth." It is not our intention to enter into the debate of each of these topics, but some of them deserve special attention.

The politically perverse nature that accompanies value bias begins to diminish when we shift the focus from conformity or authoritarianism to issues like discrimination, racism, violence, and exclusion. In this context, prescriptions lose the untamed character that Gergen attributes to them and become intervention instruments capable of fulfilling the noble task that George Miller attributed to psychology: serving human well-being (Miller, 1969). Martín-Baró aligns with this view, distancing himself from social constructionism by emphasizing psychology's role in improving human life. He asserts that psychology's involvement in family, labor relations, education, and other fields is "an express attempt at humanization, human and cultural growth: it is about understanding people better, understanding more deeply those aspects that allow human beings to achieve a better life, to delve into the most appropriate approach to those problems that confront individuals and groups and prevent their development and fulfillment" (Martín-Baró, 2016, p. 181).

However, psychology can also serve, and has served, the exact opposite purposes: successfully applying torture, controlling and punishing dissenters, and justifying war, machismo, xenophobia, and racism (psychology at the service of power, see Teo, 2015, pp. 246–247). This misuse contravenes both scientific and ethical rationality. Solomon Asch, in his paradigmatic investigations, demonstrated that psychological knowledge from experimental studies can promote both submission and social control, as well as autonomy. In his conclusions, Asch severely critiques group and society models based on conformity (Asch, 1964, pp. 492–498). Similarly, Stanley Milgram's 18 experiments on obedience to authority were motivated by the atrocities of Nazi anti-Semitism and the statements of Adolf Eichmann, who declared himself a simple servant of the state.

In Milgram's studies, we can find arguments for obedience and for rebellion (see, e.g., experiment 17: Milgram, 1980, pp. 113–118). The famous Stanford prison study was presided over by a severe critique of the American penitentiary system: its inefficiency, the mistreatment of prisoners in many of them, its inability to fulfill the probably naive objective of rehabilitation, and its inability to adequately address the problem of crime in the United States (Haney & Zimbardo, 1998). The experiments on bystander apathy (Latané & Darley, 1971) stem from the authors' concern about the inhibition of the residents of an apartment block in response to a neighbor's call for help who was attacked (and ultimately murdered) by an individual. The intention of Jost and Banaji (1994), Jost et al. (2004) is not to promote exploitation, inequality, and social injustice, but quite the opposite: to reveal the mechanisms that serve for the justification and maintenance of a *status quo* and the social order that favors and encourages them.[3]

The objective of Lippitt and White (1973) was also not to extol authoritarian leadership styles, but to show the advantages of democratic leadership; Susan Fiske's research is clearly aimed at denouncing ambivalent sexism (Glick & Fiske, 1996). The same could be said of the studies coming from the rich empirical

[3] Jost and Banaji (1994, pp. 1–2) offer a list of empirical research lines that have shown how people seek (and usually find) justifications for social events, for their own attitudes, feelings, and actions, some of them clearly harmful to other people, of aggressive and discriminatory behavior toward members of their own group as well as, above all, toward people belonging to other groups, of their social position as well as the social position of others, and of the conditions of advantage and social prevalence. See also the monograph of Social Cognition, 2011, 29(3) on social cognition in the service of the status quo.

tradition around prejudice (Allport, 1962), subtle prejudice (see the interesting theoretical reflection by Dovidio, 2001), or infrahumanization (see the review by Rodríguez et al., 2003): their intention is not to promote these behaviors but to denounce them. Not to mention the proposals of Moscovici (1976) on the innovative capacity of active minorities, or those of Sherif and Sherif (1953) to offer solutions to intergroup conflict. A particularly significant example is offered by Morton Deutsch, one of Lewin's most enthusiastic disciples, in the short but succulent review of his academic life. His studies on cooperative and competitive relationships, prejudice reduction, or distributive justice are excellent examples of the social commitment of experimental research (Deutsch, 1999).

In short, critical psychology does not renounce the transformative potential of empirical research, with Kurt Lewin and Martín-Baró as examples (Teo, 2015, p. 248). For these and many other reasons (examples of research lines) that could have been argued, saying that traditional social psychology "is part of a whole cultural scaffolding aimed at hiding social contradictions and injustices" (Ovejero & Ramos, 2011, p. 22) does not seem to faithfully respond to what has been the development of a very significant part of this discipline. Of course, neither Deutsch nor anyone minimally versed in the contents of social psychology can hide that there are experimental studies lacking theoretical interest and far from any hint of social commitment (Deutsch uses as an example his own studies following the Prisoner's Dilemma paradigm), but this does not make the authors of the experimental studies and the defenders of quantitative methodology henchmen of the exploiting and oppressive power.

It goes without saying that all the processes involved in these studies operate in accordance with the type of society, group, and situation in which they are present, but this cannot serve as an excuse to ignore or undervalue them. All this knowledge is not disposable; it has a lot of good, said Martín-Baró in the Prologue to *System, Group and Power*, although his claim to create knowledge of universal validity may be labeled provincial (Martín-Baró, 1989a, p. 5). On the other hand, to pretend that human behavior is not, to some extent, predictable, is to condemn it to arbitrariness, to luck, to fate or to the will of any supernatural instance, and to condemn the subject to resignation and passivity; that is, to chain it to fatalism.

The relationships between knowledge and power are well known, but it is very possible that they have been exaggerated in the hands of constructionism. Tomás Ibáñez, one of its most genuine representatives, pays special attention to this aspect: if it is not possible to construct knowledge about the social without the social being affected, "we must admit that any social scientist who is really effective as a scientist (…) is inevitably acting as a *political agent*" capable of influencing social reality (Ibáñez, 1992, p. 23). Again an apodictic sentence that leaves little room for agreement. The reduction of social reality to political reality is already problematic in itself, especially when we define that reality in microsocial terms, which are the most strictly psychosocial.

The support provided by social scientific knowledge to different forms of domination is a fact that is difficult to refute; so is its opposite, as we have just pointed out; but at the same time, one might ask about the meaning of knowledge about the social if the social were not affected (an ethereal knowledge, wandering in the void), in the same way that one might ask about the meaning of knowledge about certain aspects of our health if it were not positively affected, or even worse, if we believed, as constructionism suggests by denying validity to empirical observation, that there is no greater truth in a medical diagnosis than in the horoscope. Acting as a political agent can be a manifest objective of the social scientist but also a consequence. Inevitable result of their theories and research or the use that is made of them, the essential corollary of the impossibility of asepsis and intrinsic neutrality to scientific activity itself (a moral stance), or an intention attributed by political actors (politicization of social knowledge).

The political nature of psychosocial theories can manifest in various forms, all equally legitimate, but not all equally susceptible to being labeled as 'political agents.' In the case of Martín-Baró and his colleagues, who were murdered in 1989, their stance was a moral one, significantly influenced and manipulated by Salvadoran political and economic powers. In the introduction to *Action and Ideology*, he expressed this almost prophetically: the lives of those who "intend to illuminate the problems that are at the root of the conflict or contribute to the search for its solution" (Martín-Baró, 1983) are at risk. Moreover, as noted previously, "his notion of commitment was not servile to any political force," nor was it based on political power; it was primarily a moral commitment (De la Corte, 2001, p. 216). Nevertheless, Martín-Baró recognized that his theoretical work was increasingly aligning his social psychology (his psychology of liberation) with a psychology of action, whose consequences inevitably intersect with political decisions (Martín-Baró, 1989a, p. 7).

However, political action, understood as an action that reinforces or challenges the established political order, is not the only way to influence social reality nor the strategy that intervention has used to make psychosocial knowledge productive. This would imply an impoverishment of the very concept of power and an unjustified renunciation of a psychosocial perspective in the terms proposed by Cartwright (1959), French and Raven (1974), Raven (1992), or Thibaut and Kelley (1959): power as persuasive influence and not as imposition in the Weberian sense. To influence social reality, it is not necessary to act as a political agent.

If, for example, we take as a frame of reference some of the manuals on psychosocial intervention published in recent years (Blanco & Rodríguez Marín, 2007; Fernández et al., 2011; Hombrados, 2013; Maya et al., 2007) and review the different interventions contained in them, we can observe: (a) that the political component could be inferred in cases such as social and community intervention in the field of immigration, psychosocial intervention with minors in a situation of protection, prevention of drug use in the youth population, or in programs to improve access to social services for homeless people; (b) that in cases such as the project of prevention of AIDS in temporary workers, attention to children with asthma in New York, a community intervention to increase blood donation on a university campus, the implementation of a program to delay the onset of sexual activity in adolescents, the development of a sense of community, or internet and community change in an impoverished neighborhood of Chicago, it takes a very imaginative exercise to find it; (c) that in none of the programs carried out, the intervention agents have acted as political agents nor have they used political power and (d) that the power put into practice has been the power of reward, the power of expert, or the power of information, according to the taxonomy proposed by French and Raven (1974).

It does not seem, therefore, that all these interventions are inspired by a political agent, pursue the maintenance of the *status quo*, or are at the service of a dominant minority interested in continuing to deepen inequality, social injustice, or political oppression. Neither does it seem that this has been the *Leitmotif* of Lewin, Milgram, Asch, Tajfel, Sherif, Zimbardo, among the classics, or of Susan Fiske, John Bargh, Richard Petty, or John Dovidio, among the most current reference researchers. That would be like thinking that the use of quantitative methodology inherently carries within it, as an intrinsic need, to serve the oppressive power to cover up its misdeeds.

The monograph *Critical Social Psychology and Psychosocial Intervention. Reflections and Research Experiences* (Moncayo & Díaz, 2015) does not reveal to us, despite the title, the contribution that critical social psychology of a constructionist root makes to intervention. Among the 14 chapters that make it up, some interventions are generally alluded to, but none of them are described in the agreed terms: problem addressed, participants in the intervention, activities developed, and results and evaluation of the intervention itself. The closest to this basic scheme is the chapter by Claudia Jurado in which some activities carried out in panela peasant organizations are described, but it is done as a secondary accompaniment to the history of peasant organizations in Colombia, to the different visions of participation, or to the theoretical development of the concepts of cooperation and participation (Jurado, 2015).

As for research, only the chapter by Obando et al. (2015) on patriarchal imaginaries around the female gender can be considered a "research experience" per se, with the caveat that the authors limit themselves to commenting on the results of an interesting study carried out by two of them in 2010. The rest of the monograph is dedicated to reflections and theoretical speculations on the psychosocial (the first four chapters), critical social psychology, and the difference between psychosocial care and psychosocial intervention, with a particularity that powerfully draws attention: throughout the numerous reflections on the psychosocial, references such as George H. Mead, Kurt Lewin, Muzafer Sherif, Henri Tajfel, Gordon Allport, Solomon Asch, Stanley Milgram, Philip Zimbardo, etc., are omitted, to mention just some of the most known and recognized. Probably, it is one of those "false dilemmas" that a part of Spanish-speaking social psychology has not been able to overcome: the one that opposes a reactionary psychology to a progressive psychology.

In this regard, the warning made by Ignacio Martín-Baró almost 40 years ago is relevant: "what makes a theory reactionary or progressive is not so much its place of origin as its ability to explain or hide reality and, above all, to reinforce or transform the social order" (Martín-Baró, 1998, p. 294). It is also not the method, it should be added, that defines as reactionary or progressive a way of approaching psychosocial processes. In short, reading this monograph does not shed light on what are the novelties that critical social psychology brings to traditional theory around the nature of the psychosocial or to psychosocial intervention beyond the hackneyed topics about the social construction of subjectivity and the critique of quantitative methodology.

## The World of the Real (Reality) as an Existential "a priori"

If the imprint of historical-social reality is real and how we can know it (what is real and how we can know it) is the question that Berger and Luckman ask themselves in the first pages of *The Social Construction of Reality*. The answer they advance is in perfect harmony with the epistemological positions that have been accompanying us since the beginning of this chapter (the Kantian synthesis between understanding—rationalism—and sensitivity—empiricism—the Vygotskian dialectical synthesis, Lewin's Galilean philosophy, the relationship between spirit and nature of Horkheimer, the definition of the psychic—subjectivity—by Mead, and the critical realism of Martín-Baró). That is, it is an answer that decisively moves away from the exclusive dualisms to which the idealist positions (social constructivism among them) and positivists have succumbed, ignoring the recommendations of the main figure of modern philosophy (Kant). And they do it also relying on two references of contrasted and shared authority, Durkheim and Weber, to give both of them credit.

Social facts are both things (Durkheim) and meanings (Weber). These two assumptions do not contradict each other: society "possesses objective facticity" while being based on a set of activities that "express a subjective meaning." Both Durkheim and Weber recognized the dual nature of the social. The result is not the retreat of social reality into the realm of the self-absorbed subject but the visible existence of a reality sui generis (Berger & Luckman, 1968, p. 35) constructed on the meanings we collectively ascribe to its elements. These meanings acquire objective facticity through habituation—the repetition of acts according to the sense given to the components of the stimulating situation—and the existence of behavior patterns that are reproduced more or less automatically, "with economy of efforts" on the part of the subject (Berger & Luckman, 1968, p. 74). Habituation thus provides a stable background to human activity and constitutes the necessary antecedent to the institutionalization of sociocultural patterns and structural frameworks. This structure, by acquiring regularity and stability, perfects a quality that already existed in its germ: the objectivity of its components, so that they come to be experienced as something that exists "above and beyond individuals […] and as if they possessed a reality of their own, which presents itself to the individual as an external and coercive fact" (Berger & Luckman, 1968, p. 80).

Thus, when it is rightly said that there are negotiated forms of understanding reality that have a critical meaning in social life insofar as they are connected with activities in which people are involved (assumption 4 of social constructionism: Gergen, 1985, p. 268), it seems obvious that we are talking about subjective meanings endowed with objective facticity due to their reciprocal typification, source, and origin of their stability and regularity (of their institutionalization) and their consequences on the interlocutors, thus becoming, at the same time, the result of human construction and a pre-existing condition to the subject.

The dialectical relationship between man (the producer) and the social world (the product) also implies that "the product acts back on the producer" (Berger & Luckman, 1968, p. 83), that institutions also have the ability to control human behavior "by establishing predefined patterns, which channel it in a certain direction" (p. 76). This fact is what allows predictions to be made about behavior and strategies of intervention to be formulated from there, both at the individual and collective (community) level. The human being thinks, constructs, and acts on reality to the same extent that reality thinks, interprets, and acts with respect to the human being through the models of interpersonal and intergroup relationships defined and put into practice by others, by the *homo socius* that we all carry within us.

The existence of an *existential* a priori comes back into play, which, to put it in the most modest way, frames the forms and contents of knowledge (of thought) and human action, making them sometimes necessary and obligatory thanks to the constancy and coercive regularity of some of the components of social order and structure. Martín-Baró would express it somewhat more forcefully in one of his early works previously mentioned: "we could say that man, by the fact of being so, finds himself with an existential circumstance *a priori*. That is, man, without adding or subtracting anything on his part, finds himself thrown into a world. To exist is, above all, a reference, to the world" (Martín-Baró, 2016, p. 127),[4] but not to a world in abstract, but to living conditions that the author himself specified in the studies carried out at the University Institute of Public Opinion (IUDOP). In short, "each person constructs their existence from a social system that they find as a given fact [...]. Thus, each social system is at the same time a given fact and a human product" (Martín-Baró, 1989a, p. 49).

The constructed nature of order and social structure does not prevent, therefore, some of its manifestations from ending up acquiring real dimensions *sui generis*. Many of them present themselves to the senses in terms very close to how objects of the natural order do. Let's give an example to understand. According to data provided by the Historical Memory Group (GNMH), between 1958 and 2012, the Colombian armed conflict caused the death of, at least, 220,000 people (National Center for Historical Memory [CNMH], 2013, p. 20). It would be a mistake to think that this is a fact belonging to the world of nature. It will be easy to agree that it is rather an indisputable fact (an objective fact), which is located, by its own right, in the space of social reality; of that reality paved with meanings that possess objective facticity (real beings that do not matter, remembering again Martín-Baró).

[4] With his original style, Pablo Fernández Christlieb, of whom no positivist weaknesses are known, joins the existential a priori, although without alluding to its objective nature: "by force, the situation must appear before the people and things that occupy it, because otherwise they would have nowhere to be: everyone has to be somewhere, so the side is the first." And in a gesture not condescending to social constructionism, he adds: "it is not the people who constitute the situations but the situations that constitute the people" (Fernández Christlieb, 2011, p. 52).

The discourse of the armed actors is full of excuses and justifications; "for them, the population is pointed out as an extension of the enemy"; they are their "social bases," "collaborators," "traitors," etc. (CNMH, 2013, p. 38). Meanings turned into facts that have cut short the lives of hundreds of thousands of people in Argentina, El Salvador, Guatemala, or Chile. The well-known theorem of William Thomas reveals the secret: "if individuals define situations as real, they end up being real in their consequences." Robert Merton consecrates this theorem as one of the great milestones of social science because "it is instructively applicable to many, if not most, of the social processes" (Merton, 1964, p. 419). The interpretations that people make of social situations and their protagonists have their continuation in the actions, interactions, and mutual relations that they carry out. So much so that an originally false definition (e.g., stereotypes) can end up becoming true due to the behavioral consequences that it generates. Remember in this regard the wide range of social phenomena associated with so-called self-fulfilling prophecies analyzed by Merton.

The objects with mind that we humans are characterized by their ability to create, learn, use, and transmit meanings and to attribute these same qualities to others. The development of the consciousness of meaning is the key to subjectivity, says George H. Mead. But this development is only possible under one condition: others. The *socii*, both on a personal level and, above all, social (the "generalized other": the community or organized social group), thus become a pre-condition of consciousness, a necessary condition to incorporate into consciousness the meaning of things, so that "the process from which the person arises is a social process that involves the interaction of the individuals of the group and involves the pre-existence of the group" (Mead, 1972, p. 193), and it is there when, without losing its subjective character, the meaning becomes a social fact in the terms of Durkheim's *The Rules of Sociological Method*: facts that "do not have the individual as their substrate," that "partly reproduce a collective model" and are recognized by the "power of external coercion that they exert or are susceptible to exert on individuals" (Durkheim, 1978, p. 36).

The generalized other gives meaning to objectivity; it does so by the way of the consequences that its implementation in interpersonal relationships has for people. This is how Charles Morris understands it in the introduction to Mead's most well-known publication (*Mind, Self, and Society*), although not the most significant of his theoretical production:

> [...] to the extent that what the individual does or says is understandable, acceptable or certain for any other individuals involved in a common activity (and without common activity there would be no community of significance), to that degree what is done or said has a new type of universality; social universality. Such universality is, in one sense of the term, a synonym for objectivity. (Morris, 1972, p. 41)

That is the objectivity that has turned into real facts (empirically verifiable): the meaning of "Jew," "jihadist," "subversive," "woman," "African American," "infidel," "Tutsi," "immigrant," and countless others. As Gergen et al. (2015) rightly point out, all of them are facts of language, which have served to oppress, discriminate, dominate, etc., but when they have done so, they have ceased to be a mere subjective symbolic representation to become facts belonging to a social reality that, through habituation, repetition, and institutionalization, possess, in part, objective facticity in the terms of Berger and Luckman (1968).

The sense, direction, and urgency of the critique should not be surprising, given that the passion for reality became one of the founding principles of social science (Nisbet, 1969). Human beings have been defined as "animals of realities" (Zubiri), where reality serves as the main source of illumination, framework, and condition of truth (Ellacuría). It is reality that must seek concepts, not the other way around (Martín-Baró). The object of social psychology is the study of "everyday reality as it is lived by the majority of the Central American population and, more particularly, Salvadoran" (Martín-Baró, 1983, p. 4). When Martín-Baró, following Kenneth Gergen's argument, asserts that it is necessary "to situate and date psychosocial knowledge" to avoid presenting local and partial insights as universal truths (Martín-Baró, 1983), he is not questioning the objective facticity of social facts nor renouncing empirical observation in favor of discourse analysis.

Quite the contrary: since it is "the concrete social history that gives meaning to human activity as ideological," what he is proposing is to define, first, the contours of the world of the real, to reveal afterward the network of ideas that support and justify (the ideological background), to finally take a step toward liberating practice (intervention), which is "not the same as asserting that social psychology is or should be simply history" (Martín-Baró, 1983, p. 25). All this with the aim of making a social psychology "scientific," but without losing "the reference to a specific context and situation."

In the case at hand, that reality was paved with situations of misery in which "most of the people have never had their most basic needs for food, housing, health and education met" (Martín-Baró, 1998, p. 162); plagued "by denials, deficiencies, uncontrolled pressures uncontrollable forces" (Martín-Baró, 1998, p. 131); crossed by a violence that became part (and still is today) "of the normal functioning of social structures" (Martín-Baró, 1983, p. 376) and defined by the "exploitative and oppressive character of social structures," which condemn the ordinary citizen to a subhuman situation (Martín-Baró, 1998, p. 208). All these, and some others, are the vicissitudes of the social process that characterized Salvadoran society. But contrary to what the third of the assumptions of the constructionist movement (Gergen, 1985, p. 268) postulates, these vicissitudes are not limited to the interpretive rules of a community of readers (Gergen, 1996, p. 316), but have shown a devastating empirical validity full of negativity (poverty, political repression, violence, death).

Martín-Baró never epistemologically distrusted reality, but of its fatalistic, unjust, oppressive condition; that is, of its victimizing condition. Reality (naturally constructed) as an epistemological principle: that is the key to the critical realism that positions Martín-Baró in an epistemological scenario far from social constructionism. Let's remember it once more to clear up any doubts:

> Let it not be the concepts that summon reality, but reality that seeks the concepts; let it not be the theories that define the problems of our situation, but let those problems demand and, so to speak, choose their own theorization. It is, in other words, about changing our traditional methodological idealism into a critical realism. We Latin American psychologists need a good dose of reality, but of that same reality that overwhelms and distresses the majority of people. (Martín-Baró, 1998, p. 314)

We find ourselves at the antipodes of the subjective interpretive repertoires that aim to reduce reality to language games: index of residential overcrowding in different colonies of San Salvador, people murdered for political reasons by the Armed Forces between 1978 and 1979 (Martín-Baró, 2016, pp. 321–359), civilian population murdered for political reasons between 1980 and 1982 (Martín-Baró, 1983, p. 361), level of unemployment among the Salvadoran population (Martín-Baró, 1998, pp. 305–308), poverty situation in Central America (Martín-Baró, 1998, p. 324), index of political polarization (Martín-Baró, 2003, pp. 139–155), etc. These are some of the dimensions of reality that serve as the basis and foundation for critical realism; this is the reality that would prevent it from renouncing the notion of truth. Its antecedents are not to be found in constructionism but in Marxist theory and, through it, in the critical theory of the Frankfurt School, in the philosophy of historical reality of Ignacio Ellacuría, and, of course, in Liberation Theology.

The critical perspective in which these authors are installed starts from the existence of an objective facticity (facts from the order and social structure) and subjective (meanings to maintain and reproduce it), which produces victims in the face of whose defenselessness, helplessness and personal and social suffering indifference is not possible (primacy of being overthinking), but an attempt to reverse the situation (the facts and the meanings) that provokes them (primacy of praxis), thus rejecting exclusive dichotomies (rejection of dualisms) and drawing a model of a socio-historical subject, a subject who does not wander in the void equipped with personal interpretive repertoires, but who, as part of the order and macro- and microsocial structure, shares these repertoires and, at certain moments, comes to naturalize them.

Far from the speculations in the social void that the absolute reign of the self over the social and material conditions of its existence gives rise to, the critical thinking of Horkheimer and Martín-Baró is definitively marked by human suffering caused precisely by these same conditions. "The true individuals of our time are the martyrs who have gone through hells of suffering and degradation for their resistance to submission and oppression. [...]. The anonymous martyrs of the concentration camps are the symbols of a humanity that aspires to be born" (Horkheimer, 2002, p. 168). The protagonists of critical realism are the victims of social disorder, the victims of "the everyday reality as it is lived by the majority of the Central American population and, more particularly, Salvadoran" (Martín-Baró, 1983, p. 4) in terms that were meticulously analyzed through the most elementary quantitative methodology (the opinion survey), without anyone daring to accuse Martín-Baró of having served "the defense of the interests of the powerful," as has sometimes been insinuated, rather unjustifiably, with respect to those who use quantitative methods in their research (Ovejero & Ramos, 2011, p. 15).[5]

It is more than doubtful, then, that Martín-Baró could inspire the qualitative movement, as Gergen et al. (2015, p. 5) claim. Firstly, because in his main research he always used quantitative methods and, secondly, because his critical position does not belong to the rhetorical tradition of discursive practices, but to the Marxist tradition that is in the social structure and in the ideological mechanisms that sustain its main theoretical reference. The aim of criticism is to unveil and unmask the ideological background in which a social order that carries within it poverty, social inequality, and numerous forms of violence finds support, sustenance, and justification. The attempt to link the constructionist movement to Martín-Baró's Liberation Psychology (Gergen et al., 2015) is therefore unfounded.

The survey methodology was the tool used by the IUDOP, under the direction of Martín-Baró himself, to analyze the living conditions (housing, education, employment, family income, etc.), economic situation, school system, health system (health problems, health institutions, expectations about the future of health), war, political opinions (party preferences, voting disposition, opinion on presidential candidates), etc., of the Salvadoran population. What is reflected there are, naturally, personal opinions (subjective perception and interpretation). However, the fact that 55.2% of the inhabitants of the marginal sectors lived in a house made of bahareque and that 26.8% lacked water and energy is not an opinion, but an objective fact: "the living conditions of people, wrote Martín-Baró in the first chapter of the second installment of the IUDOP, are not in themselves a matter of opinion, but objective realities, although they can become the object of public opinion" (Martín-Baró, 1989b, p. 9). Facts of this nature are readily available with minimal effort. "Social justice is a matter of life or death. It affects the way people live, the likelihood of getting sick and the risk of dying a premature death [...]. The life expectancy of a girl born today can be 80 years, if she is born in certain countries, or 45, if she is born in others" (World Health Organization [WHO], 2008, p. 1).

The recent report "State of the World's Children 2016" by UNICEF, for example, states that "inequality will kill 69 million children in 15 years" and that by 2030, 167 million of them will live in poverty. These are also facts. To confine their existence (that of poverty, hunger, subhuman living conditions, the lack of the most basic health resources, etc.) to the subjective deconstruction that each person may wish to make of it is like seeing reality from the shore, lazily, without wanting to know what is happening in the stormy sea within. This is, says Lucien Febvre, one of the leading names in modern historiography, the attitude adopted by some historians under the influence of postmodern epistemology, and this seems to be the attitude of social constructionism. The extreme relativism that accompanies them

[5] By the way, it is worth remembering in this regard so anecdotal (the one about the methodology used in research) that Martín-Baró used the most sophisticated measurement technique of his time (the "path analysis") in his doctoral thesis. In relation to the methodology, what critical psychology does is choose the most pertinent method to study a certain problem, not choose the problems that best suit a certain methodology (Teo, 2015, p. 247).

ends up turning into skepticism, "and skepticism justified as an objection to all theory is a suicidal theory" (Ortega y Gasset, 1983, p. 158).

This has not exactly been the case for those who have defended the events and products of history as the main dimension of social knowledge. It would not be the case, of course, for Marx, but neither was it for Mannheim and, above all, for Merton whose existential bases of knowledge can only be understood in the light of the historical products par excellence: social structure and culture (see, e.g., the chapters "The Puritan Stimulus to Science" or "Science and Social Order"). Nor would it be the case for Vygotsky, although it is well known the high price he had to pay for prioritizing culture over structure. Nor would it be the case for Martín-Baró. The presence of the social structure is a constant throughout his career, from the beginning of the sixties when in "Suffer and Be" he invokes the aprioristic nature of existential circumstances (Martín-Baró, 2016, pp. 105–163) to the eighties when he outlines his psychology of liberation and addresses the structural roots of war (class struggle, social polarization, and institutionalized lies) and its consequences on mental health (psychosocial trauma). These existential circumstances had allowed him, as a young philosophy student, to flatly reject "all essentialist apriorism": since there is "no essence that can encompass or define human existence, we come to the conclusion that each existent is its existence; that is, by existing, man comes to be" (Martín-Baró, 2016, p. 125).

The relationship between essence and existence refers us to Marx, an author without whom it is practically impossible to understand Martín-Baró's proposal. Teo (2015) cites Marx among the theoretical antecedents of critical psychology. As expected, Gergen (1985) does not take him into account when outlining the foundations of social constructionism. This relationship refers us, more specifically, to the Prologue of the "Contribution to the Critique of Political Economy." Let us remember once again the so-often-cited assumption: it is the material conditions ("the mode of production of material life") that condition social life and subjectivity; "it is not the consciousness of man that determines his being, but, on the contrary, social being is what determines his consciousness" (Marx, 1973, p. 518).

Martín-Baró takes up this well-known quote in a section dedicated to social structure belonging to the chapter in which he is unraveling the characteristics of the social disorder to which a significant part of the Salvadoran population is thrown. It is in this disorder, and precisely because of it, where the character, fatalism, violence and war, polarization, mental health, and psychosocial trauma take root. Regarding all these sequels of social (dis)order, Ellacuría says, ontological muteness is not possible, but denunciation (becoming aware of negativity) and utopia (becoming aware of the possibility of overcoming it). The first brings up a classic theme in social science: its moral aspiration, which Nisbet (1969) clearly observes in its founding fathers: "the great sociologists never ceased to be moral philosophers" (p. 34). If we start from the premise that "psychology is, as much or more than any other science, fundamentally an ethical task" (Martín-Baró, 2016, p. 185), neither will we professionals of this discipline, regardless of the method we use in our research, cease to be, modestly, moral philosophers. And until proven otherwise (and no one has done so to date), there is no reason to deny this commitment to

Lewin, Asch, Allport, Milgram, Tajfel, Zimbardo, Moscovici, Sherif, Mead, Fiske, Jost, and a long etcetera.

Social commitment, which is, in the end, a moral commitment, is as evident in Lewin who investigates leadership styles as in Susan Fiske, when she studies benevolent sexism. To label this array of studies as "socially empty experimentation" simply because it is supported by empirical data (Ovejero & Ramos, 2011, p. 11) is one of the comfortable fallacies in which social constructionism has settled, often without real knowledge of the cause.

The principle of emancipation has become a constitutive part of our work, both in terms of research and within the framework of intervention. This is not the time to describe in detail the ins and outs of the debate around the illusory freedom of values in the work of social science, but to remember that the critique of the existing social order and its most lacerating consequences on the life and existence of certain people is part of Horkheimer's critical theory (1974, 2002), Martín-Baró's critical realism (1998) and critical psychology (Teo, 2015) whose reference in this section (pp. 248–249) is not precisely social constructionism, but the two authors just mentioned (Max Horkheimer and Martín-Baró): "critical psychologists do not accept the current structures of society as fixed realities" (p. 249) because they start from assumptions clearly alien to social constructionism: (a) the existence and preeminence of social structure (the a priori). existential); (b) the impossible neutrality regarding the issues we deal with in research (gender violence, social exclusion, racism, war, terrorism, poverty, and a long etcetera): "it is absurd and even aberrant to ask for impartiality from those who study drug addiction, child abuse or torture" (Martín-Baró, 1998, p. 317), well understood that this moral partiality is not at odds with the objectivity that any research process demands and (c) the possibility and need for change.

Denunciation and utopia are the two necessary and complementary steps in the fight for human rights: "denunciation without utopia is, to a certain extent, blind, but utopia without denunciation is practically inoperative, even more, it avoids real commitment" (Ellacuría, 1990, p. 592). Denunciation of what is being done and hope and action toward what is to be done (utopia), because "the truth of reality is not what is already done; that is only a part of the reality. If we do not turn to what is being done and what is to be done, we miss the truth of reality" (Ellacuría, 1990, p. 599). Martín-Baró, who drank from the philosophical and theological sources of Ellacuría, delves into this distinction: along with the "facts," the "to be done." Critical theory has its gaze set on the future; it does not limit itself to reflecting reality as it is: "a science that wants to be historical must look both to the past and to the future and, therefore, cannot be content with more or less faithfully reconstructing what is given, but must strive to construct what is not given, but should be given; not the facts, but *the to be done*" (Martín-Baró, 1998, p. 333).

The "facts" (and the meanings, it should be added) and the "to be done" form the framework within which Martín-Baró's critical social psychology is inscribed. His focus is on change and social transformation, promoting new forms of social life that lead to new models of interpersonal and intergroup relationships. He emphasizes recovering the primacy of the conditions of existence (being) over thinking, defending the unity of theory and practice, and granting practice a preeminent role. Critical psychology aims to improve human life not only through traditional psychological tools or reflexivity but also by "improving the real conditions in which people's lives unfold without discarding the struggle for social, economic, and environmental justice" (Teo, 2015, p. 250). Martín-Baró believed that psychology "defines itself as a scientific attempt to transform personal and group acts and behaviors, and in the tension between being and ought to be lies its ethics" (Martín-Baró, 2016, p. 187).

Critical thinking is not content with merely being a silent notary of reality; it does not just describe facts as they are. Instead, it has the clear objective of "radically questioning" them to transform them, because "a science that, in an imaginary independence, sees the formation of praxis, to which it serves and is inherent, as something that is beyond it, and that is satisfied with the separation of thinking and acting, has already renounced humanity" (Horkheimer, 1974, pp. 270–271).

## Conclusions

The main hypothesis of social constructionism, namely, that the terms in which we come to know the world and relate to it are the result of active and cooperative exchange relationships between people (Gergen, 1985), has been part of social thought since at least the publication of Karl Marx's *The Poverty of Philosophy* in 1846. These relationships are always framed within a socio-historical context that plays a decisive role in the development of subjectivity. The interdependence and mutual influence between socio-historical reality and the development and functioning of higher psychic functions and various manifestations of human behavior, which social constructionism claims, are part of the most classic and solid psychosocial traditions, including those of Vygotsky, Lewin, Mead, Milgram, Tajfel, Moscovici, Asch, Zimbardo, Kelman, and Martín-Baró.

All these thinkers, from different theoretical traditions, epistemological positions, and socio-historical experiences, agree on the importance of interaction, exchange, interdependence, and mutual influence between the different levels of reality that constitute human existence. They emphasize the interaction between the differential realities that define us as individuals and the macro- and microsocial scenarios in which our lives unfold, thereby avoiding the exclusive dualisms that had dominated knowledge theory until Kant's *Critique of Pure Reason*, where he sought to reconcile sensitivity (the ability to receive representations of objects) and understanding (the ability to construct ideas and thoughts independently of experience).

When Gergen argues that it is not experience that defines the terms we use to understand the world, he revisits Kant but stops halfway. He accepts the existence of "extra-empirical reason" but denies the existence of knowledge "regulated by objects," thus aligning himself with the endogenous perspective. This return to pre-Kantian philosophy suggests a knowing subject capable of self-sufficiency, leading to the error of attempting to explain all social processes solely by referring to their genesis in the individual psyche (Mannheim, 2004). Social constructionism's recovery of socio-historical reality in the development of subjectivity has been stripped of two key features: the shared nature of this reality and its inherent structure. Berger and Luckmann highlight the "objective facticity" of social facts, emphasizing that when the social order is institutionalized, it is experienced as preexisting the subject and as an external, coercive fact, following Durkheim's classic definition.

Similarly, Martín-Baró invokes the existence of an "existential a priori" defined by the material and social conditions in which people's lives unfold, distancing himself from the assumptions of social constructionism. This framework allows him to develop his main theoretical contributions: violence, fatalism, mental health, and psychosocial trauma. Each of these is framed within the social structure, a macro- and microsocial context, that enables, reinforces, and justifies them, transmitting them from generation to generation as if they were inherent in the nature of the subject. This is how the Salvadoran civil war is understood in the context of class struggle: fatalism as the internalization of social domination, mental health as "the materialization in a person of the humanizing or alienating character of a network of social relations" (Martín-Baró, 2003, p. 338), and psychosocial trauma as the "normal consequence of a social system based on dehumanizing exploitation and oppression relationships [...], as part of a 'normal abnormality' in society" (Martín-Baró, 2003, p. 295). This social framework promotes the creation of victims, thereby becoming an object of denunciation and change.

## References


Aceros, J. C. (2011). Social construction and relationalism: A conversation with Kenneth Gergen. *Universitas Psychologica, 11*(3), 1001–1011. https://doi.org/10.11144/Javeriana.upsy11-3.scrc

Allport, G. (1962). *La naturaleza del prejuicio*. Eudeba.

Asch, S. (1964). *Psicología social*. Eudeba.

Berger, P., & Luckman, T. (1968). *La construcción social de la realidad*. Amorrortu.

Blanco, A., & Rodríguez Marín, J. (2007). *Intervención psicosocial*. Pearson.

Cartwright, D. (1959). Field theoretical conception of power. En D. Cartwright (Ed.), Studies in social power (pp. 183–220). : Institute for Social Research.

Centro Nacional de Memoria Histórica. (2013). *¡BASTA YA! Colombia: memorias de guerra y dignidad*. Author.

Corte, L. d. l. (2001). *Memoria de un compromiso. La psicología social de Ignacio Martín-Baró*. Desclée de Brouwer.

Deutsch, M. (1999). A personal perspective on the development of social psychology in the twentieth century. En A. Rodríguez & R. Levine (Eds.), Reflections on 100 years of experimental social psychology (pp. 1–34). : Basic Books.

Dilthey, W. (1985). *Crítica de la razón histórica*. Península.

Dijksterhuis, A. (2010). Automaticity and the unconscious. En S. T. Fiske, D. T. Gilbert & G. Lindzey (Eds.), Handbook of social psychology (pp. 228–267). : Wiley.

Dovidio, J. F. (2001). On the nature of contemporary prejudice: The third wave. *Journal of Social Issues, 57*, 829–849. https://doi.org/10.1111/0022-4537.00244

Durkheim, E. (1978). *Las reglas del método sociológico*. Akal.

Ellacuría, I. (1990). Historicidad de la salvación cristiana. En I. Ellacuría & J. Sobrino (Eds.), Mysterium liberationis (Vol. 1, pp. 323–373). : UCA Editores.

Fernández Christlieb, P. (2011). Lo psicosocial. In A. Ovejero & J. Ramos (Eds.), *Psicología social crítica* (pp. 48–57). Biblioteca Nueva. https://dialnet.unirioja.es/servlet/articulo?codigo=3664499.

Fernández, I., Morales, J. F., & Molero, F. (2011). *Psicología de la intervención comunitaria*. Desclée de Brouwer.

French, J., & Raven, B. (1974). Las bases del poder social. En D. Cartwright & A. Zander (Eds.), Dinámica de grupos. Investigación y teoría (pp. 285–297). : Trillas.

Gergen, K. (1973). Social psychology as history. *Journal of Personality and Social Psychology, 26*, 309–320. https://doi.org/10.1037/h0034436

Gergen, K. (1985). The social constructionist movement in modern psychology. *American Psychologist, 40*, 266–275. https://doi.org/10.1037/0003-066X.40.3.266

Gergen, K. (1996). *Realidades y relaciones. Aproximaciones a la construcción social*. Paidós.

Gergen, K. (2015). *An invitation to social construction* (3rd ed.). Sage.

Gergen, K., Josselson, R., & Freeman, M. (2015). The promises of qualitative inquiry. *American Psychologist, 70*, 1–9. https://doi.org/10.1037/a0038597

Glick, P., & Fiske, S. T. (1996). The ambivalent sexism inventory: Differentiating hostile and benevolent sexism. *Journal of Personality and Social Psychology, 70*, 491–512. https://doi.org/10.1037/0022-3514.70.3.491

Haney, C., & Zimbardo, P. (1998). The past and the future of U.S. Prision Policy. Twenty-five years after the Stanford prison experiment. *American Psychologist, 53*, 709–729. https://doi.org/10.1037/0003-066X.53.7.709

Hombrados, M. I. (2013). *Manual de psicología comunitaria*. Síntesis.

Horkheimer, M. (1974). *Teoría crítica*. Amorrortu.

Horkheimer, M. (2002). *Crítica de la razón instrumental*. Trotta.

Ibáñez, T. (1992). Prólogo. En D. Páez, J. Valencia, J. F. Morales, B. Sarabia & N. Ursúa, Teoría y método en psicología social (pp. 9–29). : Anthropos.

Jiménez Burillo, F. (1997). *Notas sobre la fragmentación de la razón*. Universidad Complutense de Madrid.

Jiménez Burillo, F. (2005). Contribución a la crítica de la teoría psicosocial imperante. *Encuentros en Psicología Social, 3*, 5–32.

Jost, J., & Banaji, M. (1994). The role of stereotyping in system-justification and the production of false consciousness. *British Journal of Social Psychology, 33*, 1–27. https://doi.org/10.1111/j.2044-8309.1994.tb01008.x

Jost, J., Banaji, M., & Nosek, B. (2004). A decade of system justification theory: Accumulated evidence of conscious and unconscious bolstering of the status quo. *Political Psychology, 25*(6), 881–919. https://www.psych.nyu.edu/jost/Jost,%20Banaji,%20&%20Nosek%20(2004)%20A%20Decade%20of%20System%20Justificati.pdf

Jurado, C. (2015). Emergencias participativas de las organizaciones campesinas paneleras en el departamento de Caldas. Una visión de la psicología social-comunitaria. In J. E. Moncayo & A. Díaz (Eds.), *Psicología social crítica e intervención psicosocial. Reflexiones y experiencias de investigación* (pp. 171–190). Editorial Bonaventuriana.

Kant, I. (1994). *Crítica de la razón pura*. Orbis.

Lewin, K. (1991). *Epistemología comparada*. Tecnos.

Latané, B., & Darley, J. (1971). *The unresponsive bystander: Why doesn't he help?* Prentice Hall.

Lippitt, R., & White, R. (1973). Estudio experimental del liderazgo y de la vida de grupo. En H. Proshansky & B. Seidenberg (Eds.), Estudios básicos de psicología social (pp. 641–660). : Biblioteca Nueva.

Mannheim, K. (2004). *Ideología y utopía. Introducción a la sociología del conocimiento*. Fondo de Cultura Económica.

Martín-Baró, I. (1983). *Acción e ideología. Psicología social desde Centroamérica*. UCA Editores.

Martín-Baró, I. (1989a). *Sistema, grupo y poder. Psicología social desde Centroamérica II*. UCA Editores.
Martín-Baró, I. (1989b). *La opinión pública salvadoreña (1987–1988)*. UCA Editores.
Martín-Baró, I. (1998). *Psicología de la liberación*. Trotta.
Martín-Baró, I. (2003). *Poder, ideología y violencia*. Trotta.
Martín-Baró, I. (2016). *El realismo crítico. Fundamentos y aplicaciones*. UCA Editores.
Marx, C. (1973). Prólogo de la "Contribución a la Crítica de la Economía Política". In C. Marx & F. Engels (Eds.), *Obras Escogidas* (Vol. 1, pp. 516–520). Editorial Progreso.
Maya, I., García, M., & Santolaya, F. (2007). *Estrategias de intervención psicosocial*. Pirámide.
Mead, G. H. (1964). The definition of the psychical. In A. Reck (Ed.), *Selected writings George Herbert Mead* (pp. 25–59). University of Chicago Press.
Mead, G. H. (1972). *Espíritu, persona y sociedad desde el punto de vista del conductismo social*. Paidós.
Merton, R. (1964). *Teoría y estructura social*. Fondo de Cultura Económica.
Merton, R. (1977). *La sociología de la ciencia*. Alianza.
Milgram, S. (1980). *Obediencia a la autoridad*. Desclée de Brouwer.
Miller, G. (1969). Psychology as a means of promoting social welfare. *American Psychologist, 24*, 1063–1075. https://doi.org/10.1037/h0028988
Moncayo, J. E., & Díaz, A. (Eds.). (2015). *Psicología social crítica e intervención psicosocial. Reflexiones y experiencias de investigación*. Editorial Bonaventuriana.
Morris, C. (1972). George H. Mead como psicólogo y filósofo social. In G. H. Mead (Ed.), *Espíritu, persona y sociedad desde el punto de vista del conductismo social* (pp. 23–48). Paidós.
Moscovici, S. (1976). *Social influence and social change*. Academic Press.
Nisbet, R. (1969). *La formación del pensamiento sociológico*. Amorrortu.
Obando, O. L., Betancourt, J., & Martínez, D. M. (2015). Imaginarios patriarcales sobre el género femenino en comerciales televisivos colombianos. In J. E. Moncayo & A. Díaz (Eds.), *Psicología social crítica e intervención psicosocial. Reflexiones y experiencias de investigación* (pp. 255–280). Editorial Bonaventuriana.
Organización Mundial de la Salud. (2008). *Subsanar las desigualdades sociales*. Author.
Ortega y Gasset, J. (1983). *Obras completas de José Ortega y Gasset*. Fundación Ortega y Gasset.
Ovejero, A., & Ramos, J. (2011). Introducción. In A. Ovejero & J. Ramos (Eds.), *Psicología social crítica* (pp. 11–24). Biblioteca Nueva.
Ratner, C. (2015). Recuperación y promoción de las ideas de Martín-Baró sobre psicología, cultura y transformación social. *Teoría y Crítica de la Psicología, 6*, 48–76. https://www.teocripsi.com/ojs/index.php/TCP/article/view/29/38
Raven, B. (1992). A power/interaction model of interpersonal influence: French and Raven thirty years later. *Journal of Social Behavior and Personality, 7*(2), 217–244. Recuperado de https://psycnet.apa.org/record/1993-01370-001
Rodríguez, R., Rodríguez, A., & Leyens, J. P. (2003). La dimensión emocional del prejuicio: ¿sienten los miembros de los otros grupos igual que nosotros? In J. F. Morales & C. Huici (Eds.), *Estudios de Psicología Social* (pp. 55–81). UNED.
Semin, G., & Smith, E. (2013). Socially situated cognition. *Social Cognition, 31*, 125–146. https://doi.org/10.1521/soco.2013.31.2.125
Sherif, M., & Sherif, C. (1953). *Groups in harmony and tension*. Harper.
Teo, T. (2015). Critical psychology. A geography of intellectual engagement and resistance. *American Psychologist, 70*, 243–254. https://doi.org/10.1037/a0038727
Thibaut, J., & Kelley, H. (1959). *The social psychology of groups*. Wiley.
Thomson, L., & Fine, A. (1999). Socially shared cognition, affect, and behavior: A review and integration. *Personality and Social Psychology Review, 3*, 278–302. https://doi.org/10.1207/s15327957pspr0304_1
Vygotski, L. (1995). Historia del desarrollo de las funciones psíquicas superiores. In L. S. Vygotski (Ed.), *Obras Escogidas* (Vol. 3, pp. 11–325). Visor. Original paper published in 1931.

# Factors that Facilitate and Hinder the Reintegration Processes of Former Combatants and Their Families

**Irene Giovanni, Alicia del Socorro Durán, Diego Mauricio Aponte, and Diana Janneth Laverde**

The Disarmament, Demobilization, and Reintegration (DDR) processes are integral to promoting stability and security by eliminating weapons and aiding the social and economic reintegration of military structures. These processes must be flexible and adapt to the specific circumstances and evolving contexts of each situation. As Fisas (2011) argues, while DDR processes do not directly bring peace, they are crucial facilitators within broader peace and reconciliation efforts. They aim to transform ex-combatants into instruments of peace, normalizing the lives of individuals who have been engaged in armed conflict for years.

DDR programs represent a crucial transition for combatants who surrender their arms, governments seeking conflict resolution, and communities hosting demobilized individuals, as noted by Theidon and Betancourt (2006). These programs navigate the delicate balance between truth and justice, reparation, and reconciliation, often emphasizing disarmament and demobilization at the expense of reintegration. Özerdem (2012) highlights a significant gap in the literature, particularly a lack of detailed understanding of the reintegration process, its challenges, and its

*This chapter is the English translation of an article originally published in Spanish as*: Giovanni, I., Durán, A. del S., Aponte, D. M., & Laverde, D. J. (2020). Factores que facilitan y dificultan los procesos de reintegración de excombatientes y sus familias. *Universitas Psychologica, 19,* 1–17. https://doi.org/10.11144/Javeriana.upsy19.ffdp. *Please cite the original version of the article in Spanish.*

I. Giovanni (✉) · A. del Socorro Durán
Pontificia Universidad Javeriana, Bogotá, Colombia
e-mail: igiovanni@javeriana.edu.co

D. M. Aponte
Universidad Externado de Colombia, Bogotá, Colombia

D. J. Laverde
Universidad Santo Tomas, Bogotá, Colombia



W. López-López et al. (eds.), *Trends in Latin American Psychology*,
https://doi.org/10.1007/978-3-031-87554-0_3

implementation strategies. Furthermore, Rodríguez López et al. (2015) critique many reintegration programs for being overly welfare-oriented, neglecting the deeper social and political dimensions inherent in these processes.

In the Colombian context, the reintegration approach has been a process by which ex-combatants acquire civilian status; it is essentially a social and economic process aimed at ensuring that people in the reintegration process (PPR) obtain sustainable employment or regular income and their families adapt economically, socially, and politically to civilian life. This task is carried out by the Agency for Reintegration and Normalization (ARN),[1] attached to the Presidency of the Republic, to coordinate, advise, and execute the social and economic reintegration of people demobilized from illegal armed groups.

Until the creation of the ACR, the Colombian government offered a reintegration program focused on the demobilized person, providing psychosocial care, academic training, access to the national health system, and a monthly economic allowance. With the creation of the Agency, the focus of reintegration, and later reincorporation,[2] has been transformed. Thus, the reintegration process has been nourished both by its own process and by the research carried out on it, which indicates that to achieve a successful process a critical element is that the accompaniment not only focuses on the individual but also develops ways of working with the main support group of ex-combatants, that is, their families. Thus, the ARN emphasizes that the reconstruction or construction of family ties is part of the acquisition of intangible assets, understanding the value of ties as a source of social capital and, consequently, a contribution to human development (ACR, 2017).

This chapter presents the findings of a collaborative research project conducted by Pontificia Universidad Javeriana, Universidad Externado de Colombia, and Universidad Santo Tomas, in partnership with the Agency for Reintegration and Normalization (formerly the Colombian Agency for Reintegration). The study focuses on assessing the needs for family support in the reintegration process of individuals from illegal armed groups in Colombia. This research is particularly timely and significant as it not only addresses ongoing individual reintegration efforts but also coincides with the current government's renewed initiative for individual demobilizations. The results highlight critical areas for intervention, aiding in the refinement of strategies for both the individuals and their families during the reintegration phase.

[1] Formerly known as the Colombian Agency for Reintegration (ACR). The name change corresponds to the collective demobilization process carried out after the signing of the Peace Agreement between the Government and the FARC-EPL.

[2] The reincorporation process is the collective process agreed with the FARC-EPL, after the signing of the Peace Agreement, in 2016.

## The Family from a Complex Systemic Perspective

In order to understand the trajectories and unique configurations of families in reintegration contexts, it is necessary to construct an understanding of the family that goes beyond the grouping of individuals, blood ties, and cohabitation, to assume a complex and relational view of the concept. In this sense, this research understands the family as a living and open system in which its totality is made up not only by its elements (family members) but also by the relationships that they establish among themselves (Espinal et al., 2004).

By conceiving the family as a system, the focus is on connectivity, relationships, and context, as it is based on the idea that its properties emerge from the interactions and relationships between the parts. This implies a contextual view since the properties of the parts can only be understood in the context of a larger set (Capra, 1996) and in different macro-contexts in which the systems are circumscribed. This complexity perspective calls researchers to interdisciplinary, contextual, and situated dialogue, which favors an ecological view of families in the process of reintegration.

Along the same lines, Bateson (1998) explains that systemic thinking, which understands the behavior of the subject from a relational perspective, focuses on finding the pattern that connects for the definition of human interactions that one wants to see or study. Likewise, Minuchin (2003) states that the focus of the systemic paradigm is on the feedback circuit of the effects that the behavior of one individual has on another, the reactions of this one, and the context in which this relationship is generated.

In line with the above, Bowen et al. (1991) point out that a systemic reading of the family implies understanding that the relationship between individual behavior and the family group goes beyond seeing the parts separately, focusing on interactions, roles, ways of functioning, communication, and organization as a whole. Thus, the interactional dynamics are the analytical unit par excellence, as they give meaning to family relationships. That is, the interactions reveal ways of relating and connections of the members of a family that do not originate linearly but in a circular manner, what one does affects the other, and what the other does affects that person (Ochoa de Alda, 1995; Watzlawick, 1994). This recursive feedback circuit explains behavior as a shared responsibility, arising from patterns that provoke and maintain the actions of the individual himself (Minuchin et al., 2000).

This conceptualization allows understanding the family as an open sociocultural system that constantly constructs and reconstructs its operating patterns; that is, it is in permanent processes of change in response to external (contextual) and internal (group) demands that result in reorganizations of roles, structures, and rules, among others (Minuchin, 2003). This constant process of transformation and self-organization allows understanding of how the participation of one or more family members in an organized armed group outside the law (GAOML) and, in the process of reintegration, reorganizes the family system and generates new ways of functioning that can be explored from the interactional dynamics.

## Family in the Context of Reintegration

From a systemic perspective, each family is unique because its constitution involves elements that interact within the framework of its own history. In reintegration, these family histories have been woven into the logic of war, which, according to Palacio (2004), has an impact on the emotional stability of the family and on the dynamics, practices, and meanings they have constructed. Similarly, Rodríguez et al. (2002) point out how the scars of war in Colombia disrupt the lives of families, generating mistrust among people and poverty in intra-family communication. For his part, Cifuentes (2009) points out how in the same family, each member can suffer various impacts, such as kidnapping, widowhood, displacement, death, threats, and extortion, which erode family life and force the group to reconstitute itself through dismemberment and changes in the structure of relationships, functions, roles, and the management of authority. The author emphasizes that boundaries are transformed, becoming more rigid or more permeable depending on specific circumstances, and interactional patterns, both internal and external, are modified as an adaptive survival resource of the family nucleus.

In this regard, the review of studies and interventional experiences in DDR processes shows that families play a dual role in this process; on the one hand, they are the engine that leads people in the process of reintegration to demobilize and stay in it, understanding this as a protective role; on the other hand, many difficulties are observed in family relationships where a large amount of conflicts and intra-family violence is evident (Durán et al., 2018).

According to Velasco and Londoño (2011), the negative incidence in the course of reintegration corresponds to fragile or non-existent family networks. Gordillo and Niño (2009) identified factors that led people to voluntarily belong to an illegal armed group: intra-family violence, lack of communication, little demonstration of affection from parents to children, daily life in the midst of armed conflict, the participation of some relatives in armed groups in the territory (Ugarriza & Nussio, 2016), and poor interpersonal relationships. Despite this, Berrío and Cañón (2007) pointed out that the family is fundamental in the process of adapting to civilian life; however, emphasis is made on how functions within the home tend to be rigid—the man provider and the woman caregiver; this lack of flexibility, in many cases, is a source of tension and discomfort.

Amar-Amar et al. (2011) established the family as the primary network that gives physical and psychological quality of life to the demobilized and to the community, as the space of the greatest generation of networks. Kaplan and Nussio (2015) also point out participation in community organizations as a key element of successful reintegration; however, they observe that often this is constrained by security issues and in disorganized and fragmented communities.

Sierra et al. (2019), inquiring about personal support networks among victims, demobilized, and receiving communities, found that an important factor for reintegration is the new relationships that these people manage to make in their new environment. For their part, González and Guzmán (2016) found tensions and crises regarding security and marital, economic, and parenting conflicts. McFee (2016) records that ex-combatants keep their condition hidden for security in work and family environments, or because of the socially ingrained stigma; Nussio (2011) notes that the lack of personal security in members of the United Self-Defense Forces of Colombia (AUC) can lead ex-combatants to rejoin armed or criminal groups. In the same vein, Aguilar (2015) refers to concealment as a consequence of stigma and security measures against armed groups. In addition, the author highlights the difficulties regarding the security of the family and the existence of very small social networks. Additionally, Kaplan and Nussio (2018) describe how the recidivism of ex-combatants is strongly influenced by antisocial personality traits, weak family ties, lack of educational achievements, and the presence of criminal groups in the areas. These investigations on social networks determine that it is usually the relatives who are most frequently reported as members of the networks or to whom union and intimacy are more expressed (Ávila-Toscano & Madariaga, 2010).

Berrío and Cañón (2007) and Betancur et al. (2012) agree that economic conditions are an indispensable element for family tranquility and quality of life; Gordillo and Niño (2009) conclude that the family has been the primary axis for continuity in the process of reintegration into civilian life of former AUC combatants, as the bonds within that group do not constitute a trust network (Aguilar, 2015).

Lara (2015) suggests that the family environment provides the opportunity to strengthen bonds or create new ones by finding a partner and having children, generating paternal, affective care, security, and protection ties, and that in the family is where women begin a rediscovery of their feminine identity, since their previous reference was the masculinity associated with military life in the armed group.

Regarding the issue of gender in the context of DDR in Colombia, this research indicates that this perspective should not only be limited to the role of women but also to that of men (Theidon, 2009), understanding that there is a relational process constitutive of gender within armed groups, which entails logics of regime and hegemonic masculinity. These aspects are indispensable both for understanding the deconstruction of identity in war to a civic reconstruction in DDR processes and for achieving a more complex view of the family dynamics of people in the process of reintegration (Esguerra, 2013). For his part, Williamson (2006) points out that the return to the family is one of the most important elements of the healing and forgiveness process in reintegration processes, as reconciliation begins in the family nucleus, and therefore working with it is key. As López et al. (2016) have pointed out, forgiveness by the different armed actors is necessary for the construction of a stable and lasting peace.

Finally, it cannot be forgotten that ex-combatants, whether from self-defense, paramilitary, or guerrilla groups, come, in many cases, from rural areas where various armed actors (state and non-state) exercised a domination that anchored life to the logic of survival (García et al., 2005), and many were victims of a violence that prevented them from becoming creative actors and creators of their own existence, to the point of turning them into armed actors. This participation in the conflict can be understood as part of a victimization process in which one is both victim and perpetrator. Direct violence is experienced when being recruited and exposed to the dehumanizing logics of war, where symbolic violence is suffered (Martínez, 2016) and being stigmatized for their war past; violence is experienced from the most everyday relationships such as families and communities.

The family is recognized as a crucial space for reconciliation, repair, and reintegration. However, it raises the question of what type of support is most appropriate for the unique characteristics and needs of families undergoing this process. This research aimed to identify the primary needs of the family systems of ex-combatants to develop tailored support and accompaniment strategies. By doing so, the study intends to create comprehensive care processes that extend beyond the ex-combatant-centric approach, actively involving families as cohesive systems and key political actors.

## Method

### *Type of Study*

This research employed grounded theory as its qualitative method, which systematically applies a set of techniques to inductively construct a theory about a particular area of interest (Glaser & Holton, 2004). Data was systematically collected, coded using the NVivo software, and analyzed for reliability with Cohen's kappa coefficient. We utilized a triadic coding system to analyze the data, a method praised for its rigor in ensuring precise data interpretation (LaRossa, 2005).

### *Participants*

A convenience sampling method was used for this study, facilitated by the Colombian Agency for Reintegration (ACR), which selected families and individuals undergoing the reintegration process. The selection was based on the geographical distribution of territorial groups, their willingness to participate, and the logistical capacity of ex-combatants to travel from rural areas to urban centers where the research was conducted. Although the support processes by the Agency for Reintegration and Normalization (ARN) take place in urban centers, at least half of the participants reside in rural areas. This approach allowed us to include a diverse range of participants, reflecting the varied settings of the reintegration process.

There was a heterogeneity of PPR in terms of the time of participation in the GAOML (more than 5 years) and in the process of reintegration (minimum 2 years in the process). The participants came from different armed groups, and regardless of the group they participated in, they had common sociodemographic characteristics. According to published statistics (Agencia Colombiana para la Reintegración (ACR), 2017; Thorsell, 2013), the majority of this population comes from highly vulnerable rural or urban areas throughout the country; approximately half of them were recruited by the armed group as children; they have low levels of education (primary and early years of secondary), and there is a large proportion of single mothers who do not receive any economic support (Rodríguez López et al., 2015; Thorsell, 2013).

Of the 67 participants, 39 were women. Prior to the start of the interviews and focus groups, participants were informed about the purpose and scope of the research, the voluntary nature of their participation, and their right to withdraw at any time. They were also provided with information about the recording devices used and the handling of the confidentiality of the information, making clear that their identities would not be revealed but kept in anonymity. Along with the verbal explanation, they were provided with a consent form for their signature (Table 1). As for the reintegrating professionals, they were volunteers who had been working in the Agency for more than six months, and there was a heterogeneity of time of employment with the ARN. Both men and women participated, aged between 20 and 48 years.

## *Instruments*

Initially, 9 focus groups were conducted, with a total of 67 participants. Subsequently, 16 in-depth interviews were conducted with 16 people in 3 cities in Colombia: Villavicencio, Ibague, and Bogotá, with families of people in the process of reintegration, ex-combatants in the process of reintegration (PPR) and with reintegrating

**Table 1** Families participating in the project

| Strategy | Villavicencio | Ibague | Bogota |
|---|---|---|---|
| Interviews | 5 different families, 8 participants in total: 4 individuals in reintegration process, 4 family members of PPR (3 mothers and 1 father) | 5 different families, 10 participants in total. Four men in reintegration process and their wives; one woman in reintegration process and her husband | 6 different families, 10 participants in total. Two men in reintegration process and their partners; two brothers, both ex-combatants in reintegration process who were together in the armed group. Two women in reintegration process and their husbands |
| Focus groups | 7 ex-combatants, men and women in reintegration process | 8 ex-combatants, men and women, in reintegration process | 7 ex-combatants, men and women, in reintegration process |
| | 2 couples, both in reintegration process | 6 family members (1 father, 4 mothers, 1 brother) | 8 family members of PPR |
| | 13 reintegration professionals from ARN | 7 reintegration professionals from ARN | 7 reintegration professionals from ARN |

professionals, who are in charge of the monitoring of each PPR's process. Focus groups, as a method of data collection, allow for a deeper understanding of the opinions, beliefs, representations, and ways of constructing and understanding the knowledge of the participants (Marková, 2007). Likewise, semi-structured interviews allowed for expanding the information on personal aspects of the participants that were not addressed in the focus groups. The thematic guide of these groups sought to collect the opinions of the participants regarding the need for the support of the families of people in the process of reintegration. To avoid possible effects such as social desirability among the participants, they were assured that the focus groups had a strictly academic purpose and were independent of the ARN program. Likewise, it was emphasized that there were no correct or incorrect answers and that the interest of the groups was to generate conversation spaces where their experiences regarding the process could be addressed. For the family interviews and the focus groups, scripts were used that were constructed and validated by the different researchers from the participating universities. The guide consisted of open questions, distributed in three axes, namely: (a) family dynamics and structures, (b) the family in the reintegration process, and (c) support needs.

## *Procedure*

The present research consisted of five phases. Phase 1: Development of interview scripts and focus groups, taking into account all the work previously done by the participating universities and the ARN. Phase 2: The ARN selected the sample based on the availability and willingness of the participants. The interviews and focus groups were conducted between June and December 2018. Phase 3: Transcription of interviews and focus groups, and open coding in which the aim was to organize the data into categories. For open coding, the concept-indicator model proposed by Glaser and Holton (2004) was used, which is based on the regular identification of similarities and variations in the texts, with the aim of coding an indicator for each selected concept. Subsequently, the indicator was compared with others previously coded in the same way, and questions were formulated about the phenomena reflected in the data.

All of the interviews and focus groups were coded jointly by the study researchers to ensure the consistent application of the codes in all of them. Phase 4: For axial coding, a theoretical coding was used, which included looking for causes, contexts, contingencies, consequences, and conditions around the central categories. This involved the hierarchical organization of concepts to represent various relationships between the data, as well as the organization of the codes into broader categories. Phase 5: In this final phase, a selective coding was carried out, which involved the identification of several central categories, that is, those that had the analytical capacity to form an explanatory whole. Through the process, three central categories were identified, which are described in the results section.

# Results

During the data analysis process, three main categories emerged that are crucial for understanding the reintegration of families. The first category, "Internal and External Family Dynamics that Favor Adjustment to Civilian Life," encompasses interactions within the family and with wider social systems (meso, exo, and macrosystemic relationships) that facilitate the reintegration process. The second category, "Family and Contextual Dynamics that Hinder Adjustment to Civilian Life," includes internal family dynamics and their interplay with external factors that impede adaptation to civilian life. The third category, "Needs of Families in the Context of Reintegration," focuses on the specific support required by families during reintegration. The following sections detail the contents of each main category along with the emerging subcategories.

## *Family Dynamics that Favor Adjustment to Civilian Life*

### The Couple as a Linking Unit

Regarding the formation of couples, it was evident that this occurs mainly during and after the armed group. When it is formed during their stay in the armed group, the relationships are intermittent, as the members of the couple were moved from zone to zone. Also, within their history, the support received by one or another member of the couple, during the exit from the group and the start of the reintegration process, was identified as an indispensable element to stay within legality. Additionally, when the formation of the couple occurs after participation in the armed group, it often originated in peace homes, which is the first place where ex-combatants arrive after demobilization and where reintegration and socialization activities are carried out. In this category, the need to consolidate a couple and emotional bonds quickly was found; this type of dynamic emerges as a way to face the loneliness that people are subjected to once they demobilize and as a way to meet the emotional and economic needs that the armed group provided. Regarding the couple, the reintegration process becomes a family achievement and a promise. When one of its members is not an ex-combatant, the importance of not judging, understanding the reasons why they were in the armed groups and, above all, understanding the present of that person, what they are currently, both in the relationship and in the reintegration process, is highlighted.

The couples that result during participation in the armed group differ from those that are structured afterward in matters such as the handling of the stories of said group. Something significant in those formed in the context of reintegration is the revelation of the experiences within the armed group; the ex-combatants point out the moment of sincerity as a significant milestone in the couple that occurs after a thorough analysis that the PPR makes of the other person, to be sure and not expose their safety. It is also evident that the support of the couple in the reintegration process and the non-stigmatization are elements that strengthen the relationship and, in turn, the very process of reintegration, due to mutual acceptance and trust. Similarly, when a member of the couple knows about their partner's participation in the armed group and the reintegration process, there is greater adherence by the ex-combatant to the process.

Another of the most recurring themes in this subcategory is that of the construction of joint projects. While difficulties may arise in harmonizing the interests of the members, when the couple manages to have a conscious and common life project (children, business, housing, to study), it helps to strengthen the relationship and to face the difficulties of adjusting to civilian life. The construction of joint projects gives meaning to what the couple projects, plans, and imagines for the future; gives coherence and meaning to life in the legality; and gives a greater sense of well-being, security, and satisfaction. It was also found that couples with moderate and high adaptability and flexibility achieve better adjustment and greater capacity for construction of joint projects.

## Family of Origin

The family of origin also represents a bond of great importance for ex-combatants, even when, in many cases, for security issues, the relationship with the family of origin is distant. In cases that have closer ties with the family, less anxiety is observed to face the challenges of civilian life and greater capacity for adaptation. This indicates that strengthening ties with the families of origin becomes imperative. In most cases, the families of origin are aware that their children, siblings, or grandchildren have been in an armed group, even more so when the stories come from forced recruitment, escapes from violence, among others; however, on many occasions it is handled as a family secret, and it is not told to the people of the community for fear of generating exclusion and disapproval of the PPR.

Some of the demobilized, especially those who started the process as minors, managed to generate new ties with the foster families who supported them while the reception and adaptability process was taking place. On many occasions, when they finish the process of the PPR, they go to live near their foster mother to avoid losing the bond, which indicates the value that these families have for the construction of bonds. Also found within the armed group are strong networks and ties with different people. In this regard, several of the people interviewed expressed great appreciation and esteem for individuals with whom they established emotional ties of various kinds throughout their participation in the conflict. These, on many occasions, are named as their family.

While these types of relationships are not blood-related, the bonds built within the armed group, as with foster families, generate security and trust that determine forms of relationship, social expectation, and emotional contact. In addition, social bonds, solidarity, and more empathetic forms of relationship are created that favor the motivation of ex-combatants to continue the reintegration process.

### Relationship of the Family with the Community

The relationships between the community and the PPR and their family were analyzed, taking into account the relationships (of acceptance or rejection) with neighbors or groups in the community, participation in community spaces, the absence or presence of stigmatization, and the community's knowledge of the reintegration process.

In relationships with neighbors or groups, dynamics were found that oscillate between acceptance and rejection. The dynamics of exclusion, which were majority, will be presented in the following section. Families who claimed to feel welcomed by their neighbors and the community, argued that approval toward them increased when in their community lived people who were in the same process, or who had gone through similar situations before starting their demobilization process. Feeling welcomed allowed the families and ex-combatants to feel comfortable to actively participate in the various community spaces. Within the community spaces most frequented by the PPR and their family were found to be regular attendance at church, in addition to participation in cultural and recreational activities in parks or nearby public spaces.

## *Family and Contextual Dynamics that Hinder Adjustment to Civil Life*

### Territory, Displacement, and Concealment

In this category, it was found that, for the most part, the participants and their families had a rural upbringing where, upon arrival in the city, they found adaptation difficult. For security reasons, the vast majority of participants are relocated to urban centers and areas different from their regions of origin; therefore, the first hindering dynamic found refers to the longing for the territory, the experiences, and the meanings of the space in which they grew up and to which they could not return. The first meaning given to the territory is that the countryside is the space where they meet their basic needs and, therefore, it is the space of survival. This territoriality of the family and of the ex-combatants is expressed in their stories about life in the countryside, with different logics than those of life in the city and implies different daily routines. Arriving in a new territory implies a change in relational dynamics and lifestyles that are not easily assimilated. Thus, the differences between the contexts, added to the economic difficulties they encounter and the stigmatization by the receiving community, have led to the reintegration processes being experienced as a difficult experience to face that increases tensions and crises at the family level.

The constant feeling of stigmatization due to their condition as ex-combatants, added to security issues that make them move to different cities, produces a feeling of displacement and loss; in addition, the need for families to keep the identity of the people secret does not favor the construction of networks and leads to social encapsulation. On several occasions, the desired return to the land represents a danger to their lives and those of their relatives, resulting in a life away from their family nucleus and context. In the same direction, rumors about their participation in the armed conflict in the community lead to new displacements. Security then becomes one of the main tensions of the family.

The change of territory, the laying down of arms, and stigmatization generate the emergence of different emotions and feelings that end up shaping particular forms of relationship within the family. Among the situations mentioned is the moment of looking for a job, as shown in the following fragment:

> So, my wife went to help where I worked and then the boss somehow found out that my wife is demobilized and then she started: "No, those guerrillas must be kept away". (Participant 03, Personal communication, 2019)

The most common imaginaries of the community regarding the past of the PPR are observed in stories that stereotype them as "they only come to the city to do harm and to become hitmen" (Participant 01, Personal communication, 2019), causing situations of rejection and exclusion for the fact of "carrying that cross" (Participant 02, Personal communication, 2019). In addition to this, a small group of these families describe certain disagreements about the "special" treatments they receive in schools and community spaces from people who know the process in which they are currently immersed, but which has the effect of exposing them more to stigmatization.

The impact of relocation in a territory alien to them and the stigma suffered by these families generate patterns of relationship aimed at clustered interactions within the family system as a form of protection from the outside world. This encapsulation of the system favors social isolation, which in turn feeds more encapsulation of the family and relationships of dependence among them, which limits their establishment of other relationships and their integration into other contexts.

## Parenting Guidelines

In this subcategory, it was found that children are the greatest motivation to enter and stay within the law; providing them with better living conditions than they had is a constant desire of people in the process of reintegration. In the stories of the PPR, early abandonment, mistreatment, forced recruitment, or joining the group due to family ties that they do not want to repeat with their own children were identified. In other words, there was a clear interest in not repeating with their children the family detachment and the forms of care received from their families during their childhood. Although this can be considered a protective factor, the analysis of the data shows how family histories and the history of the conflict establish complex relationships with parenting guidelines in several ways. In some cases, overprotective and boundary-less parenting styles are observed, accompanied by a narrative in which they do not wish to repeat the military discipline experienced within the armed group or the domestic violence experienced in the previous family nucleus.

In other cases, parenting styles linked to the group's discipline and associated with morality, discipline, compliance, and honesty instilled in the armed groups were observed. This parenting guideline is often perceived by the PPR's partner as violent, which creates tensions within the family system. Linked to this, it is perceived that physical aggression toward minors is accepted and legitimized as a way to correct and educate.

The tendency to overprotection was found particularly in the case of women with children in the armed group and often with histories of abortion. Mothers express a deep fear of loss and therefore prefer not to give freedom and autonomy to their children to explore the world on their own. This pattern is the origin of amalgamated relationships within the family system, which shows the importance of addressing the fear of loss underlying the mother-child dyad.

#### Gender Roles and Domestic Violence

There was a tendency for the women in the family to fulfill caregiving roles and the man to be the provider. Women feel discomfort when moving away from the role they played in the armed group and also express how, once demobilized, they have felt questioned by their partners when they move away from the traditional female role.

These gender expectations are one of the strongest tensions within the couple. Ex-combatants also express that in the context outside the armed conflict, there is more machismo and inequality than in the armed group, where they could perform types of activities that could traditionally be considered masculine. In this sense, the expressions of domestic violence evidenced are related to ideas of what it means to be a man or woman in each specific context and the feeling of relational inequality, which involves disqualifying communication patterns, that is, a set of elements in the interaction that denotes pejorative behaviors that discredit or incapacitate a family member.

Related to the above, women point out the importance of coordination and balance in household chores as a way to promote coexistence.

### *Needs of Families in the Context of Reintegration*

In this category, the stigmatization and rejection that these families receive and the need to strengthen work with receiving communities reappear. Tensions with communities such as violent events, selective threats, and security issues are observed, which make people have to move again to other areas. Faced with this problem, the professionals in charge of the accompaniment only suggest new relocations. In terms of security, this strategy seems to be successful; however, the data show that it has many implications for the family system.

On the other hand, it seems that the focus that is privileged in the attention to families is centered on the "mechanization of work," as it is characterized by interventions aimed at homogenizing the process of attention, where it is necessary to meet certain goals. This results in families and ex-combatants not feeling understood or accompanied during the process. Likewise, it is observed that the accompaniment lacks a greater explanation of the phases of the reintegration process and greater demands, as several of the participants indicate that this is not clear to them or that it lacks meaning, which in turn brings with it false expectations, dissatisfactions, and little adherence to the process. Some families indicate that their needs, fears, or concerns are not fully understood; this misunderstanding is associated with the little time they can share with the reintegration professional, the constant rotation of staff, and the professionals' eagerness to meet the institutionally established goals.

In terms of accompaniment, although a large part of the families recognize the work of the ARN, the majority mention the constant change of staff as one of the main obstacles in their process and their relationship with the Agency, expressing dissatisfaction at the time of having to restart the process. Among the needs that the interviewed families emphasized the most is the work on the life project of the PPR, more than on resuming aspects of life in the armed group, which is why a large part of the interviewed families demanded some type of economic funding, either to get housing, start a business, or face their personal plans after the completion of the process. Additionally, several families expressed the need for the reintegration program to take into account that due to work issues it is difficult to attend follow-up meetings, which makes, on the one hand, the accompaniment not constant and perceived as impersonal and distant, and on the other hand, that the reintegrators understand this as a lack of commitment to the process on the part of the PPR.

## Discussion

From this research, we wanted to stimulate a reflection to try to make sense of the different family experiences in the context of reintegration. These discussions do not pretend to be finished, but they do seek to offer some guidelines for the accompaniment. First of all, it is essential to reiterate that the family cannot be a passive subject, intervening indirectly from the actions planned to meet the particular needs of the ex-combatants. In relation to the needs of the participants and in line with what was proposed by Velasco and Londoño (2011), it is found that one of the reasons that drives the decision to demobilize, is the need to reunite with the family, including partner, children, parents, siblings, and others. This reunion constitutes a need at the initial moment of the demobilization and reintegration, as is also the desire for their children to have different possibilities than joining an armed group.

The above poses several challenges in working with families. On the one hand, it is essential to know the bonds that the person has built to strengthen them, rebuild them, and motivate new bonds with other people. On the other hand, it is also necessary to heal significant relationships and painful bonds, address stigmas that emerge from the family and that hinder the transition to a life in the legality, as well as reconstruct or build less hierarchical and closer family relationships.

Now, within the different subsystems that make up the family, the importance of strengthening the couple was observed, which assumes a different structure than that of the family with children, as it has its own dynamics that must be studied and addressed in a particular way. In this study, it was possible to see how the process of reintegration constitutes a moment of renegotiation of power relations between couples to cooperate under different conditions. The above is closely related to the findings of González and Guzmán (2016) who reported tensions and crises regarding marital, economic, and parenting conflicts in the reintegration processes. In the present work, it was important to find how this negotiation process can be transformed in one direction or another by the actors involved and, especially, by the reintegration professionals, which demarcates an ethical-political action in working with families, where those who accompany are of vital importance in relational transformation.

On the other hand, the need to address gender identities was also found, as these play an important role in the way of assuming violence and in the conduct of conflicts within the family. Although Esguerra (2013) already emphasized the complexity of gender work in DDR contexts, this study agrees on the importance of addressing stereotyped and dichotomous conceptions of gender roles, as these originate in relational contexts marked by power inequality within the family. Likewise, this research allowed us to observe that relational equality in the couple is linked both to gender roles and to the attention and validation of the needs of both members equally. In this order of ideas, and in accordance with the findings of the research conducted by Lara (2015), the accompaniment should take into account the influence of gender, attending to the experiences of the armed group and demobilization as a starting point, in order to co-construct more equitable relational dynamics.

Regarding family communication, it is recognized that, depending on the configuration of communication, interactions will be different (Watzlawick et al., 1967). Likewise, the members of the family will have different tools to face the situations of daily living. In this regard, it was observed how, when the ends of family communication are not materialized, family dynamics and communication patterns can be created that alter interactions in such a way that different types of domestic violence are triggered, opposing functional communication and the construction of coexistence bonds between family members and their environment. The above is in line with the proposals of Cifuentes (2009), who emphasizes the impact that armed conflict has on the interactional patterns of families. In this sense, it is important to bear in mind that when there is no assertive, or effective, communication in family dynamics, characterized by the presence of rigid boundaries and hierarchies formed by power struggles, difficulties begin to emerge in the functioning of the system (Valdés, 2007). These communication difficulties have a relationship with the dynamics of armed groups where, as Esguerra (2013) points out, communication is mediated by militarized relational dynamics with hierarchies and power relations that are rigid and marked by violence.

Therefore, regarding family communication patterns, the importance of promoting generative forms of communication stands out, which facilitate the achievement of individual and interpersonal objectives of the family system with a minimum of wear and tear and personal growth congruent with its values, and where their communicative relationships are aimed at mutual respect, dialogue, and reflection.

Linked to this work of couple and communication, the need to accompany parenting processes becomes evident to avoid the repetition of violent intergenerational patterns that, in many cases, are responsible for the PPR joining the armed groups and, at the same time, promote patterns of loving relationship but without overprotection, to achieve secure bonds that allow the children of ex-combatants to have life experiences different from those of their parents.

Another aspect that acquires great relevance in terms of accompanying families are the bonds. This research showed how these are a form of relationship that is updated at each moment of life and can be shaped from the ways of configuration and organization of families, ex-combatants, and the contexts they inhabit. Unlike Aguilar (2015), who points out that the bonds within the group do not constitute a network of trust, in this research, the importance of some bonds with other ex-combatants was observed, especially with those who share in peace homes and substitute mothers. In this sense, many times the bonding power is not given by consanguinity; therefore, it is the duty of professionals to explore for each case and determine which bonds can be activated and strengthened. In this regard, it is important not to lose sight of the findings of Kaplan and Nussio (2018), who point out the risks of social encapsulation when ex-combatants maintain social relationships exclusively with other ex-combatants. In this measure, the accompaniment to families should be focused on understanding, evaluating, and even intervening in the functions, potentialities, risks, and attributes of each bond with the objective of promoting healthier bonds that generate greater trust, autonomy, better social interactions, more solidarity, and better adherence to the reintegration route.

On the other hand, the accompaniment processes must address the constant feeling of stigmatization and uprooting of the ex-combatants and their families. In line with Aguilar (2015) and with Kaplan and Nussio (2015), who identify concealment as a consequence of stigma and security measures against armed groups, prioritize working with receiving communities, as these are an essential element for the adjustment process of the families of ex-combatants. Likewise, it is necessary to take into consideration the findings of Shnabel et al. (2008), who point out the need for recognition and social acceptance that ex-combatants have. In this regard, working on the empowerment of ex-combatants, along with the receiving communities, is a necessary step to favor successful reintegration processes (Sierra et al., 2019).

It is essential that all interventions include an initial evaluation and a complete vision of the families and their context, being very thorough in their background, investigating where they are now, where they want to be, what their strengths are, and what is the life project they want to build within the framework of legality.

Finally, this work highlighted how reconciliation and forgiveness begin in the family and the need to work on forgiveness, heal family wounds, and resolve security situations that keep them away from families with the intention of protecting them. The above implies knowledge of family life stories before joining the group, during their stay in the group, and at the time of reintegration, where there is a reunion and/or a new family is formed.

In conclusion, it is necessary to accompany families, understood as a series of intentional actions in which collaborative reflections are produced in people so that they identify their difficulties and resources, in order to seek possibilities for change that lead to improvements in quality of life. For this purpose, it is essential to recognize the uniqueness and integrity of people, as each one has their own history, context, relationships, and ways of understanding the world that traverse the different dimensions and areas of life. The above is a very important element to take into account, as the information collected indicates that work with families has been centered on the "mechanization of work," that is, working with the family to thus avoid desertions or interruptions in reintegration processes. However, it is from this vision that we seek to distance ourselves, as it is characterized by interventions that homogenize the care process. At this point, a key to guiding the work is to understand how ex-combatants and their families understand, signify, and live the reintegration process.

In this sense, reintegration professionals are tasked not with imposing changes based on preconceived notions of what constitutes a "good" or "normal" family. Instead, their role is to respect the uniqueness of each family and to collaboratively create conditions that enable families to self-organize and realize their potential (Giovanni & Jaramillo, 2018). This approach involves a process of resignification, viewing families through their capacity for change. Crucially, this process emphasizes the reflexivity of families—their ability to critically examine their reintegration journey within the context of their relationships and to see outcomes as part of an ongoing process, rather than an end goal. This reflective perspective facilitates the creation of relational contexts for accompaniment, which support the development of meaning and empowerment for ex-combatants and their families as they navigate the reintegration path.

**Acknowledgments** This research was funded by the ARN.

## References

Agencia Colombiana para la Reintegración. (2017). *Dimensiones de la ruta de reintegración. conceptualización, logros, metas y categorías de avance*. Author.

Aguilar, V. H. (2015). Representaciones y procesos de construcción familiar y laboral. *Caso de personas en proceso de reintegración ACR Sumapaz* (Master's thesis). Pontificia Universidad Javeriana, Cali.

Amar-Amar, J., Abello-Llanos, R., Ávila-Toscano, J. H., & Madariaga, C. (2011). Relación entre redes personales y calidad de vida en individuos desmovilizados del conflicto armado colombiano. *Universitas Psychologica, 10*(2), 355–369. https://doi.org/10.11144/Javeriana.upsy10-2.rrpc

Ávila-Toscano, J. H., & Madariaga, C. (2010). Redes personales y dimensiones de apoyo en individuos desmovilizados del conflicto armado. *Psicología desde el Caribe, 25*, 179–201. https://www.redalyc.org/pdf/213/21315106009.pdf

Bateson, G. (1998). *Pasos hacia una ecología de la mente*. Ediciones Lohlé-Lumen.

Berrío, D. M., & Cañón, S. L. (2007). El rol que desempeña la familia de la población en situación de desmovilización en su proceso de inclusión al programa de atención humanitaria (PAHD) en un Hogar de Paz de exguerrilleros del ministerio de defensa durante el segundo semestre de 2016 (Undergraduate's thesis). Universidad de la Salle, Bogotá.

Betancur, E. Y., Chaparro, L. C., & Vargas, M. F. (2012). *Resiliencia familiar en el proceso de reintegración en la ciudad de Bogotá (Undergraduate's thesis)*. Universidad de la Salle.

Bowen, M., Andolfi, M., & De Nichilo, M. (1991). De la familia al individuo: la diferenciación del sí mismo en el sistema familiar. Paidós.

Capra, F. (1996). *The web of life: A new scientific understanding of living systems*. Anchor Books.

Cifuentes, M. R. (2009). Familia y conflicto armado. *Trabajo Social, 11*, 87–106. https://dialnet.unirioja.es/servlet/articulo?codigo=4070931

Durán, A. S., Giovanni, I., Aponte, D. M., Laverde, D. J., Zapata, J. G., Agudelo, D., Gaitán, D., & Granados-García, A. (2018). *Encuentros humanizantes. Implementación de una propuesta, en perspectiva de salud mental, para la atención de personas desmovilizadas de grupos armados en proceso de reintegración, sus familias y comunidades*. Editorial Universidad Externado de Colombia.

Esguerra, J. (2013). Desarmando las manos y el corazón: transformaciones en las identidades de género de excombatientes de FARC y AUC en Colombia (2004–2010), (Undergraduate's thesis). Pontificia Universidad Javeriana, Bogotá.

Espinal, I., Gimeno, A., & González, F. (2004). El enfoque sistémico en los estudios sobre la familia. *Revista Internacional de Sistemas, 14*, 21–34. https://dialnet.unirioja.es/servlet/articulo?codigo=5042892

Fisas, V. (2011). Educar para una cultura de paz. *Quaderns de Construcció de Pau, 20*, 1–8. https://www.fondodeculturaeconomica.com/PDF/Caja%20de%20herramientas/Educar%20para%20la%20paz.pdf

García, M., Alvarado, M. A., Vásquez, M. L., & Sánchez, A. (2005). Acción colectiva contestataria en contextos de conflicto armado en Colombia. In *Sociedad de emergencia: Acción colectiva y violencia en Colombia* (pp. 153–195). Defensoría del Pueblo.

Giovanni, I., & Jaramillo, D. (2018). Collaborative peace education in contexts of sociopolitical violence. In M. Walid & C. Toffolo (Eds.), *Handbook of research on promoting peace through practice, academia, and the arts* (pp. 79–97). IGI Global.

Glaser, B., & Holton, J. (2004). Remodeling grounded theory. In forum qualitative Sozialforschung/forum. *Qualitative Social Research, 5*(2), 1–22. http://www.qualitative-research.net/index.php/fqs/article/view/607/1316.

González, J. C., & Guzmán, K. V. (2016). Construcción de identidad de género de una pareja conformada al interior de las FARC a partir de contextos de socialización relevantes en sus historias de vida. Repositorio Institucional USTA. (pp. 1–161). https://repository.usta.edu.co/bitstream/handle/11634/3302/2016juangonzalez.pdf?sequence=1&isAllowed=y.

Gordillo, L. C., & Niño, A. V. (2009). *La familia parte significativa dentro del proceso de resocialización a la vida civil de dos excombatientes de las AUC* (Undergraduate's thesis). Corporación Universitaria Minuto de Dios, Bogotá.

Kaplan, O., & Nussio, E. (2015). Community counts: The social reintegration of excombatants in Colombia. *Conflict Management and Peace Science, 35*(2), 1–22. https://doi.org/10.1177/0738894215614506

Kaplan, O., & Nussio, E. (2018). Explaining recidivism of ex-combatants in Colombia. *Journal of Conflict Resolution, 62*(1), 64–93. https://doi.org/10.1177/0022002716644326

Lara, L. M. (2015). ¿Y después de la guerra qué? Avatares en el tránsito a la vida civil de jóvenes desmovilizados de las FARC. *Universitas Humanística, 82*, 49–73. https://doi.org/10.11144/Javeriana.uh82.dgat

López, W., Andrade, A. F., & Correa, A. (2016). The process of asking for forgiveness as a necessary condition in order to build peace amidst the Colombian armed conflict. *Revista Argentina de Clínica Psicológica, 25*(2), 187–194. https://www.redalyc.org/pdf/2819/281946990009.pdf

LaRossa, R. (2005). Grounded theory methods and qualitative family research. *Journal of Marriage and Family, 67*(4), 837–857. https://doi.org/10.1111/j.1741-3737.2005.00179.x

Marková, I. (2007). *Dialogue in focus groups: Exploring socially shared knowledge*. Equinox Publishing.

Martínez, A. (2016). La violencia. Conceptualización y elementos para su estudio. *Política y Cultura, 46*, 7–31. http://www.scielo.org.mx/pdf/polcul/n46/0188-7742-polcul-46-00007.pdf

McFee, E. (2016). The double bind of "playing double": Passing and identity among ex- combatants in Colombia. *Peace and Conflict: Journal of Peace Psychology, 22*(1), 52–59. https://doi.org/10.1037/pac0000146

Minuchin, P., Colapinto, J., & Minuchin, S. (2000). *Pobreza, institución, familia*. Editorial Amorrortu.

Minuchin, S. (2003). *Familias y terapia familiar*. Gedisa.

Nussio, E. (2011). How ex-combatants talk about personal security. Narratives of former paramilitaries in Colombia. *Conflict, Security & Development, 11*(5), 579–606. https://doi.org/10.1080/14678802.2011.641725

Ochoa de Alda, I. (1995). *Enfoquesenterapia familiar sistémica*. Editorial Herder.

Özerdem, A. (2012). A re-conceptualisation of ex-combatant reintegration: 'Social reintegration' approach. *Conflict, Security & Development, 12*(1), 51–73. https://doi.org/10.1080/14678802.2012.667661

Palacio, M. C. (2004). Familia y violencia familiar: de la invisibilización al compromiso político. Un asunto de reflexión sociológica (Master's thesis). Universidad de Caldas, Manizales.

Rodríguez, J., De La Torre, A., & Miranda, C. T. (2002). La salud mental en situaciones de conflicto armado. *Biomédica, 22*(2), 337–346. https://www.redalyc.org/articulo.oa?id=84309603

Rodríguez López, M., Andreouli, E., & Howarth, C. (2015). From ex-combatants to citizens: Connecting everyday citizenship and social reintegration in Colombia. *Journal of Social and Political Psychology, 3*(2), 171–191. https://doi.org/10.5964/jspp.v3i2.388

Shnabel, N., Nadler, A., Canetti, D., & Ullrich, J. (2008). The role of acceptance and empowerment in promoting reconciliation from the perspective of the needs-based model. *Social Issues and Policy Review, 2*(1), 159–186. https://doi.org/10.1111/j.1751-2409.2008.00014.x

Sierra, Y. C., Saludo, J. P., Madariaga, C., & Ávila, J. H. (2019). Redes personales de apoyo entre víctimas, desmovilizados y comunidad receptora. *Revista Hispana para el Análisis de Redes Sociales, 30*(1), 43–53. https://doi.org/10.5565/rev/redes.793

Theidon, K. (2009). Reconstrucción de la masculinidad y reintegración de excombatientes en Colombia. Editorial Fundación Ideas para la Paz.

Theidon, K., & Betancourt, P. A. (2006). Transiciones conflictivas: combatientes desmovilizados en Colombia. *Análisis Político, 58*, 92–111. http://www.scielo.org.co/pdf/anpol/v19n58/v19n58a04.pdf.

Thorsell, S. (2013). Towards people-centred economic reintegration? An analysis of the economic reintegration strategy of demobilised combatants in Colombia. *Colombia International, 77*, 177–215. https://doi.org/10.7440/colombiaint77.2013.07

Ugarriza, J. E., & Nussio, E. (2016). Are guerrilla fighters different from paramilitary members? A systematic integration and validation of motivational studies in Colombia. *Análisis Político, 28*(85), 189–211. https://doi.org/10.15446/anpol.v28n85.56254

Valdés, A. A. (2007). *Familia y desarrollo: intervenciones en terapia familiar*. Manual Moderno.

Velasco, R. M., & Londoño, C. (2011). Calidad de vida objetiva, optimismo y variables sociojurídicas, predictivos de la calidad de vida subjetiva en colombianos desmovilizados. *Avances*

*en Psicología Latinoamericana, 29*(1), 114–128. https://revistas.urosario.edu.co/index.php/apl/article/view/506/1462
Watzlawick, P. (1994). *La realidad inventada*. Gedisa.
Watzlawick, P., Beavin, J., & Jackson, D. D. (1967). *Pragmatics of human communication. A study of interactional patterns, pathologies, and paradoxes*. W. W. Norton & Company.
Williamson, J. (2006). The disarmament, demobilization and reintegration of child soldiers: Social and psychological transformation in Sierra Leone. *Intervention, 4*(3), 185–205. https://doi.org/10.1097/WTF.0b013e328011a7fb

# Revisiting Social Class in the Study of Collective Action: The Case of a Chilean Socio-Environmental Movement

**Nicolás Muñoz, Rodrigo Asún, and Claudia Zúñiga**

In recent years, there has been a notable increase in social protests worldwide, spanning a wide range of issues and regions. Notable examples include uprisings against oppressive regimes in the Middle East, movements against austerity policies in Europe, a global push for women's rights, popular uprisings in several South American countries in 2019, and massive protests against racism in the United States during the COVID-19 pandemic (Akaev et al., 2017). Alongside these, environmental concerns have risen to prominence, particularly in Latin America, where the extractivist economic model has deepened. These environmental protests are distinguished not only by their frequency and scope but also by their ability to engage actors traditionally not involved in collective actions, highlighting a significant shift in the nature and reach of mobilizations (Poma, 2014; Poma & Gravante, 2015; Svampa, 2013).

Social psychology has made significant contributions to understanding the factors that motivate people to get involved in collective action (Klandermans & van Stekelenburg, 2007; van Zomeren et al., 2008), and among the identified predictors are group identity (e.g., McGarty et al., 2009; Tajfel & Turner, 1979; Thomas et al., 2012), evaluations of injustice (e.g., Becker & Wright, 2011; Wright & Taylor, 1998), emotions such as anger or indignation (e.g., Hayward et al., 2018; Leonard et al., 2011), and collective efficacy, that is, confidence that one's own group has the

*This chapter is the English translation of an article originally published in Spanish as*: Muñoz, N., Asún, R., & Zúñiga, C. (2020). Recuperando la clase social en el estudio de la acción colectiva. El caso de un movimiento socioambiental chileno. *UniversitasPsychologica, 19,* 1–15. https://doi.org/10.11144/Javeriana.upsy19.rcse. *Please cite the original version of the article in Spanish.*

N. Muñoz · R. Asún · C. Zúñiga (✉)
Universidad de Chile, Santiago, Chile
e-mail: cczuniga@u.uchile.cl



W. López-López et al. (eds.), *Trends in Latin American Psychology*,
https://doi.org/10.1007/978-3-031-87554-0_4

ability to achieve the desired changes through collective action (e.g., Hornsey et al., 2006).

The great explanatory power of these variables has meant that psychosocial models that aim to explain individuals' participation in collective actions do not consider the material living conditions of the participants. This is understandable since, on the one hand, grievance theories, which assumed that it was the existence of material deprivations that motivated people to get involved in collective actions, proved to be inadequate, or at least not sufficient, to explain protest behavior (Tyler & Smith, 1998; Van Zomeren et al., 2008); on the other hand, empirical research has also shown that those who tend to protest more are those who have more resources to do so, whether economic resources (Dalton, 2017; Verba et al., 1995) or biographical conditions that facilitate time for it (Wiltfang & McAdam, 1991). Consequently, the evidence seems to indicate that participation is a matter of the privileged and not of the most deprived classes.

However, most of the research on participation in collective actions has been carried out in Western Europe, North America, or Australia (Ayanian & Tausch, 2016), that is, in countries characterized by a certain material abundance. In circumstances where there is evidence of crisis contexts or material shortages, the participation of the most affected becomes more relevant (Galais & Lorenzini, 2017), and it is known that the population with lower incomes and jobs more dependent on ecosystem resources is the most vulnerable to environmental disasters (Carter et al., 2007).

For these reasons, it is worth asking whether in a context of environmental crisis, greater socioeconomic deficiencies, and deep inequalities, such as in Latin America, it is possible that material living conditions, expressed in social class, have a relevant role in predicting participation in collective actions. To answer this question, the present study aims to identify the predictors of participation in the case of a set of environmental protests carried out on the Island of Chiloé, in southern Chile, during the month of May 2016.

## Psychosocial Predictors of Participation in Collective Actions

According to Wright et al. (1990), a member of a group gets involved in a collective action whenever he or she acts on behalf of that group and the action is aimed at improving the conditions of all members. This action usually aims to challenge group discrimination or disadvantage or to end or prevent injustice.

The most recognized psychosocial models currently used to explain people's participation in collective actions are the Social Identity Model of Collective Action (SIMCA) by van Zomeren et al. (2008) and the Motivational Model of Collective Action by van Stekelenburg et al. (2011). Both models (whose graphical representations and comparisons can be found in Chan, 2016) include among the predictors of participation, people's social identity, the perception of suffering an injustice, and the perception that protests can be an effective means to achieve desired goals.

Other variables that have been shown to be associated with participation in collective actions are the degree of legitimacy assigned to the protest behavior (Simon & Klandermans, 2001) and politicized social identity (Sabucedo et al., 2010). The latter refers to a form of collective identity that motivates individuals to engage in the struggle for power and is characterized by the group members perceiving that they suffer grievances and injustices due to their group membership and attributing to an outgroup the responsibility for these grievances (Sabucedo et al., 2010). For all the above, we will include in our model the most relevant of these psychosocial predictors of collective participation.

## Measurement of Social Class

The position of individuals in the productive system has shown a high capacity to explain past social struggles (De la Garza, 2016), even at times when class conflict is not explicit (Schmidt, 2011). However, given the evolution and complexity of society, a traditional notion of social class does not allow an understanding of the current social structure, but it is necessary to resort to a perspective that incorporates the growth of the middle classes of the population. In this sense, the neo-Marxist proposal of Olin Wright (1994, 2000) allows this complexity and, at the same time, respects the traditional notion of social class linked to the position in the structure productive.

Wright (2000) argues that classical Marxism was wrong to limit the problem of social classes to the dichotomy between the bourgeoisie and the proletariat (as a reflection of the capital-labor dialectic), arguing that currently between both poles it is possible to find a series of contradictory positions since the position of managers and supervisors, as well as that of the petty bourgeoisie, does not necessarily coincide with the ownership of the means of production, the control of capital investments, and work processes (Wright, 1994). From this, the author reworks the model of social classes moving to a three-dimensional model that considers the appropriation and exploitation of various types of goods: (a) ownership of the means of production; (b) hierarchy occupied in productive processes; and (c) dominion of credentialed educational certifications.

The class structure that emerges from this model can be observed in Fig. 1, where 12 social classes are presented, ordered first by owning or not means of production (a category that divides the bourgeoisie, small employers, and petty bourgeoisie from the rest), then by having credentialed skills, and, finally, by their dominion of organizational goods (managerial skills and capabilities). Given the ability of this class model to discriminate intermediate positions between the bourgeoisie and the proletariat, it will be the one we will include in our model.

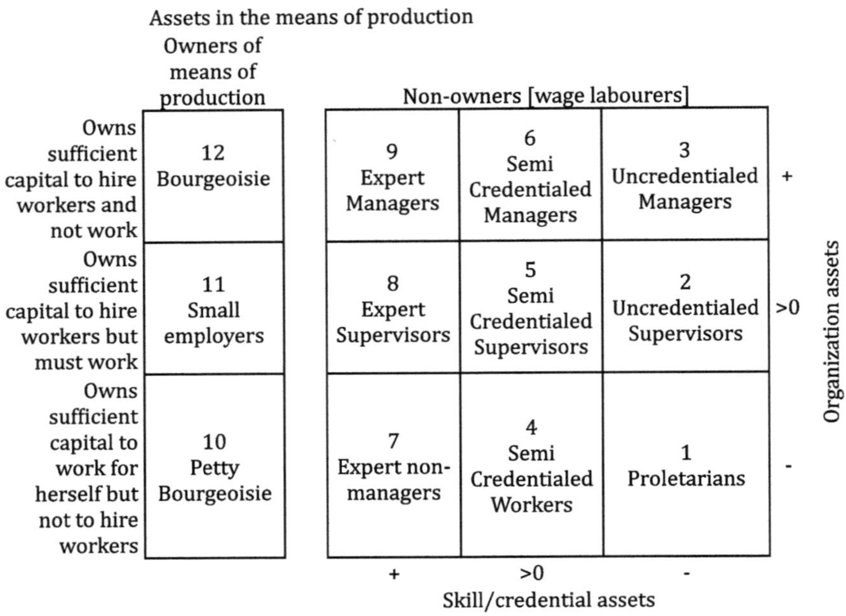


**Fig. 1** Wright's 12 class model

## The Case Studied: Socio-Environmental Protests on the Island of Chiloé

Socio-environmental movements have been understood as part of the *new social movements*, which would be characterized by actions of mobilization and political organization outside the usual margins of social conflict. That is, it would be a type of movements that construct demands that exceed the classic labor or union claims, call more diverse people than traditional militants, and, in addition, generate organizational forms usually more horizontal and democratic (Berrio, 2006).

However, some authors dispute both the novel nature of these movements (Pichardo, 1997) and their democratizing and non-"classist" character (Gledhill, 1990). Supported by these criticisms and the evidence that indicates that it is the sectors with the least capital that are most affected by environmental disasters (Carter et al., 2007), we propose to incorporate social class into the explanation of the movement that occurred on the island of Chiloé.

This movement is part of a long series of socio-environmental conflicts that have occurred in the history of Chile (Folchi, 2001). However, until recently, these were characterized by mobilizing only small sectors of the population, occurring in very specific and localized territories (Aliste & Urquiza, 2010). This situation has tended to change in recent years, with more than 100 environmental conflicts identified in Chile between 2005 and 2014. In most cases, these conflicts are associated with the centralized extractivist model dominant in the country, which tends to exploit the natural resources of the regions, without leaving an equivalent proportion of the benefits of such extraction in them (Delamaza et al., 2017).

The island of Chiloé, in the south of Chile, is a typical case of this type of development model: it has experienced major changes in the last 40 years, integrating a growing extractive-export industry (Barton & Román, 2016), among which stands out, for its social, ecological, and economic importance, the salmon industry (Bustos-Gallardo & Prieto, 2019). With the salmon industry, a process of accelerated modernization begins on the island, insertion into global dynamics and productive linkages, under the economic imperatives of comparative advantages and territorial specialization (Román et al., 2015). This process, initiated during the military government, deepens after the recovery of democracy, and to the continuous expansion of aquaculture concessions are added accusations regarding the management and preservation of the marine environment, allegations of *dumping*,[1] overmedication of salmon, poor environmental management, and a crisis due to the uncontrolled spread of a virus that sickened millions of salmon (Barton & Fløysand, 2010; Bustos, 2012; Fløysand, 2015).

During the month of May 2016, the area experienced a severe environmental and social crisis following the decree to close fishing and aquaculture operations due to the so-called "red tide",[2] which threatened the livelihood of hundreds of families by directly impacting the development of the economic activities of the island's artisanal fishermen. These fishermen attributed the responsibility for such problems to the poor waste management of the area's salmon industry and, therefore, to the government for the lack of supervision, initiating a scientific debate that remains unresolved to this day (Valdebenito, 2018).

In response to this situation, massive protests by fishermen and other sectors of the citizenry took place, paralyzing the area for almost 3 weeks, in what was called the "Chilote May" by its protagonists, becoming one of the most important mobilizations in the history of this region and positioning the socio-environmental problem in the public debate. Among the demands of this mobilization were calls for everything from economic compensation for families affected by the suspension of their sources of income to deep transformations of the extractivist development model (Cabello et al., 2018).

Parallel to the mobilizations by the inhabitants of Chiloé, a media campaign was generated, organized by environmental groups, under the *hashtag* #ChiloeResiste. Along with this, the introduction of new actors in the discussions is observed, such as environmental groups and university students, who support demonstrations for the fishermen and rejection of the government's management of the conflict, were organized in different regions of the country (Valdebenito, 2018).

---

[1] Anti-commercial practice in which a product is sold below its cost. In recent years, the concept has been extended to cover previously unconsidered issues, such as dumping social or environmental.

[2] Natural phenomenon caused by the massive proliferation of microalgae in the water, which can cause damage to the health of people who consume the mollusks that feed on them.

The mobilizations concluded after the signing of an agreement between the government and the fishermen and traders unions, leaving as a consequence a deep discussion about the natural and human causes of the disaster and a certain division between the two strands of the movement: the movement of the fishermen and seafarers and the environmentalist movement made up of organizations and collectives of various types (Cabello et al., 2018).

## Proposed Model

Based on the background presented, it was decided to study the participation of people in the socio-environmental protests of Chiloé in 2016, testing a model that considers the psychosocial variables with the most evidence of association with participation in collective action and adds a variable forgotten by social psychology: social class.

As illustrated in Fig. 2, the model posits social identity as a central but indirect exogenous factor influencing protest participation. It suggests that the pathway from social identity to protest involvement is mediated by several key perceptions: the belief that the group suffers significant grievances, the attribution of responsibility for these grievances to an outgroup, the group's perceived collective efficacy in achieving desired changes, and the degree of legitimacy assigned to protest behavior. Additionally, the model proposes that social class functions similarly to social identity, serving as an exogenous variable that indirectly affects protest participation through the same mediators. The hypothesis is that those with fewer

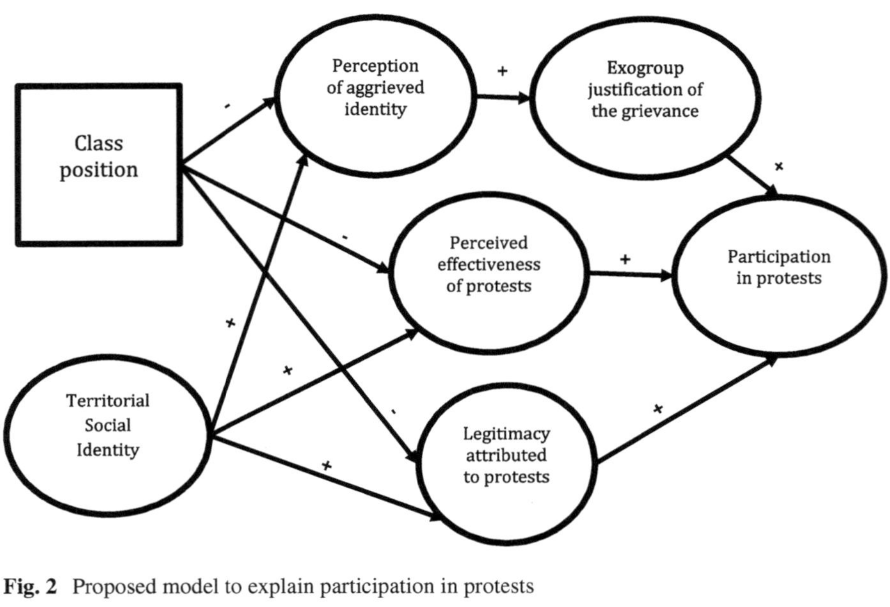


**Fig. 2** Proposed model to explain participation in protests

capitals, particularly those affected by the red tide, show greater participation in protests.

In Fig. 2, the class position is graphed with a rectangle, unlike the rest of the variables for which ovals are used, because it has been measured as an observed variable, while the others have been considered latent variables, as explained in the Method section.

## Method

### *Participants*

During the months of May and June 2017, a survey was applied to 400 people over 18 years of age, from the 2 main cities of the Big Island of Chiloé: Ancud and Castro, which that year had 61,500 inhabitants between the 2 (Instituto Nacional de Estadística, 2017). The sampling process was random, with a multi-stage cluster design and a sampling error margin of 5%, with a 95% confidence level. Of the total participants, 50.2% were men and 49.8% were women. The age range was from 18 to 94, the average was 49.8 years, and the standard deviation was 16.8 years. From an educational point of view, a very heterogeneous sample was obtained, where 33% of the sample had only basic education (8 years of study or less), the next 14% between 8 and 11 years of studies (not reaching the 12 years of compulsory education of the Chilean system), while 26% had complete secondary education and 27% had technical or university higher studies. From a socioeconomic point of view, the average income of the sample was approximately USD 800, but with high heterogeneity, as the standard deviation was USD 864.

### *Instruments*

*Regional Identity Scale (RIS-2).* A 17-item version of this Likert-type scale, adapted for Chiloé, was used, which has five response categories, from *strongly agree* to *strongly disagree*, with the intermediate category *neither agree nor disagree*. The RIS-2 has demonstrated very good psychometric properties in the Chilean population. Alpha for ordinal data = 0.95 (McDonald, 1985), a very good fit to the proposed model ($\chi^2_{116} = 664.51$; RMSEA = 0.07; TLI = 0.98; CFI = 0.99; SRMR = 0.04) and evidence of convergent validity (for more details see Asún et al., 2018). Examples of items are: "I feel proud to be part of Chiloé" and "With its good and bad things, this is the place and the culture to which I belong".

*Participation in Collective Actions.* An adapted version of the collective action participation index developed by Asún and Zúñiga (2013a) was used. Based on a press analysis in which the type of protest actions carried out during the studied demonstrations was identified, a set of 15 items was selected, each one of which refers to one of the protest tactics used in this movement. Respondents were asked if they had participated in these actions, and the response alternatives were *never*, *once*, or *more than once*. Examples of items are Marches, Demonstrations, Collection of signatures and/or money, Support for protesters, Strike, Occupation of buildings or public spaces, Barricades or route block, and Confrontation with the police.

In addition, a set of ad hoc scales was constructed, whose characteristics are described below. Since these are instruments without previous validity evidence, in the first part of the results section, their psychometric properties are analyzed.

***Perception of Aggrieved Identity*** To measure this construct, four Likert-type items were constructed based on the concept of mobilized identity by Simon and Klandermans (2001) and Sabucedo et al. (2010). It measures the degree to which life in Chiloé is perceived to be harder than in other places in the country, and the response alternatives were five, ranging from *strongly agree* to *strongly disagree*. An example of an item is: "We inhabitants of Chiloé have to face many problems just because we live here".

***Exogroup Attribution of Grievance*** Also following the concept of politicized identity by Simon and Klandermans (2001) and Sabucedo et al. (2010), six Likert-type items were constructed with five response categories, ranging from *strongly agree* to *strongly disagree*, which measure the degree to which external actors are perceived, in this case the central government, to be responsible for the shortcomings of Chiloé. An example of an item is: "The Government is the responsible for most of the problems that Chiloé has".

***Collective Efficacy*** Based on the discussion about the concept of efficacy by Hornsey et al. (2006), six Likert-type items were constructed, with five response categories, ranging from *strongly agree* to *strongly disagree*, which measure the degree to which it is perceived that it was possible to achieve the desired objectives through the protests. An example of an item is: "We inhabitants of Chiloé had the capacity to organize ourselves to achieve our objectives".

***Legitimacy Attributed to Protests*** Based on the conceptualization by Simon and Klandermans (2001) about the importance of people seeing protests as legitimate, four Likert-type items were constructed, with five response categories, ranging from *strongly agree* to *strongly disagree*, which measure the degree to which protests are perceived as a legitimate pressure tool to achieve socio-political objectives. An example of an item is: "Social movements are a valid way to influence authorities".

***Class Position*** The profession or trade of the person who contributes the most income to the household, the educational level, and the number of workers that person has under their charge were consulted. To classify this information, a combination of three systems of economic activity categorization was used: (1) the *Classification of Economic Activities* (CAE) developed by the Chilean Internal Revenue Service; (2) the *Chilean Classifier of Economic Activities*, in its fourth version (CIIU4.CL) and (3) the *Uniform Classification of Occupations* (CIUO-88) developed by the International Labour Organization (ILO). The reason for considering these three classification criteria is based on the caution made by Wright (1994) about the operationalization of his proposal, given that there are different criteria regarding the theoretical limits between the petite bourgeoisie and the proletariat. For example, the author proposes that traditionally extractive and traditional activities, such as artisanal fishing, correspond to proletarian class positions, even though they may or may not own a boat. Different is the case of shipowners and owners of larger vessels, given their ability to hire labor.

## *Data Analysis*

To determine the internal consistency of the measured variables, their reliability was calculated using the Omega index ([to adapt to the ordinal nature of Likert-type items]; McDonald, 1999), and a series of confirmatory factor analyses were applied to the items that measured each construct, except for class position, which was not treated as a latent variable but observed. Regarding the latter, an evaluation of the possibility of attributing a class position to each surveyed subject and its frequency distribution was carried out, that is, to describe the class structure of the sample.

After estimating the psychometric properties of the instruments used, the proposed model was tested, using a Structural Equations Model, since this technique seeks to establish causal relationships between latent and observed variables (Rdz-Navarro & Asún, 2016). As an estimation procedure, weighted least squares (WLSMV, for its acronym in English) were used, which has proven to be a very good procedure for estimating the relationship between variables measured with ordinal items (Asún et al., 2016). All statistical analyses were performed using the Mplus software (Muthén & Muthén, 2011).

# Results

## *Psychometric Properties of the Instruments*

To evaluate the psychometric properties of the version adapted to Chiloé, of the Regional Identity Scale (RIS-2), a unidimensional model with its 17 items was tested. The results indicated a good fit ($\chi^2_{119} = 352.71$; RMSEA = 0.07; CFI = 0.978; TLI = 0.974), with almost all items with factorial loads above 0.5. Only one item had poor performance (factorial load −0.43), so it was eliminated. The Omega index with the remaining 16 items was very adequate (ω = 0.962).

Given that the perception of aggrieved identity and the exogroup attribution of grievance together make up the construct of politicized identity (Sabucedo et al., 2010), it was decided to test a two-dimensional factorial model of two correlated constructs. This model showed a very good fit ($\chi^2_{19} = 48.95$; RMSEA = 0.063; CFI = 0.991; TLI = 0.986), with all items from the first instrument having factor loadings above 0.6 and four of the six items from the exogroup attribution of grievance having loadings above 0.5. The two items that did not fit well were eliminated. Finally, it should be noted that the relationship between both instruments was quite high ($r = 0.865$) indicating that those participants who believe that people in Chiloé live harder lives than inhabitants of other regions tend to attribute the cause of these problems to the central government. The Omega for the perception of aggrieved identity was 0.82, while for the instrument of exogroup attribution of grievance it was 0.647, which is considered adequate reliability.

Regarding collective efficacy, the fit of the original one-dimensional seven-item model was not good, so items with low factor loadings were eliminated until a one-dimensional model with three items with high factor loadings was obtained. Unfortunately, with only three items, it is not possible to obtain measures of model fit, as it is a completely determined one (without degrees of freedom). However, the factor loadings of these items were above 0.87, indicating that they are highly associated with each other, which is reflected in a very high Omega (ω = 0.931). That is, it is a brief but reliable instrument.

In relation to the legitimacy attributed to protests, the original one-dimensional model with six items had a poor fit, so two items were eliminated, obtaining a model with four items with a very good fit ($\chi^2_1 = 0.138$; RMSEA = 0.001; CFI = 1; TLI = 1) and factor loadings of all items above 0.6. The Omega was adequate (ω = 0.728), indicating good reliability.

Finally, regarding participation in collective action, six of the behaviors asked about had a very low frequency (those that involved violence or highly disruptive behaviors), so they were grouped into a single variable of "radical behaviors". In addition, "giving support to the protesters" was eliminated due to the generic nature of the behavior that did not necessarily imply participating in protests (it could consist of passive support). With the remaining eight items, plus the one that merged violent behaviors, a one-dimensional model was tested, obtaining a very good fit ($\chi^2_{27} = 35.472$; RMSEA = 0.028; CFI = 0.993; TLI = 0.99), factor loadings above 0.44 and a high Omega (ω = 0.921).

## *Participants' Class Position*

With the questions asked, it was possible to classify the social class of all the respondents. The relative frequency of each class is shown in Fig. 3, and as can be seen, almost half of the sample was classified as proletariat. The next most frequent

| | Assets in the means of production: Owners of means of production | Non-owners [wage labourers] | | | |
|---|---|---|---|---|---|
| Owns sufficient capital to hire workers and not work | 12 Bourgeoisie 1,5% | 9 Expert Managers 1% | 6 Semi Credentialed Managers 0,5% | 3 Uncredentialed Managers 1,8% | + |
| Owns sufficient capital to hire workers but must work | 11 Small employers 3,3% | 8 Expert Supervisors 1% | 5 Semi Credentialed Supervisors 0,8% | 2 Uncredentialed Supervisors 3,5% | >0 Organization assets |
| Owns sufficient capital to work for herself but not to hire workers | 10 Petty Bourgeoisie 15,8% | 7 Expert non-managers 9,3% | 4 Semi Credentialed Workers 13,8% | 1 Proletarians 48% | - |
| | | + | >0 | - | |
| | | Skill/credential assets | | | |

**Fig. 3** Class structure of the sample

classes were the petite bourgeoisie and skilled workers. This is consistent with available data, which indicates that the island has a situation of income and poverty greater than the predominant in Chile, highlighting that in 2015, the level of multidimensional poverty (which includes dimensions of health, education, work, housing, and social cohesion) reached 32%, much higher than the national 25.8% (Ministerio de Desarrollo Social, 2018).

For the purposes of the structural equation analysis, it was considered that social class was an observed ordinal variable, where higher scores correspond to classes possessing more goods and means, while lower scores correspond to the most dispossessed classes.

## Adjustment and Explanatory Capacity of the Proposed Model

Using Structural Equation Models, the model described in Fig. 2 was applied. The model's fit indicators were very good ($\chi^2_{808} = 1075.47$; RMSEA = 0.029; CFI = 0.983; TLI = 0.982), indicating that the proposed relationships are capable of adequately reproducing the observed variance and covariance structure among the items.

Figure 4 shows the regression coefficients between the different latent variables and the unexplained variances of each endogenous construct. It can be seen that the constructed model explains 46% of the respondents' participation in protest actions, indicating a very good explanatory capacity. However, it can also be seen that group identity does not seem to play a relevant role in this explanation, as the relationship between this identity and collective efficacy and the legitimacy attributed to protests is not significant. Meanwhile, while the relationship between regional identity and the perception of aggrieved identity and exogroup attribution of grievance are significant, the latter has no relationship with the participation in protests, thus breaking the causal chain. All of the above is manifested in that the total indirect effect between regional identity and participation in protests is not significant ($p = 0.075$).

Regarding class position, it does have a significant total indirect effect ($p < 0.001$) and strong ($r^2 = 0.29$) on participation in protests, which is manifested in two causal paths that relate these variables: on the one hand, people's class position is associated with the perception of collective efficacy, and this perception significantly explains participation; while on the other hand, people's class position is associated with the legitimacy attributed to protests, and this legitimacy also significantly explains participation. Conversely, the significant relationship between class position and the perception of aggrieved identity and from this with the exogroup attribution of grievance does not contribute to the explanatory capacity of the class position, due to the lack of a significant relationship between the exogroup attribution and participation in protests that has already been pointed out.

In total, social class explains almost 30% of participation in protests. But it is noteworthy that the direction of the relationship between social class and participation is contrary to what was hypothesized: the signs of the coefficients indicate that

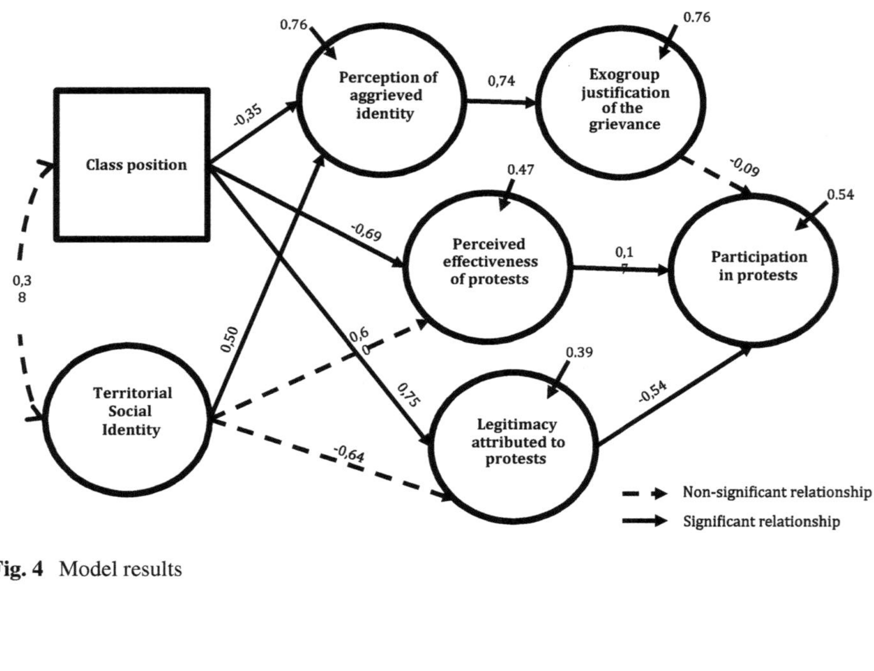


**Fig. 4** Model results

it is the classes possessing more capital and goods who attributed more legitimacy to the protests, who perceived the protests as more effective, and who participated more in the protests.

In total, it can be noted that the proposed model was only partially correct, as, although it fits the data well and most of the proposed relationships were significant, group identity did not influence participation in protests, and the direction of the relationship between social class and participation was different from what was expected.

## Discussion and Conclusions

The main results of this research show that the proposed model has a good fit to the data and predicts significantly and strongly the participation in the protests of the case studied. Evidence obtained confirms findings from other studies in the sense that collective efficacy, that is, the confidence in that one's own group has the capacity to achieve the desired changes through collective action (Hornsey et al., 2006) and the legitimacy attributed to protests as a strategy to achieve these changes (Simon & Klandermans, 2001), predicts people's participation in collective action.

However, two discoveries are contrary to what was hypothesized. On the one hand, identity with the regional group does not have a significant association with participation, unlike what was reported in multiple studies in other contexts (e.g., van Stekelenburg & Klandermans, 2013; van Zomeren et al., 2012), and the class position of individuals, although it turned out to be one of the most relevant variables to explain participation, did so in the opposite direction to what was expected.

To try to explain why group identity does not play a relevant role in predicting participation in this case, it is necessary to remember that this result has been reported in other studies in different Chilean regions, where it has been found that regional identity does not have a significant association with participation in collective actions in favor of the respective regions (Asún & Zúñiga, 2013a). The evidence would indicate that regional identity in the Chilean population is high and has an inclusive relationship with national identity; that is, a person can feel very identified with their regional group and, at the same time, feel part of the more inclusive national group (Asún & Zúñiga, 2013b), and this regional identity would be associated with values of universalism and benevolence (Zúñiga & Asún, 2010), which are not necessarily values that drive collective action. It is possible to hypothesize, therefore, from these findings, that the social norms associated with belonging to Chilean regions, that is, the unwritten rules that guide our behavior as members of a group (Smith & Louis, 2009) are not norms that include activism as a prototypical characteristic of the group.

In this line of argument, it could then be suggested that the identity as an inhabitant of Chiloé corresponds to what Williams (1984) defined as "passive identities", that is, identities that can be very strong and important for people (e.g., like that of a housewife), but that have not been politicized, in the sense that they do not generate a discourse that drives those who subscribe to this belonging to take actions to change their position in the power structure of society. A similar reflection is proposed by other studies that show that the inhabitants of Chiloé have not yet managed to politically capitalize their identity to modify development patterns toward a less vulnerable and extractivist economy (Ramírez et al., 2012).

On the other hand, the fact that the classes possessing greater capitals were the ones that participated most in the protests, is consistent with the literature that indicates that participation in collective actions requires resources of different types, including economic ones, so it is precisely the most advantaged who tend to participate in majority (Dalton, 2017; Verba et al., 1995).

However, in the case of a socio-environmental conflict like the one studied, whose main immediate effect was to put at risk the livelihoods of sea workers, it is less intuitive that it was not these proletarian sectors that most participated in the protests. In this sense, it is necessary to remember that the results show that more than 40% of the respondents belonging to this class position did report having participated, but there were other segments with greater relative participation.

The results of this study show that the social classes with the highest participation were those located in middle-high positions, characterized by their possession of credentialed skills and organizational goods (specifically the "expert workers", the "qualified managers", and the "expert supervisors"). In other words, the groups that were most committed to the mobilizations were the professional and more educated sectors of society, who seem to have more clearly appropriated the ecological demands raised by social organizations formed mainly by young people, several of them with university studies (Cabello et al., 2018).

The other side of the movement, of union origin, arises from the world of sea workers, organized by productive subsectors (fishermen, seaweed collectors, shellfish gatherers, divers, and small seafood traders), and specifically seeking the defense of workers through obtaining compensations. The demands raised by environmental organizations, on the other hand, moved away from the "petitioning" view of the workers to focus on the construction of a public problem, the search for social change, and the questioning of the extractivist development model (Cabello et al., 2018). But for the lower classes, it is precisely this model that sustains the industry, that it currently offers greater job opportunities in the area.

This highlights the difficulty also reported in other research in different contexts (Harter, 2011), of reconciling different worldviews, projects, and needs within the same movement and the challenge faced by socio-environmental movements to gain support in popular sectors, as if their discourses appear linked to claims typical of privileged segments or negatively affect workers dependent on the questioned industries; they will not have the necessary strength to drive the expected social changes.

As main limitations of this study, the number of participants stands out, as despite being a representative sample, it was relatively small in size, so there were very few subjects from the most privileged classes, which prevented the realization of a more sophisticated analysis, such as, for example, to detect relationships non-linearly between variables. Future studies could delve into the relationship between social class and participation in protests with larger samples, which would allow non-linear analysis and interclass comparisons.

**Acknowledgments** This research was funded by the National Fund for Scientific and Technological Development, Fondecyt, through Projects 1160303 and 1191295.

## References

Akaev, A., Korotayev, A., Issaev, L., & Zinkina, J. (2017). Technological development and protest waves: Arab spring as a trigger of the global phase transition? *Technological Forecasting and Social Change, 116*, 316–321. https://doi.org/10.1016/j.techfore.2016.08.009

Aliste, E., & Urquiza, A. (2010). *Medio ambiente y sociedad: conceptos, metodologías y experiencias desde las ciencias sociales y humanas*. RIL Editores.

Asún, R., Rdz-Navarro, K., & Alvarado, J. M. (2016). Developing multidimensional Likert scales using item factor analysis. The case of four point items. *Sociological Methods and Research, 45*(1), 109–133. https://doi.org/10.1177/0049124114566716

Asún, R., & Zúñiga, C. (2013a). ¿Por qué se participa? Explicando la protesta social regionalista a partir de dos modelos psicosociales. *Psicoperspectivas, 12*(2), 38–50. https://doi.org/10.5027/PSICOPERSPECTIVAS-VOL12-ISSUE2-FULLTEXT-260

Asún, R., & Zúñiga, C. (2013b). National identity and regional identities in today's Chile: Complementarity or conflict? *Estudios de Psicología, 34*(1), 95–100. https://doi.org/10.1174/021093913805403183

Asún, R., Zúñiga, C., & Morales, J. F. (2018). Design and validation of the revised regional identity scale (RIS-2). *Revista de Psicología Social, 33*(2), 357–389. https://doi.org/10.1080/02134748.2018.1439691

Ayanian, A. H., & Tausch, N. (2016). How risk perception shapes collective action intentions in repressive contexts: A study of Egyptian activists during the 2013 post-coup uprising. *British Journal of Social Psychology, 55*(4), 700. https://doi.org/10.1111/bjso.12164

Barton, J. R., & Fløysand, A. (2010). The political ecology of salmon aquaculture, 1982-2010: A trajectory from economical development to sustainability. *Global Environmental Change, 20*(4), 739–752. https://doi.org/10.1016/j.gloenvcha.2010.04.001

Barton, J. R., & Román, A. (2016). Sustainable development? Salmon aquaculture and late modernity in the archipelago of Chiloé, Chile. *Island Studies Journal, 11*(2), 651–672. https://www.islandstudies.ca/sites/islandstudies.ca/files/ISJ-11-2-MS369-Barton+Roman.pdf.

Becker, J. C., & Wright, S. C. (2011). Yet another dark side of chivalry: Benevolent sexism undermines and hostile sexism motivates collective action for social change. *Journal of Personality and Social Psychology, 101*, 62–77. https://doi.org/10.1037/a0022615

Berrio, A. (2006). La perspectiva de los nuevos movimientos sociales en las obras de Sydney Tarrow, Alain Touraine y Alberto Melucci. *Estudios Políticos, 29*, 218-236.https://www.redalyc.org/pdf/164/16429057009.pdf.

Bustos, B. (2012). Brote del virus ISA: crisis ambiental y capacidad de la institucionalidad ambiental para manejar el conflicto. *EURE Revista de Estudios Urbano Regionales, 38*(115), 219–245. http://www.eure.cl/index.php/eure/article/view/177/590.

Bustos-Gallardo, B., & Prieto, M. (2019). Nuevas aproximaciones teóricas a las regiones-commodity desde la ecología política. *EURE Revista de Estudios Urbano Regionales, 45*(135), 153–176. https://doi.org/10.4067/S0250-71612019000200153

Cabello, P., Torres, R., & Mellado, C. (2018). Conflicto socioambiental y contienda política: encuadres de la crisis ambiental de la marea roja en Chiloé (Chile). *América Latina Hoy, 79*, 59–79. https://doi.org/10.14201/alh2018795979

Carter, M. R., Little, P. D., Mogues, T., & Negatu, W. (2007). Poverty traps and natural disasters in Ethiopia and Honduras. *World Development, 35*(5), 835–856. https://doi.org/10.1016/j.worlddev.2006.09.010

Chan, M. (2016). Psychological antecedents and motivational models of collective action: Examining the role of perceived effectiveness in political protest participation. *Social Movement Studies, 15*(3), 305–321. https://doi.org/10.1080/14742837.2015.1096192

Dalton, R. J. (2017). *The participation gap: Social status and political inequality*. Oxford University Press.

De la Garza, E. (2016). La metodología configuracionista para la investigación social. Gedisa.

Delamaza, G., Maillet, A., & Neira, C. M. (2017). Socio-territorial conflicts in Chile: Configuration and politicization (2005-2014). *European Review of Latin American and Caribbean Studies, 104*, 23–46. https://doi.org/10.18352/erlacs.10173

Fløysand, A. (2015). Chiloé en la globalizacion: salmonicultura, inversiones y flujos de capital. En A. Román, J. Barton, B. Bustos & A. Salazar (Eds.), Revolución Salmonera: paradojas y transformaciones territoriales en Chiloé (pp. 27–53). RIL Editores.

Folchi, M. (2001). Conflictos de contenido ambiental y ecologismo de los pobres: no siempre pobres, ni siempre ecologistas. *Ecología Política, 22*, 79–100. http://repositorio.uchile.cl/bitstream/handle/2250/122793/folchi_m2.pdf?sequence=1&is Allowed=y.

Galais, C., & Lorenzini, J. (2017). Half a loaf is (not) better than none: How austerity-related grievances and emotions triggered protests in Spain. *Mobilization, 22*(1), 77–95. https://doi.org/10.17813/1086-671X-22-1-77

Gledhill, J. (1990). El campo y los nuevos movimientos sociales: una crítica de algunas tendencias teóricas de moda. *Revista Relaciones. Estudios de Historia y Sociedad, 12*(45), 147–179. https://www.colmich.edu.mx/relaciones25/files/revistas/045/JohnGledhill.pdf.

Harter, J. H. (2011). *New social movements, class, and the environment: A case study of Greenpeace Canada*. Cambridge Scholars Publishing.

Hayward, L. E., Tropp, L. R., Hornsey, M. J., & Barlow, F. K. (2018). How negative contact and positive contact with Whites predict collective action among racial and ethnic minorities. *British Journal of Social Psychology, 57*, 1–20. https://doi.org/10.1111/bjso.12220

Hornsey, M., Blackwood, L., Louis, W., Fielding, K., Mavor, K., Morton, T., & White, K. M. (2006). Why do people engage in collective action? Revisiting the role of perceived effectiveness. *Journal of Applied Social Psychology, 36*, 1701–1722. https://doi.org/10.1111/j.0021-9029.2006.00077.x

Nacional, I., & de Estadística, C. (2017). *Censo de población y vivienda 2017*. Author.

Klandermans, B., & van Stekelenburg, J. (2007). Individuals in movements. A social psychology of contention. En B. Klandermans & C. Roggeband (Eds.), Handbook of social movements across disciplines (pp. 157–204). Springer.

Leonard, D. J., Moons, W. G., Mackie, D. M., & Smith, E. R. (2011). "We're mad as hell and we're not going to take it anymore": Anger self-stereotyping and collective action. *Group Processes & Intergroup Relations, 14*(1), 99–111. https://doi.org/10.1177/1368430210373779

McDonald, R. P. (1985). *Factor analysis and related methods*. Erlbaum.

McDonald, R. P. (1999). Test theory: A unified treatment. *Erlbaum*.

McGarty, C., Bliuc, A.-M., Thomas, E. F., & Bongiorno, R. (2009). Collective action as the material expression of opinion-based group membership. *Journal of Social Issues, 65*(4), 839–857. https://doi.org/10.1111/j.1540-4560.2009.01627.x

Ministerio de Desarrollo Social, Chile. (2018). *Informe de estimaciones comunales de pobreza, con datos de Casen 2015* (Serie Documentos Metodológicos Casen N.° 35). Author.

Muthén, L. K., & Muthén, B. (2011). *Mplus version 6.11*. Muthén & Muthén.

Poma, A. (2014). De la oposición a la emancipación: un análisis de los conflictos ambientales desde abajo. *Ambiente & Sociedade, 17*(1), 41–58. https://www.scielo.br/scielo.php?pid=S1414-753X2014000100004&script=sci_abstract&tlng=es.

Poma, A., & Gravante, T. (2015). Analyzing resistance from below: A proposal of analysis based on three struggles against dams in Spain and Mexico. *Capitalism Nature Socialism, 26*(1), 59–76. https://doi.org/10.1080/10455752.2014.995688

Pichardo, N. A. (1997). New social movements: A critical review. *Annual Review of Sociology, 23*(1), 411–430. https://doi.org/10.1146/annurev.soc.23.1.411

Ramírez, E., Modrego, F., Yáñez, R., & Claire Macé, J. (2012). La industria acuícola del salmón en Chiloé, Chile: del crecimiento económico al desarrollo sostenible. En J. A. Berdergué & F. Modrego (Eds.), De Yucatán a Chiloé: dinámicas territoriales en América Latina (pp. 567–600). Teseo.

Rdz-Navarro, K., & Asún, R. (2016). Desarrollos recientes en estadística: aportes teórico-metodológicos a la investigación sociológica. *Sociología y Tecnociencia, 1*(6), 1–13. https://revistas.uva.es/index.php/sociotecno/article/view/651.

Román, A., Barton, J., Bustos, B., & Salazar, A. (2015). *Revolución salmonera. Paradojas, transformaciones territoriales en Chiloé.* RIL editores.

Sabucedo, J., Durán, M., & Alzate, M. (2010). Identidad colectiva movilizada. *Revista de Psicología Social, 25*(2), 189–201. https://doi.org/10.1174/021347410791063822

Schmidt, A. (2011). El concepto de naturaleza en Marx. Siglo XXI.

Simon, B., & Klandermans, B. (2001). Politicized collective identity: A social psychological analysis. *American Psychologist, 56*(4), 319–331. https://doi.org/10.1037/0003-066X.56.4.319

Smith, J., & Louis, W. (2009). Group norms and the attitude–behaviour relationship. *Social and Personality Psychology Compass, 3*(1), 19–35. https://doi.org/10.1111/j.1751-9004.2008.00161.x

Svampa, M. (2013). "Consenso de los commodities" y lenguajes de valoración en América Latina. *Nueva Sociedad, 244*, 30–46. https://nuso.org/articulo/consenso-de-los-commodities-y-lenguajes-de-valoracion-en-america-latina/.

Tajfel, H., & Turner, J. C. (1979). An integrative theory of intergroup conflict. En W. G. Austin & S. Worchel (Eds.), The social psychology of intergroup relations (pp. 33–47). Brooks-Cole.

Thomas, E. F., Mavor, K. I., & McGarty, C. (2012). Social identities facilitate and encapsulate action-relevant constructs: A test of the social identity model of collective action. *Group Processes & Intergroup Relations, 15*(1), 75–88. https://doi.org/10.1177/1368430211413619

Tyler, T. R., & Smith, H. J. (1998). Social justice and social movements. En D. T. Gillbert, S. T. Fiske & G. Lindzey (Eds.), Handbook of social psychology (pp. 595–629). McGraw-Hill.

Valdebenito, J. (2018). Twitteo, ¿luego resisto? Movilización popular y redes sociales en Chile: la marea roja de Chiloé (2016). *Izquierdas, 40*, 185–201. https://doi.org/10.4067/S0718-50492018000300185

Van Stekelenburg, J., Klandermans, B., & van Dijk, W. W. (2011). Combining motivations and emotion: The motivational dynamics of protest participation. *Revista de Psicología Social, 26*, 91–104. https://doi.org/10.1174/021347411794078426

Van Stekelenburg, J., & Klandermans, B. (2013). The social psychology of protest. *Current Sociology Review*, 1–20. https://doi.org/10.1177/0011392113479314

Van Zomeren, M., Postmes, T., & Spears, R. (2008). Toward an integrative social identity model of collective action: A quantitative research synthesis of three socio-psychological perspectives. *Psychological Bulletin, 134*, 504–535. https://doi.org/10.1037/0033-2909.134.4.504

Van Zomeren, M., Postmes, T., & Spears, R. (2012). On conviction's collective consequences: Integrating moral conviction with the social identity model of collective action. *British Journal of Social Psychology, 51*, 52–71. https://doi.org/10.1111/j.2044-8309.2010.02000.x

Verba, S., Schlozman, K. L., & Brady, H. E. (1995). *Voice and equality. Civic voluntarism in American politics*. Harvard University Press.

Williams, J. (1984). Gender and intergroup behaviour: Towards an integration. *British Journal of Social Psychology, 23*, 311–316. https://doi.org/10.1111/j.2044-8309.1984.tb00646.x

Wiltfang, G., & McAdam, D. (1991). The costs and risks of social activism: A study of sanctuary movement activism. *Social Forces, 69*(4), 987–1010. https://doi.org/10.2307/2579299

Wright, E. O. (1994). Classes. Siglo XXI.

Wright, E. O. (2000). *Class counts. Studies in Marxism and social theory*. Cambridge University Press.

Wright, S. C., & Taylor, D. M. (1998). Responding to tokenism: Individual action in the face of collective injustice. *European Journal of Social Psychology, 28*(4), 647–667. https://doi.org/10.1002/(SICI)1099-0992(199807/08)28:4<647::AID-EJSP887>3.0.CO;2-0

Wright, S. C., Taylor, D. M., & Moghaddam, F. M. (1990). Responding to membership in a disadvantaged group: From acceptance to collective protest. *Journal of Personality and Social Psychology, 58*(6), 994–1003. https://doi.org/10.1037/0022-3514.58.6.994

Zúñiga, C., & Asún, R. (2010). Identidad social y discriminación intergrupal. ¿Una relación inevitable? El caso de las identidades regionales en Chile. *Revista de Psicología Social, 25*(2), 215–230. https://doi.org/10.1174/021347410791063778

# Dimensions of Social Integration in Colombian and Cuban Population Living in Quito, Ecuador

**Carlos Reyes Valenzuela, Francisco Jaramillo Tejada, Liliana Jayo Suquillo, Marie-France Merlyn Sacoto, and María José Martos-Méndez**

The notion of social integration (SI) represents a complex social process that reveals the relationships and links between social groups. Although historically its origin can be related to the ideology that originates the French Revolution in relation to equity, equality, and fraternity among citizens, it was Emile Durkheim one of the first to address it in relation to the development of modern states. Durkheim installs the discussion around the way how modern societies produce and maintain social order. SI, following the author, would refer to the means and ways of organization and regulation of society through norms that promote social order (Durkheim, 1989). The lack of these norms, therefore, reveals the social disintegration of a society.

Social Integration (SI) is initially conceived as both a process and an endpoint within sociological frameworks. According to Cohen et al. (2000), and House et al. (1988), SI involves the transition of individuals into a social structure, aiming to achieve and maintain social order. However, the weakening or breaking of social ties, as discussed by Castel (1997) and Laparra et al. (2007), leads to social

*This chapter is the English translation of an article originally published in Spanish as*: Reyes Valenzuela, C., Jaramillo Tejada, F., Jayo Suquillo, L., Merlyn, M. -F., & Martos, M. J. (2017). Dimensiones de integración social en población colombiana y cubana que vive en Quito. *Universitas Psychologica,16*(5), 1–14. https://doi.org/10.11144/Javeriana.upsy16-5.disp. *Please cite the original version of the article in Spanish.*

C. R. Valenzuela (✉)
Universidad Politécnica Salesiana, Cuenca, Ecuador
e-mail: creyes@ups.edu.ec

F. J. Tejada · L. J. Suquillo · M.-F. M. Sacoto
Pontificia Universidad Católica del Ecuador, Quito, Ecuador

M. J. Martos-Méndez
Universidad de Málaga, Málaga, Spain

 
W. López-López et al. (eds.), *Trends in Latin American Psychology*,
https://doi.org/10.1007/978-3-031-87554-0_5

exclusion, ultimately revealing a pattern of social disintegration. This highlights the critical role of social connections in maintaining the cohesion of society.

## A Psychosocial Perspective of Social Integration

Coinciding with a sociological approach, the psychosocial perspective of SI conceives the relationship between the individual and the social from a dynamic of mutual constitution (Asún et al., 1994). However, what is distinctive in this conception is the importance attributed to the processes of subjective perception in the dynamics of relationship with social objects, so this interaction is not mechanical nor is it predetermined solely by socioeconomic aspects (Asún et al., 1994; Asún et al., 1998). Thus, SI is understood not only in a dimension of opportunity and access to the socio-economic structure (objective plane), but also considers the exchange that the individual makes with his symbolic and cultural environment (subjective plane). Together, the notion of SI is constituted in the relationship established in these planes, in terms of macro- and microsocial dimensions, in a historical-cultural context. In this way, a theoretical-methodological definition addresses SI as "a position, state or form of relationship between collective or individual subjects and the social whole, which occurs on different planes of social, economic and cultural organization" (Asún et al., 1998, p. 58). This definition makes it possible to recognize two areas of SI: one subjective-objective and another micro- and macrosocial.

SI can be observed in its objective dimension through the degree of active participation of an individual in the social media where his development takes place, that is, the level at which the individual makes use of the social media that would allow him to achieve certain ends. The objective/microsocial dimension proposes to describe how individuals perceive their social network and whether it provides them with support, while the objective/macrosocial dimension explores how people participate in social scenarios. In this way, an objective plane is evaluated through the structure of the social network and social participation, respectively. Meanwhile, SI from a subjective dimension is understood in relation to the individual's perception of the sociocultural environment, that is, to the value or interpretation that the individual assigns to the social context where he positions himself. Thus, it is related to the attitudes, motivations, behavior patterns, life projects, and emotional relationships that individuals build within the network of social relationships in which they are inscribed. Hence, a subjective/microsocial dimension identifies perceived social support, and a subjective/macrosocial dimension is approached through the notion of subjective anomie (Asún et al., 1998). This operationalization initially evaluates SI in young people, both in relation to drug use (Asún et al., 1998) and delinquent behavior (Valdenegro, 2005). The previous works focused mainly on assessing the subjective dimension of SI, based on the interest in evaluating young people with and without risk behaviors and the difficulty of configuring measurement instruments in the variable of social networks. For the study proposed here of the migratory phenomenon, this line is the one that is maintained in the present work.

## Studies on Social Integration in Migrant Population

There are numerous investigations that address social integration in immigrants, mainly developed in Spain, among others, with the Latin American population. Herrero et al. (2012) consider that social integration is related to the psychosocial well-being of immigrants, becoming an important support for these people, especially newcomers to the community. Likewise, social integration can indicate a level of adaptation and participation in the host society, as it has been observed that social isolation and little contact with the native community can negatively affect the health and well-being of migrants. Their stress levels can increase as they do not have social support to resolve stressful life situations (Cohen et al., 2000). Numerous studies show that immigrants are a group particularly vulnerable to stress due to the process of adapting to the host society (Cuellar et al., 2004; Zarza & Sobrino, 2007), and social participation has for them a significant meaning (Herrero & Gracia, 2007) by increasing their satisfaction with life and contributing significantly to their process of integration into the host society.

Thus, migrants can increase their psychological well-being through social support from close people (partner, family, and close friends), although their integration into a broader social context is also important for their satisfaction and overall well-being (Cowen, 2000; Herrero et al., 2012). On the other hand, some contextual influences, for example, the characteristics of the neighborhoods where immigrants live, constitute an important factor that can significantly influence the levels of social integration (Gracia et al., 1995; Gracia & Herrero, 2004). Therefore, understanding those factors that can promote or hinder their level of integration becomes a fundamental area of research (Herrero et al., 2012).

## Situation of Migration in Ecuador for Colombian and Cuban Population

Ecuador has historically established itself as a receiving country for migration, especially since the second half of the twentieth century. This dynamic was abruptly modified at the end of the 90s, which led simultaneously to a massive exodus of Ecuadorian nationals—mainly to the United States, Spain, and Italy—as well as to the arrival of migrants from bordering countries, predominantly from Colombia. Until 2006, the vast majority of Colombian migration was related as a result of the armed conflict, of which a minority lived in a condition of refuge recognized by the Ecuadorian State. With the arrival of Rafael Correa Delgado's Government, from

2007, a policy of reception and recognition of the displaced population and migrants in general was implemented, with deep reforms in plans and regulations—including the Constitution in 2008—recognizing free mobility, universal citizenship, and equality of rights. These changes have positioned Ecuador as the country that provides the most refuge in Latin America, of which 98% of this contingent comes from Colombia (United Nations High Commissioner for Refugees [UNHCR], 2014). According to UNHCR figs. (2016), 57,312 Colombian people are recognized refugees, 233,049 are asylum seekers, and around 500 people per month are applicants, of which the female population is slightly higher (Herrera, 2008). However, in recent years, the reception situation for displaced Colombian population has undergone abrupt changes that currently fall within a context of double exclusion for displaced people. First, because a dynamic of an expelling context in Colombia is identified (Jaramillo, 2008) and, subsequently, of a progressively excluding reception in Ecuador. The trigger for the flight continues to be the state of widespread violence, characterized by threats, selective assassinations, forced recruitment, and economic harassment from armed actors, which forces people to leave their place of origin. Contrary to what might be expected, these aspects continue occurring even after the signing in 2016 of the Final Agreement for the Termination of the Conflict and the Construction of a Stable and Lasting Peace signed between the Government of the Republic of Colombia and the Revolutionary Armed Forces of Colombia (FARC). Together, the permanence of displaced Colombian population has been altered by the current political and economic conditions of Ecuador, which is showing a gradual fragility in its economy, based on the dollar, which makes it more adverse for the subsistence and access to work for these people (Sozanski et al., 2016). In addition, with the signing of the aforementioned agreement, there is insecurity in the displaced population due to a decrease in the support that UNHCR has dedicated, and, similarly, a progressive decline in acceptance of asylum requests has been observed.

Regarding the Cuban population living in Ecuador, the vast majority are there for "economic reasons," a migration that has occurred over the last decade, precisely endorsed by the constitutional regulations of Ecuador (Correa, 2013). According to figures from the Ministry of Foreign Affairs and Human Mobility (2016), between 2012 and 2016, 26,936 visas have been granted for temporary residents, 16,738 visas for permanent residents, and 697 people have adopted Ecuadorian nationality. According to Arcentales (2012), the Cuban migrant population is concentrated in Quito, is predominantly male, aged between 20 and 49 years, and is characterized by having qualifications in their studies. Despite these characteristics, there is a perception of overestimation in the number, which has promoted a sense of alarm in the host society regarding Cuban migration (Correa, 2013). Added to this is that the experience of Cuban migration in Ecuador presents a permanent vulnerability, either labor or regularization of their migratory status. Precisely, despite the current legal order, processes of exclusion and deportation have been carried out, one of which occurred massively in July 2016. As Correa points out, "the (Ecuadorian) context promotes a traumatic reality that not only delays any process of social integration, but favors the reproduction of ghettoization logics and inverted rejection of migrant groups against host societies" (Correa, 2013, p. 45).

In this migratory context, Ecuador has issued an Organic Law of Human Mobility (National Assembly of Ecuador, 2017) that continues to reaffirm the constitutional principles of recognition of rights for the migrant population, the right to migrate, the rights of asylum and refuge, and the non-return of people. It also recognizes the principles of universal citizenship, free human mobility, prohibition of criminalization, equality before the law, and non-discrimination, which promotes rights and obligations to all foreigners. However, criticisms have arisen regarding the real recognition of equality, as it recognizes only foreigners with visas, limits the definition of South Americans to UNASUR member countries, and, in this way, hierarchizes a category of South Americans and another of foreigners (Arcentales, 2017). Therefore, a regular migratory condition is required to access the rights established in the Organic Law of Human Mobility, a permanent orientation in many countries but which under the Ecuadorian Constitution is equivalent to a violation of the principles of equality and non-discrimination (Arcentales & Chávez, 2020).

Taking into account these considerations, it is proposed as pertinent and relevant that research on social mobility inquire about the mechanisms that explain the dimensions of social integration, examining micro- and macrosocial variables that influence the migratory process. In the present study, the objective is to explore the conditions that promote anomie and social roots of the Colombian and Cuban population residing in Quito and to investigate what factors are intervening in their presence or absence. An adaptation of the works that have been carried out with the migrant population is presented, and the operationalization of IS from a psychosocial perspective is adopted, which will be oriented only to the subjective plane and its relationship with the micro- and macrosocial dimensions. The link with the host society for the migrant population can be identified from a conflicting and/or satisfaction dynamic that conditions their integration. Thus, from a plane of a dynamic of difficulties, IS considered in the migrant population on a subjective/microsocial plane as the problems perceived with the host society and on a subjective/macrosocial plane as subjective anomie. On the other hand, from a satisfaction perspective, IS in migrants on a subjective/microsocial plane corresponds to a satisfactory perceived link with the host society and, on a subjective/macrosocial plane, to social roots. These relationships will be mediated by characteristics and customs of the migrant population and by contextual factors of the host society. In this way, two objectives are proposed for each group of migrants, that is, the Colombian and Cuban population: to explore the conditions that describe a problematic relationship of these groups with the host society and subjective anomie (objective 1) and the variables that mediate the relationship between satisfaction and social roots (objective 2). It is expected to explore the influence that specific characteristics of the migrant population, such as the origin of migration, customs, and lifestyle, have on a problematic or satisfactory dynamic with the host society in Quito. Finally, the influence of contextual factors such as access or not to a paid work activity is evaluated.

# Method

## *Participants*

The study consists of 253 participants, 139 men (54.9%) and 114 women (45.1%). Their ages range between 18 and 75 years ($M = 33.67$ and $SD = 8.99$). The Colombian participants ($N$ = 105) come from the departments of Cundinamarca (Bogotá), Nariño, Valle del Cauca, and Antioquia, among others. The main reason for leaving Colombia is the situation of violence that has led them to the request for refuge in Ecuador, which is why they are attended at the institution Asylum Access Ecuador (AAE). On the other hand, the Cuban participants ($N$ = 148) come from Havana, Santiago, and Pinar del Río, among other cities. The main reason for leaving the country is economic (89%) and the remaining 11% argue the Cuban political situation. Table 1 shows the main characteristics of the sample.

**Table 1** Descriptives about participant characteristics

| | | Colombia | | Cuba | | |
|---|---|---|---|---|---|---|
| Variables | | N | % | N | % | $\chi 2$ |
| Sex | Male | 48 | 45.7 | 91 | 61.5 | 6.172* |
| | Female | 57 | 54.3 | 57 | 38.5 | |
| Age | 18–29 | 34 | 32.4 | 61 | 41.8 | |
| | 30–39 | 43 | 41 | 55 | 37.7 | |
| | 40–49 | 24 | 22.9 | 20 | 13.7 | |
| | 50–59 | 4 | 3.8 | 10 | 6.8 | |
| Marital status | Single | 32 | 30.5 | 45 | 31 | 14.936** |
| | Married/common law | 44 | 41.9 | 72 | 49.7 | |
| | Separated | 15 | 14.3 | 25 | 17.2 | |
| | Widower | 5 | 4.8 | 3 | 2.1 | |
| Time of stay in Ecuador | Less than a year | 28 | 26.7 | 46 | 31.3 | 31.959** |
| | 1 to 3 years | 38 | 36.1 | 46 | 31.3 | |
| | 3 to 6 years | 21 | 20.1 | 41 | 27.9 | |
| | + 7 years | 18 | 17.1 | 14 | 9.5 | |
| Academic level | Elementary school | 13 | 12.4 | 1 | 0.7 | 107.333*** |
| | High school | 60 | 57.2 | 73 | 49.3 | |
| | Higher education | 32 | 30.4 | 61 | 41.2 | |
| | Technical education | 0 | 0 | 12 | 8.1 | |
| Employment status in Ecuador | Working | 56 | 53.3 | 100 | 68 | 5.608* |
| | Unemployed | 49 | 46.7 | 47 | 32 | |

*Note.* *$p < 0.05$, **$p < 0.01$, ***$p < 0.001$

## *Instruments*

### Sociodemographic Data

Aspects such as sex, age, place of origin, marital status, and educational level are investigated.

### Migratory Condition

Colombian participants were consulted according to the refuge request they make in Ecuador. The possible response options were five: recognized refuge, request, denial, undocumented, and another visa. Among the Cuban participants, the response options were two: regularized legal situation and not regularized.

### Time of Residence in Ecuador

The following question was asked: "What is the year of arrival in Ecuador?", this allowed to group the answers into three categories: 1 = less than 3 years, 2 = between 3 and 6 years, and 3 = more than 7 years.

### Employment Situation

It was made up of three response options: self-employment, employment by others, and unemployed.

### Maintenance of Cultural Customs

Three items were created that evaluated three aspects of cultural customs: family traditions, meals, and celebrations of the country of origin. The following items were designed: "Do you keep in Quito the customs associated with family traditions?", "Do you keep in Quito the customs of meals from your country of origin?", and "Do you keep in Quito the customs of the celebrations of your country of origin?" The internal consistency was satisfactory ($\alpha = 0.83$). The response options are scored with 0 (*No*) and 1 (*Yes*).

### Adaptation to Local Lifestyle ([SCAS], Ward & Kennedy, 1999)

Adapted to Spanish by De Luca et al. (2011). Five items of the Cultural Learning and Communication factor were evaluated, in which the following items were consulted: "Getting used to the local food," "Understanding the jokes and sense of humor of the local people," "Understanding the local accent, language, language," "Understanding the point of view of the local culture," and "Getting used to the pace of life." It obtains a satisfactory internal consistency ($\alpha = 0.84$). The response options range from 1 (*no difficulty*) to 5 (*extreme difficulty*).

### Perceived Problems in Connection with Host Society

Four items were designed that evaluated problems with people from Quito. The following questions were asked: "Do you think that Ecuadorians reject foreigners?", "Have you had problems in Quito because you are a foreigner?", "Where did that problem occur?", "Have you ever been denied the rental of a house because you are a foreigner?". The internal consistency was acceptable ($\alpha = 0.71$). The response options are scored with 0 (*No*) and 1 (*Yes*), except in items where a specification of the problem was requested.

### Satisfactory Perceived Link with the Host Society

Three items were designed that assess the satisfactory perceived link that the participant has with the Ecuadorian population living in Quito. These questions were asked: "Do you have friends among Ecuadorians?", "Have you had help from Ecuadorians when you have problems? Have you visited Ecuadorian friends in their homes?" A good internal consistency was found ($\alpha = 0.83$). The response options correspond to 0 (*No*) and 1 (*Yes*).

### Scale of Subjective Anomie (Asún et al., 1998)

Social integration was evaluated through subjective anomie, with 20 items. The scale presents four subdimensions: estrangement, social exclusion, uncertainty, and degradation. The recoding procedure was followed, indicated in a study with young people (Aceituno et al., 2009), where a high score is associated with greater anomie. An acceptable internal consistency was found ($\alpha = 0.75$). The response alternatives vary as follows: 1 (*agree*), 2 (*I don't know*), and 3 (*disagree*).

### Scale of Social Rootedness (Torrente et al., 2011)

The social rootedness used in the immigrant population was measured in three dimensions: cultural, ecological, and social/work. The authors' instruction was maintained: "Next, a series of statements related to your life in Quito (Ecuador) are presented. Please, indicate to what extent you feel connected or feel as your own each of them." The scale presents an excellent internal consistency ($\alpha = 0.91$). The response options range from 1 (*Not at all*) to 5 (*A lot*).

## Procedure

Initially, a pilot test was carried out with the migrant population in Quito to evaluate the relevance and understanding of the items. Small changes were made to the original instrument, although it was observed the need to clarify the objective and source of the study, given some perspicacity in some participants. In a second stage, contact was made with institutions that work with the migrant population in Quito. With the Colombian population, meetings were established with Asylum Access Ecuador (AAE), an entity that established a normative to apply the surveys within their activities. Five surveyors were trained, who also received training from the AAE team. In this case, the application period was carried out between the months of May and July 2014.

In relation to the Cuban population, contact was established through a key informant who facilitated the initial approach, specifically in a neighborhood of Quito. The aforementioned surveyors established personal contact with the Cuban population, which facilitated the application of the survey. The procedure included the description of the study objectives, the reading and signing of an informed consent. Then, sociodemographic data, migration status, length of residence in Ecuador, conflict and satisfaction in the relationship with the population of Quito, the subjective anomie scale, and, finally, they answered the social rooting scale. The duration varied between 30 and 50 min.

In response to these considerations, the sample selection was determined as nonprobabilistic intentional. Participation was voluntary, and participants were identified by numerical codes, which maintained anonymity in data processing.

## Results

Table 1 presents the descriptives of the sample and an analysis of the comparison of the groups. Differences were observed in aspects such as sex, marital status, length of stay, academic level, and employment situation in Ecuador, with the exception of age. The differences found in sex respond to the indicated characteristic: the Colombian female population is slightly larger, while the Cuban one is mainly male.

Although significant differences emerged in marital status, both populations presented a condition of married/free union, followed by singles. Likewise, differences were found in the time of connection to Ecuador, where Cuban participants present a more recent migration compared to the Colombian sample. On the other hand, Cuban participants showed greater labor insertion than Colombians, which suggests that this last characteristic is not associated with the length of stay.

Then the correlations in the different scales are presented, where a direct correlation was observed between anomie and problems in the bond with the host society and an inverse correlation between these variables and almost all of the other scales (Table 2). However, it is noted that no significant relationships are established between subjective anomie and satisfactory bond with the local population. The variable problems with the host society only presented significant relationships with subjective anomie and social rooting.

When making comparisons in the different scales and dimensions that compose them between the two groups of participants, the following was found: there are no significant differences in the evaluated scales (all the $p > 0.05$), which reveal the apparent similarity of the samples in relation to social integration. However, the differences occurred in some of the dimensions that compose them. In relation to the subjective anomie scale, significant differences were observed in the dimensions of social exclusion, $t$ (252) = −2.214, $p = 0.028$, being higher in Cubans, $M_{col} = 6.84$ and $M_{cub} = 7.43$. In the dimension of estrangement, $t$ (252) = 2.83, $p = 0.005$, the trend is contrary, $M_{col} = 7.48$ and $M_{cub} = 6.8$. In relation to the social rooting scale, differences were observed in the dimension of cultural attachment, $t$ (253) = −3.11, $p = 0.002$, being higher in Cubans, $M_{col} = 2.75$ and $M_{cub} = 3.16$. When making comparisons in the dimensions of problems with the host society, differences were found in relation to the places where it has occurred, $\chi^2 = 11.765$, $p = 0.038$; mainly in Colombians it occurs in public places and in Cubans at work. Differences were also observed in the difficulties for the adaptation to the lifestyle in Ecuador, $t$ (253) = 2.996, $p = 0.008$, the difficulties being greater in Colombians.

Regarding objective 1, a mediation analysis was carried out (Hayes, 2013; Preacher & Hayes, 2004) where subjective anomie was established as the dependent variable and the perceived problems in the bond with the host society as the independent variable. The mediation variables introduced corresponded to current work,

**Table 2** Correlations between the variables under study

| Variables | Subjective anomie | Social participation | Rooting | Satisfactory bond with host society | Problems in bond with host society |
|---|---|---|---|---|---|
| Subjective anomie | – | −0.14* | −0.32** | −0.04 | 0.2** |
| Social participation | – | – | 0.18** | 0.14** | 0.08 |
| Social rooting | – | – | – | 0.15** | −016** |
| Satisfactory bond with host society | – | – | – | – | −0.04 |

*Note.* *$p < 0.05$, **$p < 0.01$

difficulty in adapting to the lifestyle of Quito, and the level of studies. In the case of the Colombian population, it was found that the problems in the bond were positively associated with subjective anomie ($B = 0.42$, $t\ (105) = 2.91$, $p = 0.004$). A significant relationship was also observed with current work ($B = -1.36$, $t\ (105) = -2.12$, $p = 0.036$) and adaptation to lifestyle ($B = 0.05$, $t\ (105) = 4.91$, $p = 0$). The results indicated that the lifestyle adaptation mediator was significantly associated with subjective anomie ($B = 3.94$, $t\ (105) = 3.08$, $p = 0.002$). Thus, the results confirmed the mediation of the identified variables between the perceived problems with the host society and subjective anomie ($B = 0.2$, SE = 0.09, *CI* [0.12, 0.5]). In addition, the results indicated that the direct effect of perceived problems with the host society on subjective anomie became non- significant ($B = 0.16$, $t\ (105) = 1.04$, $p = 0.29$), when controlling for intervening variables, suggesting complete mediation. Figure 1a shows the results.

Thus, adaptation to lifestyle more than the absence of work is set up as the main mediating variable in the case of the Colombian displaced population. This result is striking because it would imply that Ecuadorians and Colombians share customs and that this factor was not related to subjective anomie. In other words, it could be expected that the absence of work was the variable that mediated the problems with the host society and the perception of anomie, showing that the patterns of Ecuadorian culture are perceived as adverse in Colombians.

In relation to the Cuban population, there was no significant association between perceived problems in the bond with the host society and subjective anomie. A significant relationship was found between problems in the bond with the host society and current work ($B = 0.02$, $t\ (142) = 2.32$, $p = 0.021$) and between current work and subjective anomie ($B = -2.26$, $t\ (142) = -2.02$, $p = 0.044$). The results confirmed a model of complete mediation at this point ($B = 0.09$, SE = 0.05, *CI* [0.21, 0.1]). The results are presented in Fig. 1b.

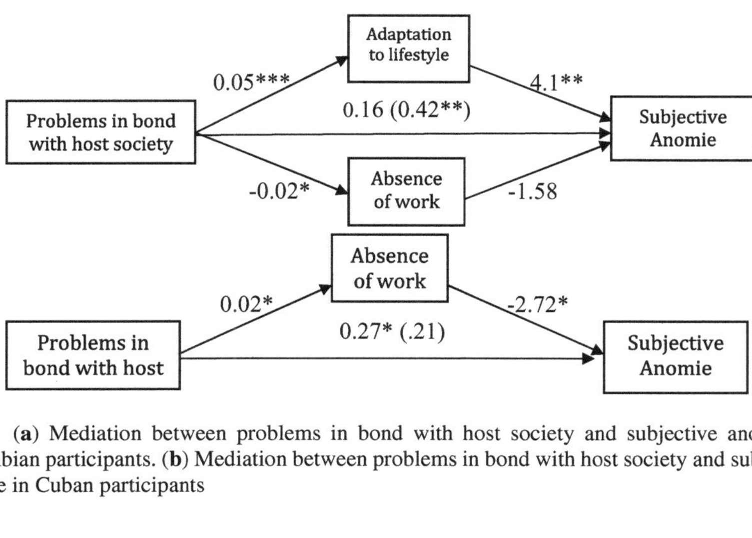


**Fig. 1** (**a**) Mediation between problems in bond with host society and subjective anomie in Colombian participants. (**b**) Mediation between problems in bond with host society and subjective anomie in Cuban participants

In this case, the model reveals that in that Cuban population that has problems with the host society, the absence of work is the variable that determines the perception of anomie. As was pointed out earlier, this population is highly qualified, and those who have work are mainly oriented in service areas, while the unemployed population is the most exposed to evaluate that they will not meet their social goals.

Finally, in relation to objective 2, the mediation analysis was carried out, establishing social roots as the dependent variable and the satisfactory perceived bond with the host society as independent. The intervening variables were made up of current work, maintenance of cultural customs, and origin of the migration. In the case of the Colombian population, this last variable stood out in relation to the migratory condition in Ecuador (i.e., recognized refugees or asylum seekers). First, a significant relationship was found between the satisfactory bond with the host society and roots ($B = 0.53$, $t\ (80) = 3.76$, $p = 0$). The bond with the host society was associated with the migratory condition ($B = 0.61$, $t\ (80) = 2.77$, $p = 0.007$). Subsequently, this condition was related to social roots ($B = 0.17$, $t\ (80) = 2.43$, $p = 0.017$) and current work ($B = 0.45$, $t\ (80) = 2.39$, $p = 0.019$). The adjustment levels formed a partial mediation ($B = 0.28$, SE = 0.07, *CI* [0.04, 0.35]). The results are presented in Fig. 2a.

These results suggest that among Colombians who perceive a satisfactory bond with the host society, the migratory condition in which they find themselves in

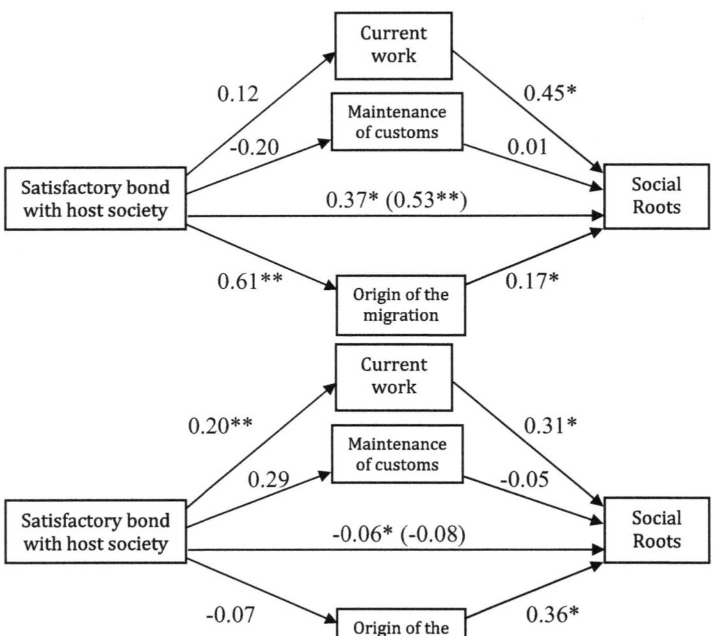


**Fig. 2** (**a**) Mediation between perceived satisfactory bond with host society and social rooting in Colombian participants. (**b**) Mediation between satisfactory bond with host society and social roots in Cuban participants

Ecuador is what allows for greater social roots. This greater rooting is observed in refugees more than in other migratory statuses, given that such population has stayed longer, has better working conditions, generally lives with their family, and perceives fewer possibilities of returning to Colombia.

In the Cuban population, the reason for leaving their country of origin was introduced as a mediating variable. No relationship was found between the satisfactory bond perceived with the host society and social roots. An association was observed between a satisfactory bond with the host country and current work ($B = 0.2$, $t$ $(140) = 3.35$, $p = 0.001$). Then, an association was found between current work and social roots ($B = 0.31$, $t\ (140) = 2.09$, $p = 0.037$) and with the reason for leaving ($B = 0.36$, $t\ (140) = 2.29$, $p = 0.023$). Despite these relationships, there is no confirmation of the mediation model ($B = 0.07$, SE = 0.06, $CI$ [−0.09, 0.14]). The results are shown in Fig. 2b.

In this case, it is observed that the presence of work also does not constitute a variable that favors the social roots of Cubans, which questions what circumstances would promote integration conditions in this population.

## Discussion

The social integration of the population in mobility condition is a challenge for societies, especially Latin American ones, given the great movement that is taking place today. News from different contexts report situations of exclusion and discrimination for migrants, in access to social services and jobs that configure them as a highly vulnerable group, especially those who migrate due to expulsion conditions from their countries of origin. The Colombian population, victim of an armed conflict that still does not cease, and the Cuban population, exposed to conditions of a system that continues in political and economic transition and that sanctions those who decide to emigrate, constitute two of the groups that are presenting high mobility in Latin America and, consequently, in Ecuador.

In this context, the objective of this study was to explore the conditions that promote the exclusion and social integration of Colombian and Cuban migrant population, in the city of Quito, through the operationalization of micro- and macrosocial variables on a subjective plane.

In this regard, the results suggest that the bond perceived with the host society is a key aspect in how social integration or exclusion of the studied groups is promoted, in which the variable of work activity is especially relevant. In the case of the Colombian population, when difficulties arise in accessing work and in adapting to the local lifestyle, they lead to anomalous perceptions of social exclusion. It is surprising that, given the cultural proximity between Colombia and Ecuador, Colombian participants perceive a distance in the lifestyle compared to the indigenous population, a situation that can be related to the discriminatory perception that exists in Quito toward Colombians. Meanwhile, in the Cuban population, only the absence of work conditions an anomie perception.

On the contrary, social rootedness is conditioned by a perception of satisfaction in the bond with the host society, which appears mediated in the Colombian population, by the presence of work activity and migratory status. In this case, the recognized refugee migratory status is more significant, which would facilitate carrying out a work activity. In contrast, social rootedness in the Cuban population is not associated with any variable of the measures in this work. Here, the statement regarding the difficulties in the social integration of groups in human mobility reveals the relationship established with the members of the host society. These results confirm what was stated by Correa (2013) regarding the relational dynamics that the Cuban population residing in Ecuador has been implementing.

The present results provide a signal about the difficulties that arise in the integration processes for people in a condition of social mobility in Latin America. It could be considered, in a quick reading, that certain similarities in language and the cultural richness of the societies of origin would encourage greater possibilities of social integration in Quito for the Colombian and Cuban population, especially with an unprecedented Ecuadorian constitutional legislation in the region. However, these findings are a wake-up call to Latin American societies regarding the plans and policies of integration on populations in a condition of mobility since their absence or delay in implementation leads these groups to various conditions of social vulnerability. For Ecuador, there is a double standard on mobility that, despite having a level of participation of certain collectives, includes a dangerous inequality among those considered migrants. Complementary to this, there is a need to observe the imaginaries that the indigenous populations present of the growing human mobility present in the region, whether it comes from the States or is aroused by the media. The experiences of social exclusion exhibited in northern hemisphere countries that had difficulties in managing the arrival of migrant population were resolved in many cases through the criminalization of collectives. This situation, even without being a trend, is progressively being implemented in Latin America, which leads to increasing dynamics of discrimination, racism, or collective expulsion. Hence, it is essential that states implement human mobility policies, which do not focus only on aspects of administrative regularity in the stay, but on generating social conditions both political and awareness in the citizenship, for a real integration of people in mobility.

## Limitations and Future Studies

The current study has several limitations that should be noted. Firstly, the sample selection inherently included participants with a high likelihood of integration difficulties due to their low social connections and perceived discrimination from the indigenous population. This could skew the results toward more negative outcomes. Future studies should consider more diverse mobility groups from different cultural backgrounds, potentially including a comparative group from the Ecuadorian population, to provide a broader perspective on social integration.

Secondly, unlike other studies that emphasize the objective dimensions of Social Integration (SI) (Gracia et al., 1995; Gracia & Herrero, 2004), our study did not examine structural factors such as socioeconomic status or cultural stress that could influence anomie or social rootedness. This omission limits our ability to fully understand the dynamics affecting SI.

Despite these limitations, the study's insights into the integration experiences of Colombian and Cuban nationals contribute valuable perspectives to the discourse on integration, particularly concerning economic migrants and those facing forced displacement. Notably, this study also examined social support and social network structure, though these aspects are not discussed in this text. Future research should consider these and other related factors to provide a more comprehensive understanding of the challenges and dynamics of social integration.

Lastly, recent research in Latin American countries in relation to the population in mobility conditions has focused on the adjustment to sociocultural stress and its negative and positive effects (Bobowick et al., 2015; Urzúa et al., 2015; Yáñez & Cárdenas, 2010; Zlobina et al., 2006). Despite these findings, it is essential to address not only these effects, but their implication in the relationship of the population in mobility conditions with the host society and in the aspects that require an IS policy. This last point is especially relevant for societies in Latin America and, in this case, Ecuador in particular, a country that has shown an inclusive migration policy in the region, given its legal incorporation, but which at the same time, is limited by organic law regulations that pose restrictions on equality processes. States need to promote the rights contemplated for the population in mobility conditions, in such a way that it contemplates an education and sensitization to the native population and does not appear as benefits granted to foreigners. The results emerged here confirm that efforts are required in this sense in groups with high vulnerability.

**Acknowledgments** This work was funded by the Pontificia Universidad Católica de Ecuador, code: K13165, named "Level of Social Integration in immigrants of Colombian and Cuban nationality residing in the City of Quito from February to November 2014." Likewise, the collaboration of Asylum Access Ecuador is appreciated, which made possible the contact with the Colombian population and Ahmed Correa with the Cuban population. This work is dedicated to Professor Domingo Asún Salazar (1943–2015), a prominent social and community psychologist in Chile, a pioneer in research on social integration.

## References

Aceituno, R., Asún, R., Ruiz, S., Venegas, J. I., Corbalán, F., & Reinoso, A. (2009). Anomia y alienación en estudiantes secundarios de Santiago de Chile: Resultados iniciales de un estudio comparativo 1989-2007. *Psykhe, 18*(2), 3–18. https://doi.org/10.4067/S0718-22282009000200001

Arcentales, J. (2012). *Migración cubana: recomendaciones de política pública para Ecuador incluyente*. Defensoría del Pueblo.

Arcentales, J. (2017). *¿Por qué la Ley de Movilidad Humana no es una buena noticia para la igualdad de derechos?*. [Unpublishedmanuscript].

Arcentales, J., & Chávez, G. (2020). La Ley Orgánica de Movilidad Humana del. Ecuador: los límites de la regularidad e irregularidad de la movilidad. In N. Caicedo (Ed.), *Tendencias y retos de las políticas y reformas migratorias en América Latina. Un estudio comparado*. Fondo Editorial de la Universidad del Pacífico.
Asún, D., Alfaro, J., & Morales, G. (1994). Análisis crítico del uso de categorías y estrategias para el estudio e intervención psicosocial con jóvenes en Chile. *Revista Chilena de Psicología, 15*(1), 5–14.
Asún, D., Alfaro, J., Fernández, P., Báez, X., Pérez, L., & Vergara, R. (1998). *Construcción de un modelo teórico-metodológico para la medición de la integración social (Proyecto FONDECYT N° 1980190)*. FONDECYT.
Bobowick, M., Basabe, N., & Páez, D. (2015). The bright side of migration: Hedonic, psychological, and social well-being in immigrants en Spain. *Social Science Research, 51*, 189–204. https://doi.org/10.1016/j.ssresearch.2014.09.011
Castel, R. (1997). *Las metamorfosis de la cuestión social. Una crónica del salariado*. Paidós.
Cohen, S., Gottlieb, B., & Underwood, L. (2000). Social relationships and health. En S.
Correa, A. (2013). Inserción laboral y producción de espacios: la migración cubana en Ecuador (Experiencias latinoamericanas). *Cuestiones Urbano Regionales, 1*(3), 39–64. https://repositorio.flacsoandes.edu.ec/bitstream/10469/6461/1/REXTN-QUR3-03-Correa.pdf
Cowen, E. (2000). Community psychology and routes to psychological wellness. In J. Rappaport & E. Seidman (Eds.), *Handbook of community psychology* (pp. 79–99). Kluwer/Plenum.
Cuellar, I., Bastida, E., & Braccio, S. M. (2004). Residency in the United States, subjective well-being, and depression in an older Mexican-origin sample. *Journal of Aging and Health, 16*, 447–466. https://doi.org/10.1177/0898264304265764
De Luca, S., Bobowick, M., & Basabe, N. (2011). Adaptación sociocultural de inmigrantes brasileños en el País Vasco: bienestar y aculturación. *Revista de Psicología Social, 26*(2), 275–294. https://dialnet.unirioja.es/servlet/articulo?codigo=3626413
Durkheim, E. (1989). *El suicidio*. Akal.
Gracia, E., & Herrero, J. (2004). Determinants of social integration in the community: An exploratory analysis of personal, interpersonal and situational variables. *Journal of Community & Applied Social Psychology, 14*, 1–15. https://doi.org/10.1002/casp.746
Gracia, E., García, F., & Musitu, G. (1995). Macrosocial determinants of social integration: Social class and area effect. *Journal of Community & Applied Social Psychology, 5*, 105–119. https://doi.org/10.1002/casp.2450050204
Hayes, A. F. (2013). *Introduction to mediation, moderation, and conditional process analysis: A regression-based approach*. Guilford Press.
Herrera, G. (2008). *Ecuador: la migración internacional en cifras*. UNFPA y Flacso Ecuador.
Herrero, J., & Gracia, E. (2007). Measuring perceived community support: Factorial structure, longitudinal invariance and predictive validity of the PCSQ (Perceived Community Support Questionnaire). *Journal of Community Psychology, 35*, 197–217. https://doi.org/10.1002/jcop.20143
Herrero, J., Gracia, E., Fuente, A., & Lila, M. (2012). Desorden social, integración social y bienestar subjetivo en inmigrantes latinoamericanos en España. *Anales de Psicología, 28*(2), 505–514. https://doi.org/10.6018/analesps.28.2.148721
House, J. S., Umberson, D., & Landis, K. R. (1988). Structures and processes of social support. *American Review of Sociology, 14*, 293–318. https://doi.org/10.1146/annurev.so.14.080188.001453
Jaramillo, A. M. (2008). Contextos explicativos del desplazamiento interno y del refugio de colombianos en Ecuador y Canadá. In P. Riaño & M. Villa (Eds.), *Poniendo tierra de por medio. Migración forzada de colombianos en Colombia, Ecuador y Canadá* (pp. 37–69). Corporación Región.
Laparra, M., Obradors, A., Pérez, B., Pérez, M., Renes, V., Sarasa, S., Subirats, J., & Trujillo, M. (2007). Una propuesta de consenso sobre el concepto de exclusión. Implicaciones

metodológicas. *Revista Española del Tercer Sector, 5*, 15–57. https://dialnet.unirioja.es/servlet/articulo?codigo=2376685

Preacher, K. J., & Hayes, A. F. (2004). SPSS and SAS procedures for estimating indirect effects in simple mediation models. *Behavior Research Methods, Instruments, & Computers, 36*(4), 717–731. http://quantpsy.org/pubs/preacher_hayes_2004.pdf

Sozanski, A., Sarmiento, K., & Reyes, C. (2016). Derecho al trabajo en personas refugiadas y solicitantes de asilo en Ecuador: dificultades y propuestas. *Forced Migration Review, 51*, 93–95. http://www.fmreview.org/sites/fmr/files/FMRdownloads/en/destination-europe/sozanski-sarmiento-reyes.pdf

Torrente, G., Ruiz-Hernández, J. A., Ramírez, M. C., & Rodríguez, Á. (2011). Construcción de una escala para medir el arraigo en inmigrantes latinoamericanos. *Anales de Psicología, 27*(3), 843–851. https://revistas.um.es/analesps/article/view/135591

Urzúa, A., Vega, M., Jara, A., Trujillo, S., Muñoz, R., & Caqueo-Urízar, A. (2015). Calidad de vida percibida en inmigrantes sudamericanos en el norte de Chile. *Terapia Psicológica, 33*(2), 139–156. http://www.scielo.cl/pdf/terpsicol/v33n2/art08.pdf

Valdenegro, B. A. (2005). Factores psicosociales asociados a la delincuencia juvenil. *Psykhe, 14*(2), 33–42. https://doi.org/10.4067/S0718-22282005000200003

Ward, C., & Kennedy, A. (1999). The measurement of sociocultural adaptation. *International Journal of Intercultural Relations, 23*(4), 659–678. https://doi.org/10.1016/S0147-1767(99)00014-0

Yáñez, S., & Cárdenas, M. (2010). Estrategias de aculturación, indicadores de salud mental y bienestar psicológico en un grupo de inmigrantes sudamericanos en Chile. *Salud y Sociedad, 1*(1), 51–70. http://www.redalyc.org/pdf/4397/439742462006.pdf

Zarza, M. J., & Sobrino, M. I. (2007). Estrés de adaptación sociocultural en inmigrantes latinoamericanos residentes en Estados Unidos vs. España: una revisión bibliográfica. *Anales de Psicología, 23*(1), 72–84. http://www.um.es/analesps/v23/v23_1/10-23_1.pdf.

Zlobina, A., Basabe, N., Páez, D., & Furnham, A. (2006). Sociocultural adjustment of immigrants: Universal and group-specific predictors. *International Journal of Intercultural Relations, 30*, 195–211. https://doi.org/10.1016/j.ijintrel.2005.07.005

# Ethnic Identity and Social Behaviors in Mapuche Indigenous Adolescents Sanctioned by the Juvenile Criminal Responsibility Law in Southern Regions of Chile

**Raúl Alberto Jiménez Bustos, Ricardo Xavier Pérez-Luco Arenas, and Gonzalo Eugenio Bustamante Rivera**

## Introduction

### *Contextualization*

In Chile, the incorporation of the Mapuche people into the state was carried out through what official historiography calls the "Pacification of Araucanía," from the mid-nineteenth century until 1880. From this military-type process of annexing Mapuche territory, Chilean society has promoted the assimilation of the Mapuche within society. This process was characterized by the use of violent strategies that ended with the creation of indigenous reductions, militarization and dispossession of their lands, and attempts to eliminate aspects of the Mapuche culture (Correa & Mella, 2010).

Currently, the effects of the "Pacification of Araucanía" have generated processes of marginalization in the Mapuche people, such as forms of social exclusion, negatively impacting various areas. On one hand, economically, it has been observed that of the total number of Mapuche (604,349) living in the country in 2002, 33% lived in the Araucanía Region, and a third of them were below the poverty line (Agostini et al., 2010). On the other hand, low levels of schooling are reported; specifically, between basic and secondary education, 30% of Mapuche children

*This chapter is the English translation of an article originally published in Spanish as:* Jiménez Bustos, R. A., Pérez-Luco Arenas, R. X., & Bustamante Rivera, G. E. (2017). Identidad étnica y conductas sociales en adolescents indígenas Mapuche sancionados por la Ley de Responsabilidad Penal Adolescente en regions del sur de Chile. *Universitas Psychologica, 16*(1), 1–21. https://doi.org/10.11144/Javeriana.upsy16-1.iecs. *Please cite the original version of the article in Spanish.*

R. A. J. Bustos · R. X. P.-L. Arenas (✉) · G. E. B. Rivera
Universidad de la Frontera, Araucanía, Chile
e-mail: ricardo.perez-luco@ufrontera.cl



W. López-López et al. (eds.), *Trends in Latin American Psychology*,
https://doi.org/10.1007/978-3-031-87554-0_6

drop out of school (Instituto Nacional de Estadística [INE], 2002). This is partly explained by the fact that many young people start to work to support their parents in household maintenance tasks and participate in sowing and harvesting, among other activities (Organización Internacional del Trabajo [OIT], 2006).

Likewise, the migratory processes of the Mapuche have been directed from rural areas, reduced in the nineteenth century, toward urban areas; migration that is greater in these than in other indigenous peoples. Despite the idea that greater contact with urban sectors leads to greater socioeconomic well-being, it has been observed that among the Mapuche, poverty in urban sectors is greater than in rural areas (Agostini et al., 2010), thus generating vulnerable conditions for the families, facilitating stronger acculturation processes, disconnecting family members from the territory, as well as losing the use of the language and traditions.

Related to the above, a central aspect that amplifies and reproduces social exclusion is the non-recognition of the Mapuche, by the Chilean State, of the status of people (Correa & Mella, 2010), which implies denying the sense of identity and therefore denying the possibility of being a different people sharing a common territorial space with the rest of Chilean society.

As a result of widespread negative stereotypes (Saiz et al., 2008), a detrimental social image of the Mapuche has been established, leading many within the community to internalize these perceptions (Saiz et al., 2009). This internalization often results in a denial or devaluation of their own identity, disconnecting from their cultural roots and exacerbating individual conflicts and tensions about their belonging to their native people. Given this context of vulnerability, marginalization, stigmatization, and poverty, it is particularly pertinent for this article to explore the identity formation processes of Mapuche adolescents and their impact on social behaviors.

Adolescence is recognized, following Erikson (1968), as a critical period for identity resolution. For Mapuche adolescents, this developmental challenge is compounded by the need to reconcile their personal identity with their cultural heritage, which often stands at a disadvantage relative to the dominant culture (Schwartz et al., 2007). This complex "dual" identity process occurs within a context that not only is inherently unfavorable but also exacerbates the psychosocial tensions typical of adolescence. These conditions can lead to the emergence of maladaptive and/or delinquent behaviors among these young individuals.

These behaviors, at a psychological level, can be understood as adaptation strategies while identity is resolved, but also as survival strategies in this context (Alarcón et al., 2005). However, in a study where the mediating capacity of self-esteem between the relationship of ethnic identity and externalizing behaviors in Turkish-Danish and Moroccan-Danish adolescents was analyzed, it was observed that in the latter group a greater development of ethnic identity was related to higher self-esteem, and this latter with a lower degree of externalizing behaviors (Wissinka et al., 2008). In other words, a defined identification toward the culture of origin can function as a factor that attenuates the existence of maladaptive behaviors.

## Adolescence and Antisocial Behaviors

As previously mentioned, adolescence emerges as a characteristic period of identity formation; concurrently, during this period, an increase in the risk of antisocial behaviors is observed (Farrington, 1996). Specifically, the concept of antisocial behaviors refers to a variety of acts that violate social norms and the rights of others (Kazdin & Buela-Casal, 2002). Additionally, it has been argued that antisocial behavior ranges from aggressive behaviors and problems with peers to theft and breaches of social coexistence norms in various socializing contexts (Peña & Graña, 2006).

Many of these antisocial behaviors become law-breaking behaviors, as they are classified as crimes in legislation; however, the sanctions are specific to this age group. In Chile, between 1986 and 2002, the number of young offenders under 18 who were apprehended by the police increased by 369% (Méndez & Barra, 2008); by 2010, the two southern regions of Chile, where this study is conducted (La Araucanía and Los Ríos), had 1435 adolescents sanctioned under the criminal responsibility law, 91% of whom were men (Servicio Nacional de Menores [SENAME], 2010), reaching 2.7% of the total adolescent population of both regions for that year (Instituto Nacional de Estadísticas [INE], 2014).

Two forms of adolescent delinquency have been widely described: a common or transient one, characterized by fleeting criminal behaviors, associated with the adolescent process and that naturally desists over time, representing between 68% (Solís et al., 2015) and 95% (Fréchette & Le Blanc, 1998) of adolescent delinquency; another form, called persistent or distinctive, which represents between 5% and 28% of adolescents who commit crimes, doing so from an early age (prior to adolescence), with a large volume of various types of crimes, high frequency, increasing severity, and projection into adult life (LeBlanc et al., 1991; Fabio et al., 2011; Fréchette & Le Blanc, 1998; Loëber & Farrington, 2001; Moffitt, 1993; Pérez-Luco et al., 2014; Piquero & Moffitt, 2005). In this group, differentiated trajectories have been identified that are expressed in distinctive patterns of criminal behavior, in specific criminogenic risk contexts, and with characteristic personality configurations (Alarcón, 2015; Alarcón et al., 2014; Fréchette & Le Blanc, 1998; Pérez-Luco et al., 2012).

In Chile, SENAME has adopted an intervention model that seeks the social reintegration of adolescent law offenders and is based on a paradigm of restorative justice, understood as the option of justice aimed at repairing the social, individual, and relational damage caused by the committed crime (Ward & Langlands, 2009). In this way, it is considered that an essential aspect is to be able to detect and modify the risk and protection factors toward antisocial and criminal behavior. From this perspective, various authors have identified multiple factors that predispose toward antisocial behaviors, as well as their prevention or reduction.

It has been observed that, at the family level, the presence of negligent and authoritarian parenting styles are associated with a higher presence of antisocial and criminal behaviors (Hoeve et al., 2008), the effect of living in a context of prolonged poverty (Eamon & Mulder, 2005), the influence of peers (Monahan et al., 2009), peer rejection, and previous aggressive behavior (Coie et al., 1995).

In Chile, as a result of a collaboration project with the University of Quebec in Outaouais and a subsequent applied research project funded by the National Council for Science and Technology, CONICYT (Pérez-Luco et al., 2009), there are methodologies that allow the evaluation of the presence of antisocial behaviors and their risk and protective factors in adolescents. However, there are still particularities that have not been investigated; specifically, if we consider that some adolescent offenders come from various indigenous peoples, it becomes necessary to study the role that cultural aspects that have not been addressed play. In particular, when studying adolescents belonging to the Mapuche people, one of the differentiating elements would be to integrate aspects of the development of ethnic identity as a risk or protective factor toward the presence and persistence of antisocial behaviors.

## *Ethnic Identity in Adolescence*

The concept of identity is complex and multifaceted. From a psychological standpoint, it refers to an individual's idiosyncrasies and the manner in which a person identifies with personal traits or in relation to others (Northoff & Heinzel, 2003). Conversely, from an anthropological perspective, identity is seen as a sense of belonging to a collective or a specific reference group, a process that is self-evaluated by the individual (Van Meijl, 2008).

This study was based on the theory of the development of ethnic identity in adolescence proposed by Phinney (1989), which indicates that it is a process characterized by the search for identity, where the need to integrate the perception of oneself, the identity imposed by the family and society (French et al., 2006), being a process of self-constructed internalization of the meaning of belonging to an ethnic group, which is accompanied by emotional reactions, thoughts, and actions (Lerner & Steinberg, 2009). From the above, Phinney (1989) proposes a model that focuses on the successive transformations of this stage, where the formation of identity comprises two interacting dimensions: that of *exploration*, which is associated with learning processes, the result of seeking information and experiencing experiences associated with one's own culture and that of *affirmation*, which refers to the affective bond, characterized by feelings and emotions that arise toward the group.

From the result of the interaction of both dimensions, the author explicates that stages of development in adolescence can be established. On the one hand, there is a period of *diffuse ethnic identity*, where adolescents lack a positive or negative view of their ethnic group; that is, there is no affective bond with the group, nor have they explored the meaning of this. On the other hand, there is a stage called *moratorium*, where they begin to explore what it means to be a member of a group, but without yet having a clear affective bond that allows valuing the relationship of himself with the group in affective terms. Also, there is a stage called *delegation*, which consists in identifying affectively, but without a greater understanding of what it means to belong to a specific ethnic group; that is, there are feelings toward the group, but that are not based on the understanding of the culture resulting from an active search by the adolescent. Finally, there is a stage called *achieved*, characterized by a more elaborate sense of belonging, a product of the exploration about the own culture, generating an evaluation and deep reflection of the meaning of being a member of their culture, which also generates positive feelings and security from and toward the ethnic group.

Considering the above, the process of development of ethnic identity in adolescence is dynamic and complex; it implies a concrete and experiential relationship of the person with their social and cultural environment, which generates feelings of belonging, which causes personal and relational changes that affect the behavioral sphere, the cognitive field, and the affective one.

In accordance with the above, empirical evidence has shown that ethnic identity is not static, but it is subject to modifications as time goes by (Hallett et al., 2008). Being socially constructed, it can change according to the context, varying according to moments and situations that occur during life (Hallet et al., 2008), as well as the bond that is established between the reference group and its relationship with other groups.

A longitudinal study (Hallet et al., 2008) showed that Canadian indigenous adolescents initially identified themselves as indigenous, but in a second measurement, about 50% did not consistently identify themselves as such; in addition, there was a difference in self-identification depending on whether the subjects belonged to an aboriginal reserve or not. Specifically, the researchers report that almost all students living on a reserve did not change their ethnic identification, and 68% of the sample living outside the reserves modified their pattern of self-identification. Considering this, according to the scholars, in aboriginal adolescents the identity is variable over time and being surrounded by people of the same culture is associated with less change in self-identification, contrary to being immersed in a different culture.

## *Ethnic Identity as a Protective/Risk Factor in Adolescents*

Various studies have shown the relationships between identification with the group of origin and the presence of antisocial behaviors. It has been observed that, in the United States, adolescents belonging to ethnic groups with an established self-identity have a more positive sense of ethnic identity and are associated with greater psychosocial well-being (Saint Louis & Liem, 2005).

From the perspective of risk and resilience, a study examined the degree to which self-esteem, ethnic identity, and cultural orientations mediated or moderated the relationship between perceived discrimination and depressive symptoms, in Latino adolescents. The results indicated that an increase in levels of exploration of ethnic identity and positive resolution of identity predicted higher levels of adolescent self-esteem (Umaña-Taylor & Updegraff, 2007).

Brook and Phal (2005) examined the potential protective effect of ethnic identity toward drug use in an African American adolescent population in the United States. The results showed that ethnic identity variables explained 7% of the variance in drug use and were inversely related to it, as well as aspects of ethnic identity attenuated risk factors and increased protective ones. On the other hand, a study shows that adolescents who identify more strongly with their culture of origin have higher self-esteem (Martínez & Dukes, 1997; Phinney et al., 1997).

Similarly, in adolescents from minority cultures, it has been identified that a strong sense of ethnic identity, coupled with a consistent sense of personal identity, functions as protective elements in the presence of behavioral problems (Yasui et al., 2004), risky sexual behaviors (Belgrave et al., 2000), and substance abuse (Marsiglia et al., 2004).

On the other hand, another study analyzed a population of Filipino adolescents residing in Hawaii, the relationships between criminal behavior with low cultural identification and decreased family support, which are considered important risk factors toward delinquency. The results showed that criminal behavior correlated positively with acculturative stress, with a low identification with their ethnic group and negative influence of their peers. Finally, it was determined that the most important variables are the influence of peers and absent parents, compared to low ethnic identification, low self-esteem, and decreased religiosity. The authors conclude that it is not only important to culturally link the adolescents, but this should be accompanied by a connection with their families and the reduction of peer influence (Guerrero et al., 2010).

The literature also indicates that the relationship between identification with one's own ethnic group and maladaptive behaviors may be influenced by mediating variables. A study found that self-esteem moderately mediated the relationship between low ethnic identification in adolescents who exhibited antisocial behaviors (Schwartz et al., 2007). In the same sense, it has been observed that a greater sense of ethnic identity was related to higher levels of self-esteem, which in turn corresponded to fewer problem behaviors (Wissinka et al., 2008).

The literature shows that adolescents who maintain identity links with both their culture of origin and the foreign culture (biculturalism) display better behavioral adjustment compared to those who do not identify with either or both of these (DeBerry, 1996; Steinberg & Sheffield, 2001). Finally, it has been observed that the presence of factors associated with enculturation, such as participating in cultural activities and maintaining higher self-efficacy, functions as protectors against mental problems in indigenous adolescents (Bals et al., 2001).

In conclusion, these studies, collectively, indicate that in adolescents of various ethnic origins, identification with their own ethnic group is associated with an increase in psychosocial well-being, that is, a better quality of the relationships they establish with their environment, promoting the healthy development of their personality, in addition to preventing the emergence of problem behaviors. Likewise, a low level of identification with the culture of origin is associated with antisocial behaviors and psychological problems.

However, the evidence of this relationship has not been studied in depth in groups of adolescents who have committed crimes and who therefore present a high psychosocial vulnerability, as they are exposed to criminal risk contexts at the community, family, and personal levels, affecting the relational quality and psychological development of the adolescent.

## *Ethnic Identity in Indigenous Juvenile Offenders*

Despite the scarce literature that analyzes variables of ethnic identification in indigenous juvenile offenders, researchers consider it important to delve into this dimension. Rugge (2006), in an article on risk assessment in indigenous offenders, argues that despite some consensus on the existence of protective and risk factors that are similar among indigenous and non-indigenous juvenile offenders, it is necessary to consider other specific ones, of which cultural variables related to ethnic identity and the need for cultural belonging of adolescents within their own population of offenders are among the most important.

A study in New Zealand aimed to identify specific risks and protective factors associated with law infringement among the Maori indigenous population. The research highlighted the development of ethnic identity and the presence of intercultural conflicts as primary variables. It also emphasized the importance of the ways in which individuals relate to their extended family (Whãnau) and the nature of these relationships (Whakawhãnaunga) (Maynard et al., 1999). Furthermore, the authors found that a secure ethnic identity can foster positive behavioral changes among Maori offenders, whereas a confused ethnic identity may lead to negative emotions such as anger, negative self-perceptions, and depressive feelings.

From another angle, to analyze the determining factors of reintegration in a sample of adult Maori aboriginal ex-offenders, in a study they were asked about aspects of their reintegration into society after leaving jail. The results showed that, of all the stories, 94% of the subjects responded that learning about personal values and their ethnic identity was paramount for achieving reintegration (Heckbert & Turkington, 2001).

Together, these investigations suggest that in adolescents belonging to various indigenous peoples, the degree of identification with their own culture is related to an increase or decrease in behavioral problems, as well as the presence of antisocial behaviors in indigenous juvenile law offenders. Moreover, it has been observed qualitatively that offenders who have already served their sentence indicate it is important for personal development and behavioral change to recognize and participate in their own culture of origin, indicating that this relationship tends to be inverse: the greater the development of ethnic identity, the fewer antisocial and criminal behaviors.

Currently, there are Mapuche adolescents sanctioned by the Adolescent Criminal Responsibility Law in Chile; however, their level of ethnic identity development and its relationship with their behavior is not precisely known. From this, it is necessary to analyze the development of ethnic identity as a risk or protection factor toward the emergence or maintenance of antisocial behavior, especially in Mapuche adolescents who present high social vulnerability, thus becoming an important focus of analysis.

Considering that the study of risk and protective factors of maladaptive behavior in juvenile offenders mainly focuses on common psychosocial variables with the general population, these cultural differences would be becoming invisible among people from and participants of different cultures and peoples.

On the other hand, while the relationships between identification with the ethnic group of origin in adolescents have been studied, there are few investigations that focus specifically on associating the development of ethnic identity with these behaviors in the adolescent population belonging to indigenous peoples.

From the above, the general objective of this research is to analyze the degree of linkage that exists between the development of ethnic identity in Mapuche adolescents who have broken the law in Chile and the presence of social behaviors. As a specific objective, the relationship between prosocial and antisocial behaviors with the dimensions of affirmation and exploration of ethnic identity in Mapuche adolescent law offenders will be analyzed. On the other hand, it analyzes whether there are differences in the degree of development of ethnic identity between Mapuche adolescent law offenders and student adolescents who do not present criminal behaviors.

Likewise, as a specific objective, the differences in social and criminal behaviors between law-breaking adolescents identified as Mapuche and non-Mapuche are studied. The hypothesis is that a higher degree of ethnic identification is associated with a lower presence of antisocial behaviors and a higher presence of prosocial behaviors; likewise, it is expected that a lower degree of development of ethnic identity, there is a greater presence of antisocial behaviors and a lower presence of prosocial behaviors.

## Method

### *Participants*

From a total population of 345 adolescents enrolled in programs under the SENAME network in the Araucanía and Los Ríos regions of southern Chile, a purposive sample of 60 Mapuche adolescents was selected for the FONDEF D08i-1205 project. The criteria for selection included: (a) residency in the study regions during 2011; (b) ages between 14 and 18; (c) self-identification as Mapuche; and (d) expressed consent to participate in the study.

From a total population of 195 adolescents attending municipal secondary schools in the commune of Ercilla, Araucanía region, a purposive sample of 115 was selected based on several criteria: (a) ethnic self-identification, ascertained through questions such as “Are you Mapuche?” and “Do you feel Mapuche?”; (b) age between 14 and 18 years; and (c) expressed consent to participate in the study. Ercilla was chosen for its notably high proportion of rural Mapuche population according to official statistics. The sample was drawn from three educational establishments that differ in their demographic composition: one predominantly Mapuche, one mixed, and one predominantly non-Mapuche.

## *Design*

A quantitative cross-sectional design was used to establish relationships between the levels of the variables ethnic identity and antisocial and prosocial behavior, variables that will be described below along with the instruments used for this research.

The non-parametric Pearson correlation test was used; in addition, Student's *t* comparisons were used to analyze the group differences between those identified as Mapuche and non-Mapuche in the aforementioned variables. The decision to use this design is due to the fact that the objective is not to find causality between the variables, but the association between them and the comparison between the groups, since, given the scarce previous empirical evidence, it is not possible to propose a causality hypothesis if there is no analysis that establishes the relationships between the variables in advance, this being the methodological objective of this research.

## *Instruments*

### Multigroup Ethnic Identity Measure (MEIM)

Currently, in Chile there is no adaptation of this instrument, nor for the cultural group of Mapuche adolescents, so for its use in this work, the psychometric properties obtained from international research that used it in Spanish-speaking, English-speaking, and various ethnic origin groups were reviewed. Various studies account for its consistent psychometric stability; therefore, the decision to apply it was due to the empirical need and the absence of research that could evaluate the relationship of identity development as a protective factor against antisocial behaviors in adolescents, whose results could impact, at a second level, intervention strategies with this group of adolescents.

An instrument that measures the ethnic identity development of adolescents is the Multigroup Ethnic Identity Measure (Phinney, 1992), adapted to Spanish by Esteban (2010), an instrument that is currently considered as a general measure of the development of ethnic identity. This scale also collects the dimensions of exploration and affirmation as central aspects of ethnic identity development (Phinney & Ong, 2007).

The instrument is a self-report questionnaire composed of 12 statements, rated on a Likert scale from "strongly disagree" to "strongly agree." It is designed to measure two dimensions: affirmation, with 5 items assessing feelings of belonging to the group; exploration, with 7 items evaluating knowledge of and participation in cultural practices. This instrument has demonstrated adequate psychometric properties, including a confirmed bifactorial structure across various ethnic groups in the United States (Phinney, 1992), Australia (Dandy et al., 2007), among African Americans (Pegg & Plybon, 2005), Latin Americans, and European Africans (French et al., 2006). Additionally, Roberts et al. (1999) observed a strong correlation between the exploration and affirmation constructs. Upon its translation into Spanish, Esteban (2010) found that the instrument also showed good internal consistency for both the global scale and its dimensions among mestizo and indigenous groups in the Spanish-speaking population.

### Self-Report Questionnaire of Social Behavior in Adolescents (SRQSA)

Validated in Chile to evaluate antisocial behaviors, both in the population of law-breaking adolescents and non-offenders (Alarcón et al., 2010), it consists of a self-administered scale that evaluates three main areas of social behavior: prosocial behavior, total antisocial behavior, and victim of abuse of power. In turn, the dimension of antisocial behavior is composed of six subscales: (a) Crimes, (b) Transgression against Property, (c) Transgression against People, (d) Abusive Behavior with Peers, and (e) Alcohol and Drug Use. The validation analyses in a Chilean sample showed that as a whole the instrument shows good internal reliability and stability, in addition to presenting internal (convergent) and external (discriminant) validity. On the other hand, it was observed that there is a significant inverse correlation between antisocial and prosocial behavior, indicating that whenever greater antisocial behavior is observed, prosocial behavior will be lower, and vice versa (Alarcón et al., 2010).

### Self-Reported Delinquency Scale (EDA)

It consists of a semi-structured interview guide that allows to know the delinquent behaviors that adolescents have presented, observed through 63 items associated with different crimes grouped into three categories: (a) thefts and robberies, (b) assaults, and (c) other crimes. These items are scored by placing their occurrence chronologically according to seven age ranges and indicating the number of times the behavior has occurred. Finally, it contains a list of 26 self-referential and hetero-referential descriptors that define the role within the criminal context (Pérez-Luco et al., 2011).

At the statistical level, this instrument shows adequate internal consistency indices ($\alpha = 0.95$) for theft and robbery crimes, for assaults ($\alpha = 0.8$), and for other crimes ($\alpha = 0.61$). It has been pointed out that this instrument is valued for identifying persistent criminal patterns, indicating specialization and polymorphism of criminal behaviors and allowing to explore the formation of criminal trajectories in adolescents (Pérez-Luco et al., 2012).

### Risk and Resources Evaluation Form (FER-R)

Structured professional judgment instrument built in Chile (Alarcón, 2001). It uses a dichotomous record (presence/absence) to estimate a global risk assessment index. It is composed of 51 items distributed in 7 factors, in addition to a global index of resources for intervention, composed of 2 factors with 17 items in total. Statistically, the 2 scales present a high internal consistency for Global Risk ($\alpha = 0.94$) and for Protective Resources ($\alpha = 0.81$) and also for each of the 9 factors ($\alpha =$ between 0.64 and 0.88).

## Procedure

The total population of adolescents was evaluated using the Differentiated Evaluation Protocol of the FONDEF D08i-1205 project, which includes a total of 14 self-report instruments of crimes, social behaviors, ethnic identity, risk assessment, and personal, family, and community resources, among others. To identify the adolescents belonging to the Mapuche people within this protocol, the criterion of ethnic self-identification was used based on the questions "Are you Mapuche?" and "Do you feel Mapuche?" and the ethnic identification judgment of the professionals responsible for the intervention was also collected.

In parallel, ethnic self-identification among secondary school students in the commune of Ercilla was assessed using two key questions: "Are you Mapuche?" and "Do you feel Mapuche?" This dual approach was chosen to explore whether the affective aspect of ethnic belonging, elicited by the second question, produces different responses compared to the first question, which might prompt self-observation of ethnic identification potentially influenced by external factors such as context or the presence of a Mapuche surname. This method aims to discern the nuances in how students identify with their ethnicity on both cognitive and emotional levels.

On the other hand, in the sample of students, the Multigroup Identity Scale was applied, with the aim of knowing the degree of development of the ethnic identity of these adolescents, which allowed to carry out comparative analyses in the degree of development of the ethnic identity between the group of offending adolescents and the group of students. Once the information was obtained, a database was built where the responses of the adolescents were recorded for statistical analysis.

## Data Analysis

Data processing involved three types of analyses. Initially, descriptive analyses were used to detail the frequency and percentages of ethnic self-identification and professional judgments within both the groups of adolescent students and the offenders. Group comparisons were then conducted using the Student's t-test to explore differences in ethnic self-identification between Mapuche adolescent students and Mapuche offenders. This test was also used to contrast the groups of non-Mapuche and Mapuche offenders, including both those charged and not charged with crimes. Additionally, comparisons were made between law-offending adolescents who self-identified as non-Mapuche and those self-identifying as Mapuche, specifically in terms of social behaviors. Lastly, correlational analyses were performed to examine the relationships between ethnic identity and social behaviors within the group of offending adolescents who identified as Mapuche.

### Ethical Safeguards

Since the sample consists of underage adolescents sanctioned by the juvenile criminal responsibility law, the right to voluntary participation in the study was safeguarded, in addition to the complete confidentiality of the identity of the participants in this research. For this, each adolescent was informed, through informed consent, about the reasons for the research and the confidentiality of the information obtained, a protocol that was signed by the adolescent and the person in charge of data collection. Also, since information was obtained about identity aspects related to the culture of origin, it was possible that the adolescents had concerns that needed to be addressed after the application of the tests, for which the commitment was established to answer the questions and provide all the necessary information to satisfy the demands of the young people, an aspect that is also described within the informed consent that the adolescents signed.

## Results

## *Selection Criterion by Self-Identification*

### Law-Breaking Adolescents Identified as Mapuche

The descriptive analyses indicated that 17.4% of the adolescents answered affirmatively to the question "Are you Mapuche?". On the other hand, the adolescents were asked "Do you feel Mapuche?", observing that of the total sample, 15.1% of them feel Mapuche. Likewise, through professional criteria, it was observed that of the total adolescents in the sample, 11.9% were identified as Mapuche; however, there are missing data (61 cases) when analyzing this criterion (18.3%), so from now on, only self-descriptive criteria were used for the analyses. Considering only the self-identification criteria, it was analyzed if there was independence between them through the chi-square test. The results show that the criteria have a high correlation ($\chi = 0.725$) in the sample of law-breaking adolescents self-identified as Mapuche, this being significant ($p < 0$).

## Student Adolescents Identified as Mapuche

On the other hand, of the total of 195 adolescents in the student sample, it was observed that 59% answered affirmatively to the question "Are you Mapuche?". To the question "Do you feel Mapuche?", 54.5% answered affirmatively. Also, considering both self-identification criteria, it was analyzed if there was independence between them through the chi-square test. The results indicated that these criteria have a high correlation ($\chi = 0.772$) being also significant ($p < 0$) (Fig. 1).

On the other hand, a lower proportion of self-identified Mapuche is observed in the sample of offenders than in the sample of students (Fig. 2).

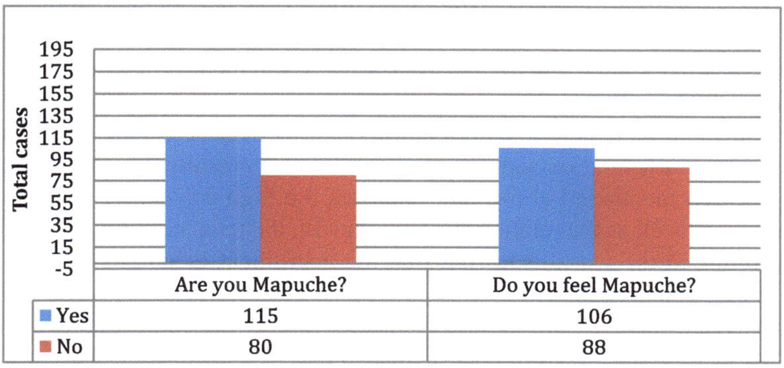


**Fig. 1** Teenagers' response to Mapuche identification criteria in a sample of offenders and students

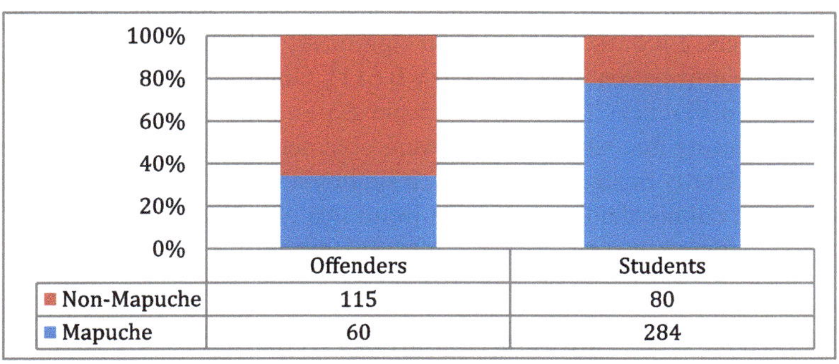


**Fig. 2** Percentage proportion of self-identified Mapuche teenagers in samples of offenders and students

## Group Comparisons Between Samples of Mapuche Student Teenagers and Mapuche and Non-Mapuche Offenders

### *Ethnic Identity Among Mapuche Offender Teenagers and Mapuche Student Teenagers*

To analyze the association between total ethnic identity and the exploration and affirmation dimensions in both groups, a Pearson correlation analysis was performed, where it was observed that there is a high correlation ($r = 0.971$) between the affirmation dimension and the total ethnic identity ($p < 0$), as well as a high correlation ($r = 0.929$) between the exploration dimension and the total ethnic identity ($p < 0$).

With the aim of analyzing the relationship between the affirmation and exploration dimensions, a Pearson correlation analysis was also carried out, where the results show that there is a high correlation ($r = 0.814$) between the dimensions of affirmation and exploration significantly ($p < 0$). Both results confirm the international research mentioned above that indicates the high correlation between both dimensions, as well as the relationship of both with the total scale found in different ethnic groups in the world, showing that the instrument behaves similarly in the group of Mapuche teenagers.

To analyze if there are differences in the development of ethnic identity between the group of Mapuche law offender teenagers and Mapuche student teenagers, a *t* test was performed to compare the means of both groups in the development of total ethnic identity and the dimensions of affirmation and exploration. The analyses indicate that there are no significant average differences ($t = 0.133$) ($p > 0.894$) regarding total ethnic identity between Mapuche offender teenagers and Mapuche student teenagers. Likewise, there are no significant differences ($t = 0.511$) in the averages of the affirmation dimension ($p > 0.611$). On the other hand, there are also no significant differences ($t = -1.05$) in the exploration dimension ($p > 0.296$). Finally, considering that similar means were obtained in both groups in the scores of the Ethnic Identity Scale, qualitatively, a slight tendency to show greater affirmation toward the culture than exploration toward it is observed (Fig. 3).

### *Non-Mapuche and Mapuche Offenders in Judicialized Crimes and Self-Reported Crimes*

To evaluate differences in the amount of crimes committed between non-Mapuche and Mapuche juvenile offenders, a mean difference test was conducted using the *t* test. The results indicate that there are no significant mean differences ($t = -0.542$) ($p > 0.588$) in the number of judicialized crimes between both groups.

To observe if there are differences in the number of self-reported crimes between the non-Mapuche and Mapuche offender group, a significative difference test was

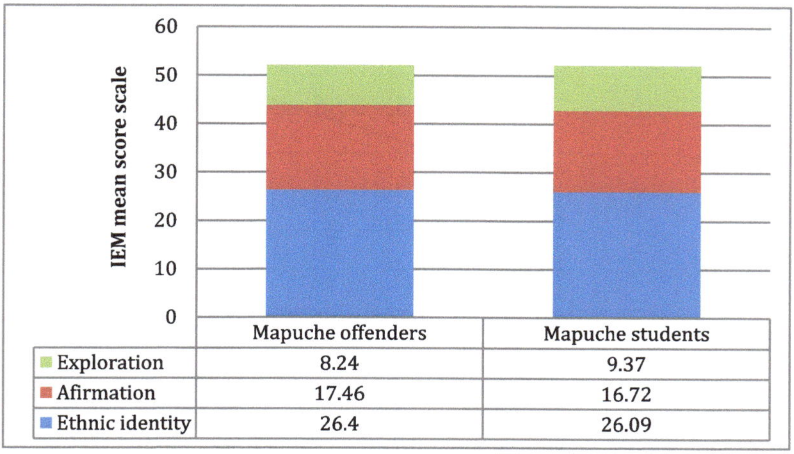


**Fig. 3** Compared average between Mapuche students and offenders on the Ethnic Identity scale

conducted using the *t* test. The results indicate significant differences ($p < 0.001$) between the total average number of self-reported crimes among non-Mapuche offenders (m = 356) and those self-identified as Mapuche offenders (m = 96). Regarding the most frequently self-reported crimes, it is qualitatively observed that on average both show more theft crimes (non-Mapuche m = 293; Mapuche m = 74); however, there are no significant differences between both groups regarding specific crimes, such as property crimes ($t = 2.941$; $p > 0.186$), crimes against persons ($t = 0.969$; $p > 0.334$), and other crimes ($t = 1.141$; $p > 0.255$). The above indicates that while both groups have a similar number of judicialized crimes, those self-reported by the adolescents themselves are significantly different, observing that, despite having fewer self-reported crimes, Mapuche adolescents are equally sanctioned as non-Mapuche, who have a higher number of self-reported crimes. This would lead to a more exhaustive analysis and hypothesis formulation that respond to these differences in both groups (Fig. 4).

## *Social Behaviors Among Mapuche and Non-Mapuche Juvenile Offenders*

To compare if there are differences in social behavior between law-breaking adolescents identified as Mapuche and non-Mapuche, a *t* test was used to compare the means of both groups, both for antisocial and prosocial behaviors, using the CACSA instrument. The analyses show that there are no significant mean differences ($t = -0.098$) ($p > 0.929$) in the means of the prosocial behavior scores between the Mapuche and non-Mapuche group. When comparing antisocial behaviors between both groups, no significant mean differences are observed ($t = 0.129$) ($p > 0.898$)

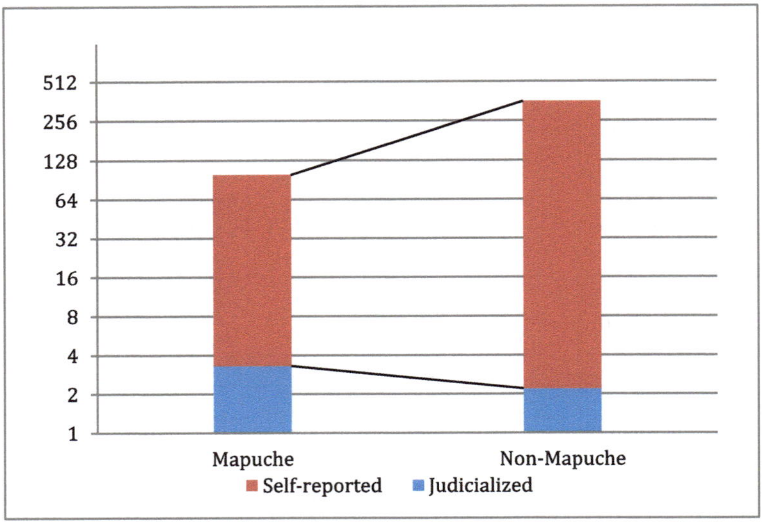


**Fig. 4** Significative differences between Mapuche and non-Mapuche juvenile offenders in judicialized and self-reported crimes

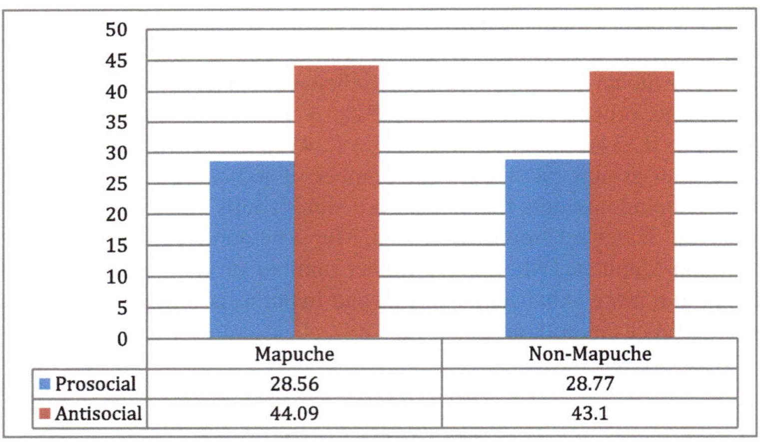


**Fig. 5** Differences in prosocial and antisocial behaviors (CACSA) between Mapuche and non-Mapuche offending adolescents

between Mapuche and non-Mapuche adolescents. The above indicates that in comparison in both groups there is a balance between social and antisocial behaviors, a fact that contrasts with the differences in self-reported crimes between both. This is associated with the fact that the antisocial behaviors analyzed by the CACSA instrument encompass not only criminal behaviors, but those against norms in general, but when focusing on the former, group differences are important, indicating that the differentiating aspects between both groups are the specific criminal behaviors and not the antisocial behaviors in general (Fig. 5).

**Table 1** Correlation matrix between total ethnic identity, its dimensions of affirmation and exploration of the IEM with the prosocial and antisocial behaviors of the CACSA

| Variable | Exploration | Affirmation | Prosocial | Antisocial |
|---|---|---|---|---|
| IET | 0.930<br>0.000 | 0.979<br>0.000 | 0.121<br>0.094 | −0.200<br>0.006 |
| Exploration | | 0.835<br>0.000 | 0.115<br>0.107 | −0.226<br>0.002 |
| Affirmation | | | 0.113<br>0.119 | −0.181<br>0.014 |

### *Association Between Ethnic Identity and Social Behaviors in Offending Adolescents Self-Identified as Mapuche*

The study sought to establish relationships between ethnic identity and social behaviors in offending adolescents self-identified as Mapuche. A Pearson correlation analysis revealed a low but significant inverse relationship between ethnic identity and antisocial behaviors; specifically, a stronger ethnic identity was associated with fewer antisocial behaviors. However, no significant correlation was found between ethnic identity and prosocial behavior.

Further analyses were conducted to examine the relationships between the dimensions of ethnic identity—exploration and affirmation—and social behaviors. Results indicated a low but significant inverse relationship between the exploration dimension and antisocial behaviors. Similarly, a slight but significant inverse relationship was observed between the affirmation dimension and antisocial behaviors. Conversely, no significant relationships were detected between either dimension of ethnic identity and prosocial behaviors, as detailed in Table 1.

## Discussion

The objective of this research was to analyze the relationship between social behaviors and ethnic identity in Mapuche indigenous adolescents who have broken the law, with the aim of empirically evaluating whether ethnic identity could be considered a protective factor associated with antisocial behavior in this group of adolescents.

The initial results show that the degree of development of the ethnic identity among Mapuche student and offending adolescents is similar. Likewise, in both a medium level of development of ethnic identity was observed, which in light of the model proposed by Phinney (1989) means that both groups would be in a state of identity situated between delegation and moratorium, indicating that in the first, adolescents identify affectively with their own culture, but have not made an active search to know and participate in it. This could also be due to the scarce possibility in the socializing context that allows exploration, knowledge, and participation in cultural practices. In the second, they participate in it, but affectively they have not yet linked with their culture, therefore without yet valuing it as their own, which could be due to the processes of stigmatization and discrimination mentioned above.

From another perspective, despite the fact that 46.5% of the population of the commune of Ercilla, where the secondary school student adolescents of the sample reside are Mapuche, has one of the highest percentages at the national level (Economic Commission for Latin America and the Caribbean [ECLAC], 2012), the degree of development of ethnic identity in both samples is on average similar. This could indicate that both in judicialized contexts and in those territorially dense in Mapuche population, the low degree of development of the ethnic identity in these adolescents could be associated with acculturation processes that impact transversally the Mapuche adolescent population. From a historical and contextual perspective, the above is consistent with what Hart (2002 cited in Howell, 2008) states, mentioning that when the experiences of colonization have been internalized by the people belonging to indigenous peoples, these influence all areas: emotional, mental, and spiritual. This generates a perception of confusion and weakening, as they feel pressured to dissociate from what they are, and to the extent that they are more internalized, there is a greater tendency to stop recognizing themselves as such, generating the loss of their identity. Therefore, for adolescents belonging to indigenous peoples, there is a factor that adds complexity to the already critical task of negotiating the formation of identity in a culturally asymmetric interpersonal context, since they are confronting the status of indigenous people within the dominant culture, while having to resolve their ethnic identity, which tells them who they are in society (Umaña-Taylor & Updegraff, 2007).

The descriptive analyses of the total population indicated that of the 345 adolescent law offenders (17.4%), identified themselves as Mapuche, a percentage lower than those self-identified as Mapuche from the sample of students (40.6%). If only both samples were compared, it could be preliminarily concluded that there is an underrepresentation in the judicial system of adolescents belonging to the Mapuche people. However, as mentioned earlier, the town of Ercilla has one of the highest percentages of people belonging to the Mapuche people at the national level (Comisión Económica para América Latina y el Caribe & Alianza Territorial Mapuche, 2012), which explains the identity characteristics of the population of secondary school students, a demographic situation that is not representative of the Mapuche adolescent population of the country.

However, when comparing the sample of Mapuche offenders and the adolescent population identified as Mapuche at the national level, it is observed that approximately 7% identify with this people (Instituto Nacional de Estadísticas [INE]. 2009). From this perspective, the 17.4% of Mapuche adolescent offenders implies an overrepresentation of Mapuche adolescents in the judicial system. This overrepresentation would be consistent with what is observed in the penal system in other countries, such as Australia (Allard et al., 2010), Hawaii (Hishinuma et al., 2005), Canada (Rojas & Gretton, 2007), among others. According to these authors, this phenomenon is associated with processes of marginalization, poverty, and the difficulties of adolescents to adapt to the dominant society, aspects linked to the process of colonization suffered for several centuries.

Considering these results, and integrating them with what was observed in the criminal behaviors of the adolescents in this study, the comparisons between the groups of non-Mapuche and Mapuche offenders, regarding the judicialized and self-reported crimes, indicate that, if well the judicialized in the group of non-Mapuche adolescents do not differ from the Mapuche group, the number of crimes self-reported by the latter are significantly lower, indicating the existence of less complex criminal trajectories, despite presenting, on average, the same number of crimes sanctioned by the penal system.

When analyzing the results from the perspective of risk factors and protection, these asymmetries observed in the judicialized and self-reported crimes could be associated with various phenomena. From the point of view of non-Mapuche adolescents, these differences could be explained because there are greater risks in various areas associated with criminal behavior, compared to the group of Mapuche adolescents, specifically associated with learning and development of greater skills to evade police detection and/or also because the social context could normalize these behaviors, being mostly invisible.

From the point of view of Mapuche adolescents, it could be associated with the fact that they would get involved in criminal behaviors that are more frequently punishable by law at an early age, but also that they could present fewer skills associated with criminal behavior and therefore are more often detected by the penal and police system, as well as it could be argued that culturally there is a lower tolerance toward the commission of crimes and therefore they are detected more early. These questions must be answered in future studies where the risks and resources are analyzed comparatively in both groups of adolescent offenders, considering not only those risk factors that have traditionally been described in the literature associated with juvenile delinquency but also specifically, according to cultural differences and particularities of this adolescent population. Of importance for the present research, and positioning from a culturally differentiating perspective, the fact that a lower number of self-reported criminal behaviors is observed in Mapuche adolescents could be related to the presence of protective factors at the social and individual level that prevent a greater commitment and delinquent behavior, compared to non-Mapuche adolescents.

In light of the above, considering the main objective of this research, the results confirm the existence of a relationship between the development of ethnic identity and social behaviors in Mapuche adolescents who break the law. Specifically, the hypothesis is confirmed, indicating that a higher degree of development of the ethnic identity is associated with a lower presence of antisocial behaviors. In addition, the results also indicate that there is an absence of a relationship between ethnic identity and a higher presence of prosocial behaviors.

These results may be important for intervention, as they would suggest that a balanced development of ethnic identity (based on the person's affirmation with the group, experientially exploring, knowing, and practicing the customs of their culture, together) would function as protective factors against antisocial behaviors, but without necessarily promoting greater prosocial behaviors.

On the other hand, that the dimension of exploration shows, qualitatively, a greater relationship with fewer antisocial behaviors than the dimension of affirmation, could indicate that the act of knowing one's own culture, in the action of experientially participating in it, and not just the mental process of valuing it, would be linked with a lower presence of antisocial behaviors in these adolescents. The above points to the need for a different planning in the way of implementing preventive actions and reducing antisocial behaviors in Mapuche adolescents who break the law. Specifically, it implies that the intervention should promote a greater connection of the adolescents to contexts where they can know, experience, and participate with others, in a relational and physical space of the customs of their own culture, beyond just valuing their own culture.

From the point of view of risk and protection factors, the reviewed literature indicates that at an international level, there are few studies that have empirically analyzed the relationship between ethnic identity with the processes of adolescent social maladjustment; however, the results are congruent with those studies that argue the importance of understanding the specific factors associated with the decrease of antisocial behaviors in adolescents belonging to indigenous peoples, becoming the greatest contribution of this research.

When analyzing these results, in light of the processes of intervention in the prevention or reduction of antisocial behaviors in adolescents belonging to indigenous peoples, interventions should be generated that are oriented not only to the distinction of cultural differences, but also to favor the active participation of the adolescent in cultural spaces, and thus to enable them to know, explore, and value their own indigenous culture, thus enhancing the growth of their own identity.

Considering the results of the research, at the level of public policies, it is necessary to strengthen the indigenous identity in the actions of prevention of adolescent law infringement, in addition to, at the level of specialized intervention, developing an integral view about those Mapuche adolescents who have broken the law, which includes the promotion of their ethnic identity. This ethnic identity, then, is understood as a dynamic protective factor; that is, it causes emotional, behavioral, and relational changes that co-occur with the normative emergence of maladaptive behaviors in the stage of adolescence and not as a predisposing factor of these.

At the methodological level, given that the process of constructing the ethnic identity is dynamic and therefore the relationship with social behaviors changes over time, the results partially show the link between ethnic identity and social behaviors at a particular moment, due to the nature of the cross-sectional design of the research. Therefore, future lines of work on this topic should integrate a longitudinal design, which allows analyzing the changes in the development of ethnic identity over time, the factors that influence it and the relationships that arise, observing the changes in social behaviors, especially if the adolescents are involved in intervention programs.

Finally, in this study only the situation of Mapuche adolescents was analyzed, requiring more studies in the cases of adolescents from other indigenous peoples in

Chile and in other countries, especially where the process of colonization has generated conditions of vulnerability such, that negatively impact the development and adolescent adaptation.

**Acknowledgments** This project, proposed from action-research, aimed to work directly with the interveners of the programs that execute the sanctions, providing them with the specialized training required for a differentiated evaluation and the necessary supervision to ensure the achievement of the sought competence. The process was carried out with 48 professionals from 3 different institutions that administer sanctions in the different systems, from Santiago to Puerto Montt (center-south of Chile), each of whom conducted between 5 and 10 complete evaluations of adolescents, with those they were supposed to intervene.

## References

Agostini, C., Brown, P., & Román, A. (2010). Poverty and inequality among ethnic groups in Chile. *World Development, 38*(7), 1036–1046.

Alarcón, P. (2001). *Evaluación psicológica de adolescentes con desadaptación social (Tesis de maestría inédita)*. Universidad de Salamanca.

Alarcón, P. (2015). *Una aproximación multidimensional al comportamiento antisocial durante la adolescencia (Tesis doctoral inédita)*. Universidad Pontificia de Salamanca.

Alarcón, P., Pérez-Luco, R., Salvo, S., Roa, G., Jaramillo, K., & Sanhueza, C. (2010). Validación del cuestionario de auto-reporte de comportamiento antisocial en adolescentes: CACSA. *Paidéia, 20*(47), 291–302.

Alarcón, P., Pérez-Luco, R., Wenger, L., Chesta, S., Lagos, L., Salvo, S., et al. (2014). *MMIDA. Modelo Multidimensional de Intervención Diferenciada con Adolescentes: Manual de evaluación diferenciada: Evaluar para intervenir* (Vol. 2). Ediciones Universidad de La Frontera.

Alarcón, P., Vinet, E., & Salvo, S. (2005). Estilos de personalidad y desadaptación social durante la adolescencia. *Psykhe, 14*(1), 3–16.

Allard, T., Stewart, A., Chrzanowski, A., Ogilvie, J., Birks, D., & Little, S. (2010). *The use and impact of police diversion for reducing indigenous overrepresentation*. Griffith University.

Bals, M., Turi, A., Skre, I., & Kvernmo, S. (2001). The relationship between internalizing and externalizing symptoms and cultural resilience factors in Indigenous Sami youth from Arctic Norway. *International Journal of Circumpolar Health, 70*(1) Recuperado de http://ijch.fi/aheadofprint.php

Belgrave, F., Marin, B., & Chambers, D. (2000). Cultural, contextual, and intrapersonal predictors of risky sexual attitudes among urban African American girls in early adolescence. *Cultural Diversity and Ethnic Minority Psychology, 6*(3), 309–322.

Brook, J., & Phal, K. (2005). The protective role of ethnic and racial identity and aspects of an Africentric orientation against drug use among African American young adults. *The Journal of Genetic Psychology, 166*(3), 329–345. https://doi.org/10.3200/GNTP.166.3.329-345

Comisión Económica para América Latina y el Caribe & Alianza Territorial Mapuche. (2012). *Desigualdades territoriales y exclusión social del pueblo mapuche en Chile: situación en la comuna de Ercilla desde un enfoque de derechos (Documentos de Proyectos N.° 473)*. Santiago de Chile. Recuperado de. http://www.cepal.org/es/publicaciones/3974-desigualdades-territoriales-exclusion-social-pueblo-mapuche-chile-situacion-la

Coie, J., Terry, R., Lenox, K., Lochman, J., & Hyman, C. (1995). Childhood peer rejection and aggression as predictors of stable patterns of adolescent disorder. *Development and Psychopathology, 7*, 697–713. https://doi.org/10.1017/S0954579400006799

Correa, M., & Mella, E. (2010). *Las razones del "illkun"/enojo. Memoria, despojo y criminalización en el territorio mapuche de Malleco*. Lom Ediciones/Observatorio de Derechos de los Pueblos Indígenas.
Dandy, J., Durkin, K., & McEvoy, P. (2007). Psychometric properties of multigroup ethnic identity measure (MEIM) scores with Australian adolescents from diverse ethno cultural group. *Journal of Adolescence, 31*(3), 323–335.
DeBerry, K. M. R. (1996). Family racial socialization and ecological competence: Longitudinal assessments of African-American transracial adoptees. *Child Development, 67*, 2375–2399.
Eamon, M., & Mulder, C. (2005). Predicting antisocial behavior among Latino young adolescents. *American Journal of Orthopsychiatry, 75*(1), 117–127. https://doi.org/10.1037/0002-9432.75.1.117
Erikson, E. (1968). *Identidad, juventud y crisis*. Buenos Aires: Paidos.
Esteban, M. (2010). Propiedades psicométricas y estructura factorial de la Escala de Identidad Étnica Multigrupo en español (MEIM). *Revista Latinoamericana de Psicología, 42*(3), 405–412.
Fabio, A., Tu, L.-C., Loëber, R., & Cohen, J. (2011). Neighborhood socioeconomic disadvantage and the shape of the age–crime curve. *American Journal of Public Health, 101*(1), 325–332. https://doi.org/10.2105/AJPH.2010.300034
Farrington, D. P. (1996). The explanation and prevention of youthful offending. In P. Cordelia & L. Siegel (Eds.), *Readings in contemporary criminological theory* (pp. 257–272). Northeastern University Press.
Fréchette, M., & Le Blanc, M. (1998). *Délinquances et délinquants* (8th ed.). Gaêtan Morin.
French, S., Seidman, E., Allen, L., & Aber, J. (2006). The development of ethnic identity during adolescence. *Developmental Psychology, 42*(1), 1–10. https://doi.org/10.1037/0012-1649.42.1.1
Guerrero, A., Nishimura, S., Chang, J., Ona, C., Cunanan, V., & Hishinuma, E. (2010). Low cultural identification, low parental involvement and adverse peer influences as risk factors for delinquent behavior among Filipino youth in Hawai'i. *International Journal of Social Psychiatry, 56*(4), 371–388.
Hallett, D., Want, S., Chandler, M., Koopman, L., Flores, J., & Gehrke, E. (2008). Identity in flux: Ethnic self-identification and school attrition in Canadian Aboriginal youth. *Journal of Applied Developmental Psychology, 29*, 62–75.
Heckbert, D., & Turkington, D. (2001). *Turning points: A study of the factors related to the successful reintegration of Aboriginal offenders (Informe N.° R-61)*. Correctional Services of Canada.
Hishinuma, E. S., Johnson, R., Kim, P., Nishimura, S., Makini, G., Andrade, N., et al. (2005). Prevalence and correlates of misconduct among ethnically diverse adolescents of native Hawaiian/part-Hawaiian and non-Hawaiian ancestry. *International Journal of Social Psychiatry, 51*(3), 242–258.
Hoeve, M., Blokland, A., Dubas, J., Loeber, R., Gerris, J. R. M., & Van der Laan, P. (2008). Trajectories of delinquency and parenting styles. *Journal of Abnormal Child Psychology, 36*(2), 223–235. https://doi.org/10.1007/s10802-007-9172-x
Howell, T. (2008). *The point of no return: Aboriginal offenders' journey towards a crime free life (Tesis doctoral inédita)*. University of British Columbia.
Instituto Nacional de Estadísticas (INE). (2009). *Compendio Estadístico*. Author. http://www.ine.cl
Instituto Nacional de Estadísticas (INE). (2014). *Proyecciones de población 2002–2020*. Author. http://www.ine.cl
Kazdin, A., & Buela-Casal, G. (2002). *Conducta antisocial: evaluación, tratamiento y prevención en la infancia y adolescencia*. Pirámide.
LeBlanc, M., Còte, G., & Loeber, R. (1991). Temporal paths in delinquency: Stability, regression and progression analyzed with panel data from an adolescent and a delinquent male sample. *Canadian Journal of Criminology, 1*, 23–44.
Lerner, R., & Steinberg, L. (2009). The scientific study of adolescent development. In R. M. Lerner & L. Steinberg (Eds.), *Handbook of adolescent psychology* (3rd ed., pp. 3–14). Wiley.

Loëber, R., & Farrington, D. P. (Eds.). (2001). *Child delinquents: Development, intervention, and service needs*. Sage.
Marsiglia, F., Kulis, S., Hecht, M., & Sills, S. (2004). Ethnicity and ethnic identity as predictors of drug norms and drug use among preadolescents in the U.S. Southwest. *Substance Abuse and Misuse, 39*, 1061–1094.
Martínez, R., & Dukes, R. (1997). The effects of ethnic identity, ethnicity, and gender on adolescent well-being. *Journal of Youth and Adolescence, 26*(5), 503–516.
Maynard, K., Coebergh, B., Anstiss, B., Bakker, L., & Huriwai, T. (1999). Ki Te Arotu toward a new assessment: The identification of cultural factors which may pre-dispose Māori to crime. *Social Policy Journal of New Zealand, 13*, 43–58.
Méndez, P., & Barra, E. (2008). Apoyo social percibido en adolescentes infractores de ley y no infractores. *Psykhe, 17*(1), 59–64.
Moffitt, T. E. (1993). Adolescence-limited and life-course-persistent antisocial behavior: A developmental taxonomy. *Psychological Review, 100*(4), 674–701.
Monahan, K., Cauffman, E., & Steinberg, L. (2009). Affiliation with antisocial peers, susceptibility to peer influence and antisocial behavior during the transition to adulthood. *Developmental Psychology, 45*(6), 1520–1530.
Northoff, G., & Heinzel, A. (2003). The self in philosophy, neuroscience and psychiatry: An epistemic approach. In A. David & T. Kircher (Eds.), *The self in neuroscience and psychiatry* (pp. 40–55). Cambridge University Press.
Organización Internacional del Trabajo. (2006). *Trabajo infantil y pueblos originarios en Chile. Experiencias en zonas aymara y mapuche (Tarapacá y Araucanía). (Informe 14.02.2)*. Author. http://white.lim.ilo.org/ipec/boletin/documentos/pueblos_originarios_ch.pdf.
Pegg, P., & Plybon, L. (2005). Toward the theoretical measurement of ethnic identity. *Journal of Early Adolescence, 25*, 250–264.
Peña, M., & Graña, J. (2006). Agresión y conducta antisocial en la adolescencia: una integración conceptual. *Psicopatología Clínica, Legal y Forense, 6*, 9–23.
Pérez-Luco, R., Alarcón, P., Zambrano, A., Alarcón, M., Lagos, L., Wenger, L., et al. (2014). *MMIDA. Modelo Multidimensional de Intervención Diferenciada con Adolescentes. Vol. 1. Manual de intervención diferenciada: prácticas que transforman vidas*. Ediciones Universidad de La Frontera.
Pérez-Luco, R., Alarcón, P., Zambrano, A., Bustamante, G., & Alarcón, M. (2009). *Estrategia ecosistémica especializada de intervención diferenciada para favorecer la integración psicosocial de adolescentes infractores de ley (Proyecto FONDEF D08i-1205)*. Universidad de La Frontera.
Pérez-Luco, R., Lagos, L., & Báez, C. (2012). Reincidencia y desistimiento en adolescentes infractores: análisis de trayectorias delictivas a partir de autorreporte de delitos, consumo de sustancias y juicio profesional. *Universitas Psychologica, 11*(4). https://doi.org/10.11144/Javeriana.upsy11-4.rdai
Pérez-Luco, R., Lagos, L., Chesta, S., & Báez, C. (2011). Escala de Delincuencia Autorrevelada "EDA". In *Instrumento de evaluación clínica del patrón delictivo adolescente (Proyecto FONDEF D08i-1205)*. Universidad de La Frontera.
Piquero, A., & Moffitt, T. E. (2005). *Integrated developmental and life-course theories of offending: Advances in criminological theory*. Transactions Press.
Phinney, J. (1989). Stages of ethnic identity development in minority group adolescents. *Journal of Early Adolescence, 9*, 34–49.
Phinney, J. (1992). The multigroup ethnic identity measure: A new scale for use with adolescents and young adults from diverse groups. *Journal of Adolescent Research, 7*, 156–176.
Phinney, J., Cantu, C., & Kurtz, D. (1997). Ethnic and American identity as predictors of self-esteem among African American, Latino, and White adolescents. *Journal of Youth and Adolescence, 26*(2), 165–185.
Phinney, J., & Ong, A. (2007). Conceptualization and measurement of ethnic identity: Current status and future directions. *Journal of Counseling Psychology, 54*(3), 271–281.

Roberts, R., Phinney, J., Masse, L., Chen, Y., Roberts, C., & Romero, A. (1999). The structure of ethnic identity in young adolescents from diverse ethnocultural groups. *Journal of Early Adolescence, 19*, 301–322.

Rojas, E., & Gretton, H. (2007). Background, offences characteristics and criminal outcomes of Aboriginal youth who sexual offend: A closer look at Aboriginal youth intervention needs. *Sex abuse: A journal of Research and Treatment, 19*(3), 257–283. https://doi.org/10.1007/s11194-007-9048-1

Rugge, T. (2006). *Risk assessment of male Aboriginal offenders: A 2006 perspective. (Informe 2006-01)*. Public Safety Canada.

Saint Louis, G., & Liem, J. (2005). Ego identity, ethnic identity and the psychological well-being of ethnic minority and majority college students. *International Journal of Theory and Research, 5*(3), 227–246.

Saiz, J., Merino, M., & Quilaqueo, D. (2009). Meta-estereotipos sobre los indígenas mapuche de Chile. *Interdisciplinaria, 26*(1), 23–48.

Saiz, J., Rapimán, E., & Mladinic, A. (2008). Estereotipos sobre los Mapuche: su reciente evolución. *Psykhe, 17*(2), 27–40.

Schwartz, S., Zamboanga, B., & Hernández, L. (2007). Ethnic identity and acculturation in Hispanic early adolescents: Mediated relationships to academic grades, prosocial behaviors, and externalizing symptoms. *Cultural Diversity and Ethnic Minority Psychology, 13*(4), 364–373.

Servicio Nacional de Menores. (2010). *Anuario Estadístico Institucional*. Author. Recuperado de http://www.sename.cl

Solís, A., Alvarado, A., & y Pérez-Luco, R. (2015). Caracterización de la reincidencia delictiva de adolescentes infractores de ley de la Región de Los Lagos, Chile. In *Estudio epidemiológico y de trayectorias delictivas. Tesis de Magíster en Psicología Jurídica y Forense*. Universidad de La Frontera.

Steinberg, L., & Sheffield, A. (2001). Adolescent development. *Annual Review of Psychology, 52*(1), 83–110.

Umaña-Taylor, A., & Updegraff, K. (2007). Latino adolescents' mental health: Exploring the interrelations among discrimination, ethnic identity, cultural orientation, self-esteem, and depressive symptoms. *Journal of Adolescence, 30*(4), 549–567. https://doi.org/10.1016/j.adolescence.2006.08.002

Van Meijl, T. (2008). Culture and identity in anthropology: Reflections on "unity" and "uncertaintly" in the dialogical self. *International Journal for Dialogical Science, 3*(1), 165–190.

Ward, T., & Langlands, R. (2009). Repairing the rupture: Restorative justice and the rehabilitation of offenders. *Aggression and Violent Behavior, 14*(3), 205–214.

Wissinka, I., Dekovic, M., Sengu, Y., Stamsb, G., & de Haana, M. (2008). Ethnic identity, externalizing problem behavior and the mediating role of self-esteem among Dutch, Turkish-Dutch and Moroccan-Dutch adolescents. *Journal of Adolescence, 31*, 223–240.

Yasui, M., Dorham, C., & Dishion, T. (2004). Ethnic identity and psychological adjustment: A validity analysis for European American and African American adolescents. *Journal of Adolescent Research, 19*, 807–825.

# Part II
# Education, Cognition and Developmental Psychology

# Introduction to Part II: Education, Cognition and Developmental Psychology

**Wilson López-López**

The chapters presented in this section encompass a wide range of research, reflecting the diversity of theoretical and methodological perspectives within the field in the region. These works include qualitative, quantitative and theoretical approaches, spanning from traditional cognitive frameworks to more critical perspectives. Many focus on populations experiencing human rights violations, clearly illustrating how educational psychology research is often situated within contexts of social exclusion and rights vulnerability.

The first chapter, 'The Role of the Coach in Teaching Life Skills to Young Brazilians at Risk of Social Vulnerability', explores the practices of coaches in Brazilian social projects. Using qualitative analysis, the study identifies strategies for teaching life skills to youth in socially excluded contexts. While the findings are not generalizable, the chapter provides valuable insights into working with vulnerable populations, a common issue in Latin America.

The next chapter, 'Towards a Critical Psychosocial Approach to School Violence: Contributions from a Study with Students in Córdoba, Argentina', addresses school violence from a critical psychosocial perspective. The study challenges conventional understandings of bullying by exploring conflicts in secondary schools in Córdoba. The authors suggest that school conflicts can be viewed as struggles for recognition, offering new avenues for interventions that challenge violence as a routine response to conflict.

The chapter, 'Characterization of Care Practices in Colombian Families with Children in Early Childhood in Situations of Forced Displacement', examines the impact of parenting practices on child development in the context of displacement due to armed conflict in Colombia. Using a mixed-methods approach, the study integrates observational tools and self-report measures. It supports existing research

W. López-López (✉)
Pontificia Universidad Javeriana, Bogotá, Colombia
e-mail: lopezw@javeriana.edu.co

 
W. López-López et al. (eds.), *Trends in Latin American Psychology*,
https://doi.org/10.1007/978-3-031-87554-0_7

linking domestic violence to child development and highlights the intergenerational transmission of violence, emphasizing its effects on various aspects of child development.

The chapter, 'The Perception of Parenting Styles and Their Relationship with Children's Self-Perception in Buenos Aires: Gender Differences', investigates how parenting styles affect children's self-perceptions, with a particular focus on gender differences. The study uses self-perception scales and parent-child relationship assessments, revealing important insights into gendered perceptions. This work contributes to understanding children's perspectives, an often-overlooked aspect of developmental research.

Finally, the chapter, 'Control Trajectories and Co-Variation of Variables as an Expression of Cognitive Change in Problem-Solving', explores variability in mathematical problem-solving among university students. Using a microgenetic method that combines qualitative and quantitative approaches, the study examines cognitive trajectories and changes in problem-solving abilities. The research highlights how cognitive changes manifest throughout the life cycle, offering valuable insights into educational challenges in problem-solving and cognitive development.

The first four chapters provide a nuanced and diverse approach to educational issues in contexts of social conflict. They highlight education as a catalyst for change, as in the case of the Brazilian study, and challenge traditional views of school violence, as seen in the Argentine study. The Colombian chapter underscores the transgenerational impact of violent parenting on child development in conflict settings, while the final study sheds light on cognitive issues in problem-solving, particularly in mathematical and scientific contexts, in the region. Together, these contributions from Latin American countries weave complex problems and offer critical insights that contribute to understanding the region's educational challenges. *Universitas Psychologica* has played a key role in giving visibility to these diverse perspectives, fostering dialogue and promoting research that addresses the unique challenges faced by the region.

# The Role of the Coach in Teaching Life Skills to Young Brazilians at Risk of Social Vulnerability

**Maurício Marques, Catarina Sousa, Jaume Cruz, and Silvia Koller**

## Introduction

Teaching young people has gained space within sports psychology in the last decade, generating studies and sharing publications on topics such as mental training for performance, which has characterized the area since its inception. From a social point of view, sport is more important for youth as an educational tool to promote life skills than to form a few elite athletes or achieve Olympic successes (Danish & Nellen, 1997). In fact, most boys and girls who join sports teams do not reach professionalism when they are adults.

Positive Youth Development (PYD) refers to the ways in which children and adolescents can accumulate optimal development experiences through their participation in organized activities, such as sports (Holt & Neely, 2011). Based on positive psychology, PYD is based on the belief that all youth have the potential to live productively, establish healthy social relationships, acquire skills for adult life, and avoid risk behaviors (Falcão et al., 2012). Thus, it encompasses different conceptual approaches such as Richard Lerner's 5 C's (e.g. *competence, confidence, character, caring/compassion,* and *connection*), the *Athlete Development Approach* by Côté et al. (1995) and the life skills of Steven Danish, which structure programs in

*This chapter is the English translation of an article originally published in Spanish as:* Marques, M., Sousa, C., Cruz, J., & Koller, S. (2016). El papel del entrenador en la enseñanza de competencias de vida a jóvenes brasileños en riesgo de vulnerabilidad social. *Universitas Psychologica, 15*(1), 129–140. https://doi.org/10.11144/Javeriana.upsy15-1.peec. *Please cite the original version of the article in Spanish.*

M. Marques (✉) · C. Sousa · J. Cruz
Universitat Autònoma de Barcelona, Barcelona, Spain

S. Koller
Universidade Federal do Rio Grande do Sul, Porto Alegre, Brazil



W. López-López et al. (eds.), *Trends in Latin American Psychology*,
https://doi.org/10.1007/978-3-031-87554-0_8

different contexts such as, for example, the community, school or sports, as cited in the review by Falcão et al. (2012).

In the application of any of these three frameworks in sport, the coach has the main role in establishing and organizing the environment for the positive development of young people (Falcão et al., 2012). Even today, training programs to help coaches in educational tasks are scarce and, in general, are used in more developed countries, for example, the *Mastery Approach to Coaching* (MAC) in the United States (Smith et al., 2007) and the *National Coach Certification Program* in Canada and the *Personalized Coaching Program* (PAPE) in Spain (Sousa et al., 2006). Even without adequate training, coaches feel responsible for the comprehensive education of young athletes, as highlighted by the study by Vella et al. (2011). In this study, the instructors reported teaching specific skills for the sports context and also for the social and/or personal context.

The concept of life skills addresses the skills that can be taught in an environment, like sport, and that facilitate success in other areas of life, such as school or work. These skills can be behavioral, cognitive, interpersonal, and intrapersonal, such as positive communication, goal setting, emotional control, and hard work (Gould et al., 2006). Observing the effectiveness of sport as a means for teaching life skills, the *Life Skills Center* coordinated by Steven Danish, created the SUPER Program—*Sports United to Promote Education and Recreation*—(Danish et al., 1996).

In this SUPER program, high school student-athletes participate, with the aim of teaching younger students that (a) there are effective and affordable student-athlete models; (b) physical and mental skills are important both in sport and in life; (c) goal setting and achievement in sport and in life is important; and (d) obstacles that arise on this path can be overcome (Danish & Nellen, 1997).

In the same line of work, Gould and Carson (2008) have conducted an important review of research and programs that deal with the teaching of life skills through sport. They even propose a heuristic model for understanding this training process and the needs of future research. The authors underline the importance of understanding what characteristics and strategies successful coaches have in the education of their athletes, as, for example, studied by Gould et al. (2007) in a study with outstanding school coaches from the United States. This study concludes that the coaches: (a) even though they were motivated to win, they had training philosophies that place great importance on the development of life skills in their players; (b) had the ability to form strong relationships and create bonds with the youth; (c) reported a series of consistent strategies for teaching the life skills that are considered most important; and (d) recognized that factors such as socioeconomic level and family characteristics strongly influence the development of life skills, and they took them into account.

Marques et al. (2013) found similar results in a recent study with coaches of social projects in Spain, based on the research and interview script created by Gould et al. (2007). The participating coaches reported working with life skills that foster the feeling of personal competence of the youth, good relationships among them, and comprehensive education (e.g., civility, sportsmanship, hygiene, etc.). The strategies used to achieve their goals mix the coach's communication style and their performance in managing training and matches (Marques et al., 2015) and also include in their objectives the healthy participation of all and learning that goes beyond sport, contemplating studies, fun, and life in society.

Finally, Camiré et al. (2012) used the model of Gould and Carson (2008) to interview Canadian coaches and student-athletes, with the intent of understanding both perspectives on philosophies and their strategies for teaching, as well as how the transfer of these skills occurs. The interviews revealed that the coaches took into account the previous characteristics of the youth and based their philosophies on the personal development of them. The results highlighted the need for the creation of bonds between both, which implies on the part of the coach having clear philosophies adapted to the reality of each team, in addition to using their teaching strategies with intentionality and systematically. Moreover, both coaches and students believe that the skills learned in sport can be transferred to other areas of life. In summary, the research conducted with coaches on the teaching of life skills through sport agrees that psychological skills are only assimilated after demonstration, modeling, and practice (Gould & Carson, 2008). This common aspect is reinforced by Silva (2010) when he refers to the need for a whole structure that validates the acquisition of these skills, in which the trainings are configured in a way that the youth can manifest them, under constant reinforcement and open and bidirectional communication. Larson (2000) concludes that learning for the positive development of youth is best given in structured voluntary participation activities, such as in sport and the arts, where there is the rare combination of intrinsic motivation with high attentional level; an example of these activities is the social projects that attract youth seeking sports teams.

The coaches of social projects in Brazil almost always work alone in the educational task and have scarce resources to train in neighborhoods characterized by a high degree of vulnerability/social risk. Likewise, they coordinate teams where dozens of athletes voluntarily attend and stay for many seasons. So, the objective of this study is to investigate how the coaches of social projects in Brazil teach life skills based on their philosophies, communication styles, routines, and work strategies used in their training.

## Method

### *Participants*

A total of six coaches of social projects (five men and one woman) were interviewed. Four of them (the coaches identified as 2, 3, 4, and 5) coached men's football teams, coach 3 also led a women's team. Coach 1 worked with indoor football and men's basketball, and coach 6 with mixed volleyball and women's indoor football. All competed in the leagues of the city of Porto Alegre, Brazil. They were between 29 and 56 years old (M = 39.1, SD = 9.4), and their experience as coaches ranged from 2 to 32 years (M = 12.3, SD = 11.8). Regarding their training, four coaches had some postgraduate university degree in physical education, and two others were finishing the degree in the same course. Two coaches worked in a private center, three in city council centers, while the coach ran a project independently, without institutional support. Each coach coordinated at least three teams of different age groups, with young people between 7 and 18 years old.

## *Procedure*

First, contact was made with the Municipal Sports Secretary, the city council body that organizes the city league, to check how the sports projects linked to it worked. In a meeting with the main person responsible for the municipal league, based on the process used by Gilbert and Trudel (2004), the objectives of the study were presented, and the collaboration of coaches with the following characteristics was requested: (a) who had led the same team for more than a season and a half, thus ensuring coexistence with young people throughout a category; (b) whose teams had a good reputation in terms of fair play and discipline; (c) whose participation in the teams was voluntary and free; and (d) whose teams belonged to neighborhoods known for low income and the risk of social exclusion. Telephone contact was made with the coaches confirming the information received about the teams, a meeting was scheduled for a talk and, when possible, to observe a training session. The objectives of the study were presented to the coaches in person, and all agreed to participate voluntarily. At the beginning of the interview, anonymity and confidentiality were guaranteed, as well as the possibility of not answering any questions. With the explained and signed consent, the interviews were conducted, which lasted between 41 and 157 min (M = 74 min). The interviewer was the first author, an expert in sports psychology, a certified football coach, with experience in semi-structured interviews of the same content, carried out under the supervision of the Sports Psychology Study Group of the Universitat Autònoma de Barcelona. After the analysis of results and the confirmation that the theoretical saturation described by Guest et al. (2006) had been achieved, the number of interviews conducted was considered sufficient.

## *Instrument*

For the interviews, the same script by Marques et al. (2013), translated into Portuguese and culturally adapted by two bilingual experts, was used. The script[1] contains eight blocks of open-ended questions, starting with personal, training, and sports experience data, followed by data on the teams they were coaching at the time of the interview. The third and fourth blocks addressed their philosophies and coaching styles, and the fifth asked directly about the life skills they taught and the strategies used. The sixth block, which did not exist in the previous study, was created using questions adapted from the script by Camiré (2012) with questions about how and which skills are acquired and can be transferred by young people. Subsequently, they were asked to talk about the main difficulties encountered in their training, as well as how they worked on issues such as sportsmanship, substance abuse, and the development of autonomy in the team. Finally, a global evaluation of their work as an educator and coach was requested, as well as advice and suggestions for improving the topic in the city.

## *Data Analysis*

The content of the interviews was analyzed by two experts, the first author and a psychologist member of the research group in sports psychology and life skills, with experience in qualitative analysis, who identified the *meaning units* (MU) existing in each of them, according to the qualitative analysis model for unstructured data by Côté et al. (1993). An MU is a segment of text, sentence, or paragraph that is understandable by itself and contains an idea, episode, or section of information expressed by the interviewee in a clear and objective manner. First, both experts selected the MUs from each interview discussing the relevance of each of them until reaching a consensus, in addition to naming them with a provisional label.

After selecting 270 MUs from all the interviews, these were grouped according to their labels and reorganized into categories by similarity of content. Thus, those MUs that best represented each category were chosen, considering that some explained the philosophy of the coaches and others, how they carried them out in a practical way, that is, the strategies. These 74 MUs were distributed into 28 categories that were discussed and readjusted into four higher order themes labeled inductively: Teamwork, Discipline, Performance and Bond, and Comprehensive Education. Finally, to ensure the credibility of the process, a third expert from the sports psychology and life skills research group, who had not participated in the previous stages of the research, analyzed a list of all the MUs and separately another list with the themes and their categories, choosing which philosophies and strategies were more related to each other. The discussion with the other two experts led to the

[1] The script can be requested from the first author by email.

reorganization of some categories, and to the choice of those MUs most representative of each category.

## Results and Discussion

The results of the research on how coaches think and act with respect to teaching life skills were classified into four main themes: Teamwork, Discipline, Performance and Bond, and Comprehensive Education, each with its categories[2] and strategies.

## Teamwork

All the coaches interviewed emphasized the importance of promoting teamwork and team spirit among the young people under their guidance. Cooperation was frequently mentioned as a value that must be worked on, as coach 1 comments:

> It's about having a very heterogeneous group and making them work for the same thing, the same objectives. Work for the group, even if there is little in common. What they have in common when they step on the field, is football.

Therefore, generating a positive climate in the team is essential for good relations between everyone and support instead of criticism:

> It's a button that is pressed every day. A good group relationship in collective sport is a necessity. It is not possible to work, or to do a collective sport, with a huge group without relating well to people. (E1)

> [I do] exercises in which they perceive the importance of teamwork for sport, when you have to support the colleague who makes a mistake or encourage the one who is a novice. Instead of scolding, I say: You have to encourage people who are starting, you also started once. (E6)

Care for the inclusion of everyone in the team's activities was highlighted in the process of forming a united group:

> I train for competition, I still don't forget the focus of the social project. I have to be very careful. Even so that those who are not good players do not feel harmed and do not leave the team. I always have this concern to remember that it is a social project that includes everyone. (E5)

A strategy used by coach 2 is to make everyone play with each other, even those who do not have friendship ties: "sometimes I let them choose the teams, they choose their friends, and, before starting, I change the captains".

Likewise, over time, a **friendship** is formed among the young people on the teams, as stated by coach 1:

[2] The categories are marked in bold.

> [The team] is always in contact, meeting and playing in other places with boys from private schools. I don't see any other medium other than sport where they could meet. They are in completely different neighborhoods, opposite in every sense geographically and economically.

Some coaches even try to **give the same opportunities** to everyone to practice what they have learned in training or even in competitions:

> In the match, make sure all the children can try game situations. So not only the best one will take the corner, the throw-in, the free kick. The adult who is coordinating should dissolve this in the group. (E2)

> Everyone is going to play. I had a starting team, however, I have not excluded anyone for playing better or worse. If I were in a club, with a competition focus, I would put the best to play and the others on the bench. (E6)

Then the coaches seek and achieve **personal and collective improvement** in their teams, as well explained by coach 6:

> Well, when the one who is not so good improves, the whole group improves. I make the level of the game improve and whoever is better wants to play with a higher level. (...) I try to take the most experienced ones who have more technique, more time on the team and pair them with someone. "Today you are going to warm up with that one who is starting, help him with the touch, explain to him". And it goes well.

Also in teamwork, the **responsibility with the group** as a whole is stimulated as mentioned by coaches 4 and 2:

> There are game situations, for example, where one makes a bad pass because he is lazy, and the other team goes there and scores a goal. I give this example so that everything we do has to be well done. If one does something wrong, it will harm another person, his group will be punished.

> They help to bring things to the court. Everything is a process in which you have to give your contribution to the team. It can't be that one arrives here and puts on his boots, pants, socks, to play and that's it. There has to be something more, the bond, the trajectory.

The research by Marques et al. (2013) showed that a category of life skills worked on by coaches of social projects in Spain is the relationship, which includes cooperation, companionship, and integration (cultural in the case of the European context), which seems to be in line with the practice of the Brazilian educators interviewed regarding the categories Cooperation, Inclusion, and Friendship. Giving the same opportunities is also a strategy for teaching life skills in the referred study. The establishment of a positive motivational climate by the coach is one of the guidelines of the MAC (Smith et al., 2007) intervention program for coaches that teaches guidelines for action in the search for benefits associated with a mastery-oriented climate.

On the other hand, the Self-Determination Theory (*Self-Determination Theory*; Deci & Ryan, 2000) is based on the belief that one of the bases of a self-determined motivation is the satisfaction of three basic innate needs (i.e., autonomy, competence, and relationship). This theory helps us understand why promoting relationships within the group is so important to keep young people motivated to participate in the team. The same happens with the basic need for competence, which has to do with the learning and improvement opportunities that someone perceives they have over some skill and explains the category of Personal and Collective Improvement.

## Discipline

All coaches are concerned about the discipline of their teams in all aspects. Firstly, they demand respect from their athletes, among themselves, toward opponents, the referee, and the rules, along with fair play, as well exemplified by coach 6:

> I work a lot with them on honesty in the game, I say "You saw the ball go out, admit it, it touched the hand, admit it". The goal is not to win at any cost, help and respect the referee and your teammates. (…) Because I believe that everyone who is part of a group, a sports team, at some point learns to deal with different people in a better way, because within the group there are multiple personalities. And one learns to handle differences and respect others. This is what one takes for life, for home and for school with their peers.

In addition, there is concern with knowing how to lose and win:

> From the winner greeting the loser, it's a matter of honor, a gentleman's sport, ethics, that has to happen. So the winner greets for the honor of having had the opportunity to have played with you. (E2)

The interviewees initially have a **regulation** established for allowed or not allowed behaviors in training and matches, and they use different strategies when they notice that tempers are heating up, like coach 5:

> Sometimes we do an exercise, when there is a lot of quarrel I stop "Stop! Everyone count to ten!" In the middle of the match, I don't care if it's good. Because first comes harmony, a team that fights among itself will never beat anyone.

Or when two young people argue: “I take out, and I don’t talk. What they want is to chat, take him out, keep him away and we continue here. Only later do I talk to them separately” (E4). The same happens in matches, as coach 3 reports: “I take him out, it doesn’t matter if I lose the match. But he won’t be expelled, there won’t be a fight because it never happened”.

Everyone reported having as a “golden rule” that “**whoever fights leaves the team**“, an idea summarized by Coach 2: You can’t react with violence. We must have a pact of non-violence. Perhaps this is the first basic rule, we cannot harm anyone here. Neither from a moral point of view nor from a physical point of view.

So, there is a **punishment** for those who fight, although with the possibility of **forgiveness** depending on the case:

> Of course, today he has returned to the team [a boy who was taken out for fighting], much better since his return, he suffered in his skin what it is to be excluded from the group, he had to work to return.

As coach 5 justifies: “No, it’s not worth [expelling] that child [the problematic one] is the one that interests me the most, it’s a way to keep him close to me”.

Respect for all participants in the sports scene and sportsmanship are common topics in the actions of coaches concerned with teaching life skills. The best coaches in the study by Gould et al. (2007) also hold young people accountable for their actions, in addition to punishing infractions that occur. The coaches interviewed by Camiré et al. (2012) create and use expressions to remind students that they must behave well, as they represent their school and neighborhood. The same happened with the participants in the study by Marques et al. (2013), who sought to work on a series of competencies on education and only made criticisms in their training when observing bad behaviors.

## Action and Bond

Coaches use different strategies on how to act in personal dealings with the young people on their teams with the aim of to create a good bond. Encouraging effort and reinforcing positively are the most common practices, both personally and as a group: "Speak, encourage, stimulate effort, challenge and offer situations for the child to have to think, pose problems that they have to solve within game situations" (E2). "We can lose, as we have lost many times, but we have to want it more than the others" (E4). "I support a lot, exalting and valuing their growth when I realize their dedication, their commitment and their appreciation in the training and matches" (E2).

**Encouraging autonomy** and **giving feedback** are also common practices: "I dictate the rules but respecting their opinions and trying to improve what we think is wrong, getting feedback from them too" (E4). "Give them the opportunity to choose their peers in different games. In a game, a relay race, a cooperative game, like choosing their own team" (E2). "Always, before each training we meet with them and pass some guidelines, in addition to reflecting on each practice" (E4).

Another important point for the creation and maintenance of the bond is the **coexistence** and **chatting** with the boys and girls of their teams not only in training and about the sport, as coaches 2 and 1 respectively told us:

"[From the collective meal that is after the game] it should not be something only to satisfy hunger, and meanwhile, talk about some play, or now we have to play against this team. It's more a space of socialization". There is, of course, a very strong emotional bond with the boys. There are a few who have been there 3, 4, 5 years. All year training and going out to matches every week. [...] Over time we start to create another relationship, like friendship. We talk about other things, not just basketball. We're going to talk about school, sometimes about girlfriends, or that he's not well for something, or even if there are some family dramas.

Teaching with **fun** and **affection**, in addition to **being a good example**, is also a strategy that helps in relationships with the young, as can be seen "[I get bored of training] makes no sense, nobody is obliged to come. It's not professional, you have to come with joy, have fun and play with your teammates, with your friends, but without mess" (E6).

> I see that most have suffered abuse at home and are already used to it. They came from other teams where the coach yelled and scolded. They get hit at home and fight in the street. So I reflected and thought: "I'm going to do everything different with them based only on love and affection. Even the most annoying ones, those are the most in need of affection. I see that it goes well". (E5)

> I see them there on the court as if they were a bunch of matchsticks, some can explode at any moment. So if I start yelling it's like pouring alcohol for a general explosion to occur. I try to be as calm as possible, as are my manners too, always calm to keep the team. I think that is why there were never fights on the team, they never fought on the field. (E5)

It is important to underline the fact that only coach 2 adopts captains for the choice of teams in training and values this leadership function, which is not common practice in the other teams interviewed in Brazil, and still occurs with all the coaches participating in the referred studies that were conducted in Spain, Canada, and the United States.

The coach-athlete relationship, based on their communication style, care, treatment, coexistence, and being a good model is one of the bases for the work of the coaches that appears in various studies that we expose in this research (Camiré et al., 2012; Falcão et al., 2012; Gould et al., 2007). The model of Gould and Carson (2008) offers a broader understanding, and ends up contemplating the results of these investigations. In what it calls "Direct training strategies"it talks about the quantity and quality of reinforcement and instructions, promoting leadership opportunities and decision-making by young people and to give them individualized attention. Starting from the theory of self-determination, the support for autonomy by the coach (Deci & Ryan, 2000) suggests that an instructor who offers an environment where the practitioner perceives themselves with voice, choice, and control will be facilitating intrinsic motivation and the young person's passion for the sport.

## Comprehensive Education

The coaches interviewed shared in their philosophies the concern of teaching life skills through sport, and during the learning of it. All reported that the **sport is a tool**, and not the objective of their work in the projects they are part of. Coaches 4 and 2 explain this idea "To gather the boys and offer them a school, a job, training, an education outside of school. The focus of the classes is not competitive".

> I would say it is a philosophy based on education through sport, the education of this sport, but always having a larger view of their lives. A process of education for life. So [...] I strive to be a teacher and educator before being a coach.

That's why they all worry about the education of **civility** and of **encouraging study and work** for the boys and girls they live with.

> There are many, who arrived here and who seemed like a beast, and now know how to go to a match, enter a field. They know how to play their game, and at the end, get on the bus, go home calmly. Something that many did not know. It does not exist in their homes. (E1)

> With the passage of time and with imposition, teaching some aspects, today we have boys who work in jobs that we recommended to them. (E3)

Even **maintaining contact with their parents** for school monitoring, reporting bad behaviors or influences, or even dealing with major problems such as drug use and substance abuse "Many mothers come to me because of the school. They believe that if I talk to the boy, he will do well in school. Or that I threaten the boy that he will not train anymore" (E5).

Finally, the **sports teaching**, as a practice that remains for the current and future life, also forms part of the educational work of the participating coaches: "Sport, leisure, or recreation, remain in people's lives, as a means of educating provides quality to life. To those who like to do sports, regardless of what you do to earn a living, those who love sport and have the opportunity to practice, will practice" (E1).

The use of sport as a tool to transform the lives of these young people and transmit skills that will remain and be useful in their schools, jobs, families, etc., is the incentive and the main function of all the participating coaches of this research, as well as the studies of Camiré et al. (2012), Gould et al. (2007), and Marques et al. (2013), on the subject. The incentive to study and work, the teaching of values and positive skills in an environment where boys and girls are motivated to participate and listen to the adult who manages is considered more important than winning matches and cups, as highlighted by Vella et al. (2011). This can be considered the great feature of those who dedicate themselves to carrying out a social project and not a club, which differentiates the social educator-coach, from the coach of a professional club.

## Conclusions

The results indicate that the coaches interviewed have a profile analogous to the life skills training model of Gould et al. (2007) as they have (a) grounded philosophies; (b) a bond and good relationship with the athletes; (c) consideration of the environment in which they work; and (d) strategies for teaching life skills. Compared to the study by Marques et al. (2013), the Brazilian participants have better university training and more experience, although they have the same difficulties in describing specific strategies for the education of competencies.

Like the Spanish coaches, they have goodwill and desire to perform the educational task, although they lack planning and systematics for execution as occurs with tactical, technical, and physical training in sport. In this situation, Danish et al. (2005) propose that one competency be worked on at a time, training and talking about its concept with examples of how it applies in non-sporting situations. They also suggest that opportunities be offered for young people to use the chosen competencies, reflect and exchange this experience, sharing with their peers the successes and failures in the attempt, and reinforcing their learning.

A significant limitation for this to occur is the large number of young people each coach is responsible for in addition to the lack of internal help (no one had a second coach) and external and the fact that everyone had other occupations. There is also no space for the exchange of experiences between these coaches who operate in similar realities and face the same difficulties such as poverty, drug trafficking, and lack of support for the maintenance of team activities.

With the continuation of our research, we wish to propose a training program for these coaches, inspired by those that have already shown effective results, such as MAC, SUPER, and PAPE, that is consistent with the cultural and economic reality of Latin American countries. Delving into studies of how young people acquire and transfer competencies for their lives is another challenge for future research. Finally, it is important to mention the limitation of this study with a reduced number of participants, which makes it impossible to generalize our results.

## References

Camiré, M. (2012). Facilitating positive youth development through high school sport. (Doctoral dissertation, University of Ottawa, Canada). Retrieved from https://www.ruor.uottawa.ca/handle/10393/22903.

Camiré, M., Trudel, P., & Forneris, T. (2012). Coaching and transferring life skills: Philosophies and strategies used by model high school coaches. *The Sport Psychologist, 26*(3), 243–260.

Côté, J., Salmela, J., Baria, A., & Russel, S. (1993). Organizing and interpreting unstructured qualitative data. *The Sport Psychologist, 7*(2), 127–137.

Côté, J., Salmela, J., Trudel, P., Baria, A., & Russell, S. (1995). The coaching model: A grounded assessment of expert gymnastic coaches' knowledge. Journal of Sport Exercise Psychology, 17 (1), 1–17.

Danish, S., Forneris, T., & Wallace, I. (2005). Sport-based life skills programming in the schools. *Journal of Applied School Psychology, 2*(21), 41–62.

Danish, S. & Nellen, V., (1997). New roles for sport psychologists: Teaching life skills through sport to at-risk youth. *Quest, 49* (1), 100–113.

Danish, S., Nellen, V., & Owens, S. (1996). Teaching life skills through sport: Community-based programs for adolescents. En J.L. Van Raalte & B. Brewer (Eds.). Exploring sport and exercise psychology (pp. 205–225). : American Psychological Association.

Deci, E., & Ryan, R. (2000). The "what" and "why" of goal pursuits: Human needs and the self-determination of behavior. Psychological Inquiry, 11 (4), 227–268.

Falcão, W., Bloom, G., & Gilbert, W. (2012). Coaches' perceptions of a coach training program designed to promote youth developmental outcomes. *Journal of Applied Sport Psychology, 4*(24), 429–444.

Gilbert, W., & Trudel, P. (2004). Role of the coach: How model youth team sport coaches frame their roles. *The Sport Psychologist, 18*(1), 21–43.

Gould, D., & Carson, S. (2008). Life skills development through sport: Current status and future directions. *International Review of Sport and Exercise Psychology, 1*(1), 58–78.

Gould, D., Chung, Y., Smith, P., & White, J. (2006). Future directions in coaching life skills: Understanding high school coaches' views and needs'. *Athletic Insight On-line, 3*(8), 28–38.

Gould, D., Collins, K., Lauer, L., & Chung, Y. (2007). Coaching life skills through football: A study of award winning high school coaches. *Journal of Applied Sport Psychology, 1*(19), 16–37.

Guest, G., Bunce, A., & Johnson, L. (2006). How many interviews are enough? An experiment with data saturation and validity. *Field Methods, 18*, 59–82.

Holt, N., & Neely, K. (2011). Positive youth development through sport: A review. *Revista de Iberoamericana de Psicología del Ejercicio y el Deporte, 2*(6), 299–316.

Larson, R. (2000). Toward a psychology of positive youth development. *American Psychologist, 55*(1), 170–183.

Marques, M., Nonohay, R., Koller, K., Gauer, G., & Cruz, J. (2015). El estilo de comunicación del entrenador y el clima motivacional percibido en sus equipos. *Cuadernos de Psicología del Deporte, 15*(2), 47–54.

Marques, M., Sousa, C., & Cruz, J. (2013). Estrategias para la enseñanza de competencia de vida a través del deporte en jóvenes en riesgo de exclusión social. *Apuntes Educación Física y Deportes, 112*, 63–71.

Silva, P. (2010). *Ensino e transmissão de competências de vida por via da prática desportiva* (Tesis de maestria no publicada) Universidade do Porto, Porto, Portugal.

Smith, R., Smoll, F., & Cumming, S. (2007). Effects of a motivational climate intervention for coaches on changes in young athletes' achievement goal orientations. *Journal of Clinical Sport Psychology, 1*(1), 23–46.

Sousa, C., Cruz, J., Torregrosa, M., Vilches, D., & Viladrich, C. (2006). Evaluación conductual y programa de asesoramiento personalizado (PAPE) a entrenadores de deportistas jóvenes. *Revista de Psicología del Deporte, 15*(2), 263–278.

Vella, S., Oades, L., & Crowe, T. (2011). The central role of the coach in facilitating positive youth development: Moving from theory to practice. *Journal of Applied Sport Psychology, 23*, 33–48.

# Toward a Critical Psychosocial Approach to School Violence: Contributions from a Study with Students from the City of Córdoba, Argentina

**Horacio Luis Paulín**

## A Critical Psychosocial Approach to Violence in Schools

The social problem of school violence, associated with the categories of school mistreatment and bullying (Olweus, 1998; Ortega, 1998), expressions of incivility and indiscipline (Debarbieux, 1996) has been the subject of more than 40 years of research in social sciences. In the 1970s, research on mistreatment among students began in Nordic countries. The term bullying, sometimes translated as thuggery, harassment, intimidation, or hooliganism, refers to the existence of an imbalance of forces in the form of an asymmetric power relationship where one or several students are exposed to negative actions by others and find difficulties to defend themselves, configuring a lasting situation of harassment and humiliation with the presence of verbal and physical violence (Olweus, 1998). At the end of the 1980s and beginning of the 1990s of the last century, the phenomenon called school violence began to receive more attention in research in various countries, both in those that first institutionalized research lines and programs, of national court and with an epidemiological profile of the problem like France, Germany, England, United States and Spain (Debarbieux, 1996) and in countries like Brazil (Abramovay, 2003) and Argentina (Míguez, 2008). This research approach has drawn attention to the problem of victimization and peer bullying in schools, and the accumulation of

*This chapter is the English translation of an article originally published in Spanish as*: Paulín, H. L. (2015). Towards a critical psychosocial approach to school violence. Contributions from a study with students from the city of Córdoba, Argentina. *Universitas Psychologica, 14*(5), 1751–1762. https://doi.org/10.11144/Javeriana.upsy14-5.aepc. *Please cite the original version of the article in Spanish.*

H. L. Paulín (✉)
Universidad Nacional de Córdoba, Córdoba, Argentina

 
W. López-López et al. (eds.), *Trends in Latin American Psychology*,
https://doi.org/10.1007/978-3-031-87554-0_9

reports on the prevalence and incidence of this form of violence has led to the generation of policies and prevention programs according to different countries.

## A Critical Reading of School Violence as *Bullying*

The theory of school bullying has focused on some psychological aspects that explain the use of violence to impose a hierarchical order in the *peer relationships*. The central hypothesis of the *bullying* approach is that school bullying is related to a *scheme of dominance-submission* that replaces or avoids the development of more egalitarian friendship or fraternity relationships among children and young people. This model of domination relationship—a product of learning in experiences of family and peer socialization—can emerge as a pattern of playful interaction that is then made flexible through the practices of negotiation and construction of rules of social participation mediated by language (Ortega, 1998). In this form of explanation, there is a specific attention to ways of emergence of aggression among children and adolescents from a supposed "natural" evolution that would result in rules and moral conventions appropriate to negotiation and dialogue that deviates at some point due to unjustified aggression.

In this last assumption, a normative and homogenizing view of social relationships is observed. On the other hand, if we assume that the diversity of social positions and cultural references indicate different valuations to dialogue, emotions, and the exercise of force, we can understand how aggression acquires meanings and uses situated in the relationships of different childhoods and youths (García & Madriaza, 2005). In contexts of social diversity, the negotiation and dialogue skills to resolve conflicts cannot be normatively assumed as a starting point in children and adolescents in their school relationships, but it is more productive to ask how it is possible for them to internalize these skills and when they put them into play.

In addition, the dominance-submission scheme focused on the well-known triangle aggressor/victim/spectator—from which aggression is understood as a product of personal characteristics of those involved in a situation—is reductive when thinking about the phenomenon only from an interpersonal scheme, as it becomes invisible that power relationships, domination, and violence are inserted in cultural practices and institutional devices and intergroup relationships that support them (García & Madriaza, 2005; Revilla Castro, 2003). Even it has been observed that the so-called "victims" can, under certain circumstances, resort to various forms of violence defensively and become "perpetrators", with which the original role scheme must be revised (Crick & Grotpeter, 1996; Zimmer-Gembeck et al., 2005).

On the other hand, from this approach, numerous studies have been developed on the incidence of the phenomenon with the purpose of rigorously measuring the frequency of appearance of school bullying at different ages according to sex and other considered variables; some authors have insisted on the need to "approach the phenomenon from the mentality and experience of children and young people" (Ortega Ruiz et al., 2001, p. 101). The search for connections between symbolic aspects and practices situated in cultural contexts to understand the emergence of actions intersubjectively signified as violent or solidary is part of a certain revision of the theory of *bullying*. As Ortega expresses:

> it is the mechanism of meaning elaboration that creates the bias "cognitive-moral that justifies the unjustifiable behavior of subjecting to domination and submission those who, being equal in freedom and dignity, should be treated with respect and tolerance. (2002, pp. 108-109)

However, the theory does not address the processes of elaboration of the social meaning of mistreatment. This happens because it underlies as a normative assumption a psychological and sociogroup *progressive* development of relationships between subjects that should lead to relationships of reciprocity and acceptance of differences. From the perspective of *bullying*, even in the most recent formulations, we believe that a psychological analysis persists that does not clarify why mistreatment is justified and exercised, although it may recognize the influence of culture in peer networks (Ortega, 2002; Ortega et al., 2012).

The third questionable aspect of the bullying theory is the consideration of the nature of aggression. From critical social psychology, it is assumed that in the classic vision of psychosocial theories, attention is focused on the *aggression as an individual problem* from an *aggressive personality* and the political dimension of it is hidden; that is, a depoliticization effect of the phenomenon is operated by extracting it from power relations. But also, aggression conceived in terms of *socially deviant behavior*[1] is attributed to social groups considered dysfunctional without raising the violent actions of institutionalized power on these groups (Domènech et al., 2002). In the same sense, I agree with Fernández Villanueva (2007) in that the hegemonic theoretical approach to violence in social psychology restricts it to the concept of aggression, favoring an individualistic reading of the phenomenon by reducing interaction processes to mere being with others. In addition, it is not recognized that both aggression and violence are sociomoral and evaluative concepts because they refer to different realities depending on who makes their definition.

> [Aggression and violence] are nourished by contents dependent on moral criteria and social values. The meanings of what is violence emerge at specific, punctual moments, depending on what individuals suffer or the social perception of their suffering. (Fernández Villanueva, 2007, p. 164)

---

[1] All these propositions are part of what Domènech and Íñiguez (2002) call the view of the *conventional social psychology* on integrated aggression by instinctive theories, environmental, frustration-aggression and social learning. The central criticism is that they disconnect aggressive behavior from the maintenance of social order and that they operate as an ideological device, preserving the *status quo*, by hiding the violence exerted on groups and subjects by the institutional and political power.

## Toward a Relational and Dynamic Psychosocial Approach to Violence in School

First of all, it is necessary to rethink, from critical and interactionist perspectives in social psychology (Domènech et al., 2002; Fernández Villanueva, 2007), the role of violence in human conflicts which is considered, rather than mere behavior, a whole social construction. Therefore, we understand by violence "a social relationship in which individuals, groups or institutions - separately or simultaneously - act against human beings, other living beings and/or against Nature preventing their full development" (Duarte, 2005, p. 5). The characteristic is the reduction of the subject to an object as a rectifying process that denies its subjective condition, making it dependent and deprived of autonomy.

In addition, as an evaluative and sociomoral concept, violence refers to a different definition depending on who exercises it, suffers it, or witnesses it from their cultural and social references.

> Violence is not an impulsive, mechanical act, it is always exercised against another and the effect falls on the subject itself (…). It needs a recipient, a human or humanized being, a being that is known to be suffering, with the capacity to feel physical or social harm. It is the interactive process par excellence. Violence, materialized in concrete acts of aggression, is always an interpersonal, relational issue, that is framed in a previous interaction between the actors and determines their future interaction. Acts of violence are strategies for constructing the social presence of the aggressors and reducing the importance of the victims. (Fernández Villanueva, 2007, p. 165)

This relational and dynamic approach to violence operates from the following dimensions:

- The procedural character defined as the progression of violence that goes from milder to more severe events, up to constituting more complex climates of violence. In addition to the notion of a *violent escalation*, from mild episodes to more severe ones, there can be *recursive sequences* that culminate in *naturalized violence* and do not imply an increase in violence.
- The antecedents and consequences, from a historical perspective, allow us to analyze that aggressions are constitutive acts of threats of new aggressions and as such generate effects on the social interaction of groups or individuals with other groups or individuals in the future. Thus, social damages are produced by constituting explicit threats to the lives of victimized individuals and their close ones, especially if they are acts of impunity or naturalized by other social actors.
- The social meaning or function of violence is indicated, in some way, in the justifications that those who exercise it can give.[2] Violence is intentional because it seeks to achieve something through aggressive action, which can be considered strategic to achieve certain objectives. The most basic objective is to sustain the social identity of the subject, that is, their versions of the answer to the question

[2] This aspect is crucial because in this approach it renounces the thesis of aggressive personalities since it is assumed that certain psychological traits are not triggers of aggression by themselves.

"who am I?" which are threatened by the presence of the other. What is obtained is "the sensation of dominance, the appropriation of personal value of the aggressor by the fact of exercising the dominance that the acts of aggression against the other –the victim– entail" (Fernández Villanueva, 2007, p. 166).

- The justificatory aspects constitute the meanings of violence that have a *symbolic* subdimension and another *imaginary*. Violence needs a symbolic coverage that, at a subjective level, is expressed in justifications or arguments as a founding sense provided by social identity. More complex symbolic networks such as ideologies, sometimes crystallized in social representations, collaborate in the justification of acts of aggression. The evaluation of others as deserving of violence is concretized from a set of ideological values such as authoritarianism, nationalism, or racism. The imaginary subdimension of violence reveals the aspect of meanings as a mode of knowledge embodied in bonds and identifications loaded with affectivity and motivation for social action (Fernández Villanueva, 2007).
- The consideration of different violences with respect to mistreatment and discrimination in their different forms leads us to reconsider both concepts from the perspective of recognition in this approach.

From an interactionist perspective, *discrimination* constitutes a mode of unequal exchange between individuals and groups (Giménez, 2007).

In social, ethnic, and sexogenetic discrimination, evaluative recognitions operate between social actors who occupy dominant and dominated positions in the social space. Those who occupy positions of domination impose overvalued definitions of themselves according to the identity dimension in dispute (social, ethnic, sexual, gender), and attribute from a power differential devalued identities that stigmatize the dominated. In the tradition of symbolic interactionism studies on racial prejudice and in the propositions of Goffman (2006), about the construction of the various forms of social stigma that are born and expressed in a common sense language that justifies them, are the basis of a promising psychosocial vision for analyzing a "particular type of conflicts called recognition conflicts, analytically different from interest conflicts and ideological ones" (Giménez, 2007, p.38).

In a convergent sense, the reconceptualization that Honneth (2010) makes of the Hegelian theory of recognition, provides us with an integral analysis scheme that highlights the *forms of mistreatment* and *social contempt*. Humiliation and physical abuse as counterparts of love as the first level of recognition. The deprivation of rights and social exclusion as opposed to reciprocal recognition (respect) that allows considering the other as a rights holder. The third type of contempt is the value devaluation of ways of lifestyles or ways of living. Discrimination involves superior stereotypes of living compared to others considered inferior. Its counterpart is reciprocal recognition as solidarity and acceptance of individually developed ways of life (Honneth, 2010).

## Theoretical-Methodological Strategy

In the research line "Youth sociabilities and conflicts in school"[3] (Paulín & Tomasini, 2008), we have emphasized the importance of understanding the intersubjective relationships of adolescents and young people in school as a youthful world that reflects a non-school subjectivity (Dubet & Martuccelli, 1998). The questioning of how these relationships of encounter and disagreement in schools are processed, has been the starting point of qualitative inquiries in different single case studies and in multiple case designs in different secondary schools in the city of Córdoba (Argentina). As general objectives, we set out to know what are the critical incidents for the actors in the relationships of youth sociability, as well as the everyday meanings of interpretation and action in conflicts by young people and educators from diverse socio-educational contexts.

From a psychosocial approach, we address this research problem as a complex social process, in which although different levels of analysis participate, we focus on the *sociability relationships* among students that unfold as a set of practices and meanings to coexist, constituted by relationships endowed with various conflicts (Weiss, 2009). Research on violence in school often has neglected the investigation of solidary encounter links between students in the sense of relational practices aimed at going through adolescence as vital journeys in the company of others significant. By considering young subjects unfolding their sociabilities with certain capacities for reflexivity and regulation of their conflicts—and not only as perpetrators and/or victims of different violences—the focus of attention on this problem substantially changes. Also, as part of an ethical-political positioning oriented toward the transformation of relations of domination and violence, we conceive the investigative work as articulated with actions of psychosocial intervention that seek to favor the subjectivation of the actors who inhabit the schools. Therefore, from university extension, we have contributed to the promotion of coexistence and the approach to violence with different educational actors (Paulín, 2014; Paulín et al., 2011).

The methodological strategy consists in immersing oneself in the participant observation of everyday school life to know and share processes, meanings, and emotions involved in coexistence relationships. In addition, we cultivate a disposition to listening in the stay with the participants through conversational spaces such as the discussion group and the interview. In terms of data analysis, we opt for a dialectical alternation between the conceptual analytical work and the fieldwork to construct understandings and interpretations relative to the involved scenarios (Vasilachis De Gialdino, 2007), from the strategy of grounded theory (Strauss & Corbin, 2002).

[3] While I refer to the research projects "Middle school, subjects and conflicts" and "Youth sociabilities and logics of recognition in school" in this communication, I mainly base myself on the developments of my *thesis* doctoral "Conflicts in sociability among young people. A psychosocial study of the perspectives of students and educators in high schools" (Paulín, 2013).

The fieldwork carried out in various schools in the city of Córdoba between the years 2009 and 2012, allowed us to approach the presence of everyday conflicts, centered around the dispute for the respectability of young subjects from popular and upper-middle classes in their social, cultural, and gender identities (Paulín, 2014; Paulín & Tomasini, 2008). In these studies, we have been able to observe playful situations that oscillate in blurry limits with asymmetric schemes of crystallized dominance-submission, in the style of the descriptions of harassment and *bullying* theories (Ortega, 2002). Without failing to notice that there are configurations of more continuous character of violence from some over others, we have tried to expand the field of understanding toward other recurrent forms of violence that emerge in fieldwork. We refer to the games of looks, intimidating postures, and fights, as less asymmetric confrontations than those of *bullying* and where recognition is disputed among students from imaginary and symbolic components to justify the use of violence (Paulín, 2010).

## Dynamics of Conflicts and Situational Violence in School

Regarding the dynamics of conflicts faced through certain physical aggressions, we have synthesized in Fig. 1 the processual character of these violences attending to antecedents, consequences, and certain justifying senses that young people give to their intentions. In fact, more than isolated episodes that impact the observation of physical and verbal aggressions, violences are interwoven in relationships of some previous history for students. They can derive from friendly or loving sociability relationships product of infidelities, betrayals, feelings of jealousy, and envy, as indicated by the young interviewees. They also refer to a set of situations of "discrimination" suffered and exercised[4] and the *offenses* to family honor or to mothers (suspecting their sexual morality) operate as potential antecedents of conflicts to be resolved by the way of violence.

These daily episodes are built in a naturalized context of nominations of young people as subjects devalued in some sense: social, sexual, and gender. In a process reading, language games, looks, and intimidating postures operate as triggers for these conflicts to be resolved through physical violence (either in fights or in unilateral aggressions). We can recognize the role that certain modes of communication, looks, gestures, and postures assumed by young people in front of others constructed as possible adversaries play here. We have included the possible ways of facing these conflicts by the students that show that the dynamic is not reduced to victims and victimizers. In that sense, avoiding confrontations, dialoguing, facing (which

[4] Among the categories used to classify each other, racialized prejudices stand out: "black people", "black-skinned", "black-souled", "shitty black", and homophobic prejudices: the "faggots". These categories place sameness and otherness in a symbolic network that assumes a bipolar scheme of confrontation with the opposites: the "normals", the "males", the "gringos", and the "posh people" (with economic access).

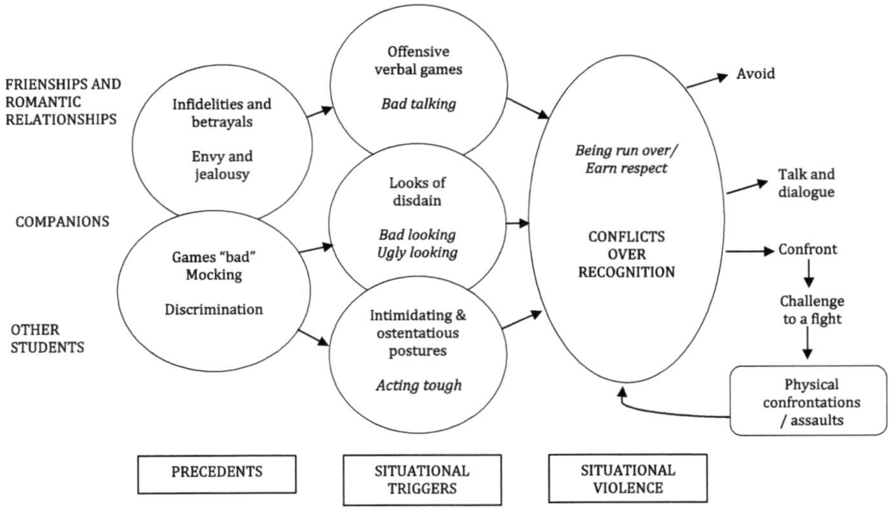


**Fig. 1** Dynamics of conflicts and situational violence

refers to verbally confronting someone in a way that ceases in their offense but without reaching aggression), and "inviting" to fight are possible actions that do not always conclude in aggressions.

Regarding the assumed postures, young people relate that "acting tough",[5] is someone who "shows off a lot, acts bad", showing their strength capacity when walking and talking. The term "acting" accounts for a subjective attempt at the construction of a position in front of others, a "personal presentation" that seeks to obtain a way of being treated with respect. In the encounter with those who generate uncertainty, the situation is sought to be controlled "acting" (and showing) in a certain way, like "tough" or "bad".

We can understand these postures as face works, aimed at the definition of social situations, preserving a safe place for the actor who seeks a certain affirmation of himself before others. (Goffman, 1970). But nothing is guaranteed in advance, and in each encounter, these challenges can be reactivated.

> Coordinator. What would it mean to act tough? To come looking for trouble. That they come and bother you. Knowing that it will bother you. To come to pick a fight with you. (Discussion group, males, private school)

The interpretation of the intentions of "acting tough" will depend on how each actor positions themselves in concrete situations. If someone "acts tough" with one, it is justifiable to "confront" them first and then fight with them, say the students.

[5] Colloquial expression in Córdoba, Argentina. The term choro has two etymologies, on the one hand it comes from caló, gypsy language, "choró" which means "thief", "robber" and on the other, from Quechua "churú" which means "bold and daring person", with which we can assume that its use oscillates between one and the other meaning (Dictionary of the Royal Spanish Academy, 2001).

But the same subject may want to "act tough" to impose respect on others who are presumed weaker (who are "less", who "are given"[6]) because it reveals pleasure in the possibility of exercising dominance over the other and a personal exaltation when being flattered by the group of friends.[7]

- That boy, I don't know what he wants to do ... it's true, you're big, but he wants to be the biggest among all ... I think he wants to act tough.
- Coordinator. When you say he wants to act tough, what do you mean?, what does he want to do?
- The boss.
- The bad guy. He acts like the bad guy. You say "ah" and he does everything to fight. He wants to show off in front of everyone, that he is ... Yes, that's how he is ... because I don't know ... he shows off. I don't like how he is. (Discussion group, males, state school).

The behavior of the other, not known, is interpreted as a signal of danger around what he might do: "because I don't know ... he shows off. I don't like how he is". Uncertainty that must be resolved since the one who adopts the pose of "acting tough" marks a potential threat in a context of violence exerted and suffered: "that he wants to take you for a fool" or "that he wants to take you for a servant". That is, some are seen as subjected to the power and superiority of others in the context of social fears that favor imaginary significations of otherness as dangerous. But at the same time, young people are clear that these are tests of courage in relation to others, facades (Goffman, 1970) built in the framework of a scenario where intersubjective relationships are key to confirm whether or not the ability to exercise a supposed dominance over others is true.

In the practice of "acting tough" there is a double sense of intimidating threat and as a way of "earning respect" from someone who persistently bothers or seeks to impose themselves.

> He was small in another school and now he is giant compared to us, that's why he acts tough now. He comes and threatens you, and what are you going to say if he beats you up.
>
> Coordinator. Does acting tough and earning respect have to do with the same thing or is there a difference? To earn respect you have to act tough. It's not the same, but to earn respect you have to act tough. (Discussion group, males, state school)

In this group of young people "acting tough" is also a construction of a facade that seeks to intimidate the other so that they back down from their taunts or accept their superiority as a man. Likewise, they recognize that many times it is not necessary to go to physical confrontation to "earn respect" due to the intimidating effect achieved with the facade of "bad" and "tough" that they build. On the other hand,

---

[6] Someone who is defenseless, without protection. It is also said that "he is given away", "he is donated".

[7] Some students explain that these act this way because "they like to do harm" or "do evil deeds". In these expressions, the search for motives or reasons to understand violence focuses on an attribution of naturalized evil in the person who harms for pleasure.

the Students from popular sectors say they also react to those who "act tough". The following conversation refers to senses of respect that translate into relationships of force and power, connoting hierarchies within groups. When these senses of respect are associated with the imposition of the same ("running you over"), they enable the option of fighting.

Camila. Everyone earns respect, and there are people who know how others are and know what others are up to, so they know that one way or another they will have to respect them.

Coordinator. And why this desire to earn respect?

Camila. And because if not, they want to run you over.

Marcos. And you're not going to let yourself be run over.

Coordinator. This is what we were talking about, let's see … when is respect achieved among you?

Marcos. When you know yourself well.

Fernando. And if not, as she said, when they start to fight …
Coordinator. So there would be two ways to earn respect …

Camila. And yes … if you seek respect, I mean you when you want to get along with a person, but if the person suddenly doesn't like you, you have to earn respect one way or another … If they want to run you over, the last option is to fight, and earn respect that way. (Discussion group, mixed state school)

"Earning respect" is also justified for some girls when they find it very offensive that another classmate provokes them with envy. The "show-offs"[8] and "those who act pretty" provoke jealousy and envy through a display of superiority, which is sanctioned by other women with confrontations or through physical violence. Blázquez (2010) interprets that some adolescents deprived of the material means to access goods that grant normality, and at the same time, established as subjects desiring these goods, would end up acting out the tension in the form of physical aggression on others. Therefore, the presence of the "show-offs" or "those who act pretty" is unbearable as it establishes a superiority of others that endangers a certain desired equality among students in the school group (Blázquez, 2010).

## Meanings of Violence

When we analyze certain justifications and arguments for violence, we see that they are linked to three issues that put this question in tension and that we maintain are not exclusive when understanding these processes: a) when there is an interpretation of intentions of domination and harm from other students; b) when feelings of envy and jealousy for material goods and resources, different relationships and cultural styles that others who "want to be more" flaunt become unbearable; and c) when

[8] Colloquial expression that means that a person "puts on airs" because they are conceited.

there are group pressures to show capacity for strength and aggressiveness crossed by the assumption of certain hegemonic gender roles in both women and men.

In these justifications, "earning respect" is a central sense expressed in a construction of subjectivity. Through the exercise of force and aggressive corporeality, it seeks to prevent the domination and possible abuse that others would embody, denying the value of their existence or the "attacks" on their social identity based on socioeconomic difference and cultural distinction, which others make feel with the display of their ostentation. Here a fear of otherness may be operating, constructed in a previous history of violation and mistreatment suffered in the most intimate relational spheres and in the social stigmatization that operates on certain young people in urban circulation outside their neighborhoods.[9]

The sense of "earning respect", as a man or woman, also sometimes involves establishing oneself through violence. The gender perspective, in terms of the role of hegemonic constructions of masculinities and femininities, is another key to interpretation that is not exclusive to the previous ones but complementary. If gender is not thought of as a trait and is not exhausted in a social role but as a performance—*performativity* (Butler, 1993), conditioned by cultural normative schemes in the daily processes of gender construction (*doing gender*, according to West & Zimmerman, 1999)—forms of being male and female are legitimized and resisted. In the case of male students, responding/resisting to the imperatives of hegemonic masculinity (exercising physical strength, emotional control, and expressing homophobic attitudes). In young women assuming/displacing submissive roles and obedience toward other subjectivities capable of exercising different forms of violence to assert themselves in front of other girls and boys.

As Fernández Villanueva (2007) expresses, there is intentionality in violence because the subject seeks to achieve something and "the most basic thing is to sustain their social identity, who am I?" (p. 166). We can say that in these processes, situational violence operates as daily materializations of structural and institutional violence, from which young subjectivities respond to the question of who they are. Subjectivities that, being crossed by the fear of otherness—as a contemporary social experience—a "sense of respect as a safeguard of their honor" (Duarte, 2005, p. 5) is present.

The sense of "earning respect", then, condenses a notion of respect restricted by fear, which operates as a safeguard of oneself and those close to them. But on the other hand, the construction of respect also presents itself as an intention to "impose respect" on others. Here, through violence, elusive recognition is obtained. It is about personal and social exaltation provided by discriminatory action, through stigmatization or exclusion of others. But this mode of recognition is fragile,

[9] I refer to the institutional violence operated by the security forces in Córdoba when young people from poor sectors are arbitrarily detained for the legal figure of loitering present in the Code of Offenses of the Province of Córdoba. The expression "face carrying" refers to the selective process of policing and control of the lives of certain young people that leads to deprivation of liberty for hours or days, to mistreatment, torture and in other cases, to death (Crisafulli & Barreto, 2011).

because it will have to be reactivated with recursive operations of symbolic and/or physical violence, every time others resist being dismissed in public.

The imposition of respect can be one of the ways to seek recognition and is exercised through force or threat. This does not mean that those who can exercise threats and violence against some are not capable of doing the exact opposite with those who are considered friends and with whom respect is not in question because trust is established in their more consolidated social relationships.

## Conclusions

In this chapter, we have tried to offer a dynamic and situated reading of the problems of violence in school as a counterpoint to descriptive studies enrolled in the approach of school violence from the theory of *bullying*. Although we recognize the contributions of the school bullying theory, we have tried to show that to understand the conflict in the processes of interaction between students, the perspective of the subjects involved and the observation of actions in the daily incidents of school coexistence is key. Our bet is for a critical review of hegemonic readings of violence in schools, to promote psychosocial interventions with a transformative will of situations of violence and discrimination among students.

We agree with Fernández Villanueva et al. (2013) that for the subject the loss of appreciation and the shame of being devalued, verified in daily interaction, can trigger violence among young people. But that does not warrant considering that they always agree with it, but that, in contexts of uncertainty and social danger, when the other behaves ambiguously, that's where violence is an available resource: "the same subjects who use it distrust its effectiveness, they assume it as a danger in which they are involved and from which there is a high probability of being punished" (p. 11). In this sense, violence is assumed as responsive-defensive to the conditions of the context and not as a personal trait of the subject that transfers it to all relational conflict.

In the case of relationships between students from the different cases under study, the emergence of violence can be understood within the framework of the notion of exclusion violence (Fernández Villanueva et al., 2013), that is, subjective manifestations resulting from the complex interplay of previous violence from structural and institutional levels that find expression in the form of actions and discourses devaluing, turned into everyday occurrences.

According to different previous analyses (García & Madriaza, 2005; Fernández Villanueva, 2007), we can conclude that in some conflicts of sociability in school, the resolution adopted by young people involves the preservation of certain personal safety, even at the cost of the mistreatment inflicted on the other. Therefore, procuring respect for oneself over the fear of others builds fragile forms of recognition that must be maintained permanently in recursive cycles of violence.

"Earning" respect in one way or another seems to be, then, an internalized imperative to resolve, present in relationships between young people from different social sectors. This respect is a social construction that is "re-staged" in school, an institution of modernity with the pretension of equal respect for all its members, but often does not promote it. This "re-staging" of the social problem of respect in school is crossed by social, racial hierarchies and gender imperatives and accounts for how young people face the social test of living with others.

Finally, we have said before (Paulín et al., 2011, 2014) that a key axis of promoting coexistence in schools should be oriented toward educational intervention in social networks and their conflicts. The understanding of relationships between young people allows us to recognize the generation of solidarities, aids, advice, and loyalties, as a kind of a group platform, which accompany the process of personal growth and indicate the importance of the presence of peers as significant referents. On the other hand, due to the emergence of situational violence to "earn respect", in which conflicts are constructed for the recognition of social diversity and ways of being among males and females, it is necessary to intervene from socio-educational practices and deliberative devices that promote the deconstruction of symbolic and imaginary arguments, justifying intolerance and violence among young people.

**Acknowledgments** This work was supported financially by the I + D Projects of the Secretary of Science and Technology of the National University of Córdoba. Project "Youth sociabilities and logics of recognition in school 2012-2013".

## References

Abramovay, M. (2003). Enfrentando a violência nas escolas: um informe do Brasil. In M. Abramovay (Ed.), *Violência na escola. América Latina e Caribe* (pp. 89–152). UNESCO.

Blázquez, G. (2010). De cara a la violencia. Agresiones físicas y formas de clasificación social entre mujeres jóvenes de sectores populares en Argentina. *Sexualidad, Salud y Sociedad, 6*, 10–40.

Butler, J. (1993). *Cuerpos que importan. Sobre los límites materiales y discursivos del «sexo»*. Paidós.

Crisafulli, L., & Barreto, I. (2011). *¿¡Cuánto falta!? Código de faltas, control social y derechos humanos*. INECIP-Advocatus.

Crick, N. R., & Grotpeter, J. K. (1996). Children's maltreatment by peers: Victims of relational aggression. *Development and Psychopathology, 8*, 367–380.

Debarbieux, E. (1996). *International survey of school climate: Secondary school students questionnaire*. Observatorio Europeo de la Violencia Escolar.

Domènech, I., Argemí, M., & Íñiguez Rueda, L. (2002). La construcción social de la violencia. *Athenea Digital, 2*, 1–10. https://doi.org/10.5565/rev/athenead/v1n2.54

Duarte, K. (2005). Violencias en jóvenes, como expresión de las violencias sociales. Intuiciones para la práctica política con investigación social. *PASOS, 120*, 3–20.

Dubet, F., & Martuccelli, D. (1998). *En la escuela. Sociología de la experiencia escolar*. Losada.

Fernández Villanueva, C. (2007). Violencia y agresiones: pinceladas para una nueva perspectiva psicosocial interaccionista. In J. Romay (Ed.), *Perspectivas y retrospectivas de la psicología social en los albores del siglo XXI* (pp. 163–171). Biblioteca Nueva.

Fernández Villanueva, C., Revilla Castro, J., Domínguez Bilbao, R., Ferreira Salles, L., & Silva, J. (2013). Explicaciones y representaciones de la violencia de jóvenes escolares brasileños. *Revista de Educación, 361*, 13–36.

García, M., & Madriaza, P. (2005). Sentido y sinsentido de la violencia escolar. Análisis cualitativo del discurso de estudiantes chilenos. *Psykhe, 14*(1), 165–180.

Giménez, G. (2007). Formas de discriminación en el marco de la lucha por el reconocimiento social. O. Gall Racismo, mestizaje y modernidad: visiones desde latitudes diversas (pp. 37–62). : CEIICH-UNAM, Centro Regional de Investigaciones Multidisciplinarias. Recuperado de http://www.crim.unam.mx/drupal/crimArchivos/Pub-crim/Libro_07_04.pdf.

Goffman, E. (1970). Sobre el trabajo de la cara. En E. Goffman, Ritual de la interacción (pp. 11–25). : Tiempo Contemporáneo.

Goffman, E. (2006). *Estigma. La identidad social deteriorada*. Amorrortu.

Honneth, A. (2010). *Reconocimiento y menosprecio. Sobre la fundamentación normativa de una teoría social*. Katz.

Míguez, D. (2008). *Violencias y conflictos en las escuelas*. Paidós.

Olweus, D. (1998). *Conductas de acoso y amenaza entre escolares*. Morata.

Ortega, R. (1998). ¿Indisciplina o violencia? El problema de los malos tratos entre escolares. *Revista Perspectivas, 28*(4), 587–599.

Ortega, R. (2002). Lo mejor y lo peor de las relaciones de iguales: juego conflicto y violencia. *Revista Interuniversitaria de Formación del Profesorado, 44*, 93–113.

Ortega Ruiz, R., Del Rey, R., & Mora-Merchán, J. (2001). Conceptos y etiquetas que definen el maltrato. *Revista Interuniversitaria de Formación del Profesorado, 41*, 95–113.

Ortega, R., Del Rey, R., & Paz, E. (2012). Violencia escolar y bullying. El estado de la cuestión y los nuevos retos investigadores. In A. Furlán (Ed.), *Reflexiones sobre la violencia en la escuela* (pp. 205–235). Siglo XXI.

Paulín, H. L. (2010). Enfrentamientos y peleas entre jóvenes escolarizados: un análisis de emociones encontradas por el reconocimiento. En Actas II Congreso Internacional de Investigación y Práctica Profesional en Psicología (pp. 153–155). : Universidad de Buenos Aires, Facultad de Psicología.

Paulín, H. L. (2013). *Conflictos en la sociabilidad entre estudiantes. Un estudio psicosocial sobre las perspectivas de jóvenes y educadores de escuelas secundarias* (Tesis de doctorado inédita). Facultad de Psicología, Universidad Nacional de Córdoba, Argentina.

Paulín, H. L. (2014). *Jóvenes y escuela. Relatos sobre una relación compleja*. Editorial Brujas.

Paulín, H. L., & Tomasini, M. (2008). *Conflictos en la escuela secundaria: diversidad de voces y miradas*. Universidad Nacional de Córdoba.

Paulín, H. L., Tomasini, M., D'Aloisio, F., López, C. J., Rodigou, M., & García, G. (2011). La representación teatral como dispositivo de investigación cualitativa para la indagación de sentidos sobre la experiencia escolar con jóvenes. *Psicoperspectivas, 10*(2), 134–155. https://doi.org/10.5027/psicoperspectivasVol10-Issue2-fulltext-149

Revilla Castro, J. (2003). La violencia de los alumnos en los centros educativos. *La Educación, 329*, 513–532.

Strauss, A., & Corbin, J. (2002). *Bases de la investigación cualitativa. Técnicas y procedimientos para desarrollar la teoría fundamentada* (2nd ed.). CONTUS, Universidad de Antioquía.

Vasilachis De Gialdino, I. (2007). La investigación cualitativa. In I. Vasilachis De Gialdino (Ed.), *Estrategias de investigación cualitativa* (pp. 23–60). Gedisa.

Weiss, E. (2009). Jóvenes y bachillerato en México: el proceso de subjetivación, el encuentro con los otros y la reflexividad. *Propuesta Educativa, 32*, 83–94.

West, C., & Zimmerman, D. (1999). Haciendo género. In M. Navarro & C. Stimpson (Eds.), *Sexualidad, género y roles sexuales* (pp. 109–143). Fondo de Cultura Económica.

Zimmer-Gembeck, M., Geiger, T., & Crick, N. (2005). Relational and physical aggression, prosocial behavior, and peer relations: Gender moderation and bidirectional associations. *The Journal of Early Adolescence, 25*(4), 421–452.

# Control Paths and Covariation of Variables as an Expression of Cognitive Change in Problem-Solving

**Hugo Alberto Escobar Melo, Rocio Abello Correa, and Jorge Castaño García**

## Introduction

Cognitive development from a microgenetic methodological perspective highlights local change within the framework of a global evolution process (Puche-Navarro, 2008, cited by Vasco & Henao, 2008). It is understood as an open transformation, which is dynamic and complex (van Geert & Steenbeek, 2005).

Within this framework of ideas, the authors of this study have been interested in asking about the characteristics that the execution patterns assume in terms of paths and trajectories when solving a physical-mathematical problem of proportionality of uniform rectilinear motion, as a theoretical-methodological alternative, to study local cognitive novelty and its complexity, framed in a global conception of development.

The central research question was as follows: how to characterize change as cognitive novelty in the solution of a linear motion problem task with constant speed in solvers that are university students?

The specific questions were expressed as follows: what are and how are the different execution patterns of the solvers characterized when facing the problem-task object of exploration? Is there intra and intersubject variability in the execution patterns when solving the problem-task object of exploration?

---

*This chapter is the English translation of an article originally published in Spanish as*: Escobar Melo, H. G., Abello Correa, R., & Castaño García, J. (2016). Trayectorias de control y co-variación de variables como expresión del cambio cognitivo en la solución de un problema. *Universitas Psychologica, 15*(1), 281–302. https://doi.org/10.11144/Javeriana.upsy15-1.tccv. *Please cite the original version of the article in Spanish.*

---

H. A. Escobar Melo (✉) · R. Abello Correa · J. Castaño García
Pontificia Universidad Javeriana, Bogota, Colombia
e-mail: escobarh@javeriana.edu.co

 
W. López-López et al. (eds.), *Trends in Latin American Psychology*,
https://doi.org/10.1007/978-3-031-87554-0_10

## Cognitive Development and Change[1]

According to Vasco and Henao (2008), development is defined as "a process that implies change or variations over time and a multiplicity or complexity in space" (p. 6); from the perspective of the cited authors, it is affirmed that this comprehensive approach to development requires an approach of intelligibility to individual variations in the trajectories that each subject lives, in terms of what remains and what changes, that accounts for complexity, multicausality and multi, micro, meso and macro level influencing factors that affect development. Such a stance is consistent with contemporary approaches by van Geert and Steenbeek (2005) on development seen from dynamic, non-linear, and complex systems.

Considering the above, it can be affirmed that there are various levels of resolution at which the macro and micro processes of development can be studied. According to Vasco and Henao (2008), it is proposed that a modality of change as a progressive process can be studied through a low-resolution level. A change as a local process, which can be progressive and at the same time regressive, requires a study at a finer resolution level. For the purposes of the base research, the interest focused on the microprocess in terms of a fine exploration scale in which the change was asked as cognitive novelty.

Cognitive change, according to Pozo and Gómez Crespo (2009a), requires distinguishing at least three types of transformations that have to do with the breadth and depth of change: enrichment that implies new information; adjustment that in a certain sense modifies cognitive structures without producing a new order; and restructure that completely reformats them. From this perspective, conceptual change, in the strict sense of the term, does not constitute an accumulation of knowledge; it is, above all, a reorganization that reformats cognitive structures.

Posner et al. (1982), cited by Pozo and Gómez Crespo (2009b), affirm that four conditions are required for a cognitive change to occur: the subject's dissatisfaction with his explanations; having a new conception, either because the subject can construct it or because it is mediated by an educational process; that it is plausible and, finally, that it is more powerful in its explanatory possibilities. Cognitive change then requires the subject to feel dissatisfaction in explaining the world from his previous references, in addition to glimpsing in the process of constructing new ideas, a different and more convincing understanding alternative.

Cognitive change turns out to be one of the central axes when studying areas such as development and learning, which is why its study and how to approach it has been a topic of great interest (Bermejo, 2005). However, the difficulty faced when studying the change itself and knowing its causes and mechanisms has led to the creation of models and approaches that aim to understand the nature of this phenomenon. Among these approaches is the model of dynamic systems.

---

[1] With the collaboration of Ana María Rodríguez and Ursula Hinostroza, Research Assistants, Psychologists, Pontifical Javeriana University, Bogotá-Colombia.

The field of psychological development, as evolutionary change, involves states, actions, and some type of mechanism (Escobar, 2003). The final state is well known: when we find it in terms of complex, defined, efficient behaviors, and we do not hesitate to affirm that there has been evolution. When such development has not occurred and the subject operates in an apparently primitive way, it is asserted that there has been a regression or an oscillation. Thus, development is opposed to regression. However, the latter can legitimately be a certain "evolutionary vection". This way, two types of evolutionary change will be differentiated: the "transformational" and the "variational". The first resembles what has been described through known metaphors, such as the line, the ladder, or even the ascending spiral. It implies new structures and a direction with certain continuities and discontinuities. The second type, variational change, refers to modifications in functioning that involve continuities, reversibilities, and, in particular, local and specific learnings within a complete structure (Overton, 1997).

It should be emphasized that we are not talking about any change. It is about the change that transforms and integrates. That is, a change that produces novel relationships and behaviors. Substructures in competition with totalities and explainable direction. In this process of transformation and integration, two unsuspected elements are anchored. The choice and the loss. The choice does not necessarily evoke something of a democratic and conscious nature. It can be forced, as in the situation of having reached the edge of the abyss, where instead of returning and extinguishing, there is nothing left but the eloquent and dignified alternative of jumping into the void. The choice always implies a *conditio* sine qua non in terms of loss. If one chooses a direction with possible achievements, accidents, and losses, one begins to travel some path that will in turn lead the subject through unsuspected places, with possibilities of successes and failures, but having chosen there will always be a possible inevitable loss. Evolutionary change must therefore be understood as a probabilistic epigenesis (Piaget, 1977). Often, these probabilities are not available to be a good subject in evolution; it depends, sometimes, on whose hands the arbitrator is in. You lose and you win, it depends on the increase in probabilities and the conditions for or against.

Evolutionary change as probabilistic epigenesis leads to the existence of levels and clusters. In this way, the representation of development is not possible through a simple figure, but of four dimensions, including the temporal, with various directions that lead to breaking, consequently, with the metaphor of the ladder that ascends to infinity. Networks of several levels, found spider webs, chosen paths and trajectories, and inflection points. A picture of issues like this does not limit us to being eternal replicating automatons. In fact, we have explicit and implicit performances that speak of ascents and descents, punctuated balances with successful jumps or colossal failures; exchanges and innovations that lead to diversity (Pinker, 2013).

As in physics, nothing is destroyed, everything is transformed, and something remains invariant; there is a game between what remains and what changes. Here the new and the old coexist. And in that dialectic, new relationships are created that are expressed in the novel change of behavior, which becomes more explicit and, at the same time, encrypted against contents and representations to which one does not have access, which reveals the presence of complex behavioral fields (Karmiloff-Smith, 1994).

As evidence of the above, there are various studies and research, for example, related to microgenesis and cognitive change in the acquisition of the numeric cardinal in Bermejo (2005); Bayesian models and complex inferential functions in Ossa and Puche-Navarro (2010); transition matrices and patterns of cognitive variability in Ossa (2013); understanding gear systems and cognitive change in 4-year-old children in Navarro-Roldán (2008), all of them under a methodological approach that resorts to microgenetic analysis for the study of change in specific problem-solving situations.

According to Siegler (1996), since the 1970s, developmental theorists in their study of change have emphasized two aspects: firstly, they have highlighted the importance of change as a means to understand development and learning, and secondly, they have expressed the difficulty of addressing it, suggesting that understanding cognitive change is limited. In response to this, over the years, models and methods have emerged that have allowed an approach to understanding this process, enabling its study and understanding to be increased.

Torbeyns et al. (2004) address cognitive change from Siegler's (1996) perspective, stating that:

> [...] the development of cognitive strategies has traditionally been portrayed in terms of the staircase metaphor. This metaphor depicts cognitive change as a series of 1:1 equations between ages and ways of thinking. Children of a given age use a particular strategy to solve a cognitive task; cognitive change involves a relatively brief period of transition, during which multiple strategies conflict with each other, leading to the substitution of the previously used strategy for a qualitatively better one. (p. 188)

According to the above, Siegler (1994, cited by Ossa, 2013) considers that cognitive change can be evidenced in the emergence of new strategies and that the "why" of the presence of variability can be found in the processes of this phenomenon itself. Hence the importance of studying change through the various processes that the subject carries out during each of the transformations, as happens in the present investigation.

In response to traditional models of cognitive change, Siegler (1996) proposes his overlapping waves theory as a new perspective for understanding development, which is responsible for explaining the variability that exists in children's problem-solving. According to this theory, subjects have access to a wide range of strategies for problem-solving and can choose which strategy to use depending on the nature of the problem; these strategies range from the most basic to the most advanced (Farrington et al., 2009).

Considering what change implies and understanding problem-solving as "the higher psychological function, intertwined with abstract thinking, reasoning, and working memory, among others" (Montealagre, 2011, p. 120), problem-solving has been used as a means to study cognitive change in a specific task, as it involves the use of a series of processes and heuristic strategies used to find the solution.

Evolutionary studies have focused on studying what is stable and universal within the patterns generated by change and not on identifying the factors or processes generating change. Thus, the central objective of the dynamic systems approach is to recognize and analyze the variability that occurs in human cognitive and behavioral functioning, which is characterized by being complex and non-linear. In this sense, this perspective describes the nature of development not in terms of simple rules, but in terms of equations that predict families of irregular and diverse curves (Gutiérrez et al., 2002).

For Ossa (2013), variability has been extensively studied and various authors have contributed to the definition from different approaches. Among these authors are Piaget (1979), Yan and Fischer (2002), van Geert and van Dijk (2002), and Puche-Navarro et al. (2003), among others. Each of these theorists' definitions is different, yet in general terms, it can be said that they understand variability as a characteristic of development and cognitive functioning that is presented in trajectories with a constant flow of change that reflects non-linear dynamics.

The problem-solving perspective has helped to understand change with specific methods for its study, to which the microgenetic method is added as one of the most significant. This analysis focuses on the study of individual changes, "of small magnitude that occur in the psychological processes of interest during a single observation or experimental session. The objective is to be able to "study the change as it occurs" (Gutiérrez & Carriedo, 2002, p. 78). This analysis is based on three basic premises: to study the dynamics of change processes and not static results, to explain these processes and not just describe them, and only through this approach can we come to understand how higher psychic functions have been formed.

By considering development as a non-linear, irregular, and variable phenomenon, set in a perspective of dynamic systems, it is accepted that the method to explore these phenomena must be one that is capable of capturing and accounting for the uneven and dynamic paths and trajectories that are presented.

## Objective

Identify and characterize intra and inter-subject variability in relation to execution patterns in the resolution of the task-problem under exploration.

## Method

### *Categories*

- Variable control dimension: refers to keeping the value of a variable constant for two or more attempts while changing the value of the other.
- Covariation: refers to the relationship between the variables speed and duration of the event to produce an effect on the distance traveled.
- Execution patterns: regularity in the control or covariation dimensions in a succession of attempts.

## Participants

The sample of participants in the base research, of an intentional non-probabilistic type, was made up of 136 university students, both women and men, between the ages of 17 and 25, distributed as follows: 42 from the Faculty of Sciences, 35 from the Faculty of Arts and 59 from the Faculty of Psychology.

## Type of Study

The type of study is descriptive under a methodological approach of microgenetic analysis that allows both a qualitative and a quantitative analysis of the data collected on the solution of the task-problem.

According to Siegler and Crowley (1991), microgenetic analysis enables direct observation, recording, and analysis of cognitive novelty and change mechanisms. To achieve this purpose, two characteristics must be attended to: first, the observation of the solver's procedure, which must be done from the beginning of the change until it acquires stability; second, a high density of observations is required to comprehensively approach cognitive change.

## Instrument

The task-problem proposed to be solved in this study is a typical problem of rectilinear motion at constant speed. Specifically, it consists of determining the constant speed that must be imparted to a mobile and the time that the event-movement must last to cover a distance that is previously set on a segment of straight line. Both the speed and the time are given in "scalar" values (that is, the value indicating their extension is given without any unit). The solver must determine the speed (V) and the duration of the movement (T) of a mobile so that it covers the distance D that separates the starting point and the arrival point (the goal) with an error of plus or minus 2.5% of the distance D. Up to 15 attempts can be made to execute the task.

The problem to be solved was designed in an interactive software that combines various expressive languages, graphic, numeric, and written, captures the values that the solver gives to the variables V and T in the different attempts, immediately feeds back the procedure done and, once the task is finished, allows recording the subjects' verbalizations about their procedure. Additionally, it has a toolbox that can be used to help in the resolution of the task-problem, as well as a screen where they can write or draw and a calculator (Fig. 1). The URANUS software analyzes and graphs the procedures of segment solvers for the dimensions of variable control and covariation.

This problem is presented under a compiled and programmed application in object-oriented JAVA language. It has a complex data repository that allows meticulous tracking of the subject's activity and automatic classification.

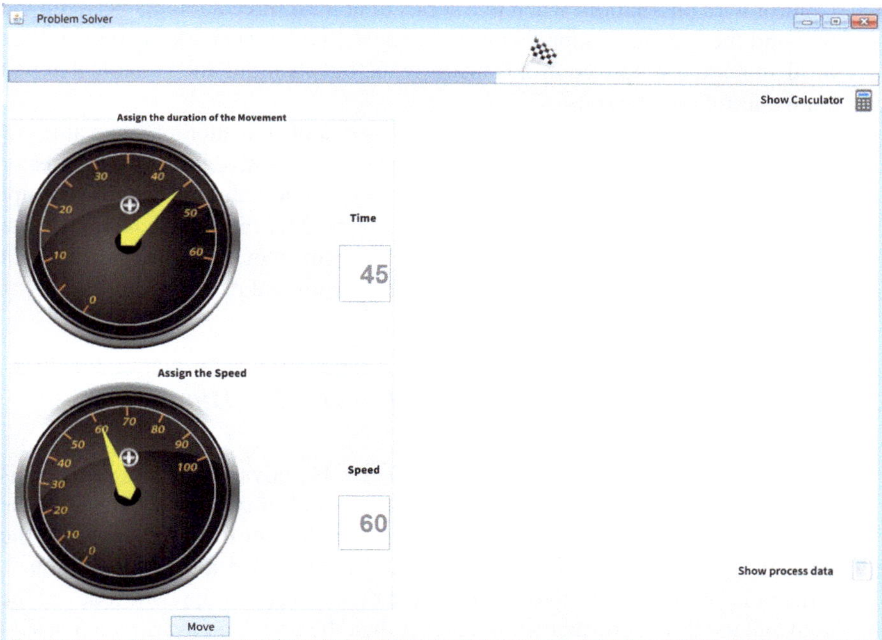


**Fig. 1** Software interface URANUS

## *Methodology*

From the microgenetic analysis used, the types of variable control and covariation used by the subjects in their approach to solving the task problem were identified. From this microgenesis, the types of paths and trajectories of the solvers were characterized.

## *Execution Patterns for the Control Dimension*

(a) No control: when from one attempt to the next, the values of both variables are changed without any apparent control by the solver, in the sense of keeping one of the variables constant.
(b) Simple control of two attempts: when in a series not exceeding two attempts, the solver keeps one of the two variables constant and changes the value of the other.
(c) Simple control of more than two attempts: when in a series of three or more attempts, the solver keeps one of the two variables constant and changes the value of the other.

(d) Control with alternation: when in a series of at least three attempts between the first and the second, a simple control is made, and between the second and the third attempt, a simple control is made again, but changing the variable that had been controlled, and so on.
(e) Controlled change of variables: when in a series of two attempts the values of both variables are changed in terms of positive or negative increase not greater than two (2) units. It is observed that the solver assigns values in the new attempt based on the immediately previous one to produce a subtle change in the mobile's displacement. The criterion of a positive or negative increase not greater than two (2) units is defined based on empirical evidence.

## *Execution Patterns According to the Covariation Dimension*

(f) No Covariation: three cases are distinguished. No covariation 1: a segment is classified as no covariation 1 when it is composed of two (2) attempts on the same side of the goal, and the second attempt is further from the goal than the previous one. No covariation 2: a segment is classified as no covariation 2, when it is composed of three attempts, the first two are on opposite sides of the goal and the third is further from the goal than the first. No covariation 3: a segment is classified as no covariation 3, when it is composed of three attempts, all on the same side of the goal and the third is further from the goal than the second.
(g) Increasing Covariation: constitutes an increasing series of three or more attempts where in each attempt it gets closer to the goal than the previous one, even if in the last one it goes to the other side of the goal. There can be a segment of increasing covariation of two (2) attempts when these are the last two leading to the goal.
(h) Decreasing Covariation: constitutes a decreasing series of three or more attempts where in each attempt it gets closer to the goal than the previous one, even if in the last one it goes to the other side of the goal. There can be a segment of decreasing covariation of two (2) attempts when these are the last two leading to the goal.
(i) Mixed Covariation: a segment is classified as mixed covariation, when it is composed of three attempts, the first and the second on opposite sides of the goal, with the second being a point of inflection[2] and the third being closer to the goal than the first. Special case: in the presence of trajectories with four attempts in which the last three form a segment of mixed covariation and with the first two it is not possible to classify them as f1; the four attempts will be considered as a single segment of mixed covariation.

[2] Inflection point: when from one attempt to another the sense of the approximations to the goal changes.

The subject's procedure is segmented according to each dimension and in accordance with the defined criteria. A segment is then understood as a succession of attempts that have the same execution pattern. The segments form paths that are configured as part of a trajectory that shows one or more segments. Finally, the total procedure of the subject constitutes a trajectory that refers to the entire sequence that the subject follows.

## Procedure

The task-problem was applied under the URANUS software to the population under study and, based on the results, the paths and trajectories were characterized according to execution patterns for the control and covariation dimensions in order to identify intra and intersubject variability.

## Results

As previously stated, this research aimed to identify and characterize intra and intersubject variability in relation to execution patterns in solving the task-problem under exploration. This objective was achieved as the results express the variability of the subjects when using at least five clearly identified forms of variable control, in addition to four types of covariation. This use is not uniform, which emphasizes change, as each subject is ultimately characterized by a defined trajectory that expresses their procedure. Small groups of subjects that share it can also be found (see Figs. 2, 3, 4, 5, 6 and 7).

Subjects can start with the use of some type of control and change it throughout the problem solution. Thus, there are trajectories without variable control (without covariation), with variable control (with covariation), and these latter can be consolidated or not consolidated. It was also observed that the trajectories show improvement, that is, they start without control or without covariation and at some point move to segments that show some type of control or covariation, and these can be intermittent, that is, they have intermediate segments of no control (no covariation), in addition to trajectories without intermittence, in which it is observed that there are indeed no intermediate segments of no control (no covariation, see Table 1).

The qualitative analysis allowed to characterize a trajectory as a sequence of execution patterns, according to control (a, b, c, d, and e) or according to covariation (f, g, h, i) described in the methodology. In Table 1 it is observed that 33.1% of the trajectories in relation to the variable control dimension are of "consolidated control", while in the covariation dimension 72.1% are of "consolidated covariation" (Table 2). These trajectories indicate that the subjects start and finish the task with some type of control different from "a" (no control) or with some type of

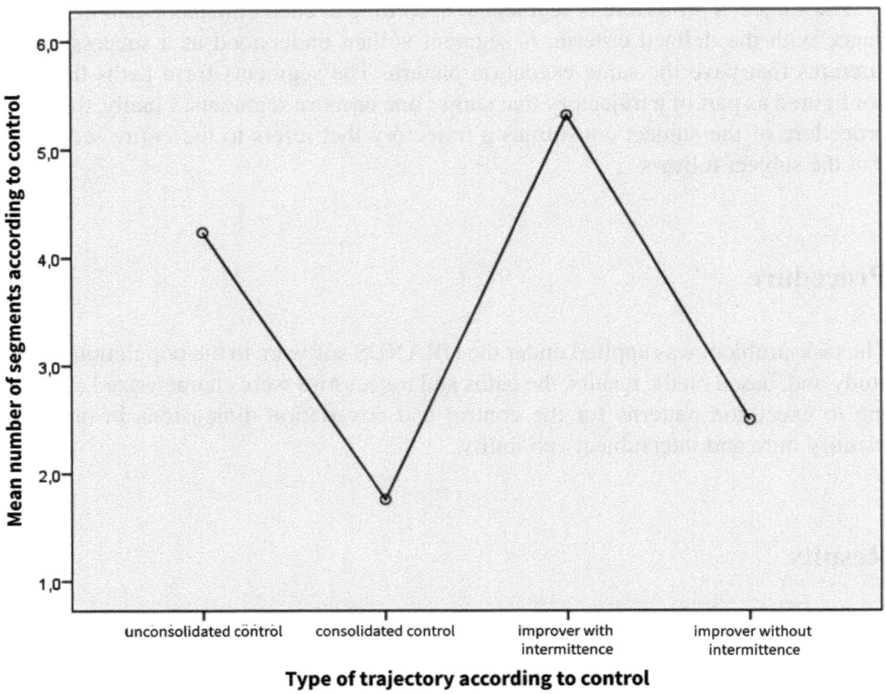


**Fig. 2** Average segments according to variable control

covariation different from "f" (no covariation) and that throughout their trajectories, there is no segment without control or without covariation.

Although these trajectories do not present changes that go from control to no control or from covariation to no covariation or vice versa, some of them do present less drastic changes, that is, from a type of control different from "no control" (or from a type of covariation different from "no covariation") to another type of control different from "no control" (or of covariation' no covariation'), in other words, from control to control or from covariation to covariation. For example, a trajectory like "bcb", which is of consolidated control, shows two changes: it goes from controlling one of the variables in two attempts to controlling the other variable in more than two attempts (b = > c) and then, again, it goes back to controlling the first variable in two attempts (c = > b).

In this way, it could be affirmed that a little more than 2/3 of the trajectories show some type of change when studying the control dimension and a little more than ¼ when studying the covariation dimension. These data highlight the change and variability in the way subjects approach the task.

The trajectories of "unconsolidated control" (10.3%, Table 1) and those of "unconsolidated covariation" (8.8%, Table 2) also do not show global changes because they only compare the first and last segments; it may happen that some of

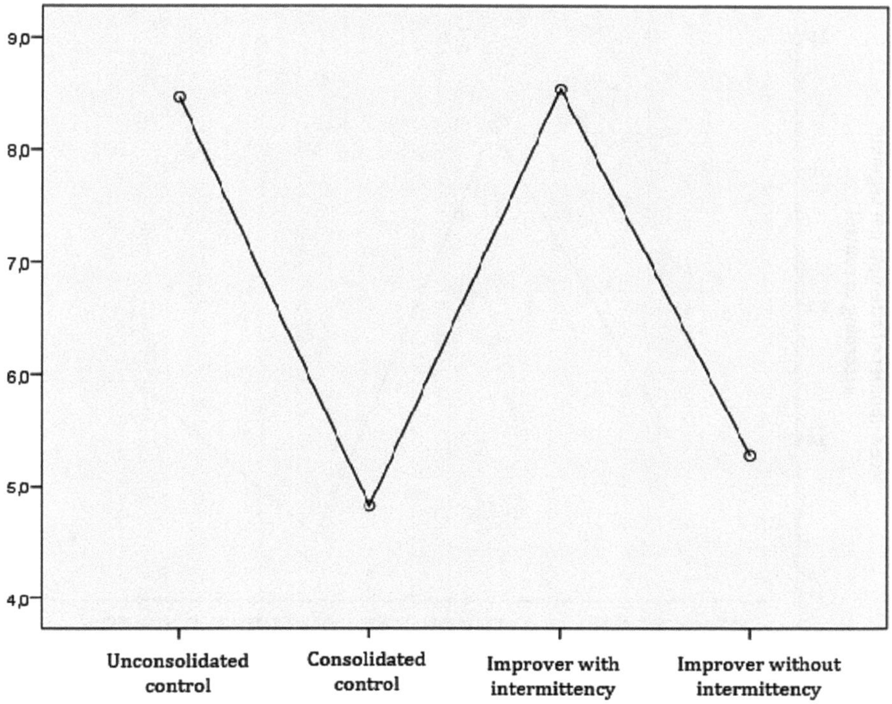


**Fig. 3** Number of attempts per trajectory according to variable control

them have changes in intermediate segments; if they are trajectories of more than two segments it may happen that in the transition from one segment to another a drastic change from control to no control[3] or from covariation to no covariation, or vice versa, or from no control to control, or from no covariation to covariation.

Clearly, improving and worsening trajectories indicate these drastic changes in one of the two dimensions. 51.5% of the trajectories show these types of changes in the control dimension (Table 1) and 14% in the covariation dimension (Table 2).

Reading Table 3 requires understanding the measure of the "average segment size", which is the result of dividing the number of attempts by the number of segments. This value is an indicator of the frequency of change. It is interpreted as follows: a lower value means fewer attempts between changes, and a higher value means more attempts; for example, the value 3.3 of the trajectories without control means that on average every 3.3 attempts the type of control changes.

[3]To simplify, whenever it is not indispensable, "no control" will be used to refer to a segment whose control is of type "a" and "control" to refer to a segment whose type is different from "a" (b, c, d, or e). Similarly, it will be done with covariation: "no covariation" is "f" and "covariation" is different from "f" (g, h, e, i).

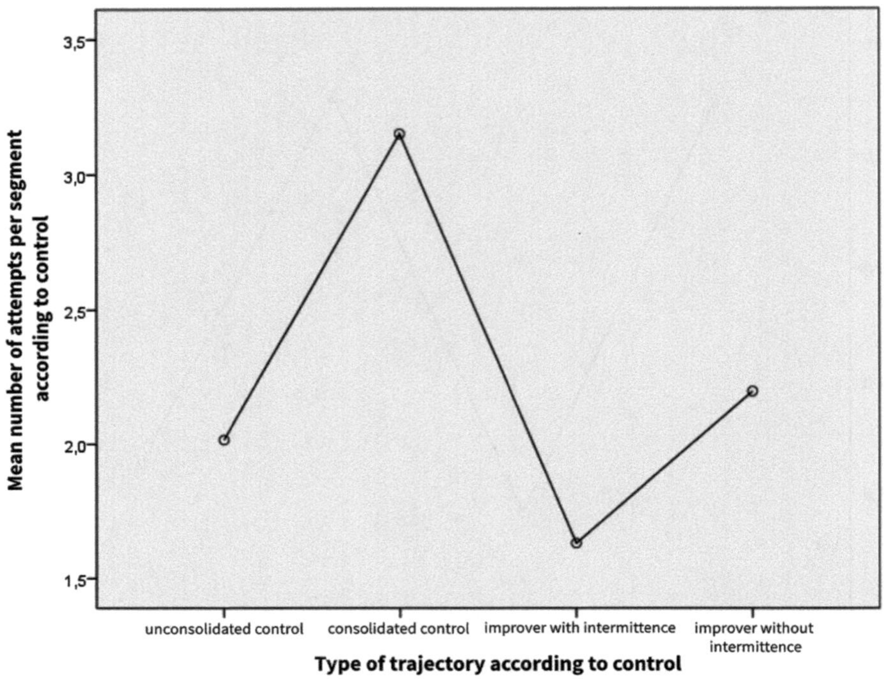


**Fig. 4** Average segment size according to variable control

In this table, it can be observed that the average size of the segments in the improving trajectories with intermittence according to the control dimension is the smallest value (1.6 attempts/segments). This data can be interpreted in terms of those trajectories in which the subject shows that they do not have control at the beginning, but tries to find it and ends up succeeding, are precisely those in which changes in control types occur more frequently. This fact seems to be corroborated with the trajectories of unconsolidated control (2 attempts/segments) which, as their name suggests, are trajectories in which although the subject starts the task showing control, they lose it a few attempts later to regain it later. In contrast, the trajectories that show little frequency of change are the trajectories without control (3.3 attempts/segments) or with consolidated control (3.1 attempts/segments).

Similarly, this happens with the covariation dimension, as can be seen in Table 3. Precisely the improving trajectories with intermittence (2.9 attempts/segments) and unconsolidated covariation (2.6 attempts/segments) are those that have the smallest value in the average segment size, an indicator of higher frequency of change, in contrast with the trajectories without covariation (9 attempts/segments) and with consolidated covariation (3.8 attempts/segments) with lower frequency of change.

When comparing the different trajectories by the average number of attempts (Table 3), which is the measure of the lesser or greater efficiency to solve the task, it can be seen that the trajectories of consolidated control (4.8 attempts, the smallest

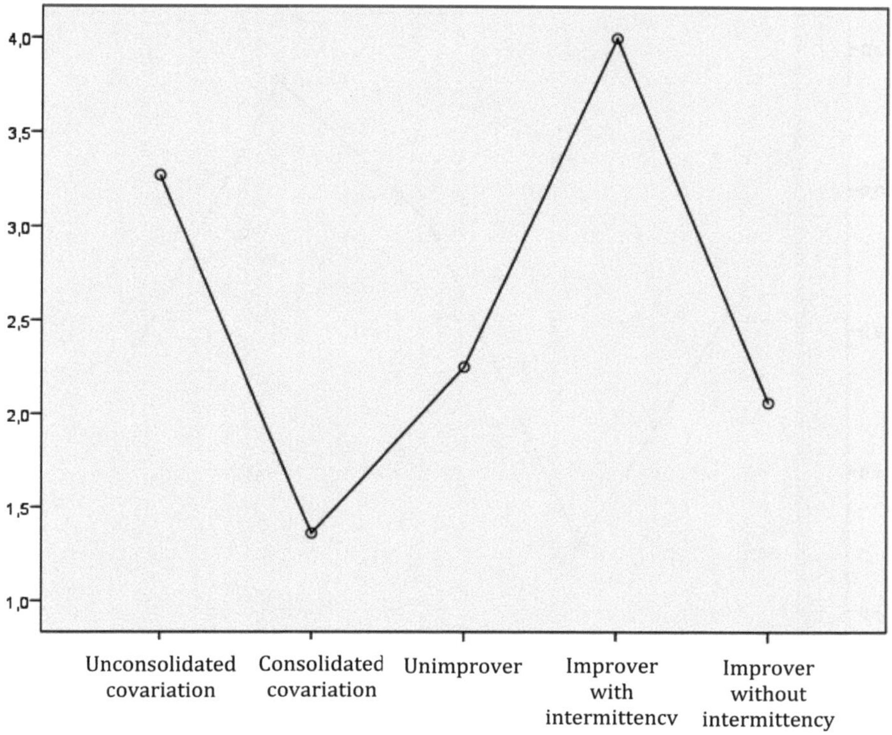


**Fig. 5** Average segments according to covariation

value) and of consolidated covariation (4.5 attempts, the smallest value) and those of improving control without intermittence (5.2 attempts, the third smallest value) and improving covariation without intermittence (7.2 attempts, the second smallest value), are the most efficient. While the improvement with intermittence (8.5 attempts according to control, the highest value and 11.5 according to covariation, the second highest value) are the least efficient.

The incidence of the two dimensions in the lesser or greater efficiency with which the task is solved, is corroborated in the difference in the average number of attempts between the trajectory that has some segment with no control or no covariation with those in all their segments are of control and covariation. Upon reviewing the data, it is found that, according to the control dimension, 91 trajectories are identified with some segment of no control (control type a) that use on average 6.3 attempts, while there are 45 trajectories with all their control segments (control type b, c, d, or e) that on average need 4.8 attempts. According to the covariation the situation is analogous, although in this case the difference is even more marked: 38 trajectories have some segment with no covariation and need on average 8.2 attempts, and 49 of no segment of no covariation that on average need 4.9 attempts. Although in this sample the covariation dimension marks a greater difference than

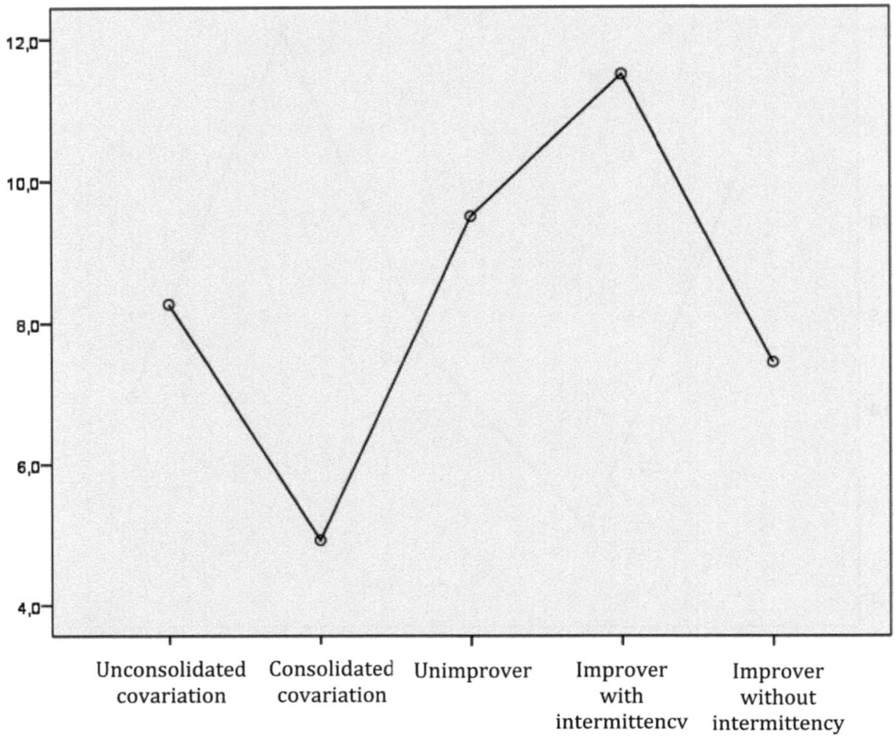


**Fig. 6** Number of attempts per trajectory according to covariation

the control dimension between the trajectories that always handle covariation or control of those that at least in one segment do not do it, it cannot be affirmed that the subject who is in the position of the covariation dimension, but not of control, solves the task more efficiently than the one who does not handle covariation and does control. Before making any statement about it, it is advisable to analyze the trajectories simultaneously according to the two dimensions.

In Table 4, there is a single trajectory that, at the same time, presents no control and no covariation. This trajectory exhausts the 15 attempts that were given to try to solve the task. While there are 51 trajectories that present control and covariation, either consolidated or improving without intermittence (40 of control and consolidated covariation and 11 of control and covariation, improving without intermittence), the average number of attempts is 5.2; these data show a clear difference in the efficiency with which the task is solved when both dimensions are not handled than when they are.

ANOVA measures were performed with post hoc HSD Tukey test to verify if there were significant differences between the various types of trajectories to attest with solidity and significance the evidence of variability. Indications of this have already been found (see Tables 1, 2 and 3), and this is evidenced by the indicators of

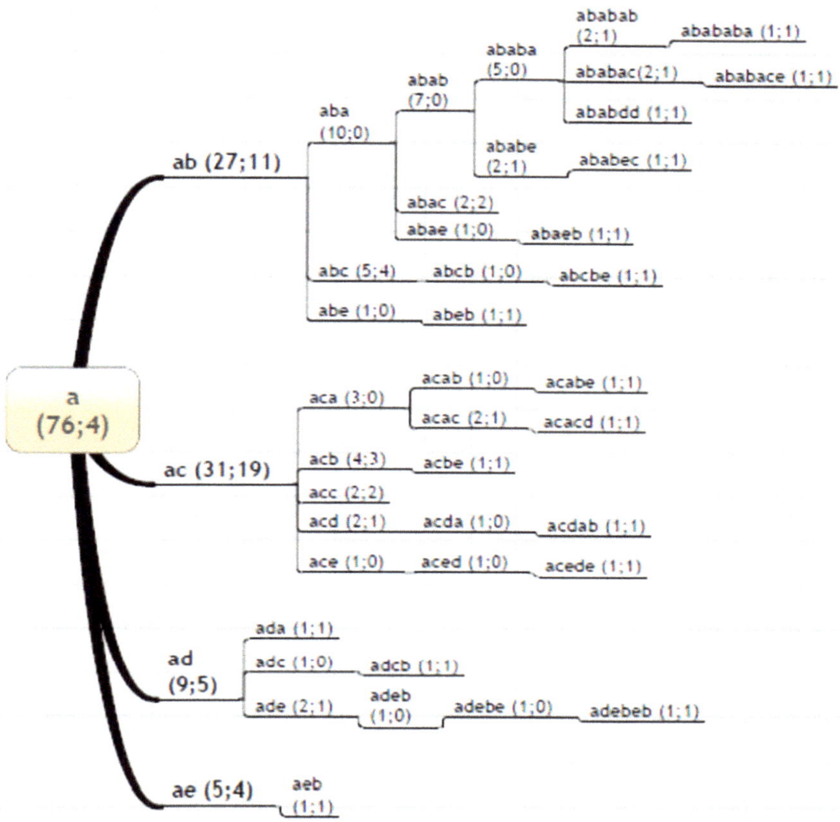


**Fig. 7** Map of paths and trajectories according to control and that start with "a"

**Table 1** Change in trajectories according to the control dimension

| Type of trajectories | | Number of subjects | % |
|---|---|---|---|
| WITHOUT CONTROL. Starts and ends without control | | 6 | 4.4 |
| WITH CONTROL. Starts and ends with control | UNCONSOLIDATED (there are intermediate segments of non-control) | 14 | 10.3 |
| | CONSOLIDATED (there are NO intermediate segments of non-control) | 45 | 33.1 |
| UNIMPROVER. It starts with control and ends without control. | | 1 | 0.7 |
| IMPROVER. Starts without control and ends with control. | WITH INTERMITTENCE (there are intermediate segments of non-control) | 13 | 9.6 |
| | WITHOUT INTERMITTENCE (there are no intermediate segments of non-control) | 57 | 41.9 |

**Table 2** Change in trajectories according to the covariation dimension

| Type of trajectories | | Number of subjects | % |
|---|---|---|---|
| NO COVARIATION starts and ends without covariation | | 2 | 1.5 |
| WITH COVARIATION. Starts and ends with covariation | UNCONSOLIDATED (there are intermediate segments of non-covariation) | 12 | 8.8 |
| | CONSOLIDATED (there are NO intermediate segments of non-covariation) | 98 | 72.1 |
| UNIMPROVER. Starts with covariation and ends without covariation. | | 5 | 3.7 |
| IMPROVER starts without covariation and ends with covariation | WITH INTERMITTENCE (there are intermediate segments of non-covariation) | 2 | 1.5 |
| | WITHOUT INTERMITTENCE (there are no intermediate segments of non-covariation) | 17 | 12.5 |

**Table 3** Average of segments, attempts, and average segment size according to the two dimensions

| Type of trajectories | | Control | | | Covariation | | |
|---|---|---|---|---|---|---|---|
| | | Average segments | Average attempts | Average segments size[a] | Average segments | Average attempts | Average segments size |
| Without control or without covariation | | 2.3 | 6.2 | 3.3 | 2.0 | 12.0 | 9.0 |
| With control or with covariation | Unconsolidated | 4.4 | 8.5 | 2.0 | 3.2 | 8.4 | 2.6 |
| | Consolidated | 1.8 | 4.8 | 3.1 | 1.3 | 4.5 | 3.8 |
| Unimprover | | 2.0 | 5.0 | 2.0 | 2.0 | 7.8 | 3.9 |
| Improver | With intermittence | 5.3 | 8.5 | 1.6 | 4.0 | 11.5 | 2.9 |
| | Without intermittence | 2.4 | 5.2 | 2.2 | 2.1 | 7.2 | 3.5 |

[a] The average segment size is first calculated for each subject and then the average is taken for the subjects of the corresponding trajectory type

the average number of segments, the average number of attempts of the trajectories, and the average size of the segments.

The average number of segments expresses the greater or lesser homogeneity of the trajectories, as it offers a measure of the number of changes that are identified throughout the trajectory. The average number of attempts of the trajectory accounts for the effectiveness, that is, how many attempts were necessary to solve the task. The average number of attempts per segment accounts for the average size of segments, denotes the speed of change and that can be taken as another measure of variability.

**Table 4** Contingency table type of trajectory according to control * type of trajectory according to covariation

| Type of trajectory according to control | Type of trajectory according to covariation | | | | | | Total |
|---|---|---|---|---|---|---|---|
| | Without covariation | Unconsolidated covariation | Consolidated covariation | Unimprover | Improver with intermittence | Improver without intermittence | |
| Without control | 1 | 0 | 3 | 1 | 0 | 1 | 6 |
| Unconsolidated control | 1 | 2 | 6 | 0 | 1 | 4 | 14 |
| Consolidated control | 0 | 3 | 40 | 1 | 0 | 1 | 45 |
| Unimproved | 0 | 0 | 0 | 1 | 0 | 0 | 1 |
| Intermittent improver | 0 | 5 | 4 | 3 | 1 | 0 | 13 |
| Improver without intermittency | 0 | 1 | 45 | 0 | 0 | 11 | 57 |
| Total | 2 | 11 | 98 | 6 | 2 | 17 | 136 |

Both the homogeneity and the average size of the segments offer an idea of the variability and the speed with which the change occurs; in this context, a plausible hypothesis could be that the subjects who follow trajectories, according to the control and covariation dimensions, of consolidated or improving type without intermittence, would tend to be more homogeneous (that is, a lower value in the number of segments) and to be less variable (that is, a higher value in the average number of attempts per segment), while the trajectories of non-consolidated control or of non-consolidated covariation are less homogeneous (the number of segments of the trajectories is higher) and tend to have greater variability, that is, to have a lower value in the average number of attempts per segments.

Figure 2 shows that subjects with consolidated control and improving without intermittence significantly differ from the others. In this sense, they present a lower average in the number of segments compared to the other groups (non-consolidated control and improving with intermittence), which is in line with the hypothesis previously proposed.

Figure 3 shows significant differences between the groups with consolidated control and improvers without intermittency, in contrast to those who do not have variable control or are improvers with intermittency regarding the average number of attempts; the highest rate of attempts is observed in the latter and corresponds to what has been proposed in terms of efficiency in groups that do not yet fully utilize variable control. This figure also allows us to observe that the group of subjects with consolidated variable control shows a smaller number of attempts within their segments, probably because an efficient solution to the problem implies, as a rule, a smaller number of segments.

Figure 4 expresses that the subjects with consolidated control differ from the other groups regarding the average size of the segments. This figure shows that the group with consolidated control is significantly different from all the others. The subjects belonging to this group exhibit a larger segment size; for the subjects with non-consolidated control and improvers with intermittency, the average size of their segments is smaller; the above argues that the former is consistent in the application of some form of control; it should be noted that no significant differences were found in this measure in the covariation dimension.

Figure 5 shows a significant difference between the groups with consolidated covariation and improvers without intermittency, compared to those of non-consolidated covariation and improvers with intermittency, in terms of the average number of segments used. Similarly, the contrast between the group with consolidated covariation and the improving group with intermittency is observed; the latter uses more segments in the attempt to solve the problem with a variational behavior. In this case, the first groups show a lower average number of segments, as in the previous case, compared to the variable control dimension; the performance adopts a more limited trend of covariation that probably translates into an intuition of the appropriate solution that leads to success.

In Fig. 6, the place of consolidated covariation is observed compared to non-consolidated and deteriorating, respectively; in this context, subjects with consolidated covariation exhibit a lower average in the number of attempts, which translates into little variability of the type of covariation. Similarly, it is highlighted that the deteriorating and improving groups with intermittency differ from the others in the average number of attempts within the trajectories, which translates into significant differences in terms of efficiency in solving the task.

In summary, in this studied sample, the validity of the hypothesis could largely be affirmed. The trajectories of control or consolidated covariation or improvers without intermittency are significantly more homogeneous and more efficient than the trajectories of control or non-consolidated covariation or improvers with intermittency. Significant differences in the average number of attempts per segment cannot be affirmed, that is, in the speed at which change occurs.

Next, Figs. 2, 3, 4, 5 and 6 graphically show the paths and trajectories. These maps allow visualizing the diversity of trajectories that subjects follow in the face of the task-problem. The first number in the parenthesis indicates the number of subjects who end their trajectory in that path and the second the number of subjects who continue beyond.

Figure 7 highlights how many subjects started without control (a), 4 of them remained in a procedure that did not change toward forms of control and 72 continued on alternate trajectories by using different types of variable control. An unconsolidated trajectory (abababa) and improving intermittently (ababace) is observed.

Figure 8 describes the subjects who started with types of control b and c, respectively (simple control and simple control with more than two attempts). A change in the use of control forms and improving trajectories that surpass the use of the type of control they started with [(be) and (ccd)] is evident.

Figure 9 shows the initial use of the type of control change with alternation (d) and controlled change (e) as well as improving trajectories (de) and (ede), respectively.

Figure 10 shows the start without a form of covariation that in all cases configures improving trajectories.

Figure 11 expresses both improving trajectories with intermittence (gifi) and without it (gh), which also reveal cognitive change.

The maps of the trajectories according to the covariation dimension compared to the maps according to control present less diversity. The contrast between the trajectories that start with no covariation with those that start with covariation (start with g, h, or i) is not as strong as it is between those that start with no control and control.

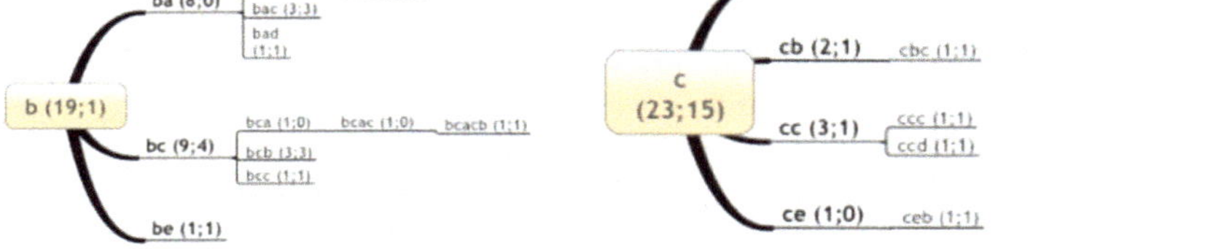


**Fig. 8** Map of paths and trajectories according to control and that start with "b" and "c"

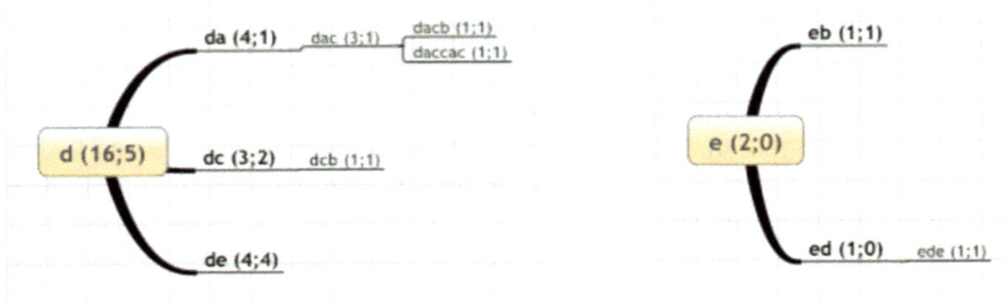


**Fig. 9** Map of paths and trajectories according to control and that start with "d" and "e"

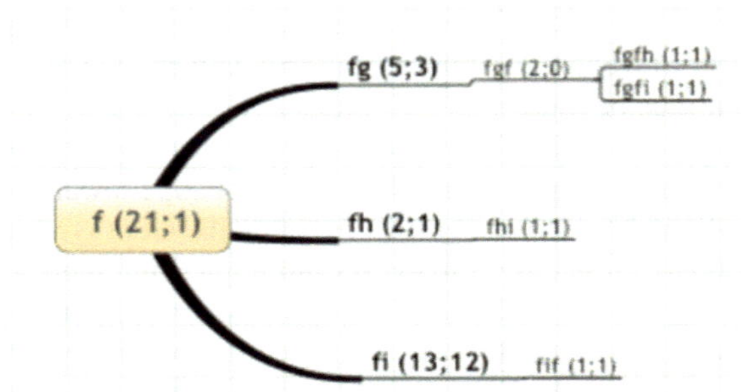


**Fig. 10** Map of paths and trajectories according to covariation and that start with "f"

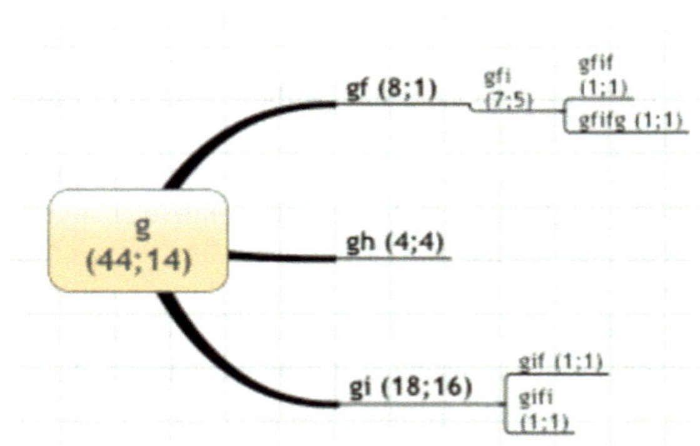


**Fig. 11** Map of paths and trajectories according to covariation and that start with "g"

Perhaps this is because in this population, the subjects exhibit from the beginning greater management of covariation; only 21 of the 136 subjects start with no covariation, while 76 start with no control.

The six maps show some changes that occur more frequently than others. According to the control dimension, in this sample, in the trajectories that start with "a" a change from a = > b or a = > c is more frequent than from a = > d or from a = > e, while according to the covariation dimension the trajectories that start without covariation more frequently move to mixed covariation (f = > i) and this, surely,

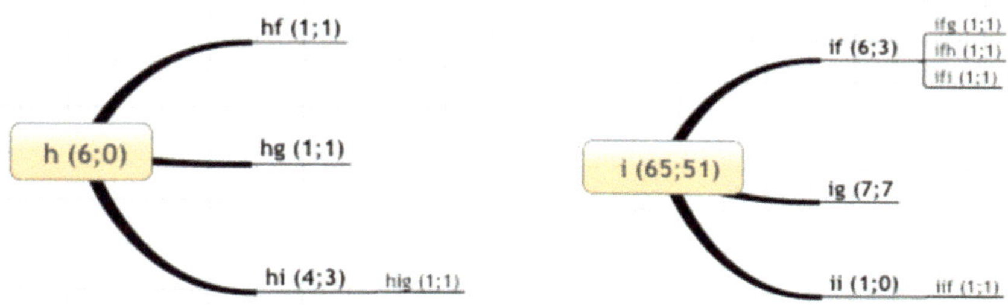


**Fig. 12** Map of paths and trajectories according to covariation and that start with "h" and "i"

**Table 5** $\chi^2$ chi-square covariation by control

| | Control | | |
|---|---|---|---|
| Covariation | High(3) | Medium(2) | Low(1) |
| High | 96 | 0 | 66.7 |
| Medium | 4 | 100 | 0 |
| Low | 0 | 0 | 33.3 |
| Total | 100 | 100 | 100 |
| *n* | 101 | 1 | 3 |
| *Chi-square* | 54.545 | | |
| *Df* | 4 | | |
| *p* | 0.000 | | |
| Ccont | 0.585 | | |

H.: statistic.: $\chi^2 = 0$. That is, there is no relationship between covariation and control. H.: alternative $\chi^2 > 0$. That is, there is a relationship between covariation and control. Critical value 18.47. $\chi^2 = 54.545 > 18.47$ $p < 0$

because with the first segment they move to the other side of the goal, so the solver gives lower values to V or T to decrease D and achieve the goal.

The control type "b" shows more instability than the other types of control. Of the 27 trajectories that change a = > b and that do not end in this path (Fig. 12), 10 have a second change b = > a, and some of these return to b or another type of control and then again to no control before finishing the task. Although the trajectories with the path ac then show a second change to no control (a = > c = > a), this is less frequent. Of the 19 trajectories that have the ac path and that do not end there, only 4 return to no control (3 from the aca path and 1 with the acda path). Of the 9 trajectories with ad path, only 1 presents the change d = > a. The 5 trajectories of ae paths do not present changes b = > a. Perhaps these data suggest a possible lower complexity of type b control than the others and that could appear in uncontrolled trajectories more frequently than the other types of control, but the data from this sample are not sufficient to make any statement about it.

The results have also suggested precursor relationships between the dimensions of variable control and covariation, so a $\chi^2$ chi-square test was performed between these dimensions. The result is expressed in Table 5.

According to the contingency coefficient (0.585) the statistical hypothesis is not assumed, so the alternative hypothesis of the relationship is fully accepted. Both the chi-square and the contingency coefficient reveal a positive and significant relationship between control and covariation. This allows us to propose that control could be a precursor of covariation.

## Discussion

Puche-Navarro (2008, cited by Vasco & Henao, 2008) and van Geert and Steenbeek (2005) express that development constitutes a changing trajectory, variable, without a fixed goal in advance to which to arrive, moving away from finalistic models. In this sense, the classical stages, while they evidenced the improving character of cognitive development, did not manage to describe and explain it, in this case, in terms of its true variable dynamism.

Clearly, in this population, the difference in the initial handling that subjects exhibit for these two dimensions, variable control and covariation, is noticeable: while a small part of the sample starts and ends controlling some of the variables when performing the task, in a large part of this sample the subjects show that from the beginning they are able to establish some relationship between speed (V) and distance traveled (D) or between time (T) and distance traveled. Overton (1997) pointed this out in terms of the variational change that expresses modifications at the level of procedural functioning.

This covariation relationship may only be of an additive type (the greater the speed, the greater the distance traveled and the greater the time, the greater the distance traveled), although in some cases it could be of a multiplicative type (to k times V or k times T corresponds k times D), but in this study, due to the information obtained, it is not possible to identify reliably when it is an additive covariation or a multiplicative one.

It could be said that these drastic changes from control to no control or from covariation to no covariation, or vice versa, occur in subjects who are seeking to improve their strategy to solve the task and are in conditions to try better strategies, while there are subjects who do not improve their strategy, either because they do not seek it or because seeking it they do not manage to find it. The above is inscribed in the theoretical approaches of Pozo and Gómez Crespo (2009a, 2009b) about cognitive development, distinguishing three types of transformations, such as enrichment, adjustment of cognitive structures, and restructuring of them. In the context of the present research, change and transformation are adjustments to the use of the dimensions of variable control and covariation.

Those trajectories that indicate greater instability in control are the ones that exhibit a higher frequency of change (lower value of number of attempts/segment), while those that indicate more stability present changes less frequently (higher value of number of attempts/segment). This stability for change can occur in two extreme cases: a) either because the subject shows that they do not manage control (or covariation) when starting the task resolution and continues this way throughout the resolution of the task or b) on the contrary, because they already managed control (or covariation) from the beginning and maintains it during the resolution. Siegler (1996) and Farrington et al. (2009) would explain the above as the superposition of strategies, forms, and types of cognitive activity according to which the subjects, if they possess varied forms in the face of problem-solving, choose the one that best suits the nature of the problem.

The greater or lesser management of the two dimensions, control and covariation, has a direct impact on the greater or lesser efficiency with which the task is resolved. The greater the control management or the greater the covariation management, the fewer attempts the trajectories have.

The data show a clear difference in the efficiency with which the task is resolved when both dimensions are not managed, compared to when they are. However, the fact of having a single trajectory of no control and no covariation gives little validity to this statement, hence it is necessary to gather more information from other samples in terms of a greater density for each category.

The data suggest a possible lower stability of type b control than the other types and could be interpreted as this type of control is less complex than the others, because it could appear in trajectories without control more frequently than the other types of control, although the data from this sample are not sufficient to make any definitive statement in this regard.

The study carried out allowed to identify a high variety of paths and trajectories determined by each of the dimensions (control and covariation). The intra and inter presence of a variety of trajectories indicates the variability of cognitive change and the majority trend of improving routes shows the progressive nature of cognitive change in solving this problem. The trajectories with management of the covariation dimension (regardless of whether they have control or not) are more efficient than those in which there is control but no covariation.

In this line of analysis, the following questions arise: Could it be affirmed that the control dimension, as a task resolution strategy, compared to the covariation dimension, as an understanding of the task, is less determinant in the efficient resolution of the task? Are the two dimensions, control of variables and covariation, precursor constructs in that order from one another and also suitable to characterize change as cognitive novelty? What are the mental representations that support execution patterns?

This inquiry suggests continuing a line of research that requires new looks and theoretical and methodological perspectives. Ossa (2011) proposes to analyze variability from regressions used in logistic growth models, which allow to account for change as they are based on different models (Malthus model, Verhulst model, Lotka and Volterra model: predator-prey relationship model) and formulas proposed from differential calculus: a mathematical method that allows studying variation and the rate at which functions vary.

In the epilogue of this inquiry, the authors adhere to a perspective of the epigenetic and probabilistic evolutionary change of psychological processes, from birth to death, as an explosion of states and development processes under starting conditions given by being members of the homo sapiens-sapiens species, typical of modern humans, supported by a mechanism of search and establishment of new choices and relationships between elements marked by inflection points, in the style of social networks, in which there are invited, accepted, waiting or inevitably excluded elements. For the developing subject, the various paths and the small never-chosen spaces, but dreamed and desired, will always be more or less explicit.

**Acknowledgments** Research Project ID 003237, "Characterization of change as a cognitive novelty in the solution of a physical-mathematical problem of proportionality in students of the Pontifical Javeriana University". Funded by the Vice-Rectorate of Research.

## References

Bermejo, V. (2005). Microgénesis y cambio cognitivo: Adquisición del cardinal numérico. *Psicothema, 17*(4), 559–562.

Escobar, H. (2003). Historia y naturaleza de la psicología del desarrollo. *Universitas Psychologica, 2*(1), 71–88.

Farrington, L., Vanuxem, S., & Stiller, J. (2009). Patterns of problem-solving in children's literacy and arithmetic. *British Journal of Developmental Psychology, 27*, 815–834. https://doi.org/10.1348/026151008x383148

Gutiérrez, F., & Carriedo, N. (2002). Métodos en el estudio del desarrollo cognitivo. In F. Gutiérrez, J. A. García, & N. Carriedo (Eds.), *Psicología Evolutiva II: Desarrollo cognitivo y lingüístico Volumen I* (pp. 50–85). UNED.

Gutiérrez, F., García, J., & Luque, J. L. (2002). Los enfoque dinámicos. El conexionismo y los sistemas dinámicos. In F. Gutiérrez, J. A. García, & N. Carriedo (Eds.), *Psicología Evolutiva II: Desarrollo cognitivo y lingüístico Volumen I* (pp. 148–177). UNED.

Karmiloff-Smith, A. (1994). *Más allá de la modularidad. La ciencia cognitiva desde la perspectiva del desarrollo*. Alianza Editorial.

Montealagre, R. (2011). La solución de problemas cognitivos en estudiantes de psicología. *Acta Colombiana de Psicología, 14*(1), 119–138.

Navarro-Roldán, C. (2008). Comprensión de sistemas de engranajes: un estudio del cambio cognitivo y las herramientas cognitivas en niños de cuatro años. *Universitas Psychologica, 7*(2), 411–424.

Ossa, J. (2011). Funcionamiento cognitivo: Un inextricable juego de pérdidas y ganancias. *Acta Colombiana de Psicología, 14*(2), 45–55.

Ossa, J. (2013). Matrices de transición y patrones de variabilidad cognitiva. *Universitas Psychologica, 12*(2), 559–570.

Ossa, J. C., & Puche-Navarro, R. (2010). Modelos bayesianos y funcionamientos inferenciales complejos. *Acta Colombiana de Psicología, 13*(2), 119–128.

Overton, W. (1997). Developmental psychology: Philosophy, concepts, and methodology. In *Handbook of child psychology: Theoretical models of human development*. John Wiley & Sons.

Piaget, J. (1977). *Biología y Conocimiento*. Siglo XXI Editores, S.A.

Piaget, J. (1979). *El mecanismo del desarrollo mental*. Editora Nacional.

Pinker, S. (2013). *La tabla rasa: La negación moderna de la naturaleza humana*. Ediciones Paidós Ibérica.

Pozo, J. I., & Gómez Crespo, M. A. (2009a). *Aprender y enseñar ciencia. Del conocimiento cotidiano al conocimiento científico*. Ediciones Morata.

Pozo, J. I., & Gómez Crespo, M. A. (2009b). Del conocimiento cotidiano al conocimiento científico: más allá del cambio conceptual. In J. I. Pozo & M. A. Gómez Crespo (Eds.), *Aprender y enseñar ciencia. Del conocimiento cotidiano al conocimiento científico*. Ediciones Morata.

Puche-Navarro, R. (2008). Érase una vez el desarrollo. In J. Larreamendy-Joerns, R. Puche-Navarro, & A. Restrepo (Eds.), *Claves para pensar el cambio: Ensayos sobre psicología del desarrollo* (pp. 30–68). Universidad de los Andes, Centro de Estudios Socioculturales e Internacionales.

Puche-Navarro, R., Combariza, E., & Ossa, J. C. (2003). La naturaleza no lineal de los funcionamientos inferenciales: un estudio empírico con base en el humor gráfico. *Avances en Psicología Latinoamericana, 30*(1), 27–38.

Siegler, R. (1996). *Emerging minds: The process of change in children's thinking*. Oxford University Press.

Siegler, R., & Crowley, K. (1991). The microgenetic method. A direct means for studying cognitive development. *American Psychologist, 46*(6), 606–620. https://doi.org/10.1037/0003-066X.46.6.606

Torbeyns, J., Arnaud, L., Lemaire, P., & Verschaffel, L. (2004). Cognitive change as strategy change. In A. Demetriou & A. Raftopoulos (Eds.), *Cognitive developmental change: Theories, models and measurement*. Cambridge University Press.

van Geert, P., & Steenbeek, H. (2005). A complexity and dynamic systems approach to development: Measurement, modeling and research. In K. W. Fischer, A. Battro, & P. Lena (Eds.), *Mind, brain and education*. Cambridge University Press.

van Geert, P., & van Dijk, M. (2002). Focus on variability: New tools to study intra-individual variability in developmental data. *Infant Behavior & Developmental, 25*, 340–374.

Vasco, C. E., & Henao, G. C. (2008). Elementos y Modelos del Desarrollo: Una revisiön del Concepto. In J. Larreamendy-Joerns, R. Puche-Navarro, & A. Restrepo (Eds.), *Claves para pensar el cambio: Ensayos sobre psicología del desarrollo* (pp. 1–27). Universidad de los Andes, Centro de Estudios Socioculturales e Internacionales.

Yan, Z., & Fischer, K. (2002). Always under construction: Dynamic variations in adult cognitive microdevelopment. *Human Developmental processes, 2*(2), 39–62.

# Characterization of Care Practices in Colombian Families with Children in Early Childhood in a Situation of Forced Displacement

**Olga Alicia María Carbonell Blanco, Sandra Juliana Plata Contreras, Milton Eduardo Bermúdez Jaimes, Liliana Catalina Suárez Baracaldo, Paola Andrea Peña Patiño, and Carolina Villanueva Betancourth**

For more than 40 years in Colombia, armed confrontations between different actors in the conflict have intensified. These confrontations have forced millions of people and their families to leave their lands, due to threats to their physical and psychological integrity, and to move to suburban and urban centers throughout the country. Bogotá is one of the cities with the highest reception of this population (Amnesty International, 2009; Consultancy for Human Rights and Displacement [CODHES], 2009).

In this scenario of armed conflict, early childhood has perhaps been the most vulnerable and exposed to violent situations, being direct and indirect witnesses of the conflict (United Nations Children's Fund [Unicef], 1996, 2014). This leads to children being the main victims, having impacts on physical security, post-traumatic stress, and sequels in emotional, social, cognitive, and affective development (Connolly et al., 2009). Although Unicef (2006) points out the importance of the family as a protective environment during and after the armed conflict, parents feel deeply affected and traumatized by the experiences they have had, and to that extent the quality of care for their children is affected. The behavioral care system refers to providing the child with physical care, and especially providing protection in situations of risk or danger through proximity and contact behaviors (Bowlby, 1993).

---

*This chapter is the English translation of an article originally published in Spanish as:* Carbonell, O. A. M., Plata, S. J., Bermúdez, M. E., Suárez, L. C., Peña, P. A., & Villanueva, C. (2015). Characterization of Care Practices in Colombian Families with Children in Early Childhood in a Situation of Forced Displacement. *Universitas Psychologica, 14* (1), 67–80. https://doi.org/10.11144/Javeriana.upsy14-1.cpcf. *Please cite the original version of the article in Spanish.*

---

O. A. M. Carbonell Blanco · S. J. Plata Contreras (✉) · M. E. Bermúdez Jaimes ·
L. C. Suárez Baracaldo · P. A. Peña Patiño · C. V. Betancourth
Pontificia Universidad Javeriana, Bogota, Colombia
e-mail: sandra.plata@javeriana.edu.co



W. López-López et al. (eds.), *Trends in Latin American Psychology*,
https://doi.org/10.1007/978-3-031-87554-0_11

The quality of care according to Ainsworth et al. (1974) has been conceptualized and evaluated from four behavioral indicators that are found on a continuum, such as cooperation-interference with the child's autonomy behaviors, the physical and psychological availability of the caregiver-ignoring/neglect with the child's signals and needs, the acceptance-rejection of the caregiver and finally, the sensitivity-insensitivity to the child's signals and communications.

From the attachment theory to understand the quality of care, it is necessary to refer to the model of intergenerational transmission of attachment relationships and parenting patterns as the process by which, intentionally or not, a previous generation psychologically influences the attitudes and behavior of the parents of the next generation (Berlin, 2007; Berlin et al., 2008).

Various studies have shown that there is a significant association between the quality of maternal care and the security of infant attachment (meta-analysis of De Wolff & van IJzendoorn, 1997; Posada et al., 2004). However, it has been found, with some exceptions, that in samples from poorer sectors of the population the association between both variables is lower, which seems to be related to stressful events in the family context and living conditions (De Wolff & van IJzendoorn, 1997).

On the other hand, parenting is a process that involves assuming a responsibility through a series of actions and interactions by caregivers, to promote emotional, social, and children's physicality with cultural particularities (Myers-Walls et al., 2005). However, environmental demands or persistent situations, such as poverty, produce stress in parenting, which has an adverse impact and reduces the family's ability to cope with parental demands, negatively affecting the quality of relationships and maternal care (Wachs, 2009), in turn, associated with children's attachment security (Hadadian & Mebler, 1996 cited by Mulsow et al., 2002).

The literature has also shown that in various contexts of psychosocial adversity, children are more likely to develop insecure attachment relationships (disorganized attachment), especially when parents transmit care patterns with abuse and neglect, as this affects basic trust in present and future adult caregivers (Gómez Muzzio et al., 2008). Likewise, children in poverty have less access to cognitively stimulating activities (Bornstein & Putnick, 2012), which affects their neurodevelopment, as well as their performance in cognitive tasks of language, memory, working memory, and cognitive control (Farah et al., 2006).

However, families in vulnerable conditions have a potential for resilience, which is defined as a process with protective factors that predict favorable outcomes and positive adaptation in the development of children and their families, despite being exposed to contexts of considerable adversity (Kim-Cohen et al., 2004). The two basic components of resilience are exposure to risk and evidence of good adaptation of the person, understood not as an individual characteristic, but as the result of a contextual, relational, and family process (Delage, 2010; Egeland et al., 1993). Among the protective factors in these contexts of adversity, such as armed conflict, studies have shown that caregivers who spend time with children and have emotional closeness with them, as well as having stable and secure attachments within families, favor resilient processes in the family (Wyman et al., 1999).

From an ecological-transactional perspective of development (Sagi-Schwartz, 2012), it is possible to appreciate reciprocal protective and/or risk influences between the systems in which the child exposed to armed conflict is immersed. The child's intraindividual system could potentially be affected at the neurological level by severe stress, as well as their ability to regulate emotional, behavioral, and social; however, close people in the family microsystem can filter these adverse experiences and reverse the negative effects of the first system, providing a protective environment, relationships of trust and a refuge of safety for the child. That is, good parental competence can moderate the negative impact of traumatic experiences and becomes a resilience factor. Similarly, in the exosystem, the community, parents' workplace, school can also become refuges of safety and support for parents, which in turn reverses into the ability to protect their children, and likewise, the child's development can be positively or negatively influenced indirectly by beliefs, values, attitudes in the macrosystem.

The problem of forced displacement has had multiple studies that consider macro and mesosocial factors; however, there are few investigations carried out in the country regarding microsocial factors, which have investigated family problems and relationships in the daily life of these families (Arango et al., 2009; González Viveros, 2004). Conducting studies that make characterizations of family relationships and child-rearing in these contexts allows recognizing the strengths, weaknesses, and resources that these families have to face in a resilient way in the upbringing of their children.

Consequently, the present study characterized the quality of care, early child-primary caregiver attachment relationships, parenting practices in the dimension of managing norms and limits, and child development in family contexts with children in early childhood, exposed to situations of forced displacement and likewise sought to establish some protective and risk factors that affect the relationships of upbringing and care in these families, from a dual perspective: the view of external observers and that of the participating caregiver.

# Method

## *Design*

The methodological design of the study was mixed-explanatory, with the aim of better characterizing the phenomenon of care and upbringing practices of children in early childhood in a family context at risk. Case studies were used to document and understand these practices more deeply, without pretensions of generalizing the findings (Hernández Sampieri et al., 2010).

## Participants

Using a non-probabilistic sampling, 10 case families were selected, in a situation of forced displacement with children between 30 and 66 months of age ($M$ = 47.7; SD = 11.26), 6 girls and 4 boys, relocated in the city of Bogotá. The main caregivers were 9 mothers and 1 father. The age of the caregivers was in a range between 21 and 30 years with $M$ = 25.3 and SD = 2.83; the educational level was in a range between 2 and 16 years of education with $M$ = 8.5 years and SD = 4. The marital status of the families was composed of 70% in a free union, 20% single and 10% married. The number of children per family was distributed in 3 children (40%), 2 children (30%), and 1 child (30%). The families belonged to socioeconomic strata 2 (80%) and 3 (20%), on a scale of 6 (Uribe-Mallarino, 2008).

## Instruments

### Quality of Care

It was observed with the Maternal Behavior Q-sort for children under 3 years old. ([MBQS], Pederson & Moran, 1995), the Maternal Behavior Q-sort for Preschoolers ([MBPQS], Posada et al., 1998) and the Qualitative Scales of Maternal Behavior (Álzate et al., 1999). The MBQS consists of 90 items based on the conceptualizations of Ainsworth et al. (1974) about the construct of caregiver sensitivity. The validation of the MBQS has been reported by (Pederson et al., 1998) and the validation of the MBPQS by Posada et al. (2007). The MBPQS is based on theoretical and empirical work on attachment relationships in infancy and early childhood, interviews and observations of mothers of preschool children (Ainsworth et al., 1974, 1978; Bowlby, 1993; Cicchetti et al., 1990; Pederson & Moran, 1995). In this study, an interobserver reliability was obtained ($M$ = 0.86, SD = 0.05, Range = 0.78–0.93).

The Qualitative Scales of Maternal Behavior are an instrument that consists of 11 sub-scales: (1) Promptness of response, (2) Effectiveness of response, (3) Behavioral consistency, (4) Balance between the baby's demands and other demands, (5) Balance between physical care and social and emotional interaction with the baby, (6) Enjoyment of interaction, (7) Interactive fluency, (8) Frequency of physical contact, (9) Quality of physical contact, (10) Frequency of verbalizations and (11) Diversity of functions in maternal verbal communications (Álzate et al., 1999). These Scales showed concurrent validity with the MBQS (Pederson & Moran, 1995; Posada et al., 2004). In this study, an average interobserver reliability was found ($M$ = 0.84, SD = 0.12, Range = 0.73–1.0).

### Attachment Relationships with the Main Caregiver

The organization of the child's secure base behavior was described with the Attachment Q-sort ([AQS]; Waters, 1995). A average interobserver reliability ($M = 0.81$, SD = 0.08, Range = 0.66–0.91).

### Parenting Practices

They were evaluated through three instruments: the Family Behavior Survey-Part 4 (Posada & Waters, 1990), the Parenting Inventory for Adults and Adolescents ([IPAA], Solís-Cámara & Bavolek, 1995), and a semi-structured interview (Strauss & Corbin, 2002). The first instrument consists of 52 items, with a 5-point Likert scale and assesses the frequency in the use of disciplinary practices, during the last 6 months. Through exploratory factor analysis, two subscales were identified: severe disciplinary practices and moderate disciplinary practices. The second instrument has four subscales: (1) Inappropriate Expectations of Development, (2) Lack of Empathy, (3) Corporal Punishment, and (4) Role Reversal Parent-Child. In the Mexican population, all the subscales have an internal reliability of 0.77 (Solís-Cámara & Díaz Romero, 2006). In this study, only the subscales of Corporal Punishment and Role Reversal Parent-Child showed adequate internal consistency (Cronbach's alpha = 0.76 and 0.79, respectively). The third instrument, the semi-structured ethnographic interview, was designed to explore in depth the domains of care and upbringing in the specific population. A content validation was made by three expert judges on the theme of forced displacement and qualitative methodologies.

### Child Development

The Abbreviated Scale of Development (EAD-1) was used to make a global assessment of four areas of development: gross motor skills, fine-adaptive motor skills, hearing-language, and personal-social, with a reliability analysis that ranges between 0.956 and 0.992 (Ortiz, 1991).

## *Procedure*

Each family was visited twice at their home with a duration of approximately 2.5 h. During the first home visit, the informed consent endorsed by the Ethics and Research Committee of the Faculty of Psychology of the Pontifical Javeriana

University was signed and a sociodemographic survey was applied to the main caregiver. Two observers, independently, were responsible for observing the child's behavior during the interactions and daily care routines and a third observer focused on the caregiver's behavior. Likewise, the child's development was evaluated with the support of the main caregiver and finally, the audio of an open interview with the main caregiver was recorded to explore care practices. During the second home visit (with an average distance of visits of 11 days), two questionnaires were applied to the main caregiver, to characterize the parenting practices. Two independent observers recorded the quality of the interactions between the child and the main caregiver, and a third observer focused on observing the child's behavior, during the interactions. In both home visits, an observer filmed the interactions between the main caregiver and the child.

### Data Analysis Plan

Being an explanatory mixed design according to the criteria of Creswell and Plano Clark (2011), the quantitative data from the Q-sorts, the questionnaires, and the child development scale were first processed, with descriptive statistics tests. Subsequently, the qualitative data that emerged from the interview were analyzed using the techniques and strategies of Grounded Theory (Strauss & Corbin, 2002). In the final part, the combination of the quantitative data with the qualitative analyses was carried out.

For the interpretation of the results, the information from the systematic observations, the questionnaires, and the interview was compared and triangulated. As part of the interpretative analyses of the study, preliminary hypotheses were proposed toward the construction of an emerging theory resulting from the qualitative inquiry. The qualitative information allowed for a broader understanding of gaps and possible inconsistencies that the quantitative data revealed. By comparing and integrating the information collected through both methods, it was possible to understand some risk and protective factors that affect parenting and caregiving relationships in these families.

## Results

Table 1 presents Pearson correlations that characterize sociodemographic and maternal care variables.

In Table 1, it is observed that the older the child, the more sensitive is the caregiver's behavior to their communicative signals and needs. Likewise, the older mothers in the sample show in their interactions less verbal communicative frequency and greater frequency of physical contact.

**Table 1** Associations between sociodemographic variables and care variables: caregiver sensitivity and subscales of maternal behavior

| Variable | 1 | 2 | 3 | 4 | 5 |
|---|---|---|---|---|---|
| 1. Age of child | – | −0.025 | 0.71* | −0.16 | 0.1 |
| 2. Age of caregiver | | – | −0.45 | 0.68 | −0.73* |
| 3. Sensibility of caregiver | | | – | −0.3 | −0.1 |
| 4. Subscale of maternal behavior—Frequency of physical contact | | | | – | −0.37 |
| 5. Subscale of maternal behavior—Frequency of verbalizations | | | | | – |

*Note.* *$p < 0.05$. ** $p < 0.01$ bilateral

**Table 2** T-tests by child's sex in severe and moderate disciplinary practices

| Variable | *N* | *M* | SD | *t* | gl |
|---|---|---|---|---|---|
| Severe disciplinary practices | | | | | |
| Girl | 6 | 28 | 24.02 | 2775* | 8 |
| Boy | 4 | 0.75 | 0.96 | | |
| Moderate disciplinary practices | | | | | |
| Girl | 6 | 40.83 | 24.7 | 2338* | 8 |
| Boy | 4 | 10.5 | 7.72 | | |

*Note.* *$p < 0.05$. ** $p < 0.01$ bilateral

**Table 3** Associations between the variables caregiver sensitivity, attachment, child development, gross motor skills, hearing and language scales, corporal punishment scales, and role reversal

| Variable | 1 | 2 | 3 | 4 | 5 | 6 | 7 |
|---|---|---|---|---|---|---|---|
| 1. Caregiver sensitivity | – | 0.63* | 0.69* | 0.65* | 0.08 | 0.13 | 0.48 |
| 2. Child development | | – | 0.92** | 0.98** | −0.09 | 0.49 | 0.62 |
| 3. Gross motor skills | | | – | 0.88** | 0.14 | 0.54 | 0.69* |
| 4. Hearing and language | | | | – | −0.14 | 0.55 | 0.6 |
| 5. Role reversal | | | | | – | 0.27 | 0.64 |
| 6. Attachment | | | | | | – | 0.63 |
| 7. Corporal punishment | | | | | | | – |

*Note.* *$p < 0.05$. ** $p < 0.01$ bilateral

Table 2 shows the use of severe and moderate disciplinary practices considered by sex; it is observed that there are significant differences between the scores obtained by boys and girls. The means of the scores on both scales are higher in girls.

In Table 3, significant and positive associations of Pearson correlations are observed between caregiver sensitivity and child development, gross motor skills, and hearing and language. A significant and positive association was also found between physical punishment and gross motor skills, as well as between the scales of role reversal and physical punishment.

In Table 4, associations are observed between the child attachment observed in visit 1, with the domains of maternal care: effectiveness of the maternal response,

**Table 4** Associations between the variables child attachment, scales of maternal behavior, and moderate disciplinary practices

| Variable | 1 | 2 | 3 | 4 | 5 | 6 | 7 | 8 | 9 | 10 |
|---|---|---|---|---|---|---|---|---|---|---|
| Attachment visit 1 | – | 0.67* | 0.67* | 0.68* | 0.7* | 0.85* | −0.06 | 0.89** | 0.97** | −0.88** |
| Behavior scales total score | | – | 0.91** | 0.94** | 0.88** | 0.7* | −0.047 | 0.46 | 0.58 | −0.68* |
| Effectiveness of the maternal response | | | – | 0.85** | 0.85** | 0.57 | −0.069 | 0.56 | 0.63 | −0.61 |
| Consistency of the maternal response | | | | – | 0.89** | 0.6 | −0.16 | 0.54 | 0.63 | −0.56 |
| Maternal interactive fluency | | | | | – | 0.62 | −0.3 | 0.46 | 0.59 | −0.57 |
| Quality of maternal physical contact | | | | | | – | 0.63 | 0.71* | 0.82** | −0.68* |
| Frequency of verbalizations | | | | | | | – | −0.2 | −0.15 | 0.34 |
| Attachment visit 2 | | | | | | | | – | −0.97** | −0.94** |
| Attachment visits 1 & 2 | | | | | | | | | – | 0.93** |
| Moderate disciplinary practices | | | | | | | | | | – |

*Note.* $*p < 0.05$. $**p < 0.01$ bilateral

interactive fluency, and quality of maternal physical contact. Likewise, moderate disciplinary practices are inversely associated with child attachment, the total score of the maternal behavior scales, and specifically to the subscale of quality of physical contact.

## *Qualitative Analysis*

For the realization of the intersubject analysis of the qualitative interview, it was taken into account how caregivers characterize their parenting practices from their own discourse. The following are presented several emerging macrocategories with their respective subcategories, using the analysis procedure (open coding—naming of categories and subcategories—axial coding, selective coding, intra-subject and inter-subject matrices) (Strauss & Corbin, 2002).

First macrocategory: Main caregiver's behaviors when the child misbehaves. With two subcategories: main forms of punishment and actions different from punishment. When inquiring about the subcategory main forms of punishment used by caregivers, it was found that they use as one of the most frequent punishments the removal of privileges, such as toys, television, outings, or what they like most; "No, then take away the things that (...) for a while the things that they like the most (...) what they love to do the most, maybe it could be not letting them watch television, not letting them play, I think that's it more than anything" (D1111). However, within this subcategory there are weak voices that express two particular and perhaps worrying ways of removing privileges, which go against the basic needs of the human being, such as food and affection. Mother D1106 in her narration exposed that one way of setting rules and limits is to take away her son's option to eat a food that he likes: "—I won't feed you, because I don't have any, where am I going to get it from?. And I punished him, I didn't give him arepas that night—and he goes to bed like that and tomorrow when he wakes up well then I give him, but that night I put him to bed like that and everything and with everything he didn't learn" (D1106). Mother D1104 tells her daughter that she "won't spoil her again", if she repeats an inappropriate behavior.

Regarding the second subcategory actions different from punishment, other ways of handling the children's bad behavior appear, such as an understanding attitude, of reflection and dialogue, different from any abusive form by the caregiver: "reflect on how he should behave" (D1108) and "try to understand him, talk to the child and explain why he can't do it" (D1107).

The second emerging macrocategory is "parental perception of their own upbringing and education", with three subcategories: type of treatment received, reflection on treatment received and caring differently to not repeat the history. First, when inquiring about the perceptions that parents have about how they were educated and raised when children, it was found that the first subcategory, the type of treatment that they received, was mainly based on violent physical abuse and with the use of objects; for example, different families exposed their experiences:

"my mom also gave me a lot, a lot of whipping" (D1101), "my dad would hit me wherever he could, for nothing" (D1108), and "punishment with stick and belt" (D1102). Similarly, other practices were identified, such as punishing with the elaboration of domestic work and with the lack of affection on the part of the mother.

However, it is relevant to show that parents reflected on the way they were treated. For example, D1108 mentioned that: "because if my dad was terrible with me, I don't, I don't want to be the same with my children"; likewise, D1109 expressed: "because if we were left very hurt that they mistreated us, they should not mistreat them because they are going to feel what we felt" and D1107 pointed out that "the same mistakes should not be made with the children". Therefore, the parents recognize that this form does influence the way they treat their children, as D1103 mentioned, "It's hard to forget and use another way to correct the children".

When comparing this subcategory with the main forms of punishment that parents use with their children, it was observed that parents establish differences between the way they were raised in their childhood and the way they raise their children today, which was recognized by most participants.

Two cases caught attention, regarding the repetition of parenting patterns: caregiver D1110 mentioned that he previously punished the children in the same way he was raised, and D1106 recognizes using physical punishment just as it was done with her and not for that reason feels hatred toward the people who raised her. There can also be seen some weak voices about the way some participants were and the perceptions they have about this fact. For example, caregivers D1101 and D1106 justified the type of treatment they received in their childhood by saying that this happened because: "their mother wanted the best for her" (D1101) or "because they did it to correct her" (D1106). On the other hand, participant D1103 recognizes that the type of treatment she received generated a series of psychological consequences, such as having felt that people tell her: "that she is bitter and antisocial", or always remembering her experiences when she punishes her son; for this reason, she states that she uses a series of strategies to not repeat the same with her son and her family, such as: "Asking God for help to understand how her children feel when she hits them" and "the mother should calm down, to talk later and solve a problem" (D1103).

Through its macrocategories and emerging subcategories, this interview allowed for a deeper understanding of the behaviors and perceptions that primary caregivers have about parenting practices and their caregiver role. When referring to these and connecting them with their own experience of being cared for by the previous generation and the treatment received from their parents, eight caregivers reported that they were physically, verbally, and psychologically abused as children, only one mother experienced lack of attention and psychological care and another mother stated that she was not abused.

Likewise, the emerging subcategory reflection on the treatment received showed that most parents had undergone a personal reflective process about the experiences lived in their own childhood and stated that they did not want to repeat them with their own children. Through subcategory 3 they want to take care of their children differently than how they were cared for and treated; they show that they want to break the intergenerational cycle of child abuse. However, narratives of the caregivers already exposed suggest that, despite the reflective process, most parents have carried out regarding their own parenting experience and the emergence of various ways of imposing rules and limits on their children, parents seem to require novel strategies to use a sensitive discipline that is not coercive, that involves positive reinforcement, negotiation, as well as understanding and empathy for the child (Juffer et al., 2008) and in this way be able to learn to co-regulate their children's inappropriate behaviors and not repeat the violent parenting pattern.

## Integrative Analysis of Quantitative and Qualitative Data: By Way of Discussion

The results of the scales of moderate and severe disciplinary practices, which were evaluated with the Family Behavior Survey-Part 4, are corroborated with the qualitative findings of the semi-structured ethnographic interview of parenting practices and caregiver role, regarding the subcategory main forms of punishment, in that physical punishment has decreased as a main disciplinary practice, if compared with the disciplinary behavioral pattern used by parents of the previous generation and is only used as a last resort, when parents consider that they have exhausted all their available disciplinary forms, generating ambivalent feelings. That is, impulsive physical punishment produced by feelings of anger, frustration, and lack of control (Thompson Gershoff, 2002). However, severe disciplinary practices, although diminished, are exercised more with girls. The findings of this study contradict most studies that show that mothers and fathers tend to use more physical punishment with boys than with girls, due to expectations regarding parenting based on gender, such as that boys should be educated with greater harshness to make them stronger (Thompson Gershoff, 2002). However, forensic medicine data in Colombia (Velasco Bernal & Lozano Mancera, 2012) show an upward growth of violence against women from the age of 5.

Likewise, the information reported by parents with the IPAA, on the physical punishment scale, corroborates the findings of the two previous instruments, on this scale six primary caregivers obtain scores that correspond to high decatypes from the raw scores obtained, which implies that they believe it is possible to use alternative disciplinary strategies to physical punishment. Four main caregivers are located in a norm decatype, according to the raw score obtained, which involves the belief of using punishment as one of the disciplinary strategies in addition to others. This is consistent with findings that show that moderate disciplinary practices are presented more frequently than severe ones, as reported by caregivers in the two self-report instruments where they report on other forms of punishment such as: withdrawal of privileges (taking away toys, not giving sweets, not allowing watching television), verbal and psychological punishment (scolding, speaking loudly and ignoring the child-no accessibility), isolation (confinement) and threats of hitting and telling the father, especially with the girls.

On the other hand, caregivers also report other actions to manage the inappropriate behavior of children, based on reasoning (dialogue and explanation of bad behavior), which allows us to assume that they have initiated a process of sensitive discipline where they show understanding, understanding, putting themselves in the child's place, which implies demonstrating empathy for him or her and giving explanations of the consequences of their actions through a method of induction (Juffer et al., 2008).

From the question about a continuity between the patterns of care and the affective relationships that are built between parents and children and whether or not they persist between several generations of the same family and what are the underlying processes, some studies reveal systematically a substantial intergenerational transmission effect of parenting styles. According to Berlin et al. (2008), it would be expected that parents who experienced a high degree of responsiveness/sensitivity in their childhood would be more open to the signals and needs of their own children, than those parents who were rejected or treated ambivalently. However, other studies have shown that parents can restructure their internal representation based on secure and meaningful attachment experiences after childhood (Hesse, 2008). It could be assumed that some of these parents who, despite not having had in their own childhood loving and understanding parents, through reflective personal processes and later affective experiences, possess an earned security in their adulthood and are capable of maintaining sensitive behaviors with their children, under conditions of high stress.

In the same vein, it was found that caregiver sensitivity is related to the quality of overall child development, the development of gross motor skills and hearing and language skills in the children of the sample. These findings confirm the evidence found in other studies that show that the quality of early child-caregiver relationships and the sensitivity of the latter are associated with the development of cognitive, linguistic, social, moral, and emotional skills in children (Shonkoff & Phillips, 2000).

It was also found that in those parents with less use of moderate disciplinary practices, the greater the attachment security of their children, the better the quality of care expressed in promptness, effectiveness, and consistency of the caregiver's response, especially in terms of the quality of physical contact, as a form for the affective and emotional expression with the children. These results are consistent with the hypothesis about the sensitivity-security connection that is empirically supported through the meta-analysis carried out by De Wolff and van IJzendoorn (1997), which shows that main caregivers sensitive to the signals and needs of children build secure attachment relationships with them, as opposed to those who abuse and are negligent in care, who generate insecure attachment relationships (Gómez Muzzio et al., 2008).

Likewise, it was found in the study that the older the child, the more sensitive is the caregiver's behavior to their communicative signals and needs. The data seem to suggest that as the caregiver has more knowledge and interactive experience with the child learns to respond and interpret their communications and needs appropriately. Similarly, an inverse relationship was observed between the age of the mother and the frequency of verbal communication. That is, the older the mother, the less frequent verbal communication. Evidence from 28 countries in the developing world, with 127,000 families with children under 5 years old, shows that the quality of verbal communicative stimulation is associated with the human development index (HDI) of the country. (Bornstein & Putnick, 2012).

These findings could also be related to the parents' own childhood experiences, daily life stressors in poverty, and their low level of education and knowledge about the importance of cognitive, social, and emotional stimulation in child-rearing, such as singing, dancing, playing, caressing, telling and reading stories, and talking to the child during care routines (Bornstein & Putnick, 2012; Kim-Cohen et al., 2004).

## Conclusions

Below are some protective and risk factors of families in situations of forced displacement and relocation in the city of Bogotá, and emerging conjectures that could be proposed, taking into account the previous analyses.

### *Protective Factors*

From the reflective processes carried out by the main caregivers about their own experiences of care and upbringing in childhood by the previous generation, it can be hypothesized that a process of breaking with intergenerationally transmitted parenting practices has begun in most caregivers. These reflective processes seem to be aimed at reducing the intensity of violent parenting patterns and seeking alternative strategies to establish norms and limits with their children. The results of the physical punishment and role reversal scales show that some caregivers think there are alternative strategies to the use of physical punishment to discipline children, and others consider it one among various strategies to establish norms and limits, showing that in these families in displacement condition, physical punishment is not the main disciplinary strategy. Most caregivers develop an adequate parental function and do not have expectations that young children will be the source of gratification for their emotional or instrumental needs.

The significant and positive associations found between caregiver sensitivity and the quality of child development, especially in the areas of gross motor skills and hearing and language, suggest that main caregivers, when sensitive to the emotional and communicative needs of children, seem to promote adequate child development.

## Risk Factors

A minority of caregivers justify physical punishment by their parents in their childhood as a parental attitude of correction or for their own good, which would lead to the assumption that parents with this perception about the treatment received by the previous generation would be more prone to repeat the parenting pattern with disciplinary strategies centered on physical punishment.

The belief reported in the discourse of many caregivers is that physical punishment is the last resort to discipline children, after exhausting other strategies for managing norms and limits, without using violence, which could favor the intergenerational repetition of violent parenting patterns.

A risk factor regarding punishment in this sample is being a girl, as a higher proportion of severe and moderate disciplinary practices were observed in girls. It would be relevant to investigate what the caregivers' representations are in relation to this population by gender, regarding appropriate behavior and ways of implementing norms and limits.

The areas of child development with lower performance levels in the children of the sample are hearing-language and personal-social. These are among the most affected in children living in contexts of poverty, due to various factors that act synergistically, impacting negatively on child development and learning, such as lower maternal educational levels, less cognitively and socio-emotionally stimulating family environments, higher levels of stress in daily life, among others (Bornstein & Putnick, 2012; Wachs, 2009).

## Limitations of the Study

Since this is an explanatory mixed study with few cases, its results are preliminary and cannot be generalized. Therefore, it is necessary to conduct a study with a sequential explanatory mixed design, expanding the sample of the population in a situation of forced displacement and relocation in the city of Bogotá, using randomized sampling.

In subsequent studies, it is important to assess the caregiver's mood, especially aspects related to maternal depression, since mothers and fathers in poverty contexts have a higher risk of suffering mental health problems (low self-esteem, negative beliefs about their ability to control, anxiety), associated with the strong and chronic stress of adverse economic conditions (Shonkoff & Phillips, 2000; Wachs, 2009) which in turn affects the quality of child care (Mulsow et al., 2002).

Likewise, it is relevant to evaluate in other studies the support networks of family, social, and community that families in a situation of displacement have since these are key factors to alleviate the stress of parenting, especially in conditions of psychosocial adversity and affect the quality of care (Wachs, 2009) and consequently, the emotional security of young children.

## References


Ainsworth, M. D. S., Bell, S. M., & Stayton, D. F. (1974). Infant-mother attachment and social development: Socialization as a product of reciprocal responsiveness to signals. In M. P. M. Richards (Ed.), *The integration of a child in the social world* (pp. 99–135). Cambridge University Press.

Ainsworth, M. D. S., Blehar, M. C., Waters, E., & Wall, S. (1978). *Patterns of attachment: A psychological study of the strange situation*. Erlbaum.

Álzate, G., Carbonell, O. A., Posada, G., & Bustamante, M. R. (1999). *Escalas cualitativas del comportamiento materno*. Manuscrito no publicado, Pontificia Universidad Javeriana.

Amnistía Internacional. (16 de julio de 2009). Colombia: Todo queda atrás. Desplazamiento interno en Colombia. Recuperado de http://www.amnesty.org/es/library/info/AMR23/015/2009/es

Arango, M., Acosta, A., & Jaramillo, M. (2009). Colombia: Historia de Marta Arango. In P. Connolly, J. Hayden, D. Levin, & L. Shulman (Eds.), *Del conflicto a la construcción de paz: el poder de las iniciativas de la primera infancia* (pp. 51–61). Editorial Visuales Dar.

Berlin, L. J. (2007). Interventions to enhance early attachments. The state of the field today. In L. J. Berlin, Y. Ziv, L. Amaya-Jackson, & M. T. Greenberg (Eds.), *Enhancing early attachments: Theory, research, intervention, and policy* (pp. 3–33). The Guilford Press.

Berlin, L. J., Zeanah, C., & Lieberman, A. (2008). Prevention and intervention programs for supporting early attachment security. In J. Cassidy & P. R. Shaver (Eds.), *Handbook of attachment: Theory, research, and clinical applications* (pp. 745–761). The Guilford Press.

Bornstein, M. C., & Putnick, D. L. (2012). Cognitive and socioemotional caregiving in developing countries. *Child Development, 83*, 46–61. https://doi.org/10.1111/j.1467-8624.2011.01673.x

Bowlby, J. (1993). *El vínculo afectivo*. Editorial Paidós.

Cicchetti, D., Cummings, M. E., Greenberg, M. T., & Marvin, R. S. (1990). An organizational perspective on attachment beyond infancy. In M. T. Greenberg, D. Cicchetti, & M. E. Cummings (Eds.), *Attachment in the preschool years: Theory, research and intervention* (pp. 51–86). The University of Chicago.

Connolly, P., Hayden, J., Levin, D., & Shulman, L. (2009). *Del conflicto a la construcción de paz: el poder de las iniciativas de la primera infancia*. Editorial Visuales Dar.

Consultoría para los Derechos Humanos y el Desplazamiento. (22 de abril de 2009). *Víctimas emergentes. Desplazamiento, derechos humanos y conflicto armado en 2008* (Boletín informativo N° 75). Recuperado de http://www.codhes.org/index.php?option=com_si&type=4

Creswell, J. W., & Plano Clark, V. (2011). *Designing and conducting mixed methods research*. Sage.

De Wolff, M. S., & van IJzendoorn, M. H. (1997). Sensitivity and attachment: A meta-analysis on parental antecedents of infant attachment. *Child Development, 68*, 571–591. https://doi.org/10.2307/1132107

Delage, M. (2010). *En el nicho familiar y la superación de las heridas*. Gedisa.

Egeland, B., Carlson, E. A., & Sroufe, L. A. (1993). Resilience as process. *Development and Psychopathology, 5*, 517–528. https://doi.org/10.1017/S0954579400006131

Farah, M. J., Shera, D. M., Savage, J. H., Betancourt, L., Giannetta, J. M., Brodsky, N. L., & Hurt, H. (2006). Childhood poverty: Specific associations with neurocognitive development. *Brain Research, 1110*(1), 166–174. https://doi.org/10.1016/j.brainres.2006.06.072

Fondo de las Naciones Unidas para la Infancia. (1996). *Estado mundial de la infancia* [Ejemplar sobre el 50.° aniversario]. Autor. Disponible en http://www.unicef.org/spanish/sowc/index_38236.html

Fondo de las Naciones Unidas para la Infancia. (2006, Mayo). Hojas informativas sobre la protección de la infancia. Autor. http://www.unicef.org/spanish/protection/files/Hojasinformativas_sobre_proteccion_infancia_Bookl.pdf

Fondo de las Naciones Unidas para la Infancia. ( 2014, Junio). *Informe anual de UNICEF 2013*. Autor. Disponible en http://www.unicef.org/spanish/publications/index_73682.html

Gómez Muzzio, E., Muñoz, M. M., & Santelices, M. P. (2008). Efectividad de las intervenciones en apego con infancia vulnerada y en riesgo social: un desafío prioritario para Chile. *Terapia Psicológica, 26*(2), 241–251.

González Viveros, C. (2004, Agosto). Transformación y resiliencia en familias desplazadas por la violencia hacia Bogotá. *Revista de Estudios Sociales, 18*, 123–130. Disponible en http://res.uniandes.edu.co/view.php/379/view.php#*.
Hernández Sampieri, R., Fernández Collado, C., & Baptista Lucio, P. (2010). *Metodología de la investigación*. McGraw Hill.
Hesse, E. (2008). The adult attachment interview: Protocol, method of analysis, and empirical studies. In J. Cassidy & P. R. Shaver (Eds.), *Handbook of attachment: Theory, research, and clinical applications* (pp. 552–598). The Guilford Press.
Juffer, F., Barkermans-Kranenburg, M. J., & van IJzendoorn, M. H. (2008). *Promoting positive parenting: An attachment-based intervention*. Psychology Press.
Kim-Cohen, J., Moffitt, T. E., Caspi, A., & Taylor, A. (2004). Generic and environmental processes in young children's resilience and vulnerability to socioeconomic deprivation. *Child Development, 75*, 651–668. https://doi.org/10.1111/j.1467-8624.2004.00699.x
Mulsow, M., Caldera, Y., Pursley, M., Reifman, A., & Huston, A. (2002). Multilevel factors influencing maternal stress during the first three years. *Journal of Marriage and Family, 64*, 944–956. https://doi.org/10.1111/j.1741-3737.2002.00944.x
Myers-Walls, J. A., Myers-Bowman, K. S., & Posada, G. (2005). Parenting practices worldwide. In B. Ingoldsby & S. Smith (Eds.), *Families in global and multicultural perspective* (pp. 147–167). Sage.
Ortiz, N. (1991). *Escala Abreviada de Desarrollo*. Ministerio de Salud.
Pederson, D. R., Gleason, K. E., Moran, G., & Bento, S. (1998). Maternal attachment representations, maternal sensitivity, and the infant-mother attachment relationship. *Developmental Psychology, 34*, 925–933. https://doi.org/10.1037/0012-1649.34.5.925
Pederson, D. R., & Moran, G. (1995). Appendix B. Maternal behavior Q-set. In E. Waters, B. E. Vaughn, G. Posada, & K. Kondo-Ikemura (Eds.), *Caregiving, cultural, and cognitive perspectives on secure base behavior and working models: New growing points of attachment theory and research* (Monographs of the society for research in child development) (Vol. 60(2–3 Serial N.° 244), pp. 247–254). https://doi.org/10.2307/1166182
Posada, G., Carbonell, O. A., Alzate, G., & Plata, S. J. (2004). Through Colombian lenses: Ethnographic and conventional analyses of maternal care and their associations with secure base behavior. *Developmental Psychology, 40*, 508–518. https://doi.org/10.1037/0012-1649.40.4.508
Posada, G., Jacobs, A., & Richmond, M. (1998). *The maternal behavior for preschoolers Q-set*. Unpublished manuscript. Purdue University at West Lafayette.
Posada, G., Kaloustian, G., Richmond, M. K., & Moreno, A. J. (2007). Maternal secure base support and preschoolers' secure base behavior in natural environments. *Attachment & Human Development, 9*, 1–19.
Posada, G., & Waters, E. (1990). *Family behavior survey. Part IV*. Manuscrito inédito, Psychology Department, Stony Brook, New York University.
Sagi-Schwartz, A. (2012). Children of war and peace: A human development perspective. *Journal of Conflict Resolution, 56*(5), 933–951. https://doi.org/10.1177/00222712446128
Shonkoff, J. P., & Phillips, D. A. (Eds.). (2000). *From neurons to neighborhoods. The science or early childhood development*. National Academic Press. Disponible en http://www.nap.edu/openbook.php?record_id=9824
Solís-Cámara, P., & Bavolek, S. (1995). *Manual del Inventario de Paternidad para adultos y adolescentes (MIPPA)*. Family Development Resources Inc.
Solís-Cámara, P., & Díaz Romero, M. (2006). Efectos de un programa de crianza para mamás y papás de niños pequeños: la importancia del nivel educativo de los padres. *Revista Infancia, Adolescencia y Familia, 1*(1), 161–176.
Strauss, A., & Corbin, J. (2002). *Bases de la investigación cualitativa: técnicas y procedimientos para desarrollar la teoría fundamentada*. Universidad de Antioquia.
Thompson Gershoff, E. (2002). Corporal punishment by parents and associated child behaviors and experiences: A meta-analytic and theoretical review. *Psychological Bulletin, 128*, 539–579. https://doi.org/10.1037/0033-2909.128.4.539

Uribe-Mallarino, C. (2008). Estratificación social en Bogotá: de la política pública a la dinámica de la segregación social. *Universitas Humanística, 65*, 139–171.
Velasco Bernal, V. L., & Lozano Mancera, N. (2012). *Comportamiento de la violencia intrafamiliar, Colombia, 2012*. Instituto Nacional de Medicina Legal y Ciencias Forenses.
Wachs, T. D. (2009, julio). La naturaleza y las consecuencias del estrés sobre las familias que viven en países con bajos ingresos. In *El estrés familiar: protegiendo el bienestar de los más pequeños* (pp. 3–10). Bernard van Leer Foundation.
Waters, E. (1995). The attachment Q-set (version 3). In E. Waters, B. Vaughn, G. Posada, & K. Kondo-Ikemura (Eds.), *Caregiving, cultural, and cognitive perspectives on secure-base behavior and working models: New growing points of attachment theory and research* (Monographs of the society for research in child development) (Vol. 60(2-3, Serial N.° 244), pp. 234–246). https://doi.org/10.2307/1166181
Wyman, P., Cowen, E. L., Work, W. C., Hoyt-Meyers, L., Magnus, K., & Fagen, D. B. (1999). Caregiving and developmental factors differentiating young at-risk urban children showing resilient versus stress-affected outcomes: A replication and extension. *Child Development, 70*, 645–659. https://doi.org/10.1111/1467-8624.00047

# Perceptions of Parenting Styles and Their Relationship to Self-Perceptions of Children in Buenos Aires: Gender Differences

María Fernanda Molina, María Julia Raimundi, and Lucía Bugallo

From birth, people develop within the family unit. In it, they grow, establish their identity, acquire responsibilities and commitments, and develop resources that allow them to enter the adult world (Minichiello et al., 2010).

Among these resources, self-concept and self-esteem play a fundamental role for healthy child and adolescent development. A positive self-perception is associated with greater subjective well-being (Rodríguez-Fernández et al., 2016), greater resilience (Cardozo & Alderete, 2009), favorable academic performance (e.g. Jiang et al., 2014; Miñano et al., 2012), a positive attitude toward school and study (Schmidt et al., 2008), greater school involvement (Ramos-Díaz et al., 2016), a lower predisposition to depression (e.g. Jiménez et al., 2007; Wu & Kuo, 2014) and suicidal ideation (De la Torre et al., 2009), lower levels of aggressive behavior (Çiftçi, 2015), and less anxiety and maladjustment (Acevedo Ponce de León & Carrillo Árcega, 2010). This shows the importance of investigating the factors that can intervene in the development of a positive self-view.

Self-perceptions are constituted from the interaction of multiple factors. Among them, early interactions in the family environment and with parents in particular

---

*This chapter is the English translation of an article originally published in Spanish as*: Molina, M.F., Raimundi, M.J., & Bugallo, L. (2017). La percepción de los estilos de crianza y su relación con las autopercepciones de los niños de Buenos Aires: Diferencias en función del género. *Universitas Psychologica 16*(1), 1–12. https://doi.org/10.11144/Javeriana.upsy16-1.pecr. *Please cite the original version of the article in Spanish.*

M. F. Molina (✉) · M. J. Raimundi
Universidad de Buenos Aires – Consejo Nacional de Investigaciones Científicas y Técnicas (CONICET), Buenos Aires, Argentina

L. Bugallo
Instituto Patagónico de Estudios de Historia y Ciencias Sociales (IPEHCS) – Consejo Nacional de Investigaciones Científicas y Técnicas (CONICET), Buenos Aires, Argentina



W. López-López et al. (eds.), *Trends in Latin American Psychology*,
https://doi.org/10.1007/978-3-031-87554-0_12

have a fundamental weight (Harter & Bukowski, 2012). It is these interactions that allow the child to gain understanding about themselves, both subjectively and objectively (Coplan et al., 2004).

Particularly, parenting styles are a key element in the constitution of children's self-concept (Harter, 1999; Muñoz Silva, 2005; Torío López et al., 2008; Vargas Rubilar & Oros, 2013) and it is the children's perception of their parents' behaviors that has the greatest influence (e.g. Ivanova & Israel, 2006; Rodríguez et al., 2009).

In this sense, the perception of acceptance, warmth, and affection in the relationship with parents is associated with the development of more positive self-perceptions in children. In turn, positive forms of control (i.e. behavioral control, provision of structure) and the promotion of autonomy are associated with higher self-esteem and a more positive self-concept, while negative forms of control (i.e. psychological control, coercion, chaos) are associated with more negative self-perceptions (e.g. Clerici & García, 2011; Frank et al., 2010; Fuentes et al., 2014; Reina et al., 2010; Richaud de Minzi, 2006a; Siffert et al., 2012).

This demonstrates the relevance of studying how the way children perceive their parents' parenting styles influences their self-perceptions. Now, do the father and mother influence their children's self-perceptions in the same way?

Research on parental patterns of upbringing has mainly focused on the mother, leaving aside the influence of the father (De La Iglesia et al., 2011). However, there is no evidence that both mothers and fathers have great psychological importance as attachment figures and that both play different roles in terms of parental functions (Lamb & Tamis-Lemonda, 2004).

On the other hand, gender differences in children must also be taken into account, as there are differences in valence and in the content of self-perceptions based on sex (Harter, 1999). Boys tend to have more positive self-perceptions than girls. However, in the domain of behavior, girls perceive themselves as more competent than boys (e.g. Gorostegui & Dörr, 2005; Molina et al., 2011).

This raises the question of whether the perception of the relationship with the father and mother has a different effect on the self-perceptions of boys and girls.

The aim of this study was to explore how the perception of the parenting style of the father and mother influences the self-perceptions of boys and girls from the Conurbano Bonaerense (Province of Buenos Aires, Argentina). The dimensional approach was adopted and the two main dimensions of parenting styles were investigated: the affective and the control.

*Hypotheses:*

1. the perception of acceptance by parents predicts more positive self-perceptions in children.
2. the perception of moderate forms of control predicts more positive self-perceptions.
3. the perception of extreme forms of control predicts more negative self-perceptions.
4. the perception of lack of control predicts more negative self-perceptions.

Finally, it was studied whether the gender of the parents and children has a moderating effect on the relationship between perceived parenting styles and children's self-perceptions. This objective was exploratory and therefore no hypotheses were proposed in this regard.

# Method

## Type of Study

A descriptive correlational study was conducted with a non-experimental transactional design (Hernández Sampieri et al., 2010).

## Participants

School-aged children of both sexes, between 8 and 12 years old, were included. The sample used was of a non-probabilistic or convenience type of voluntary subjects (Hernández Sampieri et al., 2010). It was made up of children ($n = 98$) of both sexes (56.1% female) from primary schools in the Conurbano Bonaerense with an average age of 9.86 ($SD$ = 1.28). Most of the parents were married or cohabiting (78.70%) and had a secondary education complete or higher (mothers = 84.40%; fathers = 91.60%). Most of the children belonged to a two-parent household (74.07%).

## Procedures

The children participated voluntarily and anonymously and gave their informed consent orally. Their parents previously signed a written consent. The scales were administered in groups by trained evaluators. The instructions were read aloud and explained by the evaluators, and then the questionnaires were answered individually.

## Instruments

***Sociodemographic Questionnaire*** It was constructed ad-hoc to characterize the sample based on their sociodemographic characteristics (age, sex, educational level of parents, marital status, and family composition).

***Self-Perception Profile for Children (SPPC, Harter, 1985; Adaptation: Molina et al., 2011)*** It consists of 36 items and assesses self-concept through five specific domains: academic competence, social acceptance, behavior, sports competence, and physical appearance. On the other hand, it evaluates global self-esteem with a subscale specifically designed for this purpose. This variable is defined as the degree to which the child likes himself as a person and is happy with the way he is conducting his life.

Each subscale consists of six items with four response options. The response format consists of two opposing sentences that show two groups of children with opposite self-perceptions. The children must first choose which group they resemble and, secondly, how much they resemble that group (*Really like me* or *More or less like me)*. The items are of the type: "Some kids can easily learn what they are taught in school *But* Other kids have difficulty learning what they are taught" (academic competences) or "Some kids, often, are not happy with themselves *But* Other kids are quite satisfied with themselves" (global self-esteem).

In its original version, the SPPC has shown to have adequate factorial validity and good internal consistency (Cronbach's alpha from 0.71 to 0.86) (Harter, 1985). In the local version of the scale, evidence was found in favor of construct, factorial, convergent, and discriminant validity. Regarding the reliability of the scale, the indices of internal consistency are adequate to good (Cronbach's alpha from 0.71 to 0.84) (Molina et al., 2011).

Specific domain self-perceptions can be grouped into two more general dimensions: the physical/social domain and the academic/behavioral (Harter, 1999). In this work, these domains of self-perception and global self-esteem were studied. The score for self-perceptions in the physical/social domain was obtained from the sum of the scores in the domains of social acceptance, sports competences, and physical appearance. The score for self-perceptions in the academic/behavioral domain was obtained by summing the scores on the academic competences and behavior subscales. The three subscales showed adequate internal consistency (Cronbach's alpha) ($\alpha = 0.70$).

***Argentine Scale of Perception of the Relationship with Parents for Children Aged 8–12 Years (EAPRP, Richaud de Minzi, 2007)*** It evaluates the child's perception of acceptance by his father and mother and three aspects of control in the relationship with them. The scale consists of 32 items with three response options (*always, sometimes, never*) that are divided into four subscales: acceptance, accepted control, pathological control, and extreme autonomy. The items are of the type "My mom tells me she loves me a lot" (acceptance), "My mom checks that I get home on time" (accepted control), "My mom believes that by punishing me she will correct my bad behavior" (pathological control), "My mom lets me do what I want" (extreme autonomy). The versions for the mother and the father consist of the same items.

The scale presents adequate content validity, factorial validity, and criterion validity. The indices of internal consistency (Cronbach's alpha) are adequate to very good (from 0.60 to 0.92 for the mother and from 0.60 to 0.89 for the father) (Richaud de Minzi, 2007).

In this study, the obtained internal consistency coefficients were from regular to good (acceptance, 0.68 for the mother and 0.74 for the father; accepted control, 0.51 for the mother and 0.58 for the father; pathological control, 0.69 for the mother and 0.69 for the father; extreme autonomy, 0.68 for the mother and 0.75 for the father).

## Data Analysis

Correlations were used ($r$ Pearson) to study the association between the perception of the relationship with the parents and the children‘s self-perceptions. The effect size was studied with the coefficient $r$ of Pearson, following the criteria of Cohen (1992).

Simple and multiple linear regression analyses were performed by the standard method. Different models were tested with the variables of the perception of the relationship with the parents (independent variables) that showed to have a significant or marginal relationship with the self-perceptions in the studied domains (dependent variables). Separate analyses were conducted based on the gender of the parents and children. For each of the models, the effect size was calculated with the statistic $f^2$ of Cohen (1992).

## Results

**Preliminary Analysis** When analyzing the relationship with the mother, in the case of girls, a positive association was found between the perception of acceptance and self-perceptions in the academic/behavioral domain ($r = 0.34$, $p = 0.012$) and global self-esteem ($r = 0.34$, $p = 0.011$). In the physical/social domain, a greater perception of extreme autonomy was associated with a more positive self-perception ($r = 0.46$, $p < 0.001$). The perception of pathological control negatively correlated with global self-esteem ($r = -0.31$, $p = 0.022$). In the case of boys, only a significant positive correlation was observed between acceptance and self-perceptions in the physical/social domain ($r = 0.31$, $p = 0.040$). In all cases, the effect size was medium.

Regarding the perception of the relationship with the father, in the group of girls, pathological control was negatively associated with self-perceptions in the physical/social domain ($r = -0.31$, $p = 0.027$) and global self-esteem ($r = -0.36$, $p = 0.007$). No significant correlations were found in the group of boys.

**Main Analysis** First, the adequacy of the studied models was analyzed. From the analysis of the graph of the distribution of the residuals, the normality in this distribution was verified. Through the analysis of the normal probability residual plots and scatter plots of the residuals, the assumption of homoscedasticity for all models (Chica Olmo & Frías Jamilena, 2000; Ferrán Aranaz, 1996) was confirmed. On the other hand, the values obtained by the Durbin-Watson Test (from 1.66 to 2.48) are adequate, indicating the absence of autocorrelation of the residuals (Pardo & Ruiz, 2005). Finally, in the case of the models with more than one independent variable,

**Table 1** Linear regression models of the dimensions of the relationship with the mother that predict the self-perceptions of girls

| | Predictors Data | | | Model Data | | | |
|---|---|---|---|---|---|---|---|
| Predictors | *B* | *β* | 95% CI *B* | $R^2$ | Adjusted $R^2$ | *F* | $F^2$ |
| *Self-perceptions physical/social* | | | | | | | |
| Extreme autonomy | 2.33 | 0.46*** | [1.09, 3.58] | 0.21 | 0.2 | 14.08*** | 0.26 |
| *Self-perception academic/behavioral* | | | | | | | |
| Acceptance | 1.07 | 0.34* | [0.25, 1.89] | 0.11 | 0.1 | 6.81* | 0.12 |
| *Global self-esteem* | | | | | | | |
| Acceptance | 0.07 | 0.32* | [0.02, 0.12] | 0.2 | 0.17 | 6.47** | 0.25 |
| Pathological control | −0.05 | −0.29* | [−0.09, −0.01] | | | | |

*Note.* CI = confidence interval. *$p < 0.05$; **$p < 0.01$; ***$p < 0.001$

**Table 2** Linear regression models of the dimensions of the relationship with the mother that predict the self-perceptions in the physical/social domain for boys

| | Predictors Data | | | Model Data | | | |
|---|---|---|---|---|---|---|---|
| Predictors | *B* | *β* | 95% CI *B* | $R^2$ | Adjusted $R^2$ | *F* | $F^2$ |
| Acceptance | 1.36 | 0.31* | [0.06, 2.66] | 0.1 | 0.08 | 4.49* | 0.11 |

*Note.* CI = confidence interval. *$p < 0.05$

adequate tolerance coefficients were obtained (0.95–0.99), indicating the absence of multicollinearity (Hair et al., 2001).

Table 1 presents the results of the models of the perception of the relationship with the mother, which was shown to significantly predict the self-concept and global self-esteem of girls. The main predictor of self-perceptions in the physical/social domain was extreme autonomy. The percentage of variance explained by the model was 20%. The effect size was medium. The main predictor of self-perceptions in the academic/behavioral domain was acceptance. The percentage of variance explained by the model was 10%. The effect size was low. Finally, the main predictors of global self-esteem were acceptance and pathological control. The percentage of variance explained by the model was 17%. The effect size of the model was medium.

Table 2 presents the results of the model of the perception of the relationship with the mother, which significantly predicted the self-concept in the physical/social domain of boys. The main predictor was the perception of acceptance by the mother. The percentage of variance explained by the model was 8%. The effect size was low.

In Table 3, the results of the models of the perception of the relationship with the father, which significantly predicted the self-perceptions of girls, are presented. In the physical/social domain, high acceptance and low pathological control were predictors of a more positive self-perception. The percentage of variance explained by the model was 18%. The effect size was medium. These same variables predicted

**Table 3** Linear regression models of the dimensions of the relationship with the father that predict the self-perceptions of girls

| | Predictors Data | | | Model Data | | | |
|---|---|---|---|---|---|---|---|
| Predictors | *B* | *β* | 95% CI *B* | $R^2$ | Adjusted $R^2$ | *F* | $F^2$ |
| *Self-perceptions physical/social* | | | | | | | |
| Acceptance | 1.4 | 0.33* | [0.3, 2.51] | 0.21 | 0.18 | 6.39** | 0.26 |
| Pathological control | −1.14 | −0.4** | [−1.9, −0.39] | | | | |
| *Global self-esteem* | | | | | | | |
| Acceptance | 0.55 | 0.39** | [0.19, 0.9] | 0.27 | 0.24 | 9.2*** | 0.37 |
| Pathological control | −0.43 | −0.45*** | [−0.68, −0.19] | | | | |

*Note.* CI = confidence interval. *$p < 0.05$; **$p < 0.01$; ***$p < 0.001$

the global self-esteem of girls. The percentage of variance explained by the model was 24%. The effect size was high.

Regarding the perception of the relationship with the father, no explanatory models were found for boys.

## Discussion and Conclusions

This study aimed to explore how perceived acceptance and control in the relationship with the father and mother influence the self-perceptions of boys and girls in the Conurbano Bonaerense (Province of Buenos Aires, Argentina).

From the analyses carried out, it was found that the dimensions of parenting styles, as perceived by children, differently predict the level of their self-perceptions when considering the gender of parents and children.

In the case of girls, the perception of the relationship with the mother impacts all domains of the studied self-perceptions. On the one hand, the perception of high levels of extreme autonomy predicts a more positive self-concept in the physical/social domain. On the other hand, the perception of greater acceptance predicts a more positive self-concept in the academic/behavioral domain. Finally, the perception of high levels of acceptance and low levels of pathological control predicts high global self-esteem. This same combination of variables, perceived in the relationship with the father, predicted the level of self-concept in the physical/social domain and of the global self-esteem of girls.

In the case of children, only the perception of acceptance in the relationship with the mother showed predictive power in the physical/social domain of self-concept. The perception of the relationship with the father did not have predictive power, for males, in any of the evaluated domains.

These results present evidence in favor of the first and third hypotheses: the perception of acceptance by parents is associated with more positive self-perceptions, while pathological control predicts more negative self-perceptions. These findings are consistent with those presented by other studies that show that the perception of acceptance, warmth, or affection in the relationship with parents is linked with more positive self-perceptions. On the contrary, negative forms of control (psychological control, coercion, and intrusiveness) are associated with more negative self-perceptions (Frank et al., 2010; Reina et al., 2010; Siffert et al., 2012).

On the other hand, no evidence was found in favor of the second hypothesis. The perception of accepted control did not show predictive power for any of the studied domains. This finding contradicts those indicated by studies that show that positive forms of control, such as behavioral control, the provision of structure, or firm control, are associated with more positive self-perceptions (Alonso García & Román Sánchez, 2005; Oliva Delgado et al., 2008; Reina et al., 2010). However, in a study conducted with children from our context, no relationship was found between this dimension and the children's self-perceptions (Richaud de Minzi, 2006a).

The fourth hypothesis proposed did not have evidence to support it. However, the perception of extreme autonomy had predictive power of the level of self-perceptions but in the opposite direction to the hypothesized; it predicted more positive self-perceptions in the physical/social domain. Extreme autonomy is defined as lax discipline and disinterest (Richaud de Minzi, 2007). In our context, it has been associated with negative functioning in children. High levels of extreme autonomy are associated with greater conflicts in friendship relationships (Richaud de Minzi, 2006b), an affinity for solitude, and a more negative self-perception of academic competencies (Richaud de Minzi, 2006a).

However, it is important to bear in mind that, from the perspective of the typology of parenting styles, the dimensions of acceptance and control combine to result in different types of parenting styles; depending on what other parental behaviors it is associated with, autonomy will have different consequences in child-rearing. That is, if it is accompanied by a lack of commitment to parenting, it will be characteristic of a negligent parenting style. However, it can also be characteristic of a permissive parenting style, in which the parents' demand is low, but there is a high commitment on their part and high acceptance (Muñoz Silva, 2005; Torío López et al., 2008). There are findings that show that a permissive parenting style is beneficial (sometimes even more than the authoritative) for the self-concept of young people from Latin American countries (e.g. Brazil in Martínez et al., 2007; Mexico in Villalobos et al., 2004). Therefore, future research should delve into this issue by investigating the role that extreme autonomy plays in combination with other characteristics of the relationship with parents (e.g. acceptance).

Now, the results found in this study differed depending on the sex of the parents and the children, which indicates that gender, both of the children and the parents, plays a moderating role in the relationship between the perception of parenting patterns exercised by parents and children's self-perceptions.

On the one hand, the perception of the relationship with parents has a greater influence for girls than for boys. These results coincide with those found in a study conducted with children from Entre Ríos (Argentina). In this work, it was found that maternal positive emotions predict the self-concept of girls to a greater extent than that of boys (Resett et al., 2016). These findings can be linked to the differences that exist in the way men and women perceive themselves and their world. Women are more prone to have collectivist self-schemas, assembled or connected. In these schemas, relationships with others, especially significant others, are crucial elements of the self. Men are more likely to have individualistic self-schemas, independent or autonomous. That is, others are represented as distinct from the self (Cross & Madson, 1997; Josephs et al., 1992).

As the relationship with others is an important aspect in the psychological life of women, it is expected that their self-esteem is based, to a greater extent than men's, on maintaining significant relationships with others (Josephs et al., 1992; Oyserman & Fryberg, 2006). This is consistent with what was found in a study in which it was investigated what are the main domains of self-concept that predict the self-esteem of boys and girls in our context. For girls, the main predictors of global self-esteem were the self-perception of social acceptance and behavior, while for boys the main predictor of self-esteem was the self-perception of physical appearance. This shows the relevance that social dimensions take over individual ones for girls in our culture (Molina & Raimundi, 2011). That is, social acceptance implies the perception of acceptance by peers, and the behavior is associated with behavior valued by adults. On the other hand, physical appearance, which has the greatest importance relative for boys, constitutes the external face of the self and one of its most personal aspects (Harter, 1999).

In summary, it is possible that parents have more impact on the self-perceptions of girls because they are more open to the influence of the context than boys and, therefore, their self-concept is more shaped by relationships with their significant others.

On the other hand, the perception of the relationship with the mother is the one that has the greatest influence for both sexes. Different authors agree that even today mothers spend more time with their children than fathers and have greater responsibilities linked to upbringing (Cabrera et al., 2012; Lamb & Tamis-Lemonda, 2004; Rodríguez et al., 2009). It is possible that for this reason, their behaviors have a greater impact on the development of children's self-perceptions than those of fathers.

This study presents some limitations. On the one hand, it worked with a non-probabilistic sample and, therefore, not representative. It is for this reason that the results should be replicated with other samples. Also, there are geographical limitations, the children who participated in the study were residents of the Buenos Aires suburbs. For this reason, the conclusions reached in this work cannot be generalized to other contexts in Argentina.

On the other hand, the low number of cases did not allow to combine the studied dimensions of the relationship with the parents in order to be able to establish how the type of parental style perceived by the child influences their self-perceptions. In future studies, it is recommended to complement the dimensional approach adopted in this work with the typological approach proposed by Baumrind (1991).

Finally, it is important to consider that the relationships found, mostly, have a magnitude (effect size) from medium to low. That is, there are other variables involved in the prediction of children's self-perceptions. In this sense, it is necessary to point out the complexity of the origin of self-perception and the multiplicity of factors involved in its constitution. On the one hand, in addition to social factors, there are other determining factors in its formation such as, for example, cognitive ones (Harter, 1999). On the other hand, social factors involve more than the relationship with the parents. The relationship with peers and teachers is particularly relevant for the life stage that was considered in this study (see Swann & Bosson, 2010 for a review). It is important to investigate these variables especially in the case of boys, since the perception of the relationship with parents has shown to have little influence on their self-perceptions.

Despite these limitations, this study makes both theoretical and practical contributions. On the one hand, it allows us to know in greater depth how the perceived acceptance and control in the relationship with the father and mother are linked with the self-perceptions of sons and daughters. In this way, existing knowledge about one of the main antecedents of self-concept and self-esteem is the relationship with the people who play a central role in their upbringing.

On the other hand, understanding the factors involved in the origin of self-perceptions enables the development of more appropriate interventions to improve children's self-view. There is evidence that treatments aimed at increasing self-esteem improve scores on standardized performance tests and reduce disciplinary reports in school and drug and alcohol use (see Swann & Bosson, 2010, for a review). For this reason, developing intervention programs to improve self-perceptions has been a topic of growing interest (Bos et al., 2006; Mann et al., 2004). The findings of this study contribute in this sense, as they highlight the importance of the perception of the relationship with both parents for the self-perceptions of girls. It also raises the importance of the relationship with the mother for the self-perceptions of boys in the physical/social domain and to consider other factors involved in the origin of self-perceptions when working with them.

**Acknowledgments** This research was funded by the National Council of Scientific and Technical Research (CONICET; Res. No 3609/11 Director: Dr. Schmidt. Co-Director: Dr. Leibovich de Figueroa) and by the Secretary of Science and Technology of the University of Buenos Aires (UBACyT 20020100100052; Director: Dr. Leibovich de Figueroa. Co-Director: Dr. Schmidt). Thanks are extended to the students, teachers, and authorities of the Alas-Los Pinitos School for their collaboration in this research project. Also, thanks to Lic. Mariel Giménez and Yanina Guzmán for their collaboration in the data collection for this research.

## References

Acevedo Ponce de León, J. A., & Carrillo Árcega, M. L. (2010). Adaptación, ansiedad y autoestima en niños de 9 a 12 años: una comparación entre escuela tradicional y montessori. *Psicología Iberoamericana, 18*(1), 19–29. Recuperado de http://www.redalyc.org/articulo.oa?id=133915936003

Alonso García, J., & Román Sánchez, J. M. (2005). Prácticas educativas familiares y autoestima. *Psicothema, 17*(1), 76–82. Recuperado de http://dialnet.unirioja.es/servlet/articulo?codigo=1070808

Baumrind, D. (1991). The influence of parenting style on adolescent competence and substance use. *The Journal of Early Adolescence, 11*(1), 56–95. https://doi.org/10.1177/0272431691111004

Bos, A. E., Muris, P., Mulkens, S., & Schaalma, H. P. (2006). Changing self-esteem in children and adolescents: A roadmap for future interventions. *Netherlands Journal of Psychology, 62*(1), 26–33. https://doi.org/10.1007/BF03061048

Cabrera, N. J., Fagan, J., & Schadler, C. (2012). The influence of mother, father, and child risk on parenting and children's cognitive and social behaviors. *Child Development, 82*(6), 1985–2005. https://doi.org/10.1111/j.1467-8624.2011.01667.x.The

Cardozo, G., & Alderete, A. M. (2009). Adolescentes en riesgo psicosocial y resiliencia. *Psicología Desde El Caribe, 23*, 148–182. Recuperado de http://pepsic.bvsalud.org/pdf/pdc/n23/n23a09.pdf

Chica Olmo, J., & Frías Jamilena, D. M. (2000). Regresión lineal. In T. L. Martinez (Ed.), *Técnicas de análisis de datos en investigaciones de mercados*. Madrid.

Çiftçi, H. D. (2015). Relationship between aggression and self-concept in nine and ten-year-old children. *Academic Research International, 6*(2), 181–198. Retrieved from www.journals.savap.org.pk

Clerici, G., & García, M. J. (2011). Autoconcepto y pautas de apoyo y control parental en niños escolares. In *Memorias del III Congreso Internacional de Investigación y Práctica Profesional en Psicología* (pp. 37–39). Secretaría de Investigaciones de la Facultad de Psicología de la Universidad de Buenos Aires.

Cohen, J. (1992). A power primer. *Psychological Bulletin, 112*(1), 155–159. https://doi.org/10.1037/0033-2909.112.1.155

Coplan, R. J., Findlay, L. C., & Nelson, L. J. (2004). Characteristics of preschoolers with lower perceived competence. *Journal of Abnormal Child Psychology, 32*(4), 399–408. https://doi.org/10.1023/B:JACP.0000030293.81429.49

Cross, S. E., & Madson, L. (1997). Models of the self: Self-construals and gender. *Psychological Bulletin, 122*(1), 5–37. https://doi.org/10.1037/0033-2909.122.1.5

De La Iglesia, G., Ongarato, P., & Fernández Liporace, M. (2011). Evaluación de estilos parentales percibidos: Un breve recorrido histórico. In *Memorias del III Congreso Internacional de Investigación y Práctica Profesional en Psicología* (pp. 40–43). Secretaría de Investigaciones de la Facultad de Psicología de la Universidad de Buenos Aires.

De la Torre, I. M., Cubillas Rodríguez, J. M., Román Pérez, R., & Valdez, E. A. (2009). Ideación suicida en población escolarizada infantil: Factores psicológicos asociados. *Salud Mental, 32*(6), 495–502. Recuperado de http://www.redalyc.org/pdf/582/58212267007.pdf

Ferrán Aranaz, M. (1996). *SPSS para Windows. Programación y análisis estadístico*. McGraw Hill.

Frank, G., Plunkett, S. W., & Otten, M. P. (2010). Perceived parenting, self-esteem, and general self-efficacy of Iranian American adolescents. *Journal of Child and Family Studies, 19*(6), 738–746. https://doi.org/10.1007/s10826-010-9363-x

Fuentes, M. C., García, F., Gracia, E., & Alarcón, A. (2014). Los estilos parentales de socialización y el ajuste psicológico. Un estudio con adolescentes españoles. *Revista de Psicodidactica, 20*(1), 117–138. https://doi.org/10.1387/RevPsicodidact.10876

Gorostegui, M. E., & Dörr, A. (2005). Género y autoconceptos: Un análisis comparativo de las diferencias por sexo en una muestra de niños de educación general básica (EGB) (1992-2003). *Psykhe, 14*(1), 151–163. Recuperado de http://www.scielo.cl/scielo.php?pid=S0718-22282005000100012&script=sci_arttext

Hair, J., Anderson, R., Tatham, R., & Black, W. (2001). *Análisis multivariante* (5th ed.). Prentice Hall Iberia.

Harter, S. (1985). *Manual for the self-perception profile for children*. University of Denver.

Harter, S. (1999). *The construction of the self: A developmental perspective* (1st ed.). The Guilford Press.

Harter, S., & Bukowski, W. M. (2012). *The construction of the self: Developmental and sociocultural foundations* (2nd ed.). The Guilford Press.

Hernández Sampieri, R., Fernández-Collado, C., & Baptista Lucio, P. (2010). *Metodología de la investigación [Research methodology]* (5th ed.). McGraw Hill.

Ivanova, M. Y., & Israel, A. C. (2006). Family stability as a protective factor against psychopathology for urban children receiving psychological services. *Journal of Clinical Child and Adolescent Psychology, 35*(4), 564–570. https://doi.org/10.1207/s15374424jccp3504_7

Jiang, Y., Song, J., Lee, M., & Bong, M. (2014). Self-efficacy and achievement goals as motivational links between perceived contexts and achievement. *Educational Psychology, 34*(1), 92–117. https://doi.org/10.1080/01443410.2013.863831

Jiménez, T. I., Murgui, S., & Musitu, G. (2007). Comunicación familiar y ánimo depresivo: El papel mediador de los recursos psicosociales del adolescente. *Revista Mexicana de Psicología, 24*(2), 259–271. Recuperado de http://www.redalyc.org/pdf/2430/243020637010.pdf

Josephs, R. A., Markus, H., & Romin, W. T. (1992). Gender and self-esteem. *Journal of Personality and Social Psychology, 63*(3), 991–402. https://doi.org/10.1037/0022-3514.63.3.391

Lamb, M. E., & Tamis-Lemonda, C. S. (2004). The role of the father. An introduction. In M. E. Lamb (Ed.), *The role of the father in child development* (4th ed., pp. 1–31). John Wiley & Sons.

Mann, M., Hosman, C. M., Schaalman, H. P., & de Vries, N. K. (2004). Self-esteem in a broad-spectrum approach for mental health promotion. *Health Educational Research. Theory & Practice, 19*(4), 357–372. https://doi.org/10.1093/her/cyg041

Martínez, I., García, J. F., & Yubero, S. (2007). Parenting styles and adolescents' self-esteem in Brazil. *Psychological Reports, 100*(3), 731–745. https://doi.org/10.2466/PR0.100.3.731-745

Miñano, P., Gilar, R., & Castejón, J. L. (2012). Un modelo estructural de variables cognitivo-motivacionales explicativas del rendimiento académico en Lengua Española y Matemáticas. *Anales de Psicología, 28*(1), 45–54.

Minichiello, C., Maglio, A. L., & Schmidt, V. (2010). La familia: Importancia y vigencia de sus funciones. In N. B. Leibovich & V. Schmidt (Eds.), *Ecoevaluación psicológica del contexto familiar. Aspectos teóricos y empíricos* (pp. 27–32). Editorial Guadalupe.

Molina, M. F., & Raimundi, M. J. (2011). Predictores de la autoestima global en niños de escuela primaria de la Ciudad de Buenos Aires. Diferencias en función del sexo y la edad. *Revista Argentina de Ciencias Del Comportamiento, 3*(3), 1–7. Retrieved from http://www.revistas.unc.edu.ar/index.php/racc/article/view/5201

Molina, M. F., Raimundi, M. J., López, C., Cataldi, S., & Bugallo, L. (2011). Adaptación del Perfil de Autopercepciones para Niños para su Uso en la Ciudad de Buenos Aires. *Revista Iberoamericana de Diagnóstico y Evaluación Psicológica (RIDEP), 32*(2), 53–78.

Muñoz Silva, A. (2005). La familia como contexto de desarrollo infantil. Dimensiones de análisis relevantes para la intervención educativa y social [Family as context of child development. Main components to educational and social intervention]. *Portularia, 5*(2), 147–163. Recuperado de http://rabida.uhu.es/dspace/bitstream/handle/10272/505/b1518923.pdf?sequence=1

Oliva Delgado, A., Parra Jiménez, Á., & Arranz, E. (2008). Estilos relacionales parentales y ajuste adolescente. *Infancia Y Aprendizaje, 31*(1), 93–106. https://doi.org/10.1174/021037008783487093

Oyserman, D., & Fryberg, S. (2006). The possible selves of diverse adolescents: Content and function across gender, race and national origin. In C. Dunkel & J. Kerpelman (Eds.), *Possible selves: Theory, research, and applications* (pp. 1–23). Nova Science Publishers.

Pardo, A., & Ruiz, M. A. (2005). *Análisis de datos con SPSS 13 base*. McGraw Hill.

Ramos-Díaz, E., Rodríguez-Fernández, A., Fernández-Zabala, A., Revuelta, L., & Zuazagoitia, A. (2016). Apoyo social percibido, autoconcepto e implicación escolar de estudiantes adolescentes. *Revista de Psicodidáctica, 21*(2), 339–356. https://doi.org/10.1387/RevPsicodidact.14848

Reina, C., Oliva Delgado, A., & Parra Jiménez, Á. (2010). Percepciones de autoevaluación: Autoestima, autoeficacia y satisfacción vital en la adolescencia [Self-evaluation perceptions: Self-esteem, self-efficacy and life satisfaction in adolescence]. *Psychology, Society, & Education, 2*(1), 47–59.

Resett, S., Meier, L., García Sánchez, O., & Katz, O. (2016). Predicción del autoconcepto a partir de las emociones maternas en niños de edad escolar y diferencias según sexo. *Psicodebate, 16*(1), 27–48. https://doi.org/10.18682/pd.v16i1.565

Richaud de Minzi, M. C. (2006a). Loneliness and depression in middle and late childhood: The relationship to attachment and parental style. *The Journal of Genetic Psychology, 167*(2), 189–210. https://doi.org/10.3200/GNTP.167.2.189-210

Richaud de Minzi, M. C. (2006b). Parental styles and attachment in relation with self control, social skills and coping in children at risk due to poverty-related causes. In D. M. Devore (Ed.), *New developments in parent-child relations* (pp. 87–110). Nova Science.

Richaud de Minzi, M. C. (2007). La percepción de estilos de relación con su padre y madre en niños y niñas de 8 a 12 años [Childrens' perception of parental behavior in 8-12 years-old subjects]. *Revista Iberoamericana de Diagnóstico Y Evaluación Psicológica, 1*(23), 63–81.

Rodríguez, M. A., del Barrio, M. V., & Carrasco, M. A. (2009). ¿Cómo perciben los hijos la crianza materna y paterna? Diferencias por edad y sexo. *Escritos de Psicología, 2*(2), 10–18. Recuperado de http://scielo.isciii.es/pdf/ep/v2n2/original2.pdf

Rodríguez-Fernández, A., Ramos-Díaz, E., Ros, I., Fernández-Zabala, A., & Revuelta, L. (2016). Bienestar subjetivo en la adolescencia: El papel de la resiliencia, el autoconcepto y el apoyo social percibido. *Suma Psicológica, 23*(1), 60–69. https://doi.org/10.1016/j.sumpsi.2016.02.002

Schmidt, V., Messoulam, N., & Molina, M. F. (2008). Autoconcepto académico en adolescentes de escuelas medias: Presentación de un instrumento para su evaluación. *Revista Iberoamericana de Diagnóstico Y Evaluación Psicológica, 25*(1), 81–106. Recuperado de http://www.aidep.org/03_ridep/R25/R254.pdf

Siffert, A., Schwarz, B., & Stutz, M. (2012). Marital conflict and early adolescents' self-evaluation: The role of parenting quality and early adolescents' appraisals. *Journal of Youth and Adolescence, 41*(6), 749–763. https://doi.org/10.1007/s10964-011-9703-1

Swann, W. B., & Bosson, J. K. (2010). Self and identity. In G. L. Susan, T. Fiske, & D. T. Gilbert (Eds.), *Handbook of social psychology* (5th ed., pp. 589–628). John Wiley & Sons.

Torío López, S., Peña Calvo, V. J., & Rodríguez Menéndez, M. C. (2008). Estilos educativos parentales. Revisión bibliográfica y reformulación teórica [Parenting styles. Bibliographical revision and theoretical reformulation]. *Teoría de La Educación. Revista Interuniversitaria, 20*, 151–178. Recuperado de http://gredos.usal.es/jspui/bitstream/10366/71805/1/Estilos_educativos_parentales_revision_b.pdf

Vargas Rubilar, J. A., & Oros, L. B. (2013). Parentalidad y autoestima de los hijos: una revisión sobre la importancia del fortalecimiento familiar para el desarrollo infantil positivo. *Apuntes Universitarios, 1*(1), 155–171. https://doi.org/10.17162/au.v0i1.13

Villalobos, J. A., Cruz, A. V., & Sánchez, P. R. (2004). Estilos parentales y desarrollo psicosocial en estudiantes de Bachillerato [Parental styles and psychosocial development in high school students]. *Revista Mexicana de Psicología, 21*, 119–129.

Wu, P.-C., & Kuo, S.-T. (2014). Academic achievement, self-concept and depression in Taiwanese children: Moderated mediation effect. *School Psychology International, 36*(1), 36–53. https://doi.org/10.1177/0143034314559869

# Part III
# Neuropsychology, Clinical and Health Psychology

# Introduction to Part III: Neuropsychology, Clinical, and Health Psychology

**Irene Giovanni-Aguilar**

During the last few decades, there have been strong efforts to increase mental health and well-being awareness and understand the influence of mental health in Latin American society. Despite the recent research and advances in mental health in Latin America, there are still significant challenges. High-quality psychological services are needed, along with educating qualified psychologists and expanding the profession to address mental health difficulties within communities. Findings from mental health surveys conducted in several countries in Latin America and the Caribbean show that nearly 80% of the people with mental health problems do not have access to health or mental health services (PAHO/WHO & CARICOM, 2006). In this regard, some of the most pressing needs to be reviewed fall into the categories of service provision, research, and training (Lequay, 2010; Ward & Hickling, 2004). Clearly, psychological research in clinical and health psychology and neuropsychology can play a role in closing the gap in access to care. Regarding academic research, it is important to consolidate and make evident the identity of Latin American research, based on the geopolitical context and psychosocial processes that have characterized and influence clinical and health psychology and neuropsychology. In this regard, research should be compatible and sensitive with the varying vulnerabilities across the different countries in Latin America.

Considering the above, this section of the book seeks to highlight some of the most outstanding research in the field of neuropsychology, clinical, and health psychology based on the necessities of Latin American people. One of them is adolescence, and the other one is older adulthood, specifically with Alzheimer's disease. Both are populations most often underestimated and understudied, but in developing countries, where social, gender, racial, ethnic, and territorial inequalities are so strong, may represent a greater risk and vulnerability.

I. Giovanni-Aguilar (✉)
Pontificia Universidad Javeriana, Bogota, Colombia
e-mail: igiovanni@javeriana.edu.co



W. López-López et al. (eds.), *Trends in Latin American Psychology*,
https://doi.org/10.1007/978-3-031-87554-0_13

In view of the foregoing, the main purpose of this section is to illustrate the variety and diversity of research in life cycles mentioned above and to give an account of the most representative trends and topics in clinical, health, and neuropsychology in Latin America. Also, this section seeks to highlight and disseminate the multiple contributions and meaningful developments in research in these areas.

For these reasons, the first two chapters in this section are dedicated to adolescence. The researches presented below show some of the most important challenges that psychology faces in dealing with this sensitive population, given the psychological changes it implies. It is important to highlight that in the literature, the scientific production of mental health in low- and middle-income countries represents only about 6% of this content, and this figure is even lower when specified for the mental health of children and adolescents (Saxena et al., 2006). According to the World Health Organization, physical, emotional, and social changes, including exposure to poverty, abuse, or violence, can make adolescents vulnerable to mental health problems. Additionally, multiple factors affect mental health. The more risk factors adolescents are exposed to, the greater the potential impact on their mental health. Factors that can contribute to stress during adolescence include exposure to adversity, pressure to conform with peers, and exploration of identity.

Thus, in the chapter entitled "Influence of Sex, Age, and Culture on Coping Strategies of Paraguayan and Mexican Adolescents," readers will find an analysis of the role of coping in adolescence and all the emotional, cognitive, behavioral, and physiological actions that are deployed in stressful situations and that can assume a protective role and contribute to positive adaptation. This provides highly relevant evidence for the work of psychologists, as well as for public policies on prevention and health promotion in adolescents.

On the other hand, in the chapter "Suicidal Ideation and Peer Group: Analysis in a Sample of Venezuelan Adolescents," an alarming analysis is made of the adolescent suicide rate, which, although it varies from one country to another, is a reality that challenges psychology, evidencing a public health problem. Thus, this research asks about the factors that amplify or minimize suicidal thinking in young people. For this purpose, some explanatory models are explored that have merged individual factors related to stressful life events, hopelessness, depression, self-esteem, drug use, and loneliness with contextual factors related, for example, to family conflict, family cohesion, economic problems in the family, and parental physical abuse. What is striking about this research and makes it novel in its field is that it aims to explore mainly the role played by the peer group in the likelihood of influencing adolescent suicidal ideation, leaving a reflection on the fundamental role that the peer group plays in adolescence.

Now, the other two chapters in this section address one of the most common and difficult neurodegenerative diseases in the older adult population: Alzheimer's disease. Dementia has been declared a global challenge, yet regions around the world show differences in both the nature and magnitude of such a challenge. Regarding specific health actions, most Latin American countries have minimal mental health facilities and do not have specific mental health policies or budgets specific to dementia. In addition, local regulations may need to consider the regional context when developing treatment and prevention strategies (Parra et al., 2018). In comparison with other regions, dementia prevalence in Latin America is growing rapidly, along with the consequent clinical, social, and economic burden upon patients and their families. The combination of fragile health care systems, large social inequalities, and isolated clinical and research initiatives makes the coordination of efforts imperative (Ibanez et al., 2021).

Thus, the chapter "Implementation of the Psychological Intervention Program in Resilience for Informal Caregivers of Patients with Alzheimer's Dementia PIRCA" seeks to demonstrate the different social and psychological consequences for the caregiver to assume this role, as well as the different intervention programs for them. Specifically, the research focuses on the design of a program for informal caregivers in which resilience is the central axis of the intervention.

Finally, the chapter "Analysis of the Perception of Static and Dynamic Events in People with Alzheimer's Disease" addresses the language impairments of patients with the disease and how these difficulties are related to the way AD patients perceive and understand the world around them, and observes whether differential patterns are present that may contribute to establish early predictors of Alzheimer's disease (AD).

## References

Ibanez, A., Parra, M. A., & Butler, C. (2021). The Latin America and the Caribbean Consortium on Dementia (LAC-CD): From networking to research to implementation science. *Journal of Alzheimer's Disease, 82*(s1), S379–S394. https://doi.org/10.3233/JAD-201384

Lequay, K. (2010). The role of T&T psychologists in national development. TTAP: Coming of age. In *Trinidad & Tobago Association of Psychologists 10th anniversary commemorative magazine* (p. 11). The Yearbook Company.

Pan American Health Organization/World Health Organization (PAHO/WHO) & Caribbean Community Secretariat (CARICOM). (2006). *Report of the Caribbean Commission on Health and Development*. Ian Randle Publishers. http://www.who.int/macrohealth/action/PAHO_Report.pdf

Parra, M. A., Baez, S., Allegri, R., Nitrini, R., Lopera, F., Slachevsky, A., Custodio, N., Lira, D., Piguet, O., Kumfor, F., Huepe, D., Cogram, P., Bak, T., Manes, F., & Ibanez, A. (2018). Dementia in Latin America: Assessing the present and envisioning the future. *Neurology, 90*(5), 222–231. https://doi.org/10.1212/WNL.0000000000004897

Saxena, S., Paraje, G., Sharan, P., Karam, G., & Sadana, R. (2006). The 10/90 divide in mental health research: Trends over a 10-year period. *The British Journal of Psychiatry, 188*(1), 81–82. https://doi.org/10.1192/bjp.bp.105.011221

Ward, T., & Hickling, F. (2004). Psychology in the English-speaking Caribbean. *The Psychologist, 17*(8), 442–444. https://www.proquest.com/scholarly-journals/psychology-english-speaking-caribbean/docview/211815556/se-2?accountid=13250

# Influence of Sex, Age, and Culture on Coping Strategies of Paraguayan and Mexican Adolescents

**Norma Coppari, Blanca Barcelata, Laura Bagnoli, Gerónimo Codas, Heidi López Humada, and Úrsula Martínez Cañete**

Adolescence is a stage of many biological, psychological, and social changes that are often a source of stress; however, coping is a process that can cushion its negative impact on adolescent development. Based on the transactional model of Lazarus and Folkman (1991), in general, coping is defined as a process that involves a set of emotional, cognitive, behavioral, and physiological actions, which are deployed in stressful situations and that can assume a protective role and contribute to positive adaptation (Evans et al., 2015; Simpson et al., 2018; Verdugo-Lucero et al., 2013; Wadsworth et al., 2005) or, on the contrary, be associated with psychopathology, depending on the type of coping used (Castro et al., 2014; Manne et al., 2015; Seiffge-Krenke, 2000), so its research has implications in terms of mental health.

There are different coping models for adolescents. Connor-Smith and Compas (2004) suggest that coping consists of a series of physiological, behavioral, or cognitive reactions (e.g., cognitive restructuring) that can lead to engaging with the problem, either by modifying the source of stress or the emotions related to the stressful event, or on the contrary, they may involve disengaging from the situation. There is evidence that the former is associated with mental health, while the latter

*This chapter is the English translation of an article originally published in Spanish as*: Coppari, N., Barcelata, B., Bagnoli, L., Codas, G., López Humada, H., & Martínez Cañete, U. (2019). Influencia del sexo, edad y cultura en las estrategias de afrontamiento de adolescentes paraguayos y mexicanos. *Universitas Psychologica, 18* (1), 1–13. https://doi.org/10.11144/Javeriana.upsy18-1.isec. *Please cite the original version of the article in Spanish.*

N. Coppari (✉) · L. Bagnoli · G. Codas · H. López Humada · Ú. Martínez Cañete
Universidad Católica Nuestra Señora de la Asunción, Asunción, Paraguay
e-mail: norma@tigo.com.py

B. Barcelata
Universidad Nacional Autónoma de México, México, Mexico



W. López-López et al. (eds.), *Trends in Latin American Psychology*,
https://doi.org/10.1007/978-3-031-87554-0_14

are related to emotional and behavioral problems (Barcelata et al., 2016; Frydenberg et al., 2009).

Another model (Seiffge-Krenke, 2011) proposes that coping can be basically of two types: functional or nonfunctional, and can involve various forms of reactions. Some may be centered on emotion, while others more on behavior (Eisenberg et al., 1997; Muñoz et al., 2015). The criticism of this coping dichotomy is driven by the hypothesis that, among young people affected by trauma, certain strategies, such as distraction and avoidance that were originally conceptualized as maladaptive, can be positive adaptations in some cultures and contexts (Cherewick et al., 2016).

Frydenberg et al. (2008) distinguish between styles and coping strategies. Styles refer to the personal predisposition to react in a certain way to a situation, and the strategy implies the specific action used to confront said problem. There are three types of coping styles: productive, nonproductive, and other-referenced. The first one is made up of strategies aimed at reducing stress or achieving positive results, such as problem-solving, focusing on the positive, investing in close friends, physical recreation, relaxing diversions, seeking belonging, or striving to solve the problem and succeed. On the contrary, nonproductive coping involves the tendency to use strategies whose results can be negative, as they do not contribute to reducing stress, such as ignoring the problem, keeping it to oneself, not coping, self-blaming, inappropriately reducing tension, deluding oneself, or worrying. Lastly, coping can be in reference to other individuals and constitute strategies such as seeking professional support, social support, spiritual support, or resorting to social action.

The literature shows that coping forms can vary during adolescence based on some personal variables, in particular, sex and age (Frydenberg & Lewis, 2000a; Seiffge-Krenke, 2011; Seiffge-Krenke et al., 2009), due to their association with developmental changes and also contextual factors, such as culture (Lee & Mason, 2014; Samper et al., 2008; Urzúa et al., 2017). Regarding sex, it is reported that girls, in general, tend to use a wider variety of coping strategies, with the most used ones being those related to seeking social support, while boys report the use of some distancing strategies from the problem, such as seeking relaxing activities or distracting themselves (Barcelata et al., 2016; Connor-Smith & Compas, 2004; Frydenberg & Lewis, 2000b; Seiffge-Krenke, 2000). In another study with Uruguayan university students, Scafarelli and García (2010) found that women use strategies such as seeking relaxing diversions or belonging, but also worrying and seeking social support, significantly and more than men, which coincides with previous studies (Morales et al., 2012).

Regarding age or age range, there are some data that indicate that younger or younger-aged adolescents tend to use more avoidance or disengagement strategies, centered on emotion (Eisenberg et al., 1997) and have a smaller repertoire of strategies compared to older adolescents, among other reasons, because these already have more experiences that have allowed them to try more actions and see the result (Seiffge-Krenke, 2011; Seiffge-Krenke et al., 2009; Sittichai & Smith, 2018). However, other studies report that older adolescents present less-effective strategies than those of younger age (Barcelata et al., 2014; Clemente, 2015).

In relation to the influence of context or culture on coping patterns, Frydenberg et al. (2003) show evidence in this regard, by conducting a cross-cultural research with Australian, German, Colombian, and Palestinian adolescents, in which they reported significant differences in the three coping styles (productive, nonproductive, and other-referenced), among the different groups. Palestinians and Colombians presented more nonproductive coping than adolescents from other countries, however, they did not find a significant influence between sex and culture. Similar data were found in all coping strategies, except in self-blaming, in which they also did not find an interaction effect between sex and culture. In another multicultural research conducted by Samper et al. (2008), in which adolescents from Spain, Western Europe, Eastern Europe, Arab Countries, and Latin America participated, it was found that coping responses vary according to the level of aggressiveness, sex, and culture. Aggressive people use more unproductive coping than nonaggressive ones. Women use to a greater extent coping in relation to others, and men make greater use of physical distraction, ignoring the problem, seeking professional support, and social action. Likewise, differences are pointed out in Latin American participants, who tend to not confront the problem or they focus on seeking spiritual support, compared to Spaniards who present strategies of a coping style in relation to others.

Lastly, Barcelata et al. (2014) compared coping styles in early and middle adolescents from Mexico and Paraguay, finding differences with respect to sex, age, and culture, finding significant differences in the three coping styles. Paraguayan adolescents scored higher in nonproductive coping and coping with reference to others, while Mexicans scored higher in productive coping. Regarding sex differences, men scored significantly higher in productive coping strategies, while women did so in unproductive strategies, such as worrying, reducing tension, self-blaming, and noncoping. In terms of age differences, middle adolescents scored higher in seeking social support, problem-solving, self-blaming, and worrying, while early adolescents did so in ignoring the problem and seeking physical recreation. Also, it was found that middle adolescents scored significantly higher in productive coping.

This brief state of the art highlights the importance of analyzing coping in adolescence, for its potential protective role even in situations of significant stress and its association with the mental health of adolescents (Rutter, 2007). The simultaneous study of the influence of personal variables such as sex and age and other contextual ones on coping at this stage of the life cycle, is relevant, not only because it is a stage characterized by rapid changes, but because it would allow obtaining some references from which concrete mental health actions can be proposed, taking into account these factors (Seiffge-Krenke et al., 2009). It is of particular interest to conduct more research with Latin American population, since, although there are various studies on the subject, the results cannot be generalized, given the diversity of contexts and conditions in which adolescents live throughout Latin America, whose mental health epidemiological profiles reflect that they represent a vulnerable and priority group, in terms of public mental health policies. The relevance of knowing how Paraguayan and Mexican adolescents cope with challenges in different areas of their life (e.g., new social roles, greater autonomy and independence from the family nucleus, greater academic demand, among others) according to sex, age or age group, and cultural context is raised. For this reason, the objective of this study has been to analyze the styles and strategies of coping based on sex and age, in two cultural contexts such as Paraguay and Mexico. It is expected that the findings will provide evidence that will allow the development of universal and selective programs, to promote productive coping styles and strategies that increase the resilient potential in both Paraguayan and Mexican adolescents, in the family, school, community, and broader social contexts.

## Method

It is a cross-sectional field study, ex post facto, of a comparative type with two independent samples and with a 2 × 2 × 2 design: sex * age * culture (Kerlinger & Lee, 2001), as it explores two levels of three variables: sex (male-female), age (13–15 years and 16–18 years) and culture (Paraguay and Mexico). According to previous evidence, it is expected that there will be a difference in the styles and strategies of coping by these three variables, resulting from the countries of origin of the adolescents (Paraguay or Mexico). Also, it is expected that there will be an effect in the combination of at least two variables, such as sex and age, sex and culture, age and culture or the three variables, in coping. The mentioned design was chosen, because it seeks to compare groups that were not previously randomly assigned, but were previously established naturally (McGuigan, 1996).

### *Participants*

The sample was selected in a nonprobabilistic manner, for convenience, and was comprised of 2278 adolescent students, Paraguayans ($N$ = 1188) and Mexicans ($N$ = 1090); males (Py = 538; Mex = 540), females (Py = 650; Mex = 550), aged 13–18 years ($M_{age}$ = 15.31; $SD$ = 1.48), from basic education schools (BEB) and middle schools (MEM) in the city of Asuncion, and secondary and high schools in Mexico City, capitals of Paraguay and Mexico, respectively.

### *Instruments*

To assess coping, the Coping Scale for Adolescents ([ACS]; Frydenberg & Lewis, 2000b), adapted for Mexican adolescents (Barcelata & Molina, 2013 in Molina, 2013) and also tested with Paraguayan adolescents (Barcelata et al., 2014), was applied, which obtained adequate internal consistency indicators (total alpha = 0.874). It is a scale composed of 79 Likert-type items, of five points ranging from 1 = *it never happens to me*, to 5 = *very frequently*, which assesses 18 first-order factors called coping strategies (alphas per factor from 0.642 to 0.884), integrated into three second-order factors or coping styles. Productive coping (total alpha = 0.642), which promotes actions in search of a solution or dealing with the source of stress, such as focusing on the problem solution, focusing on the positive, investing in close friends, physical recreation, seeking relaxing activities, seeking belonging and working hard and achievement. Nonproductive coping (total alpha = 0.788) includes avoidant strategies that involve distancing from the stressor and not solving, such as ignoring the problem, keeping it to oneself, not coping, self-blaming, reducing tension, worrying and magical thinking. Coping with reference to others (total alpha = 0.636) involves other people in problem solving, such as seeking professional help, social support and spiritual support, as well as social actions (Frydenberg et al., 2003).

For the collection of sociodemographic data, the sociodemographic card of the adolescent and his family (Barcelata, 2014) was used, which consists of 16 multiple-choice items (ordinal alpha = 0.0676), which explores data such as age, sex, education of the adolescent and their parents, as well as some characteristics of the housing.

## *Procedure*

Authorization was requested from the directors of the institutions for access to the last three grades of basic education and middle education in the case of Paraguay and middle education (secondary level) and higher middle education (high school level) in Mexico. The Mexican secondary level is equivalent to the last three grades of basic education (seventh, eighth, and 9th) of Paraguay, as well as the first, second, and third of high school in Mexico is with the grades first, second, and third of Paraguayan middle education. According to the ethical principles recommended by the American Psychological Association (APA, 2013), prior to the application in both countries, informed consents were obtained from the authorities of the schools and parents, as well as informed consent from the adolescent students. The application of instruments was carried out by group during their normal activity schedules, which the adolescents voluntarily attended, and they were asked to answer anonymously, guaranteeing the confidentiality of the results. The data collection was carried out within the school period of each country, from September 2016 to February 2017, considering the availability according to the calendars of each country. Trained auxiliary researchers collaborated under the supervision of the responsible researchers in both countries.

## *Analysis Plan*

Descriptive analyses were carried out, so frequency and central tendency measures were obtained to characterize the samples in terms of sociodemographic variables and to describe the study variables. According to the 2 × 2 × 2 design, a MANOVA was carried out to evaluate the possible main effects of sex (male-female), age or age group (13–15 years to 16–18 years), and according to culture or cultural context (Paraguay and Mexico), on coping styles and strategies separately, as well as the possible interaction effects between these factors: sex, age; sex, culture; age, culture; sex, age, culture, on coping styles and strategies. Prior to the multivariate analyses, normality analyses of the variables were carried out using the Kolmogorov-Smirnov indices as indicators. The analyses were carried out with SPSS 15.

## Results

The basic sociodemographic data according to sex, age, and cultural context (Table 1) allow us to observe that the samples, in general, are equivalent in terms of sex and age group. In both countries, about half of the participants were men and the other half women, although with a relatively higher number of Paraguayan women. Likewise, more adolescents from 13 to 15 years participated in both samples, although with a slightly higher number in the Mexican sample. A larger proportion of the total sample belonged to EEB in both countries, although comparatively by country, there were more EEB adolescents in Paraguay; however, it is striking that a higher percentage of students from Mexico were in EM.

**Table 1** Distribution of sociodemographic variables by country sample and of the total sample

| | Paraguay $n = 1188$ | | Mexico $n = 1090$ | | $N = 2278$ | |
|---|---|---|---|---|---|---|
| Variables | *f* | % | *f* | % | *f* | % |
| *Sex* | | | | | | |
| Male | 538 | 45.3 | 540 | 49.5 | 1078 | 47.3 |
| Female | 650 | 54.7 | 550 | 50.5 | 1200 | 52.7 |
| *Age group* | | | | | | |
| 13–15 years | 624 | 52.5 | 719 | 66 | 1343 | 58.9 |
| 16–18 years | 564 | 47.5 | 371 | 34 | 935 | 41 |
| *Marital status* | | | | | | |
| Single | 1188 | 100 | 1064 | 97.6 | 2252 | 98.8 |
| *Education* | | | | | | |
| Secondary/basic | 868 | 73.1 | 642 | 58.9 | 1510 | 66.3 |
| High school/middle | 320 | 26.9 | 448 | 41.1 | 768 | 33.7 |

*Note.* Secondary level in Mexico corresponds to the three grades of the third cycle of basic school education in Paraguay, just as high school is equivalent to the last cycle of middle education, respectively

Table 2 presents the age distribution of both countries, and it is observed that in the sample from Mexico, there is a higher proportion of students aged in the group of 13–15, specifically more than 14 years ($M_{age}$ = 14.1; *SD* = 1.45), than among those from Paraguay, where the overall proportion by age range was more or less the same, although it is observed that the highest percentage is of teenagers aged 15 ($M_{age}$ = 15.36; *SD* = 1.36). To compare the coping styles and strategies used by the Paraguayan and Mexican adolescents and analyze the influence of sex, age, and culture on the evaluated variables, preliminary analyses of the normality of the distribution were carried out; the data of which are shown in Table 2.

Multivariate analyses were also performed by styles and strategies, separately, once the normality indicators were tested, whose D values (between 0.879 and 0.975) in all variables showed probabilities of alpha greater than 0.05 (from 0.63 to 0.89), which indicated the pertinence of performing these analyses with a MANOVA. Table 3 presents the means and standard deviations of coping styles, by sex, age, and country, which indicate a greater tendency to use productive coping in both samples, especially older men, particularly Mexicans. On the other hand, nonproductive coping reveals values around the theoretical mean (2.5) in both samples; however, higher scores are appreciated in the Paraguayan sample, specifically in older women. Coping with reference to others also indicates moderate means in the Paraguayan and Mexican sample, although it is the older Paraguayan men and women who present the highest values.

With respect to coping strategies, Table 4 of descriptive data shows, in detail, that in both samples older females tend to use a higher number of strategies in general, especially Paraguayan girls. However, the means show that Mexican adolescents tend to use more productive style strategies than Paraguayan adolescents,

**Table 2** Distribution of adolescents by country according to age

| Country | 13 years *f* (%) | 14 years *f* (%) | 15 years *f* (%) | 16 years *f* (%) | 17 years *f* (%) | 18 years *f* (%) | Total |
|---|---|---|---|---|---|---|---|
| Paraguay | 140 (11.8) | 174 (14.6) | 310 (26.1) | 294 (24.7) | 219 (18.4) | 51 (4.3) | 1188 |
| Mexico | 235 (21.6) | 313 (28.7) | 172 (15.8) | 125 (11.5) | 173 (15.9) | 72 (6.6) | 1090 |
| Total | 375 (16.5) | 487 (21.4) | 482 (21.2) | 419 (18.4) | 392 (17.2) | 123 (5.4) | 2278 |

**Table 3** Means and standard deviation of coping styles according to sex, age, and culture

| | Country (*N*) | Paraguay (1188) | | | | Mexico (1090) | | | |
|---|---|---|---|---|---|---|---|---|---|
| | Sex (*n*) | Men (538) | | Women (650) | | Men (540) | | Women (550) | |
| Coping Styles | Age (*n*) | 13–15 (296) | 16–18 (242) | 13–15 (328) | 16–18 (322) | 13–15 (378) | 16–18 (162) | 13–15 (341) | 16–18 (209) |
| Productive | *M* | 3.17 | 3.26 | 3.11 | 3.21 | 3.18 | 3.35 | 3.2 | 3.31 |
| | *SD* | 0.59 | 0.53 | 0.66 | 0.62 | 0.6 | 0.56 | 0.57 | 0.5 |
| Nonproductive | *M* | 2.43 | 2.47 | 2.53 | 2.61 | 2.4 | 2.42 | 2.44 | 2.44 |
| | *SD* | 0.59 | 0.55 | 0.59 | 0.53 | 0.49 | 0.49 | 0.47 | 0.46 |
| In reference to others | *M* | 2.52 | 2.61 | 2.57 | 2.61 | 2.45 | 2.49 | 2.44 | 2.43 |
| | *SD* | 0.7 | 0.67 | 0.66 | 0.62 | 0.59 | 0.62 | 0.59 | 0.53 |

**Table 4** Means and standard deviations of coping strategies, sex, age, and culture

| | | Paraguay $N = 1188$ | | | | Mexico $N = 1090$ | | | |
|---|---|---|---|---|---|---|---|---|---|
| | | Men $n = 538$ | | Women $n = 650$ | | Men $n = 540$ | | Women $n = 550$ | |
| | | 13–15 $n = 296$ | 16–18 $n = 242$ | 13–15 $n = 328$ | 16–18 $n = 322$ | 13–15 $n = 378$ | 16–18 $n = 162$ | 13–15 $n = 341$ | 16–18 $n = 209$ |
| Coping styles | Coping strategies | Mean (SD) | Mean (SD) | Mean (SD) | Mean (SD) | Mean (SD) | Mean (SD) | Mean (SD) | Mean (SD) |
| Productive coping | Problem solving | 2.98 (0.93) | 3.17 (0.87) | 3.04 (0.91) | 3.18 (0.88) | 3.28 (0.83) | 3.52 (0.76) | 3.32 (0.83) | 3.6 (0.68) |
| | Focus on the positive | 3.32 (0.93) | 3.46 (0.88) | 3.46 (0.96) | 3.69 (0.82) | 3.15 (0.83) | 3.29 (0.8) | 3.16 (0.83) | 3.34 (0.77) |
| | Close friends | 2.84 (0.87) | 2.97 (0.85) | 2.68 (0.9) | 2.68 (0.88) | 2.98 (0.86) | 3.09 (0.79) | 2.96 (0.86) | 3.11 (0.86) |
| | Physical distraction | 3.41 (1.42) | 3.42 (0.98) | 2.96 (1.06) | 2.92 (1.07) | 3.05 (1.09) | 3.28 (1.02) | 3.09 (1.05) | 2.79 (0.98) |
| | Relaxing fun | 3.14 (0.96) | 3.26 (0.92) | 2.99 (0.89) | 3.14 (0.86) | 3.23 (0.85) | 3.47 (0.77) | 3.26 (0.82) | 3.43 (0.8) |
| | Seek belonging | 3.13 (0.81) | 3.19 (0.82) | 3.23 (0.83) | 3.32 (0.77) | 3.1 (0.77) | 3.2 (0.71) | 3.15 (0.77) | 3.2 (0.72) |
| | Work hard and succeed | 3.41 (0.81) | 3.34 (0.82) | 3.39 (0.81) | 3.54 (0.75) | 3.49 (0.78) | 3.62 (0.73) | 3.47 (0.78) | 3.69 (0.67) |

| | | | | | | | | | |
|---|---|---|---|---|---|---|---|---|---|
| Nonproductive coping | Ignore the problem | 2.23 (0.89) | 2.13 (0.81) | 1.98 (0.84) | 1.97 (0.86) | 2.04 (0.78) | 1.90 (0.66) | 1.90 (0.74) | 1.75 (0.71) |
| | Keeping it to yourself | 2.47 (0.96) | 2.51 (0.89) | 2.58 (0.98) | 2.71 (0.91) | 2.55 (0.81) | 2.57 (0.86) | 2.57 (0.89) | 2.51 (0.98) |
| | Not coping | 1.97 (0.69) | 2.06 (0.65) | 2.14 (0.72) | 2.19 (0.7) | 1.98 (0.61) | 1.93 (0.61) | 2.08 (0.65) | 1.95 (0.63) |
| | Self-blame | 2.34 (0.9) | 2.47 (0.95) | 2.55 (1.09) | 2.57 (0.95) | 2.38 (0.92) | 2.38 (0.79) | 2.44 (0.88) | 2.5 (0.83) |
| | Tension reduction | 1.82 (0.75) | 1.77 (0.76) | 2.02 (0.71) | 2.06 (0.7) | 1.93 (0.67) | 1.99 (0.73) | 2.08 (0.7) | 2.02 (0.68) |
| | Getting your hopes up | 2.96 (0.83) | 3 (0.76) | 3.06 (0.85) | 3.14 (0.82) | 2.64 (0.78) | 2.64 (0.78) | 2.71 (0.71) | 2.68 (0.73) |
| | Worry | 3.24 (0.9) | 3.37 (0.85) | 3.39 (0.85) | 3.63 (0.81) | 3.32 (0.89) | 3.51 (0.66) | 3.33 (0.75) | 3.65 (0.63) |
| Reference to others | Seek professional help | 2.51 (1.07) | 2.61 (1) | 2.44 (1.03) | 2.48 (0.99) | 2.63 (0.95) | 2.74 (0.98) | 2.61 (0.99) | 2.56 (0.87) |
| | Social support | 2.76 (0.91) | 2.83 (0.92) | 2.98 (0.91) | 3.05 (0.92) | 2.93 (0.88) | 3.12 (0.86) | 3.07 (0.85) | 3.33 (0.89) |
| | Spiritual support | 2.98 (0.93) | 3.11 (0.89) | 3.16 (0.84) | 3.21 (0.83) | 2.32 (0.78) | 2.19 (0.71) | 2.23 (0.77) | 2.2 (0.77) |

specifically in solving problems and investing in close friends, with higher scores in older women, as well as in relaxing fun and striving and succeeding, with higher values in men in the first type of strategy and in both older men and women in the last strategy. However, the older Paraguayan teenagers present the highest scores in focusing on the positive. On the contrary, Paraguayan teenagers present the highest values in several nonproductive strategies, with a greater tendency of women to keep it to themselves, not confront, self-blame, and delude themselves, although like Mexican women they also worry. The data indicate that younger Paraguayan men tend to ignore the problem.

Finally, Table 5 presents the estimated values, from which it can be affirmed whether or not the effects of sex, age, and culture on coping styles and strategies were significant.

Multivariate contrasts were analyzed to evaluate the main and interaction effects with statistical significance of sex, age, and culture on coping styles and strategies. The data show that the general model for age was significant ($F_{Roy} = 7.263$; $p = 0.001$; $\eta^2 = 0.005$), as well as for culture ($F_{Roy} = 28.519$; $p < 0.001$; $\eta^2 = 0.039$), indicating that they have a main effect on coping styles, although the model for sex was not statistically significant ($F_{Roy} = 0.571$; $p = 0.634$). However, an interaction effect of sex and culture was observed ($F_{Roy} = 3.061$; $p = 0.027$; $\eta^2 = 0.004$) in coping styles. Regarding the general models of coping strategies, it is observed that age ($F_{Roy} = 4.833$; $p < 0.001$; $\eta^2 = 0.024$) and culture ($F_{Roy} = 61.441$; $p < 0.001$; $\eta^2 = 0.035$) have a main effect, but there are also interaction effects of sex and age ($F_{Roy} = 1.827$; $p = 0.018$; $\eta^2 = 0.018$), of sex and culture ($F_{Roy} = 2.969$; $p < 0.001$ $\eta^2 = 0.025$), as well as of age and culture ($F_{Roy} = 1.912$; $p = 0.012$; $\eta^2 = 0.016$), even though the model for sex in the strategies was also not significant. It is observed that the major effects are given by culture. Roy's largest root was chosen based on possible collinearity (Rencher, 2003), although all the other statistics (Pillai-Bartlett, Wilks, and the *F* of Hotelling) yielded the same value *F* and levels of significance, as well as eta values, with respect to the multivariate contrasts.

On the other hand, the estimators of the intersubject contrasts, for each style and coping strategies (Table 5), observed main effects of culture in all coping styles and in the majority of strategies, while age has an effect on the productive coping, which indicates that Mexican adolescents tend to use more productive strategies than Paraguayans, as well as older adolescents from both countries (Table 3). No statistically significant effects due to sex were found. On the other hand, statistically significant values were found in eight of the strategies due to culture, five of them productive, such as solving problems, striving and succeeding, investing in close friends, focusing on the positive, and seeking relaxing diversions; there is a greater tendency of Mexican adolescents to use this type of strategies except in focusing on the positive, which showed an interaction effect between age, indicating that the older adolescents are the ones who use it the most (Table 3). The nonproductive strategies that showed statistically significant effects were worrying, ignoring the problem, daydreaming, and noncoping, which are the most used by Paraguayan adolescents. The strategies that involve seeking social support and spiritual support, typical of coping with reference to others, are the most used in Paraguayans,

**Table 5** Main effects of sex, age, and culture interaction on coping styles and strategies

| Coping Styles and Strategies | Sex $F(\eta^2)$ | Age $F(\eta^2)$ | Culture $F(\eta^2)$ | Sex*Age $F(\eta^2)$ | Sex* Culture $F(\eta^2)$ | Age* Culture* $F(\eta^2)$ | Sex* Age* Culture $F(\eta^2)$ |
|---|---|---|---|---|---|---|---|
| Productive coping | 0.007 (0) | 9.194*** (0.009) | 7.216** (0.007) | 0.259 (0) | 0.66 (0) | 0.607 (0) | 0.622 (0) |
| Nonproductive coping | 1.52 (0.001) | 0.804 (0) | 12.117** (0.011) | 0.132 (0) | 3.126 (0) | 1.474 (0) | 0.323 (0) |
| With reference to others | 0.006 (0) | 1.459 (0) | 17.948*** (0.015) | 0.418 (0.001) | 1.175 (0) | 0.579 (0) | 0.233 (0) |
| Social support | 2.82 (0.001) | 6.57*** (0.006) | 24.48*** (0.12) | 0.17 (0.001) | 0.25 (0) | 3.51 (0.001) | 0.22 (0) |
| Problem solving | 0.79 (0) | 15.86*** (0.006) | 72.77*** (0.033) | 0.14 (0.001) | 0.09 (0) | 1.29 (0) | 0.19 (0) |
| Work hard and succeed | 0.2 (0.001) | 5.39*** (0.015) | 17.82*** (0.089) | 2.13 (0.001) | 0.75 (0) | 3.36 (0.002) | 0.71 (0) |
| Worry | 2.6 | 17.05*** (0.016) | 1.42 (0.001) | 1.5 (0.001) | 2.7 (0.001) | 0.72 (0) | 0.01 (0) |
| Close friends | 0.25 (0) | 3.72** (0.004) | 36.412*** (0.018) | 0.18 (0) | 7.56*** (0.012) | 0.56 (0) | 1.02 (0) |
| Seek belonging | 1.69 (0.001) | 2.17 (0.002) | 2.56 (0.001) | 0.35 (0.001) | 1.68 (0) | 0.189 (0) | 0.38 (0) |
| Getting your hopes up | 1.68 (0.001) | 0.2 (0.001) | 104.7*** (0.047) | 0.26 (0) | 0.81 (0) | 1.12 (0) | 0.22 (0) |
| Not coping | 1.9 (0.001) | 0.22 (0.001) | 10.83*** (0.006) | 0.61 (0.001) | 2.89 (0) | 7.29*** (0.005) | 0.06 (0) |
| Tension reduction | 2.61 (0.001) | 0.07 (0.004) | 6.72*** (0.004) | 0.06 (0.001) | 4.96* (0.003) | 0.67 (0) | 2.6 (0.001) |
| Social action | 1.4 (0.001) | 1.1 (0.001) | 3.16 (0.001) | 2.54 (0.001) | 0.17 (0) | 3.21 (0.003) | 1.64 (0.001) |
| Ignore the problem | 0.15 (0.001) | 4.36** (0.002) | 23.29*** (0.022) | 0.46 (0) | 0.71 (0) | 1.43 (0) | 0.44 (0) |
| Self-blame | 0.26 (0.001) | 0.87 (0) | 1.72 (0.001) | 0.08 (0) | 0.73 (0) | 0.22 (0) | 0.9 (0) |
| Keeping it to yourself | 0.29 (0) | 0.28 (0) | 0.2 (0.001) | 0.06 (0) | 4.24* (0.003) | 1.62 (0) | 0.92 (0) |
| Spiritual support | 0.53 (0) | 0.09 (0) | 529.9*** (0.201) | 0.54 (0) | 5.83** (0.004) | 4.8* (0.003) | 1.18 (0.001) |
| Focus on the positive | 2.75 (0.001) | 9.49*** (0.009) | 37.78*** (0.018) | 0.84 (0) | 3.69 (0) | 13.312* (0.012) | 0.13 (0) |
| Professional help | 0.13 (0.001) | 1.59 (0.002) | 7.44*** (0.004) | 0.93 (0) | 0.45 (0) | 0.31 (0) | 0.31 (0) |
| Relaxing fun | 0.11 (0.001) | 9.45*** (0.009) | 28.38*** (0.014) | 0.06 (0) | 2.66 (0) | 0.66 (0) | 0.36 (0) |
| Physical distraction | 2.94 (0.001) | 0.43 (0.001) | 5.96** (0.003) | 4.16** (0.004) | 5.89** (0.004) | 0.31 (0) | 5.34 ** (0.003) |

*Note.* Design: Sex, Age, Culture. Intersection Sex*Culture; Age*Culture; Sex*Age; Sex*Age*Culture. $N = 2279$; * $p < 0.05$; ** $p < 0.01$; *** $p < 0.001$

especially by older girls. Interaction effects of sex and culture were observed in investing in close friends and physical distraction (productive strategies), with Mexican girls scoring higher in the first strategy, while boys scored higher in the second; as well as in tension reduction and keeping it to oneself (nonproductive strategies) with higher scores in Mexican women in the first strategy and Paraguayan women in the second type of strategy (Table 3). Finally, seeking spiritual support, the self-referential strategy had an effect of sex and culture, as well as age and culture, indicating that both Paraguayan women and older Mexican adolescents prefer it. However, no significant effects of sex alone were observed. Only physical distraction had an effect due to sex, age, and culture, with older Paraguayan men being the ones who use this coping strategy the most.

## Discussion and Conclusions

The research aimed to provide evidence on the coping styles and strategies of school-going adolescents, Paraguayans and Mexicans, through the analysis of the main effect and interaction of sex, age, and culture. No interaction effect was found between culture, age, sex, and coping. The results show an interaction effect between sex and culture; the interaction of culture and age occurred in the noncoping strategy and spiritual support. As for sex and age, interaction was observed only in the physical distraction strategy. The three evaluated variables—culture, sex, and age—interact jointly in physical distraction.

The results show that Paraguayan and Mexican adolescents differ significantly in their coping styles in risk and stress situations. This coincides with the findings of Frydenberg et al. (2003), Omar (2013), and those of Barcelata et al. (2014) that there seems to be a relevant influence of culture on the choice and use of certain coping skills. Mexicans present more productive styles (Verdugo-Lucero et al., 2013), while Paraguayans show higher average scores in nonproductive coping and with reference to others. This reveals greater fragility of Paraguayan adolescents in the face of stressors, which could be explained by a conformist, evasive, and conservative cultural environment (Veliz, 1970), when seeking to solve problems on their own, as well as scarce reinforcement for learning and application of resolutive alternatives. It should not be forgotten that until 1989 Paraguay lived under repressive dictatorship, where the right to think and decide was forbidden, and it was only possible to take refuge in religious beliefs to face difficulties. It is to be expected that the families of these young people still reproduce overprotective and authoritarian parenting styles. On this point, further research will need to be carried out in the future.

As for the age variable, it was observed that adolescents from 16 to 18 years old present significantly higher scores than those from 13 to 15 years old in productive coping styles and with reference to others; in contrast, those from 13 to 15 years old show higher scores in nonproductive coping styles. These results, although expected, as they would have a maturational explanation (Williams & McGillicuddy-De Lisi,

1999), contrast with what was reported in Barcelata et al. (2014) and Clemente (2015), where it was found that early adolescents obtained the highest scores in coping with reference to others and low scores were found in nonproductive strategies. This contradicts other results (Frydenberg & Lewis, 2000a), which indicate that it is unproductive coping that is used as age increases, but most of the evidence ultimately supports the idea that greater and better resources are acquired to deal with stress as the maturational process progresses in adolescence (Eisenberg et al., 1997; Williams & McGillicuddy-De Lisi, 1999).

An interaction effect was found between sex and culture, unlike what was reported by Frydenberg et al. (2003) and by Barcelata et al. (2014); thus, Mexican women present higher productive coping scores than Paraguayans, who score higher in unproductive coping and with reference to others, revealing greater vulnerability of the latter to stressful events. These results may respond to the cultural variables inherent in the idiosyncrasy and history of Paraguay, already mentioned. In a sample of older people, evident differences were observed depending on sex and culture (Lee & Mason, 2014); however, these could be due to the samples being less similar to those used in the present study.

Regarding coping strategies in general, and always in relation to the cultural factor, significant differences were observed by culture in almost all of them, except in social action, search for belonging, worrying, self-blaming, and keeping it to oneself, results similar to those found by Samper et al. (2008) and Barcelata et al. (2014). Also, significant differences were found by age in the strategies of solving problems, striving and succeeding, investing in close friends, focusing on the positive, seeking relaxing diversions, worrying, ignoring the problem, and seeking social support. No significant differences were observed by sex, contrary to what was reported in the studies by Scafarelli and García (2010), Samper et al. (2008), and Sanchez et al. (2013). These results contradict the idea that women use more productive strategies in relation to men (Morales et al., 2012; Morales & Moysén, 2015) and vice versa (Clemente, 2015). The tentative explanation could be given by the interaction mentioned above between culture and sex in coping styles; in this line, it is expected that the learning of coping strategies is subject to the gender roles differentially assigned by each culture. At the same time, these discrepancies, both in differences by age and by sex, differ from the results found by Barcelata et al. (2014) when comparing Paraguayan and Mexican adolescents in another sample that evaluated the same variables in association, evidencing the relevance of continuing to study them, even in interaction with other factors.

As with coping styles, results are reiterated that prove an interaction effect between culture and sex by coping strategies, such as investing in close friends, physical distraction, tension reduction, keeping it to oneself, and seeking spiritual support. These results coincide with those of Barcelata et al. (2014) regarding the tension reduction strategy; however, the effects of the other strategies were not found in that research, which, on the other hand, yielded interaction effects between others that were not found in the present.

The interaction of culture and age occurred in noncoping and spiritual support. As for sex and age, there was interaction only in the physical distraction strategy.

The three variables evaluated—culture, sex, and age—interact jointly in physical distraction. In all these cases, the results differ from what was reported by Barcelata et al. (2014).

Considering the context in which these studies are carried out, given by the line of macroresearch, it is expected that the results will contribute to the design and execution of risk prevention programs in the school and community environment, and the promotion of resilient coping patterns, considering the differential factors of age, sex, and cultural context. Above all, in the case of Mexico, it is important to strengthen the development of productive strategies in early adolescents aged 13–15 and with reference to others. In the case of Paraguay, it is necessary to promote productive coping and strengthen social support in both age groups of adolescents, especially early ones and in women. The learning of early coping skills for prevention, under the modality of training change agents in the community, as in the experiences of Prevented Adolescence Workshops (Coppari, 2013), with the own resources of the environment in sustainability, has a multiplier effect on the benefits and strengthens a healthy youth culture (Hetherington & Blechman, 2014).

There are still many aspects to continue investigating and improving, especially in the research design that, for the case, presents the limitation of a probabilistic, intentional sampling, with voluntary participation of adolescents, within public institutions that allow access, so the sample is not representative of other rural or less urbanized areas of Paraguay. Future studies should expand the scope, in order to generalize the results and have a more complete picture of the situation.

**Acknowledgments** Project 14-INV-424/PROCIENCIA/UC funded by CONACYT, Paraguay, Beneficiary Entity: Catholic University Our Lady of the Assumption.

## References

American Psychological Association. (2013). *Ethical principles of psychologists and code of conduct*. Autor.

Barcelata, B. (2014). *Cédula sociodemográfica del adolescente y su familia (Versión para investigación PAPIIT IN303714–3)*. Facultad de Estudios Superiores Zaragoza, Universidad Nacional Autónoma de México.

Barcelata, B., Coppari, N., & Márquez-Caraveo, M. E. (2014). Gender and age effects in coping: A comparison between Mexican and Paraguayan adolescents. In K. Kaniasty, K. A. Moore, S. Howard, & P. Buchwald (Eds.), *Stress and anxiety. Applications to social and environmental threats, psychological well-being, occupational challenges, and developmental psychology* (pp. 249–260). Logos-Verlag.

Barcelata, B., Luna, Q. Y., Lucio, E., & Durán, C. (2016). Personalidad y afrontamiento adolescente. Características de personalidad predictoras del afrontamiento en adolescentes de contextos marginados. *Acta Colombiana de Psicología, 19*(1), 197–210. https://doi.org/10.14718/ACP.2016.19.1.9

Castro, K., Planellas, I., & Kirchner, T. (2014). Predicción de conducta autodestructiva en adolescentes mediante tipologías de afrontamiento. *Universitas Psychologica, 13*(1), 1–22. https://doi.org/10.11144/Javeriana.UPSY13-1.pcaa

Cherewick, M., Doocy, S., Tol, W., Burnham, G., & Glass, N. (2016). Potentially traumatic events, coping strategies and associations with mental health and well-being measures among conflict-affected youth in Eastern Democratic Republic of Congo. *Global Health Research and Policy, 1*(8), 1–18. https://doi.org/10.1186/s41256-016-0007-6

Clemente, E. (2015). *Estrés, afrontamiento y bienestar psicológico en una muestra de adolescentes escolarizados (Tesis de licenciatura inédita).* Universidad de Salamanca. Recuperado de https://gredos.usal.es/jspui/handle/10366/126704

Connor-Smith, J., & Compas, B. (2004). Coping as a moderator of relation between reactivity to interpersonal stress, health status and internalizing problems. *Cognitive and Therapy Research, 28*(3), 347–368. https://doi.org/10.1023/B:COTR.0000031806.25021.d5

Coppari, N. (2013). Adolescencia prevenida: Empoderando en la promoción de la resiliencia en talleres de formación de monitores. In J. Gaxiola & J. Palomar (Eds.), *Estudios de resiliencia en América Latina* (Vol. 2, pp. 121–136). Pearson/Universidad de Sonora/Universidad Iberoamericana.

Eisenberg, N., Fabes, R. A., & Guthrie, I. K. (1997). Coping with stress: The roles of regulation and development. In S. A. Wolchik & I. N. Sandler (Eds.), *Issues in clinical child psychology. The handbook of children's coping: Linking theory and intervention* (pp. 41–70). Plenum Press.

Evans, L. D., Kouros, C., Frankel, S. A., McCauley, E., Diamond, G. S., Schloredt, K. A., & Garber, J. (2015). Longitudinal relations between stress and depressive symptoms in youth: Coping as a mediator. *Journal of Abnormal Child Psychology, 43*, 355–368. https://doi.org/10.1007/s10802-014-9906-5

Frydenberg, E., Care, E., Freeman, E., & Chan, E. (2009). Interrelationships between coping, school connectedness and wellbeing. *Australian Journal of Education, 53*(3), 261–276. Recuperado de https://research.acer.edu.au/aje/vol53/iss3/4

Frydenberg, E., Eacott, C., & Clark, N. (2008). From distress to success: Developing a coping language and programs for adolescents. *The Prevention Researcher, 15*(4), 8–13. (N.° de servicio de reproducción de documentos ERIC EJ823351).

Frydenberg, E., & Lewis, R. (2000a). Teaching coping to adolescents: When and to whom? *American Educational Research Journal, 37*(3), 727–745. https://doi.org/10.3102/00028312037003727

Frydenberg, E., & Lewis, R. (2000b). *ACS. Escalas de afrontamiento para adolescentes. Manual* (3rd ed.). TEA.

Frydenberg, E., Lewis, R., Kennedy, G., Ardila, R., Frindte, W., & Hannoun, R. (2003). Coping with concerns: An exploratory comparison of Australian, Colombian, German and Palestinian adolescents. *Journal of Youth and Adolescence, 32*(1), 59–66. https://doi.org/10.1023/A:1021084524139

Hetherington, E. M., & Blechman, E. A. (Eds.). (2014). *Stress, coping, and resiliency in children and families*. Psychology Press.

Kerlinger, F. N., & Lee, H. B. (2001). *Investigación del comportamiento: Métodos de investigación en ciencias sociales*. McGraw-Hill/Interamericana Editores S. A.

Lazarus, R., & Folkman, S. (1991). *Estrés y procesos cognitivos*. Ediciones Roca.

Lee, H., & Mason, D. J. (2014). Cultural and gender differences in coping strategies between Caucasian American and Korean American older people. *Journal of Cross-Cultural Gerontology, 29*(4), 429–446. https://doi.org/10.1007/s10823-014-9241-x

Manne, S., Myers-Virtue, S., Kashy, D., Ozga, M., Kissane, D., Heckman, C., et al. (2015). Resilience, positive coping, and quality of life among women newly diagnosed with gynecological cancers. *Cancer Nursing, 38*(5), 375–382. https://doi.org/10.1097/NCC.0000000000000215

McGuigan, F. J. (1996). *Psicología experimental. Métodos de investigación*. Prentice Hall.

Molina, G. (2013). *Análisis comparativo del afrontamiento de adolescentes y padres*. Tesis inédita de licenciatura, Universidad Nacional Autónoma de México.

Morales, B. G., & Moysén, A. (2015). Afrontamiento del estrés en adolescentes estudiantes de nivel medio superior. *Revista Digital de Investigación en Docencia Universitaria, 9*(1), 9–20. Recuperado de http://dialnet.unirioja.es/servlet/articulo?codigo=5156471

Morales, F. M., Trianes, M. V., & Miranda, J. (2012). Diferencias por sexo y edad en afrontamiento infantil del estrés cotidiano. *Electronic Journal of Research in Educational Psychology, 10*(26), 95–110. Recuperado de http://www.redalyc.org/articulo.oa?id=293123551006

Muñoz, S., Vega, Z., Berra, E., Nava, C., & Gómez, G. (2015). Asociación entre estrés, afrontamiento, emociones e IMC en adolescentes. *Revista Intercontinental de Psicología y Educación, 17*(1), 11–29. Recuperado de http://www.redalyc.org/articulo.oa?id=80242935002. ISSN 0187-7690

Omar, A. G. (2013). Predictores de resiliencia en jóvenes y adolescentes. In J. Gaxiola & J. Palomar (Eds.), *Estudios de resiliencia en América Latina* (Vol. 2, pp. 19–35). Pearson/Universidad de Sonora/Universidad Iberoamericana.

Rencher, A. (2003). *Methods of multivariate analysis*. John Wiley & Sons.

Rutter, M. (2007). Resilience, competency and coping. *Child Abuse & Neglect, 31*, 205–209. https://doi.org/10.1016/j.chiabu.2007.02.001

Samper, P., Tur, A. M., Mestre, V., & Cortés, M. T. (2008). Agresividad y afrontamiento en la adolescencia. Una perspectiva intercultural. *International Journal of Psychology and Psychological Therapy, 8*(3), 431–444. Recuperado de http://colpos.redalyc.org/articulo.oa?id=56080314

Sanchez, Y. M., Lambert, S. F., & Cooley-Strickland, M. (2013). Adverse life events, coping and internalizing and externalizing behaviors in urban African American youth. *Journal of Child and Family Studies, 22*(1), 38–47. https://doi.org/10.1007/s10826-012-9590-4

Scafarelli, L. M., & García, R. C. (2010). Estrategias de afrontamiento al estrés en una muestra de jóvenes universitarios uruguayos. *Ciencias Psicológicas, 4*(2), 165–175. Recuperado de http://www.scielo.edu.uy/pdf/cp/v4n2/v4n2a04.pdf

Seiffge-Krenke, I. (2000). Causal links between stressfull events, copying style and adolescent symptomatology. *Journal of Adolescence, 23*, 575–691. https://doi.org/10.1006/jado.2000.0352

Seiffge-Krenke, I. (2011). Coping with relationship stressors: A decade review. *Journal of Research Adolescence, 21*(1), 196–210. https://doi.org/10.1111/j.1532-7795.2010.00723.x

Seiffge-Krenke, I., Aunola, K., & Nurmi, J. E. (2009). Changes in stress perception and coping during adolescence: The role of situational and personal factors. *Child Development, 80*(1), 259–279. https://doi.org/10.1111/j.1467-8624.2008.01258.x

Simpson, D., Suarez, L., Cox, L., & Connolly, S. (2018). The role of coping strategies in understanding the relationship between parental support and psychological outcomes in anxious youth. *Child and Adolescent Social Work Journal, 35*(4), 407–421. https://doi.org/10.1007/s10560-018-0531-y

Sittichai, R., & Smith, P. (2018). El acoso y el ciberacoso en Tailandia: las estrategias de afrontamiento y la relación con la edad, el sexo, la religión, y la condición de víctima. *Journal of New Approaches in Educational Research, 7*(1), 24–30. Recuperado de https://www.learntechlib.org/p/182223/

Urzúa, A., Basabe, N., Pizarro, J. J., & Ferrer, R. (2017). Afrontamiento del estrés por aculturación: inmigrantes latinos en Chile. *Universitas Psychologica, 16*(5), 1–13. https://doi.org/10.11144/Javeriana.upsy16-5.aeai

Veliz, C. (1970). *El conformismo en América Latina*. Editorial Universitaria.

Verdugo-Lucero, J., Ponce de León-Pagaza, B., Guardado-Llamas, R., Meda-Lara, R., Uribe-Alvarado, J., & Guzmán-Muñiz, J. (2013). Estilos de afrontamiento al estrés y bienestar subjetivo en adolescentes y jóvenes. *Revista Latinoamericana de Ciencias Sociales, Niñez y Juventud, 11*(1), 79–91. Recuperado de http://www.redalyc.org/articulo.oa?id=77325885021

Wadsworth, M. E., Raviv, T., Compas, B. E., & Connor-Smith, J. K. (2005). Parent and adolescent responses to poverty related stress: Tests of mediated and moderated coping models. *Journal of Child and Family Studies, 14*(2), 283–298. https://doi.org/10.1007/s10826-005-5056-2

Williams, K., & McGillicuddy-De Lisi, A. (1999). Coping strategies in adolescents. *Journal of Applied Developmental Psychology, 20*(4), 537–549. https://doi.org/10.1016/S0193-3973(99)00025-8

# Implementation of the Psychological Intervention Program in Resilience for Informal Caregivers of Patients with Alzheimer's Dementia PIRCA

**Ara Mercedes Cerquera Córdoba, Daysy Katherine Pabón Poches, and Alexis Lorenzo Ruíz**

## Introduction

Alzheimer's disease is a degenerative disease with a progressive course most common in the elderly population (Romano et al., 2007). It is estimated that the number of people with dementia worldwide will be 65.7 million in 2030 and 115.4 million in 2050. In Colombia, by 2020, it is expected that 260,000 people over 60 years old will suffer from Alzheimer's disease (World Alzheimer Report, 2009). This disease triggers a situation of disability and dependence (Durán et al., 2010), causing the patient with dementia to require the help of others to be able to carry out daily life activities (Ruíz-Robledillo & Moya-Albiol, 2012). The family member who assumes the role of informal caregiver is described as a person who provides help in the domestic context (Aparicio et al., 2008; Lavretsky, 2005), generating in them a series of significant changes in social and psychological aspects, and other adjustments in their life (Achury et al., 2011; Espín, 2012).

Given the different consequences that assuming this role brings for the caregiver, intervention programs for them have begun to be created. The programs that have been used most frequently have been those of respite, self-help, psychoeducational,

*This chapter is the English translation of an article originally published in Spanish as*: Cerquera Córdoba, A., Pabón, D., & Ruíz, A. (2017). Implementación del programa de intervención psicológica en resiliencia para cuidadores informales de pacientes con demencia tipo Alzheimer PIRCA. *Universitas Psychologica, 16* (2), 1–12. https://doi.org/10.11144/Javeriana.upsy16-2.ipip. *Please cite the original version of the article in Spanish.*

A. M. Cerquera Córdoba (✉) · D. K. Pabón Poches
Universidad Pontificia Bolivariana, Medellín, Colombia
e-mail: ara.cerquera@upb.edu.co

A. L. Ruíz
Universidad de la Habana, La Habana, Cuba



W. López-López et al. (eds.), *Trends in Latin American Psychology*,
https://doi.org/10.1007/978-3-031-87554-0_15

and psychotherapeutic (Losada et al., 2007), although the literature reports other forms of intervention, such as self-help (Rabinovitz et al., 2006), individual and family (Mittelman, 2003; Mittelman et al., 2007), telephone support (Gallager-Thompson et al., 2007; Mittelman et al., 2007; Rabinovitz et al., 2006), psychoeducational interventions from nursing (Gerdner et al., 2002; Sánchez-Pascual et al., 2001), psychosocial interventions with relaxation techniques (Hosaka & Sugiyama, 2003), physical activity (Castro et al., 2002), and from the area of occupational therapy (Gitlin et al., 2008).

As for the results that these studies have generated, it has been evidenced through theoretical reviews that the interventions with the most significant effects have been the psychotherapeutic ones, especially those that have used the cognitive-behavioral approach (Losada et al., 2005; Zabalegui et al., 2008). The PIRCA program of cognitive-behavioral approach takes resilience as the center of intervention (Cerquera Córdoba & Pabón Poches, 2015), a psychological term defined as a positive personality trait that allows the individual's adaptation to threatening situations (Wagnild & Young, 1993); it includes the following elements: personal competence, which indicates self-confidence, independence, determination, invincibility, power, ingenuity, and perseverance; and acceptance of oneself and of life, which represents adaptability, balance, flexibility, and a stable life perspective and reflects acceptance of life and a feeling of peace, despite adversity (Salgado, 2005).

Taking into account the components of resilience and the results obtained in the study by Cerquera Córdoba and Pabón Poches (2015), in which resilience correlated positively with social support and coping strategies such as positive reappraisal and problem solving, and negatively with waiting, religion, and seeking professional support, the PIRCA program was designed. Based on these results, the implementation of the program is proposed to observe the changes presented in the informal caregivers of patients with Alzheimer's-type dementia after having participated in the program.

## Method

### *Design*

Experimental cross-sectional descriptive comparative, pretest/posttest type.

### *Participants*

This study involved the participation of 10 informal caregivers of patients with Alzheimer's-type dementia, participants in the resilience intervention program for caregivers, 9 women and 1 man, from the city of Bucaramanga, aged between 55 and 80 years, and who had been caring for their relative for at least 6 months, 8 h daily; Alzheimer's disease was within the three stages and their relative was mother, father, or wife/husband. The participants met the following inclusion criteria: not receiving remuneration for being a caregiver, nor having any type of formal training on the disease, living in the same home as the patient with Alzheimer's, and having been caring for them for at least 6 months, 8 h daily.

## *Procedure*

### Phase I: Selection of Instruments and Theoretical Review

This phase consisted of reviewing relevant literature to define key concepts of the project, choosing the most suitable instruments for the population, and subsequently contrasting results. Likewise, the Quality of Life in Old Age research group from the Universidad Pontificia Bolivariana—Bucaramanga, Colombia, final-year thesis students and young researchers from Colciencias were trained for the application of the planned tests and the semistructured interview.

### Phase II: Contact with the Sample

In this phase, the search for health institutions that work with older adults and more specifically with dementia began. Thus, the work proposal was presented to two institutions to subsequently access a database of patients with Alzheimer's. Once the database was created, caregivers were contacted to present the research and obtain informed consent in case of acceptance for participation in the study.

### Phase III: Pretest Application

Having established contact with the sample, it was verified that they met the inclusion criteria to finally arrange an appointment where they would receive a visit from the researchers, who would apply the pretest for the evaluation of the program.

### Phase IV: Execution of Intervention Program

An invitation was extended to 70 caregivers who were randomly selected for participation in the program. Of the total number of caregivers invited, 30 started and only 10 finished. This phase took place at the Family and Life Institute of the Universidad Pontificia Bolivariana—Bucaramanga, from February to April 2014. The implementation of the program was developed in ten sessions. The first session is of *presentation*; its objective is to establish the therapeutic contract and create expectations about the program. The second session, *this is me*, aims to improve the image one has of oneself by recognizing emotions and facilitating self-confidence. The third session, *accepting myself*, seeks to recognize through positive experiences the characteristics of a stable life. The fourth session, *social support*, seeks to identify the type of social support that the caregiver has to enhance personal balance. The fifth session, *this is how they see me*, aims to strengthen the caregiver's self-esteem by recognizing the qualities that others see in him. The sixth session, *wanting to do it and I achieved it*, aims to recognize perseverance and decision as developed personal competencies. The seventh, *what I would be capable of doing*, seeks to identify decision as an important characteristic of personal competence. The eighth session, *recognizing my rights and learning to ask for help*, seeks to identify the rights of the caregiver to improve his quality of life. The ninth session, *my motivational powers*, aims to inhibit undesirable actions, feelings, and beliefs so that the caregiver visualizes the appearance of achievements and objectives that lead him to develop personal resilience competencies. The tenth session, *closure*, evaluates the results of the intervention program.

#### Phase V: Evaluation of Results

After the execution of the intervention program, the process evaluation began with three self-made questionnaires and the post-test application, leading to the scoring of the tests and tabulation in the SPSS. 22 data system for the respective analysis.

### *Instrument*

#### Psychological Intervention Program for Informal Caregivers of Alzheimer's-Type Dementia Patients PIRCA (Cerquera Córdoba & Pabón Poches, 2015)

The PIRCA program, with a cognitive-behavioral approach, aims to carry out a psychological intervention in resilience for informal caregivers of Alzheimer's-type dementia patients. It consists of 10 sessions, each lasting approximately 90 min.

#### Wagnild and Young's Resilience Scale (1993)

The adapted Spanish version was taken from Novella (2002). It consists of 25 positively worded items with a Likert response system ranging from 1 to 7 points. It includes two dimensions: personal competence and acceptance of oneself and life. The scale's validity is 0.79, according to Cronbach's alpha. The higher the score, the higher the level of resilience both in the total scale and in its dimensions (Quiceno et al., 2011).

### Zarit Caregiver Burden Scale Adapted to Spanish by Martin et al. (1996)

It was designed to assess the subjective experience of overload felt by the primary caregiver of dementia patients. It is a self-administered instrument of 22 items that explores the negative effects on the caregiver in different areas of their life: physical health, mental health, social activities, and economic resources. Each question is evaluated using a Likert scale with 5 possible answers ranging from never to almost always, scoring between 1 and 5. The total score is the sum of all items, and the range, therefore, varies between 22 and 110. The internal consistency yields a Cronbach's alpha coefficient of 0.91. The reliability is 0.86.

### Modified Coping Strategies Scale (EEC-M)

Modified by Londoño et al. (2006). This scale proposes 69 items that represent different ways people cope with problems or stressful situations that arise in life. The subject must indicate the number that best indicates how common this behavior has been in stressful situations with the following values: 1 never, 2 almost never, 3 sometimes, 4 frequently, 5 almost always, 6 always. The internal consistency yields a Cronbach's alpha coefficient of 0.847.

### MOS Social Support Survey

Validated by Espíndola et al. (2005), Argentine version. The questionnaire focuses the analysis on the perception of help. It consists of 20 items with a Likert scale expressed in the following values: 1 never, 2 a few times, 3 sometimes, 4 most of the time, 5 always, with 0.919 of internal consistency according to Cronbach's Alpha.

## *Ethical Considerations*

For the realization of this research, the guidelines of Law 1090 of 2006, article 2, numeral 9, referring to research with humans and the respect for the dignity and well-being of the people who participate with full knowledge of the research, were taken into account. Likewise, what is indicated in article 50 was assumed, which states that research carried out by psychology professionals must be based on the ethical principles of respect and dignity and safeguard the well-being of the rights of the participants. Likewise, the research proposal was submitted for review by the ethics committee of the Universidad Pontificia Bolivariana—Bucaramanga.

## Results

In the following section, the process and result evaluation criteria in the implementation of the PIRCA resilience intervention program will be presented. For the process evaluation, three questionnaires were developed, a questionnaire that indicates the level of satisfaction that caregivers experience with the program in which they participated session by session. This questionnaire is developed with a Likert scale with response options where the maximum satisfaction had a rating with a maximum of five and a minimum of one for each item. The scores obtained in each category are observed, and the corresponding average for each factor per session is obtained (Table 1).

The second questionnaire evaluated the fulfillment and quality of the tasks assigned to the caregiver according to each session, taking into account two items: the first evaluated the performance of exercises and activities at home, and the second, the quality of the exercises and activities (Table 2).

The third questionnaire evaluated the caregiver's satisfaction with the intervention program through 17 items and a list of 11 incomplete sentences (Table 3).

For the evaluation of results, the posttest is applied, and the averages obtained with the pretest are compared.

In Table 4, it can be observed that the posttest scores decreased considerably, especially in state depression.

In Table 5, it is observed that the perception of material support decreased, considering that the caregivers when moving to the program required greater support from family members to care for the patient. Emotional support increased, indicating that participating in the program makes them perceive emotional support. The other MOS scale scores remained or increased minimally, thereby wanting to support the impact of psychological intervention on caregivers. In the Zarit test, a significant decrease is observed, showing the effectiveness of the program in reducing the burden, while in resilience there are no significant variations.

In Table 6, the changes referred to the posttest scores are observed, where significant variations in the strategies of seeking social support, emotional avoidance, expression of difficulty, and increasing cognitive avoidance are determined.

**Table 1** Evaluation of process criteria for program implementation and satisfaction

| Category | Level of satisfaction | | | | |
|---|---|---|---|---|---|
| Satisfaction with the theoretical content | 1 | 2 | 3 | 4 | 5 |
| Satisfaction with the practical content | 1 | 2 | 3 | 4 | 5 |
| Satisfaction with the therapists | 1 | 2 | 3 | 4 | 5 |
| Clarity of the information conveyed | 1 | 2 | 3 | 4 | 5 |
| Suitability of the exercises | 1 | 2 | 3 | 4 | 5 |
| Suitability of the materials | 1 | 2 | 3 | 4 | 5 |
| Meets expectations | 1 | 2 | 3 | 4 | 5 |
| Usefulness of what was learned | 1 | 2 | 3 | 4 | 5 |

**Table 2** Evaluation of process criteria by the therapist

| |
|---|
| **Criteria for Quantifying the Number of "Homework Tasks" Completed** |
| 0: The session exercises and homework tasks have not been completed |
| 1: Less than half of the tasks and exercises have been completed |
| 2: Half of the tasks and exercises have been completed |
| 3: More than half of the tasks and exercises have been completed |
| 4: All tasks and exercises have been completed |
| **Criteria for Quantifying the Quality of the "Registered" Task** |
| 0: The caregiver has not completed the task |
| 1: The caregiver has had difficulties completing the task (finding the right moment) |
| 2: The skills have been implemented but in a wrong way |
| 3: The skills have been implemented but adjustments are needed (not done every day) |
| 4: The skills have been implemented correctly |
| 5: The skills have been implemented correctly, and the caregiver makes observations or changes |
| 6: The skills have been implemented correctly and generalized to other situations or problems |

**Table 3** Satisfaction questionnaire with treatment

| | |
|---|---|
| 1. How would you rate the quality of the service you received?<br>a. Excellent<br>b. Good<br>c. Fair<br>d. Poor | 10. Did you receive useful knowledge for handling caregiver duties?<br>a. A lot<br>b. Quite a bit<br>c. A little<br>d. None |
| 2. To what extent has our program met your needs?<br>a. Completely<br>b. Generally<br>c. Partially<br>d. Not at all | 11. How often do you use the exercises taught in the program sessions?<br>a. Always<br>b. Almost always<br>c. Sometimes<br>d. Never |
| 3. If a friend needed similar help, would you recommend our program?<br>a. No<br>b. Probably not<br>c. Probably yes<br>d. Yes | 12. Your perception of the therapists is:<br>a. Excellent<br>b. Good<br>c. Fair<br>d. Poor |
| 4. To what extent are you satisfied with the type of help received?<br>a. Very much<br>b. A lot<br>c. Quite a bit<br>d. A little | 13. Did you complete the homework tasks from the intervention program?<br>a. Always<br>b. Almost always<br>c. Sometimes<br>d. Never |
| 5. Have the services you received helped you cope more effectively with your problems?<br>a. A lot<br>b. Quite a bit<br>c. A little<br>d. Not at all | 14. Have you been able to use the exercises and information received in the intervention program for other areas of your life beyond caregiver duties?<br>a. A lot<br>b. Quite a bit<br>c. A little<br>d. Not at all |

(continued)

**Table 3** (continued)

| | |
|---|---|
| 6. Was the information provided by the therapists clear?<br>a. Very much<br>b. Quite a bit<br>c. A little<br>d. Not at all | 15. Overall, to what extent are you satisfied with the service received?<br>a. A lot<br>b. Quite a bit<br>c. A little<br>d. Not at all |
| 7. Do you feel you adequately understood the information provided by the therapists?<br>a. Very much<br>b. Quite a bit<br>c. A little<br>d. Not at all | 16. Overall, to what extent are you satisfied with the service received?<br>a. A lot<br>b. Quite a bit<br>c. A little<br>d. Not at all |
| 8. Were the materials, content, and exercises used in the program adequate?<br>a. Very much<br>b. Quite a bit<br>c. A little<br>d. Not at all | 17. If you needed help again, would you return to our program?<br>a. No<br>b. Probably not<br>c. Probably yes<br>d. Yes |
| 9. Did the therapists have the necessary professionalism and skills to carry out the intervention program?<br>a. A lot<br>b. Quite a bit<br>c. A little<br>d. None | |
| **List of incomplete treatment evaluation phrases**<br>• The breathing practice has helped me with…<br>• The relaxation techniques help me to…<br>• Increasing pleasant activities has been…<br>• Identifying positive emotions has helped me to…<br>• The positive emotions I have experienced during the intervention treatment are…<br>• Throughout this treatment, I have learned…<br>• I would have liked to practice more…<br>• I think what has helped me the most has been…<br>• I can improve in…<br>• What I liked the most has been…<br>• What I liked the least has been… | |

**Table 4** Comparison of average depression

| Depression | | Direct score | Percentile | Direct score | Percentile | Direct score | Percentile |
|---|---|---|---|---|---|---|---|
| STATE | | Dysthymia | Dysthymia | Euthymia | Euthymia | Total | Total |
| | PRE | 6,1 | 4,7 | 8,9 | 18,9 | 15,3 | 23,2 |
| | POST | 5,9 | 5,0 | 7,5 | 8,6 | 12,8 | 11,2 |
| TRAIT | | Dysthymia | Dysthymia | Euthymia | Euthymia | Total | Total |
| | PRE | 6,1 | 3,4 | 7,6 | 8,2 | 13,9 | 8,7 |
| | POST | 5,6 | 4,4 | 6,8 | 6,8 | 12,1 | 6,7 |

**Table 5** Comparison of social support, burden and resilience averages

| Variable | PRE | POST |
|---|---|---|
| Emotional | 28,4 | 30,1 |
| Material Help | 15,6 | 14,4 |
| Social Interaction | 14,3 | 14,6 |
| Affective | 11,6 | 11,9 |
| Global | 71,8 | 71,0 |
| Zarit | 50,0 | 37,3 |
| Personal Competence | 104,2 | 102,9 |
| Self-Acceptance of Life | 46,9 | 46,4 |
| Resilience | 151,2 | 149,2 |

**Table 6** Coping strategies pretest and posttest

| Strategy | Problem-solving | Social support seeking | Waiting | Religion | Emotional avoidance | Professional support |
|---|---|---|---|---|---|---|
| PRE | 38,1 | 29,6 | 21,9 | 34,5 | 17,3 | 15,0 |
| POST | 38,3 | 23,9 | 21,7 | 24,5 | 15,9 | 14,9 |
| *Strategy* | *Aggressive reaction* | *Cognitive avoidance* | *Positive reevaluation* | *Expression of difficulty* | *Denial* | *Autonomy* |
| PRE | 8,8 | 13,8 | 21,6 | 9,1 | 7,5 | 5,4 |
| POST | 8,5 | 14,1 | 21,8 | 8,7 | 7,8 | 4,4 |

## Discussion and Conclusions

The intervention program addresses an important problem that affects a vulnerable population: the informal caregivers of Alzheimer's patients. According to Cerquera Córdoba and Pabón Poches (2015), this program was designed to be executed in 10 sessions, each of which had a specific purpose, with techniques suitable for that purpose and the adopted approach, as proposed by the authors of the program.

In the evaluation of the results of the PIRCA intervention program, it is found that caregivers show resilience in the application of the pre- and posttest; this is evident when the answers are in the average of 144.16 in total. In the subscales of self-acceptance and life, 45.70, and in personal competencies, 98.4. The data thrown are relevant insofar as to be a caregiver one must be resilient. This is confirmed by the literature in the definition of resilience, understood as "a stable trajectory of functioning healthy over time, as well as the ability to generate positive experiences and emotions" (Bonanno, 2004). For the studied sample, resilience measurements remained constant, indicating that this is a personality trait that determines the individual's peculiarities, coinciding with the explanation of the Model of psychobiological characteristics and molecular genetics of resilient adults, which confirms that positive emotions such as optimism and sense of humor, elements worked on from the intervention program, enable the regulation of autonomic activity and strengthen reward circuits, leading to resilient behavior (Quiceno & Vinaccia, 2010).

According to Saavedra and Villalta (2008), resilience is a personal trait cultivated throughout the subject's history, and possibly, it has been constituted as an early bond and is a condition for the development of a particular appropriation of life events. That is, what the subject has as a distinctive trait has been learned in relation to others, and being learned can change or is in a constant process of interpretation. In the case of caring for an Alzheimer's patient, an important situation in life, the caregiver must resort to resilience to be able to assume the caregiver role.

Regarding the results of depression, evaluated through the IDER scale, in the pretest, there was no evidence of depressive symptomatology, although state depression scores were higher than trait depression scores. In the posttest, it is noteworthy that both state and trait dysthymia increased, results consistent with the literature that states that depression is a difficult variable to intervene in informal caregivers since the symptomatology tends to increase due to the characteristics of the role (Espín, 2012). On the other hand, both trait and state euthymia decreased, which is not consistent with (Fernández-Lanzac & Crespo, 2011) who states that depression will increase as the patient's disease progresses. Considering the PIRCA program, it can be affirmed that resilient caregivers exclude depressive symptoms, so the program shows that it could influence this variable as long as depressive symptomatology is present.

Among other elements to highlight for having a direct relationship with the program's approach, it is worth mentioning those scores that increased in the coping strategies used by the subjects of the sample; among them is cognitive avoidance, defined as "a cognitive strategy in which the aim is to eliminate or neutralize thoughts valued as negative or disturbing through distraction or denial" (Londoño et al., 2006); problem-solving, described as "the sequence of actions aimed at solving the problem taking into account the opportune moment to analyze or intervene" (Londoño et al., 2006), according to the strategies implemented in the PIRCA program, allowed the subjects to identify those problems that were more complex to address and solve them at the opportune moments. This worked specifically in session No. 6, "wanting to do it and I did it." Other important results in relation to coping strategies is *the search for social support*, in which the scores decreased, with which it can be hypothesized that the subjects found a utility in the program and do not require the use of this strategy to the same extent as before. Likewise, the strategy of *waiting* decreased its score, which then determines that the subjects began to take an active position in front of the problem.

In relation to resilience, the strategy of *Positive Reevaluation* increased in its use. Londoño et al. (2006) define it as "a cognitive strategy that seeks to learn from difficulties by identifying the positive aspects of the problem, it is a strategy of optimism that contributes to tolerate the problem and generate thoughts that favor, when facing the situation." This relationship is important considering that one of the characteristics by which resilience is defined is the sense of humor and happiness (Bonanno, 2004). The search for professional support decreased; this behavioral strategy is in function of the search of professional resources to solve the problem or its consequences (Londoño et al., 2006). As for the use of this strategy, it is related to the tools provided in the program that facilitate the proper coping with the problem situation without requiring therapeutic help.

The strategy of religion decreased; the caregivers of the program sought other strategies different from those initially indicated. Prayer is considered a strategy to tolerate the problem or to generate solutions to it (Londoño et al., 2006). However, great precision must be taken when analyzing this data, as prayer is a different concept that people use today. It is also important to highlight the differences in the plurality of cults in today's society (Parker, 2008). The results of the overload variable indicate a decrease in the Zarit Caregiver Burden Scale, in which a lower score was obtained in the posttest, which indicates that the program significantly affects this variable. Group work with caregivers allowed the caregiving experience to be shared and that, according to the testimonies of each one of them, they did not feel that they alone had to face this situation.

It is worth noting that within coping strategies like other models, active coping is considered in the search for solutions and emotional control; in addition, cognitive flexibility, cognitive reevaluation, and acceptance are found as an achievement of resilient behaviors (Quiceno et al., 2011), characteristics found in the caregivers of the sample. As for the differences in means between the pre- and post-test, it should be noted that in most of the scores of the variables, the change is not greater, which is in agreement with Knight et al. (1993), Brodaty et al. (2003), Pinquart and Sörensen (2006), when referring to the effect size of interventions with caregivers is generally small and tends to be smaller in follow-up phases. The difficulty in obtaining positive effects through interventions does not mean that there have not been notable advances in research in the area, which is evident in the change in the scores of the variables depression state, euthymia state, overload, and coping strategies such as search for social support and religion in the PIRCA program.

Thus, there are data that allow us to conclude that not all interventions present the same degree of efficacy; those based on cognitive and/or behavioral models (Beck et al., 1979; Lewinsohn et al., 1978), of which there are adaptations to care (Knight et al., 2000; Losada et al., 2005), are the ones that allow greater benefits, especially when active participation is required by the caregivers (Gallagher-Thompson & Coon, 2007; Pinquart & Sörensen, 2006).

In the case of the PIRCA intervention program, the tasks that are assigned to the caregiver must be answered to corroborate personal involvement in the program. It is precisely these types of interventions that have gone from being classified, according to the criteria of the Division 12 of Clinical Psychology of the American Psychological Association (Chambless et al., 1996; Chambless & Hollon, 1998), as probably effective interventions (Gatz et al., 1998) to currently being considered as well-established or empirically validated interventions.

Regarding interventions with family or informal caregivers, there is agreement among several authors in concluding that psychoeducational or informative interventions have not been sufficient to improve the caregiver's quality of life (Espín, 2008; Losada et al., 2005) and that, on the contrary, the best way to intervene in this population is through psychological intervention (Losada et al., 2005; Orozco-Gómez et al., 2012; Zabalegui et al., 2008).

However, even when a psychological intervention like PIRCA is designed and implemented, and additionally, its effects are empirically verified, there may be limitations, such as the possibility that caregivers do not strictly attend the sessions.

This study started with 30 patients and ended with 10, which was the biggest obstacle to implementation; the caregivers generally do not have the availability of time and/or support to attend the sessions. The above opens new lines of research in respite programs for caregivers that are aimed at mitigating these limitations.

**Acknowledgments** Implementation of the PIRCA intervention program. Funding entity: General Directorate of Research, Universidad Pontificia Bolivariana—Bucaramanga, and COLCIENCIAS. Code: 090-0613-3100.

## Annex A

### *Assessment of Results: Satisfaction Questionnaire with the Treatment*

Please help us improve our intervention program for informal caregivers by answering some questions about the services you have received. We are interested in your honest opinions, whether they are positive or negative. Please answer all questions by marking the option that corresponds to your choice below each item.

| |
|---|
| 1. How would you rate the quality of the service you received?<br>a. Excellent b. Good c. Fair d. Poor |
| 2. To what extent has our program met your needs?<br>a. Completely b. Generally c. Partially d. Not at all |
| 3. If a friend needed similar help, would you recommend our program?<br>a. No b. Probably not c. Probably yes d. Yes |
| 4. To what extent are you satisfied with the type of help received?<br>a. Very much b. A lot c. Quite a bit d. A little |
| 5. Have the services you received helped you cope more effectively with your problems?<br>a. A lot b. Quite a bit c. A little d. Not at all |
| 6. Was the information provided by the therapists clear?<br>a. Very much b. Quite a bit c. A little d. Not at all |
| 7. Do you feel you adequately understood the information provided by the therapists?<br>a. Very much b. Quite a bit c. A little d. Not at all |
| 8. Were the materials, content, and exercises used in the program adequate?<br>a. Very much b. Quite a bit c. A little d. Not at all |
| 9. Did the therapists have the necessary professionalism and skills to carry out the intervention program?<br>a. A lot b. Quite a bit c. A little d. None |
| 10. Did you receive useful knowledge for handling caregiver duties?<br>a. A lot b. Quite a bit c. A little d. None |
| 11. How often do you use the exercises taught in the program sessions?<br>a. Always b. Almost always c. Sometimes d. Never |
| 12. Your perception of the therapists is:<br>a. Excellent b. Good c. Fair d. Poor |

| |
|---|
| 13. Did you complete the homework tasks from the intervention program?<br>a. Always b. Almost always c. Sometimes d. Never |
| 14. Have you been able to use the exercises and information received in the intervention program for other areas of your life beyond caregiver duties?<br>a. A lot b. Quite a bit c. A little d. Not at all |
| 15. Overall, to what extent are you satisfied with the service received?<br>a. A lot b. Quite a bit c. A little d. Not at all |
| 16. Overall, to what extent are you satisfied with the service received?<br>a. A lot b. Quite a bit c. A little d. Not at all |
| 17. If you needed help again, would you return to our program?<br>a. No b. Probably not c. Probably yes d. Yes |
| **Complete the following phrases:**<br>• The breathing practice has helped me with...<br>• The relaxation techniques help me to...<br>• Increasing pleasant activities has been...<br>• Identifying positive emotions has helped me to...<br>• The positive emotions I have experienced during the intervention treatment are...<br>• Throughout this treatment, I have learned...<br>• I would have liked to practice more...<br>• I think what has helped me the most has been...<br>• I can improve in...<br>• What I liked the most has been...<br>• What I liked the least has been...<br>Other observations: |

# References


Achury, D., Castaño, H., Gómez, L., & Guevara, N. (2011). Calidad de vida de los cuidadores de pacientes con enfermedades crónicas con parcial dependencia. *Investigación en Enfermeria: imagen y desarrollo, 13*(1), 27–46.

Aparicio, M., Díaz, J., Cuéllar, B., Fernández, M., & De Tena, A. (2008). *La Salud Física y Psicológica de las Personas Cuidadoras: Comparación entre Cuidadores Formales e Informales*. Tesis para optar el título de doctor, Universidad Complutense de Madrid.

Beck, A. T., Rush, J. A., & Shaw, B. F. (1979). *Cognitive therapy of depression*. Guilford Press.

Bonanno, G. (2004). Loss, trauma, and human resilience: Have we underestimated the human capacity to thrive after extremely aversive events? *American Psychologist, 59*(1), 20–28.

Brodaty, H., Green, A., & Koschera, A. (2003). Meta-analysis of psychosocial interventions for caregivers of people with dementia. *Journal of the American Geriatrics Society, 51*(5), 657–664.

Castro, C. M., Wilcox, S., O'Sullivan, P., Baumann, K., & King, A. C. (2002). An exercise program for women who are caring for relatives with dementia. *Psychosomatic Medicine, 64*(3), 458–468.

Cerquera Córdoba, A. M., & Pabón Poches, D. K. (2015). Modelo de intervención psicológica en resiliencia para cuidadores informales de pacientes con Alzheimer. *Diversitas: Perspectiva Psicológica, 11*(2), 181–192. https://doi.org/10.15332/s1794-9998.2015.0002.01

Chambless, D. L., & Hollon, S. D. (1998). Defining empirically supported therapies. *Journal of Consulting and Clinical Psychology, 66*(1), 7–18.

Chambless, D. L., Sanderson, W. C., Shoham, V., Bennett Johnson, S., & Pope, K. S. (1996). An update on empirically validated therapies. *The Clinical Psychologist, 49*(2), 5–18.

Durán, A., Valderrama, L., Uribe, A., González, A., & Molina, M. (2010). Enfermedad crónica en adultos mayores. *Revista Universitas Médica, 51*(1), 16–28.
Espín, A. (2008). Caracterización psicosocial de cuidadores informales de adultos mayores con demencia. *Revista Cubana salud Pública, 34*(3), 1–13.
Espín, A. (2012). Factores de riesgo de carga en cuidadores informales de adultos mayores con demencia. *Revista cubana de salud pública, 38*(3), 393–402.
Espíndola, R., Enrique, S., & Carmelo, H. (2005). Validación Argentina del cuestionario MOS de apoyo social percibido. *Psicodebate, 7*, 155–168.
Fernández-Lanzac, V., & Crespo, M. (2011). Resiliencia, personalidad resiliente y crecimiento en cuidadores de personas con demencia en el entorno familiar: Una revisión. *Clinica y salud, 22*(1), 21–40.
Gallager-Thompson, D., Gray, H., Tang, P., Pu, C., Leung, L., & Wang, P. (2007). Impact of in-home behavioral management versus telephone support to reduce depressive symptoms and perceived stress in Chinese caregivers: Results of a pilot study. *American Journal of Geriatric Psychiatry, 15*(5), 425–434.
Gallagher-Thompson, D., & Coon, D. W. (2007). Evidence-based psychological treatments for distress in family caregivers of older adults. *Psychology & Aging, 22*(1), 37–51. https://psycnet.apa.org/doi/10.1037/0882-7974.22.1.37
Gatz, M., Fiske, A., Fox, L. S., Kaskie, B., Kasl-Godley, J. E., McCallum, T. J., & Wetherell, J. L. (1998). Empirically validated psychological treatments for older adults. *Journal of Mental Health and Aging, 4*(1), 9–46.
Gerdner, L., Buckwalter, K., & Reed, D. (2002). Impact of a psychoeducational intervention on caregiver response to behavioral problems. *Nursing Research, 51*(6), 363–374.
Gitlin, L., Winter, L., Burke, J., Chernett, N., Dennis, M., & Hauck, W. (2008). Tailored activities to manage neuropsychiatric behaviors in persons with dementia and reduce caregiver burden: A randomized pilot study. *American Journal of Geriatric Psychiatry, 16*(3), 229–239.
Hosaka, T., & Sugiyama, Y. (2003). Structured intervention in the family caregivers of the demented elderly and changes in their immune function. *Psychiatry and Clinical Neurosciences, 57*(2), 147–151.
Informe mundial sobre Alzheimer. (2009). Resumen ejecutivo. Recuperado de http://www.alz.co.uk/research/files/WorldAlzheimerReport-Espanol.pdf
Knight, B. G., Lutzky, S. M., & Macofsky-Urban, F. (1993). A meta-analytic review of interventions for caregiver distress: Recommendations for future research. *The Gerontologist, 33*, 240–248.
Knight, B. G., Silverstein, M., McCallum, T. J., & Fox, L. S. (2000). A sociocultural stress and coping model for mental health outcomes among African American caregivers in Southern California. *Journal of Gerontology: Psychological Sciences, 55*(3), 142–150.
Lavretsky, H. (2005). Stress and depression in informal family caregivers of patients with Alzheimer's disease. *Aging Health, 1*(1), 117–133.
Lewinsohn, P. M., Muñoz, R. F., Youngren, M. A., & Zeiss, A. M. (1978). *Control your depression*. Prentice-Hall disfuncionales, IMSERSO.
Londoño, H., Henao, G., Puerta, I., Posada, S., Arango, D., & Acevedo, C. (2006). Propiedades psicométricas y validación de la escala de estrategias de coping modificada (eec-m) en una muestra colombiana. *Universitas Psychologica, 5*(2), 327–349.
Losada, A., Márquez-Gonzalez, M., Peñacoba, C., Gallagher-Thompson, D., & Knight, B. (2007). Reflexiones en torno a la atención a los cuidadores informales de personas con demencia y propuesta de una intervención interdisciplinar. *Psicología Conductual, 15*(1), 57 76.
Losada, A., Montorio, I., Izal, M., & Márquez, M. (2005). *Estudio e intervención sobre el malestar psicológico de los cuidadores de personas con demencia. El papel de los pensamientos disfuncionales*. IMSERSO.
Martin, M., Salvadó, I., Nadal, S., Mji, L., Rico, L., Lanz, J., et al. (1996). Adaptación para nuestro medio de ka escala de sobrecarga del cuidador. *Revista de gerontología, 6*(4), 338–345.
Mittelman, M. (2003). Community caregiving. *Alzheimer's Care Quarterly, 4*(4), 273–285.

Mittelman, M., Roth, D., Clay, O., & Haley, W. (2007). Preserving health of Alzheimer caregivers: Impact of a spouse caregiver intervention. *American Association for Geriatric Psychiatry, 15*(9), 780–788.

Novella, A. (2002). *Incremento de la resiliencia luego de la aplicación de un programa de psicoterapia breve en madres adolescentes*. Tesis de maestria, Universidad Nacional Mayor de San Marcos.

Orozco-Gómez, A., Eustache-Rodriguez, V., & Grosso-Torres, L. (2012). Programa de intervención cognoscitivo conductual en la calidad de sueño de cuidadores familiares. *Revista Colombiana de Enfermería, 7*(7), 75–85.

Parker, C. (2008). Pluralismo religioso, educación y ciudadanía. *Sociedad e estado, 23*(2), 281–353.

Pinquart, M., & Sörensen, S. (2006). Gender differences in caregiver stressors, social resources, and heath: An update meta-analysis. *Journal of Gerontology, 61*(1), 33–45.

Quiceno, J., & Vinaccia, S. (2010). Resiliencia: Una perspectiva de la enfermedad crónica en la población adulta. *Pensamiento Psicológico, 9*(17), 69–82.

Quiceno, J., Vinaccia, S., & Remor, E. (2011). Programa para potenciación de la resiliencia para pacientes con artritis reumatoide. *Revista de Psicopatología y Psicología Clínica, 16*(1), 27–47.

Rabinovitz, Y., Mausbach, B., Coon, D., Depp, C., Thompson, L., & Gallagher-Thompson, D. (2006). The moderating effect of self-efficacy on intervention response in women family caregivers of older adults with dementia. *American Journal of Geriatric Psychiatry, 14*(8), 642–649.

Romano, M., Nissen, M., Del Huerto, N., & Parquet, C. (2007). Enfermedad de Alzheimer. *Revista de posgrado de la vía cátedra de medicina, 175*, 9–12. Recuperado de http://med.unne.edu.ar/revista/revista175/3_175.pdf

Ruíz-Robledillo, N., & Moya-Albiol, L. (2012). El cuidador: una visión actual. *Revista de motivación y emoción, 1*(22), 22–33.

Saavedra, E., & Villalta, M. (2008). Medición de las características resilientes, un estudio comparativo en personas entre 15 y 65 años. *Liberabit. Revista de Psicología, 14*, 31–40.

Salgado, A. (2005). La ciencia y su respuesta frente la adversidad: Estudios desde la perspectiva de la resilencia. *Cultura, 19*(19), 394–416.

Sánchez-Pascual, P., Mouronte-Liz, P., & Olazarán-Rodríguez, J. (2001). Beneficios de un programa de formación del cuidador en la demencia: Experiencia piloto desde la enfermería especializada. *Revista de Neurologia, 33*(5), 410–424.

Wagnild, G. M., & Young, H. M. (1993). Development and psychometric evaluation of the resilience scale. *Journal of Nursing Measurement., 1*(2), 165–178.

Zabalegui, A., Monserrat, D., Cabrera, E., Fernández-Puebla, A., Bardallo, D., et al. (2008). Eficacia de las intervenciones dirigidas a cuidadores principales de personas dependientes mayores de 65 años. Una revisión sistémica. *Revista Española de Geriatría y Gerontología., 43*(3), 157–166.

# Suicidal Ideation and Peer Group: Analysis in a Sample of Venezuelan Adolescents

Juan Antonio Rodríguez Ramírez and Jesús Ángel Oduber Camacho

## Introduction

In Latin America, the adolescent suicide rate varies from one country to another, and the figures fluctuate from 2.5 to 9.3 cases per 100,000 inhabitants (González, 2007; Toro et al., 2009; Ventura-Juncá et al., 2010). Likewise, the contingent of young people who report suicidal thoughts in this region can range between 16 and 62% (Espinoza-Gómez et al., 2010; Florenzano et al., 2011; Gascón, 2005; Ventura-Juncá et al., 2010; Vera & Díaz, 2012). It is undeniable that these statistics reveal a public health problem, particularly because suicide is globally among the top three causes of death during adolescence (World Health Organization [WHO], 2014).

On the other hand, in most research, suicidal behavior—also called the suicide spectrum—is an escalation of stages that varies from less to more severe (Maris, 2002). This escalation begins with suicidal ideation, continues with the manifestation of threats, plans, and suicide attempts, and finally ends with completed or consummated suicide (Viñas et al., 2000). Although less common, other researchers argue that this process is not always sequential and that presenting any of the suicidal behaviors does not necessarily imply the manifestation of others (De Wilde et al., 1996; González et al., 2003). In any case, what seems to be better established is that suicidal ideation refers to those cognitions that range from sporadic ideas that life is not worth to live it up to thoughts of chronic and sustained self-annihilation (Goldney et al., 1989). Furthermore, it is a risk factor for both suicide attempts and

*This chapter is the English translation of an article originally published in Spanish as:* Rodríguez, J. A., & Oduber, J. A. (2015). Ideación suicida y grupo de iguales: análisis en una muestra de adolescentes venezolanos. *Universitas Psychologica, 14*(3), 1129-1140. https://doi.org/10.11144/Javeriana.upsy14-3.isgi. *Please cite the original version of the article in Spanish.*

J. A. Rodríguez Ramírez (✉) · J. Á. Oduber Camacho
Universidad de Los Andes, Mérida, Venezuela



W. López-López et al. (eds.), *Trends in Latin American Psychology*,
https://doi.org/10.1007/978-3-031-87554-0_16

completed suicide; it is even the most frequent component of the suicide spectrum, and its risk is amplified when it is chronic (Miranda de la Torre et al., 2009).

Similarly, empirical research denotes that in adolescence several individual and environmental factors converge, increasing or reducing the possibility of suicidal ideation. Some of them are depression, domestic violence, family support, and the peer group having suicidal behaviors (Espinoza-Gómez et al., 2010; Evans et al., 2004; Gascón, 2005; Miranda de la Torre et al., 2009; Sánchez-Sosa et al., 2010; Srdanović-Maraš et al., 2011; Toro et al., 2009). Regarding depression, in the Latin American case, there is a substantial number of works that point to a strong relationship between this disorder and adolescent suicidal ideation (e.g., Barroilhet et al., 2012; González et al., 2003; Miranda de la Torre et al., 2009; Toro et al., 2009). In Venezuela, for example, Gascón (2005) reports that the suicidal ideation of school adolescents is influenced by sex, social stratum, anxiety, and depression. However, in most of these studies, it is not sufficiently established whether the effect of depression on suicidal thinking is direct or indirect. Perhaps the research that offers the most solid evidence in this regard is that of Sánchez-Sosa et al. (2010) with adolescents from Mexico. Their results point out that depression is a variable that has direct effects on suicidal thinking and, in the same way, acts as a mediator in the relationship between family functioning, school integration problems, school victimization, and the dependent variable, suicidal ideation.

As for contextual or environmental variables, the type of parental practices is associated with the occurrence of adolescent suicidal ideation. In Latin America, for example, Salvo and Melipillán (2008), through a multiple linear regression analysis, find that cohesion and parental support contribute to explain the variability of suicidality and, specifically, are factors that prevent suicidal ideas of Chilean youth. Also in Chile, Florenzano et al. (2011), based on a logistic regression analysis, determine that the good relationship between father and mother, the appropriate styles of parental upbringing, and the conventional relationships between parents and children prevent the suicidal thinking of adolescents. In Mexico, González et al. (2003), examining a sample of adolescents, detect that the affection and communication of parents with their children are variables that reduce the risk of depression and suicidal ideation, particularly in males who report a good relationship with their parents. Likewise, Sánchez-Sosa et al. (2010) tested a model of relationships to explain the suicidal ideation of adolescents in that same country, and one of their main findings indicates that the effect of family functioning on suicidal thinking is indirect and is mediated by depression.

On the other hand, about conflict and family violence, González et al. (2003) document, as correlates of suicidal ideation in Mexican adolescents, the problems of the child with both parents and the discussion of these for economic problems. Espinoza-Gómez et al. (2010) report the strong association between suicidal ideation and perception of domestic violence in all its manifestations, that is, psychological, physical, and sexual violence. Also in Mexico, Sarmiento and Aguilar (2011) achieve positive correlations between fights between parents and children and the suicidal thinking of these. Moreover, the conflict with the mother is one of the predictive variables that enters the model obtained through multiple linear regression analysis. In addition, the works tend to indicate that discussion and domestic violence increase the probability of depression in adolescents and, through this, the risk of suicidal thinking (Espinoza-Gómez et al., 2010; González et al., 2003; Leyva et al., 2007; Moad, 2007).

However, it is worth noting that research in Latin America has not considered how friends who exhibit suicidal behaviors influence the suicidality of the adolescent themselves, but there are reasons to advocate that the peer group can play a significant role in the suicidal tendencies of young people. Perhaps the contribution of Sánchez et al. (2005) constitutes one of the few systematic studies in the region that evaluates the impact of peers on the suicidal ideation of adolescents. Their findings suggest that adolescents with a depressive diagnosis tend to imitate the suicidal behaviors of their friends.

With reference to other contributions outside of Hispanic America, Cerel et al. (2005), analyzing a representative sample of 5852 adolescents, observe that those young people exposed to friends with suicidal behaviors are more likely to experience suicidal ideation and attempts, as well as antisocial behavior (e.g., alcohol consumption, drug use, and aggression). Evans et al. (2004) confirm that several studies reach similar conclusions; that is, there is a significant association between having friends who exhibit suicidal behaviors and one's own suicidal thoughts. Specifically, it is the suicide attempt of the peers, and not the completed suicide, that has an effect on the suicidal ideation of young people. In contrast, Feigelman and Gorman (2008) determined that the suicide of a friend is associated with the adolescent's own suicidal thoughts and attempts and also with increased depression during the first year after the death. Similarly, Gould et al. (2004) argue that adolescents who report the loss of a friend by suicide generally present a short-term deterioration of their mental health (e.g., depression) and an increase in the incidence of completed suicide, although this study does not detail whether that death also affects the suicidal cognitions of the adolescent.

In this sense, Phillips (1974) reported that the suicidal behavior of friends is a correlate of people's suicidal tendencies. This author interprets this correlation in the following way: (1) individuals imitate the suicidal behaviors of their peers, or (2) those subjects with suicidal attitudes seek environments with such propensities. Agnew (1998) argues that the adolescent's interest in suicide can be the effect of a learning process and contact with relatives or peers who have exhibited this type of behavior, which teaches the young person that suicide is an alternative for solving problems. De Wilde (2000) argues that the suicidal behavior exhibited by a member of the peer group at school or outside of it can have an effect on the adolescent's suicidality through a suggestive process called "suicide contagion." According to Evans et al. (2004), the literature suggests that it is the modeling process of suicidal behaviors of the peer group that exerts an influence on the adolescent's own suicidal tendency. In conclusion, it seems, adolescents whose peer group exhibits suicidal ideas and attempts and/or completed suicides may be at risk of exhibiting suicidal behaviors.

# Objectives

This study is innovative because it strengthens the work in Spanish on the risk of suicidal ideation during adolescence. Given the lack of systematic studies on the subject in the region, it aims to primarily explore the role that the peer group plays in the likelihood of suicidal ideation; of course, without excluding from the analysis the interactive link of other variables related to this phenomenon. Taking into account the findings in the area, this study seeks to determine a model of relationships (Fig. 1) with which the suicidal ideation of school-going adolescents can be explained, defining the effect that the suicidal behavior of peers, depression, the support of the father and mother, and domestic violence have.

# Method

## *Participants*

The type of sampling in this research was non-probabilistic. In such a way, the sample is made up of 912 high school students who were present in the classroom at the time of applying the questionnaire. The participants were within an age range from 11 to 18 years old, with an average of 14.55 years (SD = 1.58 years). Regarding gender, 441 of these students are male (48.4%) and 471 are female (51.6%). All the adolescents were part of five public education centers conveniently selected in Mérida, Venezuela. The distribution by educational stages is as follows: 411 subjects (45.1%) were part of the basic cycle (first, second, and third year) and 501 (54.9%) of the diversified cycle (fourth and fifth year). Of the total number of school-going adolescents, 83.4% reported that they only studied, and the rest (15%)

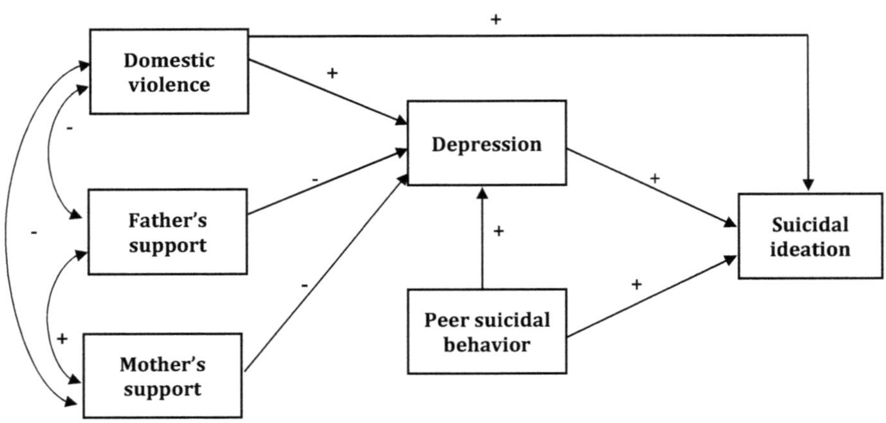


**Fig. 1** Hypothetical starting model of suicidal ideation

reported that they alternated studies with work activities. Almost half of these young people belong to two-parent families (49.7%), more than a third (36.2%) to single-parent families, and the rest live exclusively with siblings or other relatives (14.1%).

## Instruments and Variables

For data collection, a set of standardized questionnaires and some ad hoc indicators were used. All have shown satisfactory levels of reliability and validity in previous research (see in more detail Loinaz et al., 2012; Rodríguez et al., 2012; Sanz & García-Vera, 2007; Villalobos, 2009, for an analysis of both the process of adapting these questionnaires to Spanish, as well as their validity and reliability). The variables and their respective instruments are detailed below.

## Parental Support

A Spanish adaptation of the Abusive and Supportive Environments Parenting Inventory (EASE-PI) by Nicholas and Bieber (1997) was used. The parental support subscale consists of 24 items for the case of parents (12 items referring to the father's affectionate behaviors and 12 referring to the mother's affectionate behaviors). All these items evaluate the frequency with which each of the parents shows behaviors aimed at helping the young person in difficulties or to provide them comfort and affection when they need it. Any of these items are answered in a 5-point Likert format (0 = never, 1 = rarely, 2 = sometimes, 3 = often, and 4 = very frequently). In the present study, the Cronbach's alpha achieved for the mother's support was 0.92 and for the father's was 0.94.

## Domestic Violence

An adaptation of the Conflict Tactics Scales (CTS) by Straus et al. (1996) was used to evaluate the frequency with which physical violence is used as a tactic to resolve conflicts at home (e.g., "Beating or hitting the other"). The response range of the four items goes from "Never" (0) to "Always" (4). In this research, the observed Cronbach's alpha for the physical violence subscale was 0.86.

## Depression

In this study, the Beck Depression Inventory (BDI-IA) (Beck et al., 1996) was applied to evaluate depression. The Beck inventory is a self-report that consists of 21 items that assess the severity of depression. The 21 factors measured by this questionnaire are sadness, pessimism, sense of failure, dissatisfaction, guilt, feeling of punishment, self-disgust, self-accusation, suicidal ideas, crying, irritability, social disinterest, indecision, changes in body image, difficulty working, insomnia, fatigue, loss of appetite, weight loss, somatic concerns, and low libido level. Each item has four response categories ranging between 0 and 3 points. Due to the objectives of this research, the factor on suicidal ideas was excluded from the sum. The Cronbach's alpha obtained in this study was 0.87.

## Peer Suicidal Behavior

Based on the literature in the area (e.g., Prinstein et al., 2001), three items were developed referring to the occurrence of suicidal thoughts, suicide attempts, and completed suicide among peers. Specifically, adolescents were asked about the following situations: (1) How many of your friends think that suicide is the only way out of the problems in their life? (2) How many of your friends have attempted suicide in the past year? and (3) How many of your friends have committed suicide in the past year? The response category for these questions is set on a four-point Likert scale (0 = none, 1 = some, 2 = almost all, and 3 = all). A global index was estimated by totaling the three items. This variable has been called peer suicidal behavior. The Cronbach's alpha achieved was 0.72.

## Suicidal Ideation

The Positive and Negative Suicide Ideation Inventory (PANSI) by Osman et al. (1998) was the questionnaire administered to assess the adolescents'suicidal ideation. A Spanish version was validated by Villalobos (2009) in Colombia and is the one used in this study. The original instrument and the Spanish adaptation include a total of 14 items in which two factors underlie. One of these factors is related to positive suicidal ideation and consists of 6 items; the other refers to negative suicidal ideation and totals 8 items. The respondent is asked about the frequency with which they have had suicidal thoughts during the past year. The response category is formulated on a 5-point Likert scale that varies in an interval from 0 (never) to 4 (always). The reliability estimated by means of Cronbach's alpha was 0.87 in this study.

## Procedure

After requesting and obtaining authorization from the educational institutions, the instruments were collectively applied in the classroom where academic activities take place. At the beginning, the participants were explained the purpose of the research, and it was emphasized that the responses and their participation were anonymous and voluntary. The sample was taken in November 2012. Out of a total of 1187 questionnaires applied, 275 were eliminated due to inconsistencies and errors in the information provided.

## Data Analysis

To establish the general characteristics of the sample in terms of the study variables, the main measures of centrality and dispersion, that is, mean, standard deviation, and ranges, were analyzed. Also, to explore the association between each of the factors analyzed and suicidal ideation, a Pearson correlation analysis was carried out. Both analyses were performed using the statistical program SPSS (version 17.0). Then, using the program AMOS 18.0 (Arbuckle, 2009), a path analysis was developed to test the hypothetical model described in Fig. 1. In this case, the Maximum Likelihood Method was chosen for parameter estimation. Thus, the goodness-of-fit indices between the initial model and the empirical data of the sample were reviewed to observe their suitability. Specifically, both the contrast on the $\chi^2$ distribution and the rest of the goodness-of-fit indices were verified. According to Hair et al. (2000), a proposed model presents a good fit to the observed data when the product between the $\chi^2$ and the degrees of freedom is less than 3, the NFI, CFI, and GFI fit indices are equal to or greater than 0.9, and the RMSEA is less than 0.08. Finally, due to the problems of fit found, the initial model was respecified based on the following criteria: (1) the significance levels of the parameters (relationships between variables) estimated, (2) the information provided by the residual matrix, and (3) the modification indices established by the AMOS program itself.

# Results

## Descriptive and Correlations

According to Table 1, the perceived levels of parental support are, on average, high, and physical violence in the homes of these young people is rare. On average, these adolescents interact with very few friends who exhibit suicidal behaviors and, at the same time, report low levels of depression and suicidal ideation. However, it is convenient to contrast this trend with the variability present in some scores, especially

**Table 1** Pearson correlation coefficients, mean, standard deviation, and ranges of the observed variables

| Variable | 1 | 2 | 3 | 4 | 5 | 6 |
|---|---|---|---|---|---|---|
| 1. Mother's Support | – | | | | | |
| 2. Father's Support | 0.55*** | – | | | | |
| 3. Domestic Violence | −0.23*** | −0.24*** | – | | | |
| 4. Peer Suicidal Behavior | −0.13*** | −0.14*** | 0.25*** | – | | |
| 5. Depression | −0.27*** | −0.32*** | 0.27*** | 0.31*** | – | |
| 6. Suicidal Ideation | −0.28*** | −0.27*** | 0.31*** | 0.29*** | 0.53*** | – |
| Mean | 36,68 | 31,46 | 1,21 | 0,65 | 5,36 | 8,91 |
| (*SD*) | (10,20) | (13,03) | (2,68) | (1,15) | (6,72) | (8,71) |
| Theoretical range | 0–48 | 0–48 | 0–16 | 0–9 | 0–60 | 0–56 |
| Observed range | 0–47 | 0–47 | 0–16 | 0–9 | 0–59 | 0–52 |

*** $p < 0.001$ ** $p < 0.01$

**Table 2** Goodness-of-fit indices of the initial model and the final model

| Modelo | $X^2$ | *df* | *p* | $X^2/df$ | NFI | CFI | GFI | RMSEA |
|---|---|---|---|---|---|---|---|---|
| Inicial | 30,9 | 3 | 0.000 | 10.29 | 0.93 | 0.94 | 0.97 | 0.16 |
| Final | 3,2 | 4 | 0.52 | 0.8 | 0.99 | 1.0 | 0.99 | 0.01 |

the one confirmed by the standard deviation and the observed range. Simultaneously, it can be verified with the correlation analysis of Table 1 that the support of the father and the mother decreases the probability of adolescent suicidal ideation and, on the contrary, domestic violence, suicidal behavior of peers, and depression increase it.

## *Path Analysis*

Consistent with the data analysis strategy, the model proposed in Fig. 1 was tested. In Table 2, it is observed that the goodness-of-fit indices between the initial model and the empirical data were not entirely appropriate. Especially, the product between $\chi^2/gl$ and the RMSEA reveal problems of fit in the proposed model, as pointed out by Hair et al. (2000). This made it necessary to respecify the hypothetical starting model according to the criteria described in previous paragraphs. The respecification process was developed step by step until achieving a model whose fit to the empirical data was appropriate. Consequently, a final model was obtained, whose fit indices are also summarized in Table 2. According to this table, the different indices analyzed show an improvement in the quality of fit.

The final model of relationships between the variables is then configured according to the results presented in Fig. 2. Regarding this graphic representation, it is observed that there is a positive and significant correlation between the support of the father and the support of the mother ($r = 0.56$, $p < 0.001$), and a negative

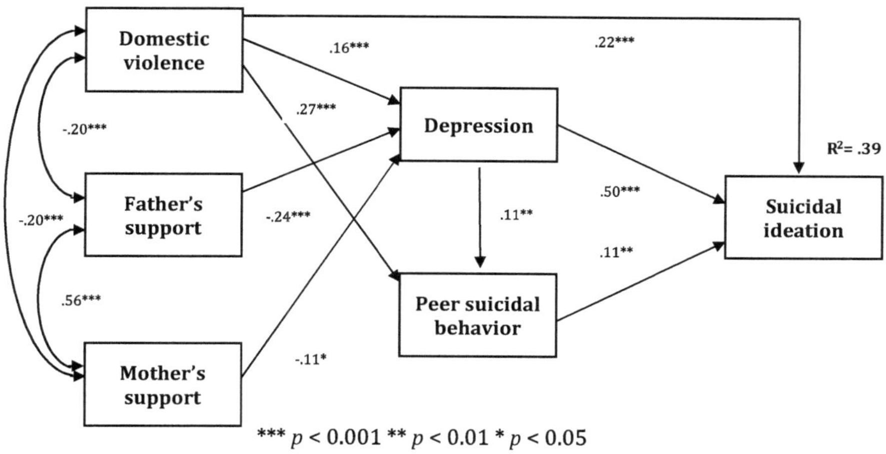


**Fig. 2** Final model of relationships on suicidal ideation ($n$ = 369) (*** $p < 0.001$ ** $p < 0.01$ * $p < 0.05$)

correlation of these two variables with domestic violence ($r = -0.2$, $p < 0.001$ in both cases).

Regarding the direct effects, in the final model it is observed that depression has a significant effect on suicidal ideation ($\beta = 0.5$, $p < 0.001$). Specifically, high levels of depression are associated with high levels of suicidal thinking. Similarly, the suicidal behavior of peers has a significant effect on the explained variable ($\beta = 0.11$, $p < 0.01$). Thus, the greater the contact with friends who exhibit suicidal behaviors (e.g., suicidal thoughts and attempts and completed suicide), the greater the probability of suicidal ideation in adolescents. Lastly, another direct effect is that of domestic violence on suicidal ideation ($\beta = 0.22$, $p < 0.001$). Perceiving physical violence at home directly increases the suicidal thinking of young people.

In addition to these, the final model shows other indirect effects of special consideration. In such a way, the support of the mother and father presents a negative and significant relationship with depression ($\beta = -0.11$, $p < 0.05$ and $\beta = -0.24$, $p < 0.001$, respectively) and the latter with suicidal ideation. Domestic violence has an indirect effect on suicidal ideation through its positive relationship with depression ($\beta = 0.16$, $p < 0.001$). Likewise, domestic violence and depression also show an indirect relationship with suicidal ideation through their effect on peer suicidal behavior ($\beta = 0.27$, $p < 0.001$ and $\beta = 0.11$, $p < 0.05$, respectively). The indirect effect of both variables was indicated by the analysis technique itself. Finally, the obtained model explains 39% of the variance in suicidal ideation.

## Discussion and Conclusion

As already explained, the main objective of this study has been to test a structural model that includes peer suicidal behavior, to estimate its influence on adolescent suicidal ideation. In response to the question about which factors amplify or minimize the suicidal thinking of young people, some explanatory models have merged individual factors related to stressful life events, hopelessness, depression, self-esteem, problem-solving, drug use, loneliness, self-efficacy, etc., with contextual factors referred to, for example, family conflict, family cohesion, economic problems in the family, paternal physical abuse, divorce, teacher support, social support, etc. (e.g., Sánchez-Sosa et al., 2010; Villalobos, 2009). However, in most of these models, the peer group is not included as an explanatory variable that indisputably plays a fundamental role in adolescence and, of course, in the psychosocial adjustment of the young person.

Based on the above, the final model of this study indicates that the peer group with suicidal behaviors has a direct effect on the adolescent's suicidal ideation. Although a similar finding was not found in other publications that have applied structural equations as an analysis technique, this data agrees with studies that achieve at the bivariate and multivariate level that the suicidality of the peer group is a predictor of the suicidal thinking of adolescents (e.g., Evans et al., 2004; Feigelman & Gorman, 2008; Prinstein et al., 2001). Of course, this empirical evidence can be interpreted in several ways. For example, adolescents learn in their peer groups with suicidal inclinations definitions, rationalizations, and motives favorable to suicide. It should be said, moreover, that in a group environment with such characteristics, the learning mechanisms that facilitate suicidal thinking are those that are generally proposed in psychology, that is, those of reinforcement and modeling. This explanatory proposal is consistent with the interpretations made by Phillips (1974), Agnew (1998), and Evans et al. (2004). However, the direct effect that the suicidality of peers generates on one's own suicidal ideation can also be explained by other group processes such as, for example, "social contagion" seen as a mechanism of suggestion (De Wilde, 2000). In any case, the findings of this research confirm that the suicidal behavior of peers has a direct effect on the probability of suicidal ideation, and since adolescence is a stage marked by constant interaction and influence from peers, this characteristic must be considered in any attempt to predict and explain suicidal behavior during this stage of development.

Also, from a group perspective, in the initial model, an indirect effect of the peer group on the dependent variable through depression was proposed. This relationship was proposed based on the findings revealed by Feigelman and Gorman (2008), which suggest that a friend's suicidality increases the depression and suicidal ideation of the adolescent. However, the path analysis indicated that such a relationship, at least in this sample, is not empirically plausible; on the contrary, the modification indices of the AMOS 18 program show that the relationship is inverse, that is, presenting depressive symptoms increases the possibility of associating with friends who show suicidal tendencies. Provisionally, this effect allows us to infer that depression instigates adolescents to seek peer groups with inappropriate behaviors, in this case, other young people who experience suicidal ideas and attempts or even friendships that end up taking their life.

In addition to this, the structural model allows us to determine that the support from both the mother and the father are variables that indirectly affect suicidal ideation through their incidence in depression. This finding is consistent with that reported by other authors such as Sánchez-Sosa et al. (2010) and Srdanović-Maraš et al. (2011). Also, from the family domain itself, the perception of domestic violence directly increases the adolescent's suicidal ideation, which coincides with the results of other authors who highlight the stressful role of this variable in suicidal ideas (e.g., Espinoza-Gómez et al., 2010). Similarly, young people who witness physical abuse in their homes experience depression, which subsequently has an effect on suicidal ideas. Moreover, perceiving problems of domestic abuse increases the risk of associating with groups that show problems of suicidality and, through these, the risk of suicidal ideation. Although this indirect effect was not established in the starting model, it was indicated by the path analysis. It is evident, then, that a dysfunctional family environment, characterized by low support and the use of physical violence, has an influence both on the onset of mental disorders and on making contact with a group of friends with inappropriate behaviors, which together increase the possibility of suicidal ideation.

Regarding depression, the model makes it clear that it is the key variable and, undoubtedly, the one that best explains suicidal ideation. The strength of such effect, in this case direct, coincides with the findings of other research (e.g., Konick & Gutiérrez, 2005; Sánchez-Sosa et al., 2010). Likewise, the mediating property and the possible indirect effects that this disorder presents in the final model allow to confirm its prominent role in the etiology of the phenomenon addressed. Therefore, and in line with what was pointed out by Konick and Gutiérrez (2005), depression is an individual variable that should not be excluded from any explanatory model of suicidal ideation in adolescence, especially if it is empirically demonstrated that 60% of males and 44% of females who contemplate suicide and who have attempted to take their life present symptoms of moderate and severe depression (Srdanović-Maraš et al., 2011). Rounding out these observations, depressed adolescents who think about suicide present a multisystemic context that includes a home with problems of affection, conflict, and physical violence; it also encompasses friendships prone to suicidality, without ruling out that other factors, such as school failure, eating disorders, impulsivity, or antisocial behavior (Sánchez-Sosa et al., 2010), are also part of it.

Based on the above, it should be clarified that it is not plausible to support or reject the order of causality of the observed variables, given the cross-sectional nature of this study; however, the relationships proposed in the model come from the literature in the area. It is not superfluous to indicate that these relationships should be understood with discretion.

Finally, looking to the future, it is proposed to replicate this structural model in other cross-sectional studies, considering that, if it is possible, it may be more valuable to test the effects found and explained here through longitudinal studies. It could also be a valuable contribution to separately contrast the effect of the three types of peer suicidal behaviors (ideation, attempt, and completion) in such a way that it is possible to specify which has a greater explanatory capacity of adolescent suicidal thinking. Similarly, it would be appropriate to test the explanatory power and the invariability of these models with other groups that may be made up of categories linked to gender, age, or even adolescents from the general and/or clinical population. Analyzing different models in these terms can guide the development of much more comprehensive intervention programs aimed at preventing suicidal ideation.

## References

Agnew, R. (1998). The approval of suicide: A social-psychological model. *Suicide and Life-threatening Behavior, 28*(2), 205–225. https://doi.org/10.1111/j.1943-278X.1998.tb00640.x

Arbuckle, J. L. (2009). *Amos 18 user's guide*. Amos Development Corporation.

Barroilhet, S., Fritsch, R., Guajardo, V., Martínez, V., Vöhringer, P., Araya, R., & Rojas, G. (2012). Ideas autolíticas, violencia autoinfligida y síntomas depresivos en escolares chilenos. *Revista Médica de Chile, 140*(7), 873–881. https://www.scielo.cl/pdf/rmc/v140n7/art07.pdf

Beck, A., Steer, R., Ball, R., & Ranieri, W. (1996). Comparison of beck depression inventary-IA and II in psychiatric outpatients. *Journal of Personality Assessment, 67*, 588–597. https://doi.org/10.1207/s15327752jpa6703_13

Cerel, J., Roberts, T., & Nilsen, W. (2005). Peer suicidal behavior and adolescents risk behavior. *Journal of Nervous and Mental Disease, 193*(4), 237–243.

De Wilde, E. (2000). Adolescent suicidal behavior: A general population perspective. In K. Hawton & K. Van Heeringen (Eds.), *The international handbook of suicide and attempted suicide* (pp. 249–259). Wiley.

De Wilde, E., Kienhorst, I., & Diekstra, R. (1996). El suicidio en la adolescencia. In J. Buendía (Ed.), *Psicopatología en niños y adolescentes. Desarrollos actuales* (pp. 309–332). Pirámide.

Espinoza-Gómez, F., Zepeda-Pamplona, V., Bautista-Hernández, V., Hernández-Suarez, C., Newton-Sánchez, O., & Plasencia-García, G. (2010). Violencia doméstica y riesgo de conducta suicida en universitarios adolescentes. *Salud Pública de México, 52*(3), 213–219. https://www.scielo.org.mx/pdf/spm/v52n3/05.pdf

Evans, E., Hawton, K., & Rodham, K. (2004). Factors associated with suicidal phenomena in adolescents: A systematic review of population-based studies. *Clinical Psychology Review, 24*, 957–979. https://doi.org/10.1016/j.cpr.2004.04.005

Feigelman, W., & Gorman, B. (2008). Assessing the effects of peer suicide on youth suicide. *Suicide and Life-threatening Behavior, 38*(2), 181–194. https://doi.org/10.1521/suli.2008.38.2.181

Florenzano, R., Valdés, M., Cáceres, E., Santander, S., Aspillaga, C., & Musalem, C. (2011). Relación entre ideación suicida y estilos parentales en un grupo de adolescentes chilenos. *Revista Médica de Chile, 139*, 1529–1533. https://www.scielo.cl/pdf/rmc/v139n12/art01.pdf

Gascón, A. I. (2005). *Ideación suicida, humor depresivo y ansiedad en la adolescencia intermedia escolarizada de la Parroquia Antonio Spinetti Dini: algunos factores de riesgo. Mérida 2005.* Tesis de especialización en Psiquiatría, Universidad de Los Andes. Disponible en https://tesis.ula.ve/post-grado/tde_busca/arquivo.php?codArquivo=2948

Goldney, R., Winefield, A., Tiggemann, M., Winefield, H., & Smith, S. (1989). Suicidal ideation in a young adult population. *Acta Psychiatrica Scandinavica, 79*, 481–489. https://doi.org/10.1111/j.1600-0447.1989.tb10291.x

González, J. (2007). Epidemiología de los suicidios. Colombia, 2007. In *Forensis 2007. Datos para la vida* (pp. 179–204). Instituto Nacional de Medicina Legal y Ciencias Forenses.

González, C., Ramos, L., Caballero, M., & Wagner, F. (2003). Correlatos psicosociales de depresión, ideación e intento suicida en adolescentes mexicanos. *Psicothema, 15*(4), 524–532. https://www.psicothema.com/pdf/1102.pdf

Gould, M., Drew, V., Kleinman, M., Lucas, C., Thomas, J., & Chung, M. (2004). Teenagers' attitudes about coping strategies and help-seeking for suicidality. *Journal of the American Academy of Child and Adolescents Psychiatry, 43*, 1124–1133. https://doi.org/10.1097/01.chi.0000132811.06547.31

Hair, J., Anderson, R., Tatham, R., & Black, W. C. (2000). *Análisis multivariante*. Prentice Hall.

Konick, L., & Gutiérrez, P. (2005). Testing a model of suicide ideation in college students. *Suicide and Life-threatening Behavior, 35*, 181–192. https://doi.org/10.1521/suli.35.2.181.62875

Leyva, J., Hernández, J., Nava, J., & López, G. (2007). Depresión en adolescentes y funcionamiento familiar. *Revista Médica del Instituto Mexicano de Seguro Social, 45*(3), 225–232. Recuperado de http://new.medigraphic.com/cgi-bin/contenido.cgi?IDREVISTA=46&IDPUBLICACION=1295

Loinaz, I., Echeburúa, E., Ortiz-Tallo, M., & Amor, P. (2012). Propiedades psicométricas de las Conflict Tactics Scales (CTS-2) en una muestra española de agresores de pareja. *Psicothema, 24*(1), 142–148. Recuperado de http://www.psicothema.com/pdf/3991.pdf

Maris, R. W. (2002). Suicide. *The Lancet, 360*(9329), 319–326.

Miranda de la Torre, I., Cubillas, M., Román, R., & Valdez, E. (2009). Ideación suicida en población escolarizada infantil: Factores psicológicos asociados. *Salud Mental, 32*(6), 495–502. http://www.redalyc.org/pdf/582/58122267007.pdf

Moad, C. (2007). Depresión en adolescentes de escuelas públicas y privadas. *Psicología Iberoamericana, 15*(1), 6–12. http://www.redalyc.org/articulo.oa?id=133915928002

Nicholas, K., & Bieber, S. (1997). Assessment of perceived parenting behaviors: The exposure to abusive and supportive environments parenting inventory (EASE-PI). *Journal of Family Violence, 12*(3), 275–291.

Organización Mundial de la Salud. (2014). *Salud para los adolescentes del mundo. Una segunda oportunidad en la segunda década*. Autor. Recuperado de http://apps.who.int/adolescents/second-decade/files/WHO_FWC_MCA_14.05_spa.pdf

Osman, A., Gutiérrez, P., Kopper, B., Barrios, F., & Chiros, C. (1998). The positive and negative suicide ideation inventory: Development and validation. *Psychological Reports, 82*, 783–793. https://doi.org/10.2466/pr0.1998.82.3.783

Phillips, D. (1974). The influence of suggestion on suicide: Substantive and theoretical implications of the Werther effects. *American Sociological Review, 39*, 340–354.

Prinstein, M., Boergers, J., & Spirito, A. (2001). Adolescents' and their friends' health-risk behaviour: Factors that alter or add to peer influence. *Journal of Pediatric Psychology, 26*(5), 287–298. https://doi.org/10.1093/jpepsy/26.5.287

Rodríguez, J. A., Mirón, L., & Rial, A. (2012). Análisis de la relación entre grupo de iguales, vinculación familiar y escolar, autocontrol y conducta antisocial, en una muestra de adolescentes venezolanos. *Revista de Psicología Social, 27*(1), 25–38. https://doi.org/10.1174/021347412798844033

Salvo, L., & Melipillán, R. (2008). Predictores de la suicidalidad en adolescentes. *Revista Chilena de Neuro-Psiquiatría, 46*(2), 115–123. http://www.scielo.cl/pdf/rchnp/v46n2/art05.pdf

Sánchez, R., Guzmán, Y., & Cáceres, H. (2005). Estudio de la imitación como factor de riesgo para ideación suicida en estudiantes universitarios adolescentes. *Revista Colombiana de Psiquiatría, 34*(1), 12–25. Recuperado de http://www.redalyc.org/pdf/806/80628403003.pdf

Sánchez-Sosa, J., Villareal-González, M., Musitu, G., & Martínez, B. (2010). Ideación suicida en adolescentes: un análisis psicosocial. *Intervención Psicosocial, 19*(3), 279–287. https://doi.org/10.5093/in2010v19n3a8

Sanz, J., & García-Vera, M. (2007). Análisis psicométrico de las versiones breves del Inventario para la Depresión de Beck de 1978 (BDI-IA). *Psicología Conductual, 15*(2), 191–214. http://www.funveca.org/revista/pedidos/product.php?id_product=288

Sarmiento, C., & Aguilar, J. (2011). Predictores familiares y personales de la ideación suicida adolescentes. *Psicología y Salud, 21*(1), 25–30. http://www.uv.mx/psicysalud/psicysalud-21-1/21-1/Carolina-Sarmiento-Silva.pdf

Srdanović-Maraš, J., Durić, O., Marković, J., & Biro, M. (2011). Family and individual factors of suicidal ideation in adolescents. *Psihologija, 44*(3), 245–260. https://doi.org/10.2298/PSI1103245S

Straus, M., Hamby, S., Boney-McCoy, S., & Sugarman, D. (1996). The revised conflict tactic scales. Development and preliminary psychometric data. *Journal of Family Issues, 17*(3), 283–316. http://pubpages.unh.edu/~mas2/CTS15.pdf

Toro, D., Paniagua, R., González, C., & Montoya, B. (2009). Caracterización de adolescentes escolarizados con riesgo de suicidio, Medellín, 2006. *Revista Salud Pública, 27*(3), 302–308. http://www.scielo.org.co/pdf/rfnsp/v27n3/v27n3a07.pdf

Ventura-Juncá, R., Carvajal, C., Undurraga, S., Vicuña, P., Egaña, J., & Garib, M. (2010). Prevalencia de ideación e intento suicida en adolescentes de la Región Metropolitana de Santiago de Chile. *Revista Médica de Chile, 138*, 309–315. http://www.scielo.cl/pdf/rmc/v138n3/art08.pdf

Vera, Ó., & Díaz, C. (2012). Suicidio en adolescentes de Sudamérica: un problema creciente. *Salud Pública de México, 54*(4), 363–364. http://www.scielosp.org/pdf/spm/v54n4/03.pdf

Villalobos, F. (2009). *Ideación suicida en jóvenes: formulación y validación del modelo integrador explicativo en estudiantes de educación secundaria y superior*. Tesis Doctoral, Universidad de Granada. http://hera.urg.es/tesisugr/1805982x.pdf

Viñas, F., Jané, M., & Domènech, E. (2000). Evaluación de la severidad de la ideación suicida autoinformada en escolares de 8 a 12 años. *Psicothema, 12*(4), 594–598. http://www.psicothema.com/pdf/377.pdf

# Analysis of the Perception of Static and Dynamic Events in People with Alzheimer's Disease

**María Fernanda Lara Díaz, Judy Constanza Beltrán Rojas, Silvia Raquel Rodríguez Montoya, Diana María Arias Castro, and Sandra Milena Araque Jaramillo**

## Introduction

Alzheimer's disease (AD) is a neurodegenerative disease, which, in recent years, with the change in population structure and the increase in life expectancy, has exponentially increased the number of people suffering from it. In Colombia, it is estimated that for every 1000 people, 13.1 are diagnosed with this disease (Pradilla et al., 2003). Currently, there is no cure and its diagnosis is based on invasive, costly, or cognitively demanding tests for patients with AD (Albert et al., 2011).

Memory failures constitute the main impairment in AD (Grady et al., 2001); however, research has found that the perception of events is affected and influences daily life activities (Mosimann et al., 2004), this being a field little researched, which is paradoxical considering the participation in the processes of event perception of cortical areas that begin their degeneration at least 3 years before people receive a diagnosis of AD (Boucart, Bubbico, et al., 2014). A fundamental element in the perception of events is visual processing.

The progressive neuropathological changes of the disease (the death of neurons, neurofibrillary tangles, and amyloid plaques) can generate corticocortical disconnections, which cause deterioration in the processing, visual attention, eye

---

*This chapter is the English translation of an article originally published in Spanish as:* Lara, M. F., Beltrán, J. C., Rodríguez, S. R., & Araque, S. M. (2016). Análisis de la percepción de eventos estáticos y dinámicos en personas con enfermedad de Alzheimer. *Universitas Psychologica, 15* (5). https://doi.org/10.11144/Javeriana.upsy15-5.apee. *Please cite the original version of the article in Spanish.*

---

M. F. Lara Díaz (✉) · J. C. Beltrán Rojas · S. R. Rodríguez Montoya · D. M. Arias Castro · S. M. Araque Jaramillo
Universidad Nacional de Colombia, Bogota, Colombia
e-mail: mflarad@unal.edu.co



W. López-López et al. (eds.), *Trends in Latin American Psychology*,
https://doi.org/10.1007/978-3-031-87554-0_17

movements and skills necessary for perception such as the speed in visual search, the identification of details in a scene, the amplitude of saccadic movements, among others (Fujimori et al., 1997; Grady et al., 2001; Hof & Bouras, 1991). Similarly, alterations in visual functions such as reading, complex exploration routes, the location of objects, and their recognition, among others, are identified (Fernández et al., 2015; Rizzo et al., 2000). Despite the fact that visual acuity is normal in the early stages of AD (Armstrong, 2009; Valenti, 2010).

Eye movements are a behavioral manifestation of the allocation of attention in a scene. They also provide real-time information about cognitive processing; therefore they can serve as a window to the understanding of higher processes (Henderson, 2003). From the eye movements, it is possible to observe variables that otherwise would be very difficult to analyze such as behavior in response to static and dynamic stimuli (Karatekin, 2007; Wang et al., 2014). Given that the neural substrates of eye movements are well established, it is possible to make inferences about how the brain processes information.

This research analyzes eye movements in relation to the perception of events. An event is defined as: "a type of information that consists of a set of functionally related entities that develop in evanescent circumstances … they are also a functional unit of action in time recognized as such thanks to previous experience, which is expressed as a unit of representation or knowledge and is operated to communicate or think" (Serra, 2013, p. 191).

Research in population with AD using technology for visual tracking (Eye tracker), like that of Mosimann et al. (2004), which compared the exploration form in clock reading, shows the influence of event perception in everyday life tasks, evidencing significant changes compared to a control group mainly in terms of fixation duration and movement amplitude. In a more recent study by Boucart, Calais, et al. (2014) the ability to detect a target within a scene (visual search) was analyzed, finding that people with AD were much less efficient in this type of task than the control group, especially in terms of the selection of relevant objects. In this regard, the relationship between visual perception and AD is promising to understand the nature of linguistic deficits.

In AD, along with the deficit of visual integration, language is affected, specifically the ability to structure sentences and encode the message to account for an observed scene. In this sense, there is a close relationship between visual perception and language (Ferreira & Tanenhaus, 2007; Miranda-Castillo et al., 2013).

Thus, the objective of this research was to describe the main characteristics of the perception of static and dynamic events in patients with Alzheimer's disease compared to their controls.

## Method and Procedure

### Participants

In the present study, 14 older adults were evaluated: seven diagnosed by consensus with probable mild or moderate Alzheimer's disease (five women, two men), recruited from the database of the Institute of Genetics of the Universidad Nacional de Colombia with the collaboration of the Neuroscience Research Group, and seven controls, namely, healthy older adults recruited from the "Mentes en Acción" group of the Human Communication Center of the Faculty of Medicine of the Universidad Nacional de Colombia.

The following inclusion criteria were considered: (1) that the patient agreed to participate in the study by giving their assent and the relative their consent. (2) Be between 60 and 80 years old. (3) Have a diagnosis of probable mild to moderate Alzheimer's disease with a global score on the Global Deterioration Scale (Scale of global deterioration) GDS equal to or less than four (Reisberg et al., 1982). As exclusion criteria, the following were taken into account: having a GDS greater than or equal to five, presenting uncorrected hearing or visual impairments, or having glasses in poor condition, that prevent the development of the task or the understanding of simple instructions.

Ethical standards in accordance with the Declaration of Helsinki (updated in 2000) and with resolution 8430 of the Ministry of Health of Colombia. The study considered all ethical aspects related to cost-benefit, assent and informed consent, voluntary participation, and the confidential handling of information.

### Instruments

Eye movements were recorded using the Eye-Tracking Tobii Tx300 visual tracking equipment. This device recognizes and stores information about the behavior of eye movements at a frequency of 300 Hz, which refers to the samples collected per second in each eye. It has a 23-inch LCD screen with a resolution of 1920 × 1080, which was used for the presentation of stimuli, and a hardware device located under the screen that emits infrared light and has cameras that capture the reflections of light emissions.

In this research, two types of tasks were carried out: search, in which the area of interest was verbally indicated in which the participant should focus their attention, and tracking, which consisted of a free exploration of the image for a predefined time. In these tasks, the metrics recorded by the Eye Tracker and relevant to the study were:

- Fixations: A fixation is the stabilization of the eye on a part of the stimulus for a period of time between 200 and 300 ms. The Eye Tracker provides fixation data, which includes a time interval and X and Y coordinates ().
- The exploration trajectory: This corresponds to a series of fixations in temporal order. An AOI is visited if there is at least one fixation in it. Researchers in psychology have shown that exploration trajectories are representative of the tasks performed by participants. (Just & Carpenter, 1976).

The above metrics can be presented through the representation of the gaze path (gaze plot) or heat map in which the sum of the eye fixations is shown, summarizing the positions in which fixations were made; the parts marked with intense red color correspond to high fixation places, and the green ones to low fixation places.

## *Procedure*

The sessions were held in the Cognitive Neuroscience and Communication laboratory of the National University of Colombia. Initially, the Montreal Cognitive Assessment (MoCa) (Nasreddine et al., 2005) was administered, which, in a period of approximately 10 min, quickly explores, as a screening, the different cognitive domains (orientation, attention, calculation, language, memory, and praxis); the maximum score is 30, and the cut-off point to consider the presence of any alteration is 23 (Nasreddine et al., 2005) as a characterization instrument. Then a series of tasks were presented through the Eye Tracker, for the performance of which the participant sat in front of the Eye Tracker in a static chair, located 65 centimeters away from the screen, under constant natural lighting conditions. Then, a brief calibration session of nine points, each located at a distance ≤18 degrees, was carried out. For calibration, the participant was given the instruction to keep the head as static as possible and only follow a moving red dot with the gaze. In this way, the equipment software calculates the accuracy of data acquisition and ensures the correct detection of the position and movement of both eyes. After calibration, the participant was presented once with the tasks that appear below:

- Search Experiment: Static perception type: they were presented with a drawn image, with defined lines, in which a cityscape is observed, with a variety of situations. The instruction given was: "Observe the word that is being named, when you locate it say: done." They were asked to locate five words, which were police, traffic light, children playing, pink dress, and cinema.
- Tracking Experiment 1: Static perception type: a color image of a kitchen was presented, drawn with defined lines, in which various animated characters (lady cooking, children studying) and inanimate objects (box, rabbit, drawer, shelf, dishwasher), and a considerable amount of additional details are shown. In this image, free exploration was allowed for 30 s.
- Tracking Experiment 2: Static perception type: they were presented with the image: "The cookie theft" (Goodglass et al., 2000), which is part of the Boston

Test and is a typical image in language evaluation. It consists of five elements that are considered critical (lady washing, cookies, falling boy, girl, water spilling). In this image, free exploration was allowed for 30 s.

- Dynamic tracking experiment: Dynamic perception type: they were presented with a video of Pingu©, which was chosen because it does not have oral language, which could interfere with the understanding of the scene, detracting from visual perception; the video has a duration of 1 min 30 s and corresponds to a sequence of events within a house by the penguin family. In this task, they were asked to narrate what they observed in the video after watching it, and the audios were recorded using a Sony ICD-BX140 digital recorder. In the video, four areas of interest (AoI) were selected, which correspond to actions expressed in verbs with different frequencies calculated from the Spanish Corpus (Davies, 2014), the verbs and their frequency were: play (1656), read (3001), assemble (269), breastfeed (8). The first three verbs are frequent in Spanish, being transitive verbs (that require a direct object), and the last verb with a low frequency is intransitive.

## *Data Analysis*

Eye movements were recorded by the Eye Tracker Tobii Tx300 and were analyzed using the Tobii Studio software through identification of areas of interest (AoI) (an area of interest is a part of the image that is considered relevant and that is susceptible to analysis) (Sharafi et al., 2015), heat maps, and gaze plot graphs.

The areas of interest identified for each image are summarized in Table 1.

The data recorded by the Tobii Studio software were transcribed into a database in Excel for subsequent analysis in the SPSS 17.0 program. Comparisons of means between the groups (EA and control) for the different tasks applied were made. These comparisons were made with the nonparametric Mann-Whitney U test for independent samples, with a significance level (alpha) of 0.05. Similarly, to assess possible relationships, the nonparametric Spearman correlation test was used.

The audio data was transcribed orthographically and they were coded following the parameters of the SALT© Software (Systematic Analysis of Language Transcripts) (Miller & Iglesias, 2012) as markers were identified: number of words produced, number of sentences, abandoned sentences, MLU (which is a measure mainly used in children but aims to present the average length of sentences produced), the type token ratio (Fergadiotis et al., 2013), which is an index that indicates lexical diversity through the relationship between the number of words and the number of different words; this indicates when speech is empty, with a high presence of circumlocutions, connectors, and fillers and the Fillers that correspond to fillers, additional expressions to language.

**Table 1** Areas of interest (AoI) identified in each of the images

| Stimulus | AoI | Task |
|---|---|---|
| Image 1: "City" |  | Search task: police, traffic light, children playing, pink dress, cinema. |
| Image 2: "Kitchen" | 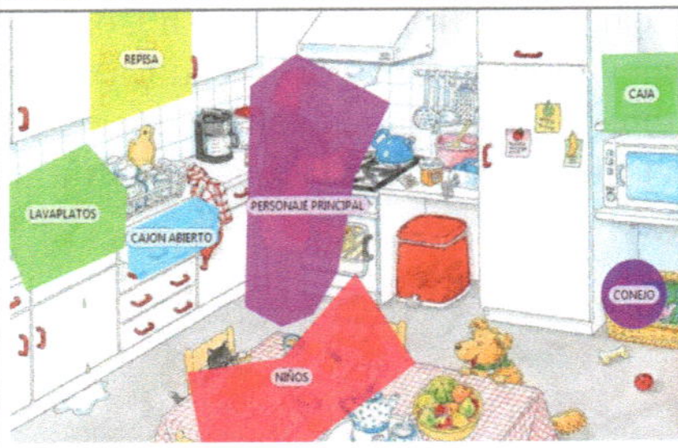 | Animated and inanimate areas of interest were identified, which were: main character (lady cooking), children, box, rabbit, dishwasher, shelf. |
| Image 3: "The theft of the cookies" | 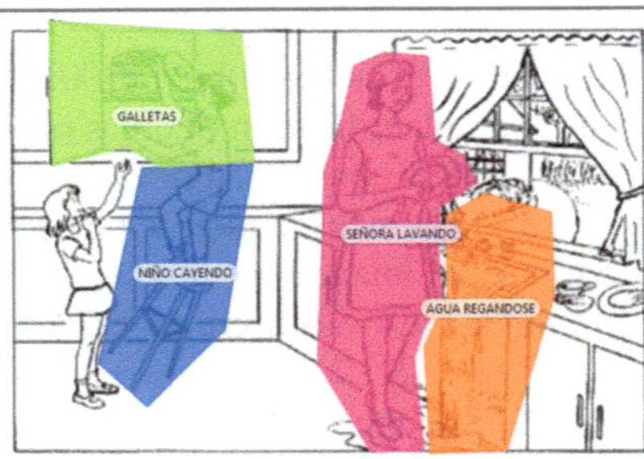 | Areas of interest that are traditionally taken into account to evaluate language narration through this image from the Boston test: lady washing, cookies, child falling, water being sprinkled. |
| Video: |  | Areas of interest in movement were identified which correspond to the actions that can be identified in the dynamic scene: reading, sliding, nursing, and assembling. |

## Results

In Table 2 the sociodemographic characteristics of the sample are described. No significant differences were found in the variables age and years of schooling; in the MLU there is a significant difference indicating cognitive function deterioration in the group with AD.

In Table 3 the results of the search experiment are shown in which the participant had to fix their gaze on an area of interest (AOI) that was verbally indicated to them. It is found that the group with AD differs significantly from the controls in terms of time to first fixation, performing the search process more effectively.

In Table 4 the results of the visual tracking of Images 2 and 3 are presented, in which they had 30 s to perform a free exploration. A significant difference is evident in image 2, "kitchen," in which the AD group identified fewer elements (of the seven marked) than their controls, in contrast with image 3, "the cookie theft," in which there is no significant difference in terms of the number of elements perceived between the two groups.

In Table 5, the results of the linguistic transcription of the narration from the dynamic scene (video) are summarized. The control group shows superior performance in linguistic expression, and statistically significant differences are evident in all chosen variables.

To observe the possible relationships between visual tasks and the analysis of linguistic production, a Spearman correlation was proposed in which a significant correlation is observed in the MOCA scores against the MLU, the fillers, the number of sentences, abandoned phrases, the number of words, verbs and arguments (Table 6).

Upon observing the heat maps of Fig. 1, it is evident that in the event of the kitchen in general, the control group perceives more details, fixing their gaze on them, than the AD group. In the "cookie theft" plate, the controls focus their attention more clearly on the agents than on the elements on which the action falls; the

**Table 2** Sociodemographic characteristics

| Variable | Alzheimer's Group | Control Group |
|---|---|---|
| Age | 76 (5.38) | 74.85 (7.1) |
| MoCa score | 13.57 (4.23) | 27.42 (1.71)* |
| Years of education | 9 (5.38) | 12.8 (3.9) |

*Note.* Score in means, standard deviation in parentheses. $*p < 0.05$

**Table 3** Results measure time to first fixation in search task

| Image | AoI | Alzheimer's Group | Control Group | U of Mann–Whitney |
|---|---|---|---|---|
| Image 1 "city" Experiment 1 Search task | Police | 5.1429(1.5735) | 0.6843(0.5245) | 0* |
| | Cinema | 26.0729(5.0062) | 13.1471(2.8602) | 0.0* |

*Note.* Results in means, standard deviations in parentheses. $*p < 0.05$

**Table 4** Number of areas of interest (AoI) in which they made fixation

| Image | Alzheimer's Group | Control Group | U of Mann–Whitney |
|---|---|---|---|
| Image 2<br>"Kitchen"<br>(7 AOI) | 4.0000(1.2909) | 6.2857(0.75593) | 2* |
| Image 3<br>"The cookie theft"<br>(4 AOI) | 3.8571(0.3779) | 4.0000(0.0000) | 21 |

*Note.* Results in means, standard deviations in parentheses. *$p < 0.05$

**Table 5** Linguistic transcription data

| Variable | Alzheimer's Group | Control Group | U of Mann–Whitney |
|---|---|---|---|
| MLU | 5.0486(1.43574) | 8.6129(1.58284) | 2* |
| Words | 15.8571(4.0590) | 48.4286(19.1994) | 1 * |
| Sentences | 5.571471(3.71612) | 13.4286(2.4397) | 1 * |
| Verbs | 5.8571(5.1777) | 20.7143(9.5169) | 2* |
| Arguments | 5.1429(5.8431) | 18.7143(4.3861) | 3* |
| Abandoned phrases | 3.7143(1.38013) | 1.1429(0.89974) | 1.5* |
| Type token | 0.7786(0.11782) | 0.6157(0.4392) | 6* |
| Fillers | 4.5714(1.2724) | 2.2857(1.4960) | 5.5* |

*Note.* Results in means, standard deviations in parentheses. *$p < 0.05$

**Table 6** Spearman correlations between linguistic and visual variables

| Variables | MoCa | Number of AoI | Time of fixation to breastfeed | Time of fixation to assemble | Time of fixation to slide | Time of fixation to read |
|---|---|---|---|---|---|---|
| MoCa | | 0.32<br>(0.295) | −0.545*<br>(0.044) | −0.299<br>(0.299) | −0.459<br>(0.098) | −0.302<br>(0.294) |
| MLU | 0.734**<br>(0.003) | 0.318<br>(0.267) | −0.361<br>(0.204) | −0.259<br>(0.372) | −0.207<br>(0.478) | −0.268<br>(0.355) |
| Type token | −0.450<br>(0.106) | −00.284<br>(0.326) | 0.032<br>(0.912) | 0.294<br>(0.307) | −0.352<br>(0.216) | 0.300<br>(0.298) |
| Fillers | −0.699**<br>(0.005) | −0.134<br>(0.648) | 0.481<br>(0.082) | 0.123<br>(0.676) | 0.576*<br>(0.031) | 0.131<br>(0.656) |
| Number of phrases | 0.753**<br>(0.002) | 0.439<br>(0.116) | −0.634*<br>(0.015) | −0.463<br>(0.096) | −0.376<br>(0.185) | −0.471<br>(0.089) |
| Abandoned phrases | −0.823**<br>(0.000) | −0.137<br>(0.640) | 0.495<br>(0.072) | 0.137<br>(0.640) | 0.590*<br>(0.026) | 0.138<br>(0.639) |
| Number of words | 0.776**<br>(0.001) | 0.220<br>(0.451) | −0.387<br>(0.172) | −0.223<br>(0.444) | −0.296<br>(304) | −0.228<br>(0.433) |
| Verbs | 0.799**<br>(0.001) | 0.253<br>(0.384) | −0.423<br>(0.131) | −0.238<br>(0.412) | −0.332<br>(0.247) | −0.246<br>(0.396) |
| Arguments | 0.813**<br>(0.000) | 0.434<br>(0.121) | −0.623*<br>(0.017) | −0.427<br>(0.127) | −0.399<br>(0.158) | −0.441<br>(0.115) |

*Note.* Level of significance in parentheses. *$p < 0.05$. **$p < 0.01$

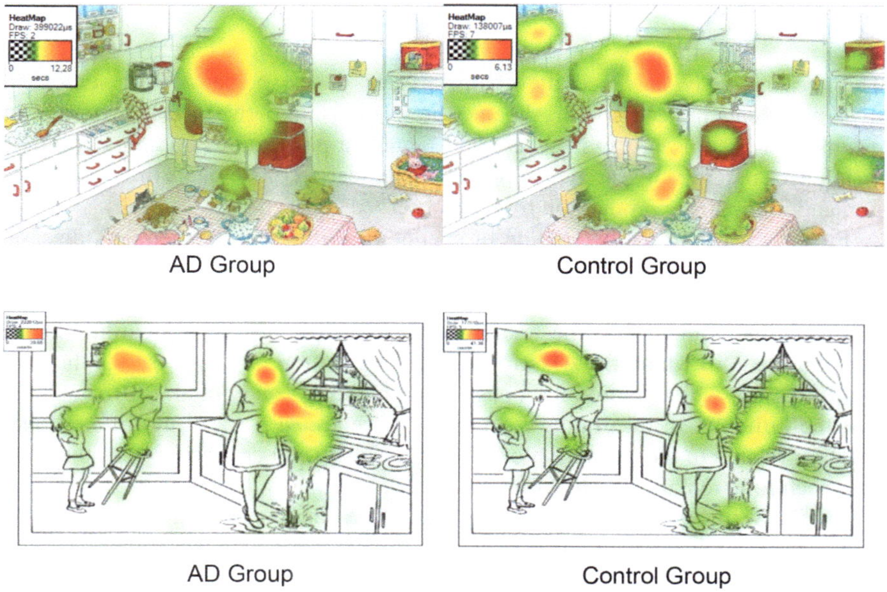


**Fig. 1** Heat map comparison of fixations between groups

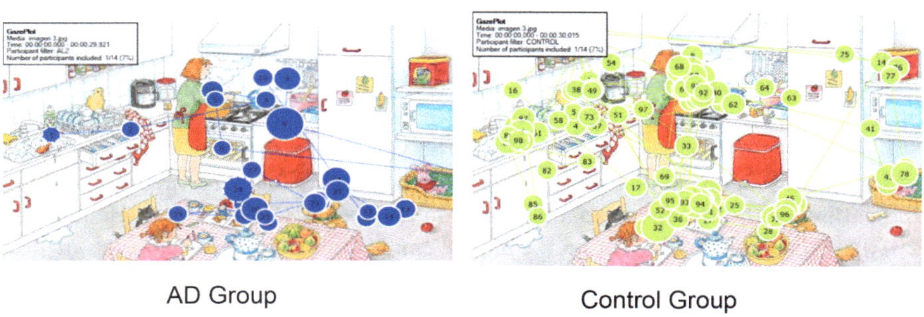


**Fig. 2** Example of fixation path in the control group and EA group (gaze plot)

controls look longer at the hands than the face of the main character; that is, they give more importance to the action (verb) than to the subject (noun).

In Fig. 2, the gaze plot is observed as an example of the visual path in which a subject with AD is compared against their age- and education-matched control. In this case, a more extensive and detailed visual path with a greater number of fixations is observed in the control subject.

## Discussion

The present study analyzed the characteristics of the perception of static and dynamic events in people with AD, and the relationship between the perception of events (how people process scenes) and language production, finding significant differences in terms of search parameters, identification of elements in visual tracking, and in linguistic production from an observed event.

Firstly, regarding the perception of events in people with Alzheimer's disease, most studies reported a longer fixation duration and less systematic exploration during visual perception (Mosimann et al., 2004). This is reaffirmed by what was evidenced in experiment 2 in the tracking task regarding the areas identified in the kitchen image in which the AD group focused attention on fewer details than the control group, who explored the image more broadly. Landy et al. (2015) express that the difficulty in integrating features of a scene and associating different elements is related to the disruption of connections between cortical regions that process each function affected in AD (Landy et al., 2015).

Similarly, in experiment 2, with the "kitchen" stimulus, in the form of observation, significant differences are evidenced between people with Alzheimer's disease and controls. Generally, patients focused attention predominantly on the main scene of the image, leaving aside the details that were perceived largely due to the controls; the heat map shows these differences. According to the research, this can be related to the ability to identify a successful exploration strategy (Boucart, Bubbico, et al., 2014; Boucart, Calais, et al., 2014).

The previous results support the hypothesis of Henderson (2003), who claims that people generally fix their gaze on the objects of a scene more than on the empty space. Likewise, there is a correlation between the place of preference of the gaze and the semantic relevance of the object. The viewers prefer to fix their gaze in the center of the objects. In this way, an exploration is carried out with predominance in the entities with greater relevance present in the scenes (Nuthmann & Henderson, 2010). These gaze paths, through eye movements, are related to the type of task being developed (search or tracking) and similarly interact with short-term memory, with semantic information, world knowledge, and objects (Hayhoe & Ballard, 2005; Vo & Henderson, 2009). In one of the tasks presented when showing them an image with different elements, the two study groups preferred the observation of animated elements (lady cooking, children) and, secondly, other objects and details of the image, in which a greater number of areas of interest detected for the control group, with a statistically significant difference in the kitchen image.

The models of visual exploration, that is, the sequence of fixations and saccadic movements, are crucial for perception (Mosimann et al., 2004). The aspects that explain the gaze path in the images used within this study have to do with the fact that all of them appear scenes that follow the regularities of the real world, do not have errors associated with the coherence of events, and the presence of inappropriate objects in the same, which allows observers to have knowledge about the scheme of the image and have prior information about what they observe (e.g., kitchens usually have stoves), in spatial categories and world knowledge categories (e.g., dishes do not float in the air); this is according to Schyns and Oliva, whose research accounts for how information is retrieved from an image immediately from the knowledge of the schemes (Schyns & Oliva, 1994).

As for the visual search task, different skills are intertwined. The parietal cortex is involved, which includes attention processes and integration of the information that is perceived (Hao et al., 2005; Tales et al., 2002); among the related skills highlighted is working memory, which can control visual attention in the search task (Huettig et al., 2011), and the ability to inhibit stimuli, or the integration of different characteristics of an object; particularly, according to these characteristics the search time can be longer if there is a deterioration (Tales et al., 2002).

In the search task for the purposes of this research, simple orders and known words were used. The objective corresponded to a visually relevant element in the image and of unique function, which means that there were no distractor objects of similar characteristics; the above facilitates the performance of people with Alzheimer's disease. However, as illustrated in Table 2, the control group found the object they had to identify within the image more quickly; in this regard, Foster et al. (1999), as well as Tales et al. (2002), report similar results in which people with Alzheimer's disease manage to perform single search tasks with increased latency; other research reports that in single search the reaction time is generally slower compared to people who do not manifest this pathology (Hao et al., 2005; Landy et al., 2015; Tales et al., 2002).

Among the results found for the image "The Theft of the Cookies" (Goodglass & Kaplan, 1996), it can be said that fixations are closely linked to the encoding of memory, both for short-term memory (Hollingworth & Henderson, 2002) and long-term memory (Nelson & Loftus, 1980); in the same way it is also related to the understanding and production of language (Ferreira & Tanenhaus, 2007; Griffin & Bock, 2000; Tanenhaus et al., 1995). Thus the differences were not significant in the perception of this image since both groups had similar performances identifying visually the critical elements. In this regard, the difficulty lies when the person is asked to express what was observed since, despite having focused their attention in that area, they do not manage to integrate it into short-term memory and encode it into a linguistic message that can be expressed.

Current theories do not specify how visual attention is guided by linguistic representations. The models predict that the interaction between language and visual attention is subject to conditions such as working memory, processing capacity, and cognitive control mechanisms.

Regarding language and its relationship with the perception of events, this observation allows to analyze aspects related to the understanding of language online, that is, to identify the relevant information for understanding, taking into account both informational and temporal aspects (Knoeferle & Crocker, 2006).

From a dynamic event (in motion) it was shown that within a linguistic task in which a scene had to be described, people with Alzheimer's disease name fewer actions, and even some of them do not manage to tell anything about what was observed, in the event in motion (Table 5), this may be due to the fact that short-term memory constitutes a link between the information perceived visually and the linguistic expressions so that when it is affected, the productions are affected (Huettig et al., 2011).

The linguistic results from the observation of the dynamic event show significant differences in terms of the following variables: MLU, number of words, number of sentences, number of verbs, and type token. This indicates that the productions of people with AD are significantly shorter, with fewer verbs and empty speech is evident in most of them. In this case, the influence of the integration of the elements of an image can be identified. Perceptually, working memory and language organization. According to Mosimann et al. (2004), the loss of exploration strategy and a longer fixation duration can put patients with Alzheimer's disease at a disadvantage for many daily tasks associated with the demand for visual exploration. Similarly, understanding how people with this pathology perceive the world is a step forward in new forms of diagnosis and intervention.

In line with the research on this matter by Fernández et al. (2014), even in the early stages of the disease, patients with AD showed a marked change in the pattern of eye movements, compared with control individuals. This suggests that the analysis of eye movements could provide new insights into the pathogenesis of AD, suggesting a promising field of research to contribute with an additional minimally invasive tool, useful for an early clinical diagnosis (Fernández et al., 2014).

## *Clinical Implications*

Intervention in neurodegenerative pathologies that directly or indirectly affect language, and therefore communication is a field of action that especially involves the speech therapist, their evaluation in the framework of an interdisciplinary team, and the intervention to promote the communicative well-being of the person become a priority. For this, the way in which people with AD especially perceive the world must be taken into account. One of the contributions is that it has been identified that in AD, performances in terms of the ability to detect movement remain the same as the control group; this can contribute in terms of being beneficial for the evaluation to include dynamic scenes in addition to static ones.

Regarding the use of the image "The Cookie Theft," which is part of the Boston Test for the diagnosis of aphasia (Goodglass & Kaplan, 1996), in the present study, this stimulus did not present significant differences in terms of tracking parameters compared to the control group which would provide evidence to limit its use in the evaluation of the language of this population and other neurodegenerative pathologies.

## Conclusions

Differences are evident in the way subjects with AD perceive events. These differences include an increase in the detection time in search tasks, fewer fixations and the nondetection of all the elements of a scene in the AD group. Similarly, differences are observed in dynamic perception compared to static. In dynamic perception both groups had similar performances in terms of the perception of the central actions.

The differential patterns in the perception of scenes indicate difficulties in understanding the events that are reflected in the language production since, despite observing all the elements of an image, the linguistic production is different. Regarding the production of verbs, the AD group produces them in smaller quantity, and in the same way the number of verbal arguments is reduced in the same proportion.

The present study also showed that the quantitative evaluation of visual perception is well tolerated by patients and viable for Alzheimer's disease, which opens the doors for new research through the Tobii eye tracker or other eye-tracking devices. In the future it would be very interesting and relevant to study people with mild cognitive impairment MCI and observe if there are differential patterns that can contribute to establishing early predictors of AD.

**Acknowledgments** To the people who participated in this study and their families for their willingness, to the Neuroscience Research Group and the Human Communication Center of the National University who facilitated contact with the participants. This study was funded by the Research Seedbeds Call of the Faculty of Medicine of the National University of Colombia (Behavioral Neuroscience Research Seedbed Hermes Code 21880 and QUIPU Code: 201010023351).

## References

Albert, M. S., DeKosky, S. T., Dickson, D., Dubois, B., Feldman, H. H., Fox, N. C., Gamst, A., Holtzman, D. M., Jagust, W. J., Petersen, R. C., Snyder, P. J., Carrillo, M. C., Thies, B., & Phelps, C. H. (2011). The diagnosis of mild cognitive impairment due to Alzheimer's disease: Recommendations from the National Institute on Aging-Alzheimer's association workgroups on diagnostic guidelines for Alzheimer's disease. *Alzheimers and Dementia, 7*(3), 270–279. https://doi.org/10.1016/j.jalz.2011.03.008

Armstrong, R. A. (2009). Alzheimer's disease and the eye. *Journal of Optometry, 2*(3), 103–111. https://doi.org/10.3921/joptom.2009.103

Boucart, M., Bubbico, G., Szaffarczyk, S., & Pasquier, F. (2014). Animal spotting in Alzheimer's disease: An eye tracking study of object categorization. *Journal of Alzheimer's Disease, 39*(1), 181–189. https://doi.org/10.3233/jad-131331

Boucart, M., Calais, G., Lenoble, Q., Moroni, C., & Pasquier, F. (2014). Differential processing of natural scenes in typical and atypical Alzheimer disease measured with a saccade choice task [Original research]. *Frontiers in Integrative Neuroscience, 8*, 60. https://doi.org/10.3389/fnint.2014.00060

Davies, M. (2014). *Corpus Español.* https://www.corpusdelespanol.org/x.asp

Fergadiotis, G., Wright, H. H., & West, T. M. (2013). Measuring lexical diversity in narrative discourse of people with aphasia. *American Journal of Speech-Language Pathology/American Speech-Language-Hearing Association, 22*(2), S397. https://doi.org/10.1044/1058-0360(2013/12-0083)

Fernández, G., Laubrock, J., Mandolesi, P., Colombo, O., & Agamennoni, O. (2014). Registering eye movements during reading in Alzheimer's disease: Difficulties in predicting upcoming words. *Journal of Clinical & Experimental Neuropsychology, 36*(3), 302. https://doi.org/10.1080/13803395.2014.892060

Fernández, G., Schumacher, M., Castro, L., Orozco, D., & Agamennoni, O. (2015). Patients with mild Alzheimer's disease produced shorter outgoing saccades when reading sentences. *Psychiatry Research, 229*(1–2), 470–478. https://doi.org/10.1016/j.psychres.2015.06.028

Ferreira, F., & Tanenhaus, M. K. (2007). Introduction to the special issue on language-vision interactions. *Journal of Memory and Language, 57*(4), 455–459. https://doi.org/10.1016/j.jml.2007.08.002

Foster, J. K., Behrmann, M., & Stuss, D. T. (1999). Visual attention deficits in Alzheimer's disease: Simple versus conjoined feature search. *Neuropsychology, 13*(2), 223–245. https://doi.org/10.1037/0894-4105.13.2.223

Fujimori, M., Imamura, T., Yamashita, H., Hirono, N., & Mori, E. (1997). The disturbances of object vision and spatial vision in Alzheimer's disease. *Dementia and Geriatric Cognitive Disorders, 8*(4), 228–231. https://doi.org/10.1159/000106635

Goodglass, H., & Kaplan, E. (1996). *Test de Boston para el diagnóstico de la afasia*. Editorial Médica Panamericana.

Goodglass, H., Kaplan, E., & Barresi, B. (2000). *Boston diagnostic aphasia examination: Short form*. Lippincott Williams & Wilkins.

Grady, C. L., Furey, M. L., Pietrini, P., Horwitz, B., & Rapoport, S. I. (2001). Altered brain functional connectivity and impaired short-term memory in Alzheimer's disease. *Brain, 124*(4), 739–756. https://doi.org/10.1093/brain/124.4.739

Griffin, Z. M., & Bock, K. (2000). What the eyes say about speaking. *Psychological Science, 11*(4), 274–279. https://psycnet.apa.org/doi/10.1111/1467-9280.00255

Hao, J., Li, K., Li, K., Zhang, D., Wang, W., Yang, Y., Yan, B., Shan, B., & Zhou, X. (2005). Visual attention deficits in Alzheimer's disease: An fMRI study. *Neuroscience Letters, 385*(1), 18–23. https://doi.org/10.1016/j.neulet.2005.05.028

Hayhoe, M., & Ballard, D. (2005). Eye movements in natural behavior. *Trends in Cognitive Science, 9*(4), 188–194. https://doi.org/10.1016/j.tics.2005.02.009

Henderson, J. M. (2003). Human gaze control during real-world scene perception. *Trends in Cognitive Sciences, 7*(11), 498–504. https://doi.org/10.1016/j.tics.2003.09.006

Hof, P. R., & Bouras, C. (1991). Object recognition deficit in Alzheimer's disease: Possible disconnection of the occipitotemporal component of the visual system. *Neuroscience Letters, 122*(1), 53–56. https://doi.org/10.1016/0304-3940(91)90191-U

Hollingworth, A., & Henderson, J. (2002). Accurate visual memory for previously attended objects in natural scenes. *Journal of Experimental Psychology: Human Perception & Performance, 28*, 113–136. https://doi.org/10.1037/0096-1523.28.1.113

Huettig, F., Olivers, C. N. L., & Hartsuiker, R. J. (2011). Looking, language, and memory: Bridging research from the visual world and visual search paradigms. *Acta Psychologica, 137*(2), 138–150. https://doi.org/10.1016/j.actpsy.2010.07.013

Just, M. A., & Carpenter, P. A. (1976). Eye fixations and cognitive processes. *Cognitive Psychology, 8*(4), 441–480. https://doi.org/10.1016/0010-0285(76)90015-3

Karatekin, C. (2007). Eye tracking studies of normative and atypical development. *Developmental Review, 27*(3), 283–348. https://doi.org/10.1016/j.dr.2007.06.006

Knoeferle, P., & Crocker, M. W. (2006). The coordinated interplay of scene, utterance, and world knowledge: Evidence from eye tracking. *Cognitive Science, 30*(3), 481–529. https://doi.org/10.1207/s15516709cog0000_65

Landy, K., Salmon, D., Filoteo, V., Heindel, W., Galasko, D., & Hamilton, J. (2015). Visual search in dementia with lewy bodies and Alzheimer's disease. *Cortex, 73*, 228–239. https://doi.org/10.1016/j.cortex.2015.08.020

Miller, J., & Iglesias, A. (2012). *Systematic analysis of language transcripts (SALT)*. Middleton.

Miranda-Castillo, C., Mascayano Tapia, F., Roa Herrera, A., Maray Ghigliotto, F., & Serraino Guerra, L. (2013). Implementación de un programa de estimulación cognitiva en personas con demencia tipo Alzheimer: Un estudio piloto en chilenos de la tercera edad. *Universitas Psychologica, 12*(2), 445–455. https://doi.org/10.11144/Javeriana.upsy12-2.ipec

Mosimann, U. P., Felblinger, J., Ballinari, P., Hess, C. W., & Müri, R. M. (2004). Visual exploration behaviour during clock reading in Alzheimer's disease. *Brain, 127*(2), 431–438. https://doi.org/10.1093/brain/awh051

Nasreddine, Z. S., Phillips, N. A., Bédirian, V., Charbonneau, S., Whitehead, V., Collin, I., Cummings, J., & Chertkow, H. (2005). The Montreal Cognitive Assessment, MoCA: A brief screening tool for mild cognitive impairment. *Journal of the American Geriatrics Society, 53*(4), 695–699. https://doi.org/10.1111/j.1532-5415.2005.53221.x

Nelson, W., & Loftus, G. (1980). The functional visual field during picture viewing. *Journal of Experimental Psychology Human Learning and Memory, 6*, 391–399. https://pubmed.ncbi.nlm.nih.gov/7391754/

Nuthmann, A., & Henderson, J. M. (2010). Object-based attentional selection in scene viewing. *Journal of Vision, 10*(8), 20–20. https://doi.org/10.1167/10.8.20

Pradilla, G., Vesga, B., Leon-Sarmiento, F., & Geneco, G. (2003). Estudio neuroepidemiologico en Colombia. *Revista Panamericana de Salud Pública, 14*, 104–111. https://doi.org/10.4067/S0034-98872002000200009

Reisberg, B., Ferris, S. H., de Leon, M. J., & Crook, T. (1982). The global deterioration scale for assessment of primary degenerative dementia. *The American Journal of Psychiatry, 139*(9), 1136–1139. https://doi.org/10.1176/ajp.139.9.1136

Rizzo, M., Anderson, S. W., Dawson, J., & Nawrot, M. (2000). Vision and cognition in Alzheimer's disease. *Neuropsychologia, 38*(8), 1157–1169. https://doi.org/10.1016/S0028-3932(00)00023-3

Schyns, P. G., & Oliva, A. (1994). From blobs to boundary edges: Evidence for time- and spatial-scale-dependent scene recognition. *Psychological Science, 5*(4), 195–200. https://doi.org/10.1111/j.1467-9280.1994.tb00500.x

Serra, M. (2013). *Comunicación y lenguaje. La nueva neuropsicología cognitiva, I*. Universitat de Barcelona, Publicacions i Edicions.

Sharafi, Z., Soh, Z., & Guéhéneuc, Y. G. (2015). A systematic literature review on the usage of eye-tracking in software engineering. *Information and Software Technology, 67*, 79–107. https://doi.org/10.1016/j.infsof.2015.06.008

Tales, A., Butler, S. R., Fossey, J., Gilchrist, I. D., Jones, R. W., & Troscianko, T. (2002). Visual search in Alzheimer's disease: A deficiency in processing conjunctions of features. *Neuropsychologia, 40*(12), 1849–1857. https://doi.org/10.1016/S0028-3932(02)00073-8

Tanenhaus, M. K., Spivey-Knowlton, M. J., Eberhard, K. M., & Sedivy, J. C. (1995). Integration of visual and linguistic information in spoken language comprehension. *Science, 268*(5217), 1632–1634. https://doi.org/10.1126/science.7777863

Valenti, D. A. (2010). Alzheimer's disease: Visual system review. *Optometry – Journal of the American Optometric Association, 81*(1), 12–21. https://doi.org/10.1016/j.optm.2009.04.101

Vo, M., & Henderson, J. (2009). Does gravity matter? Effects of semantic and syntactic inconsistencies on the allocation of attention during scene perception. *Journal of Vision, 9*(3), 24–24. https://doi.org/10.1167/9.3.24

Wang, Q., Yang, S., Liu, M., Cao, Z., & Qingguo, M. (2014). An eye-tracking study of website complexity from cognitive load perspective. *Decision Support Systems, 62*, 1–10. https://doi.org/10.1016/j.dss.2014.02.007

# Index





W. López-López et al. (eds.), *Trends in Latin American Psychology*,
https://doi.org/10.1007/978-3-031-87554-0

MIX
Papier aus verantwortungsvollen Quellen
Paper from responsible sources
FSC® C105338

If you have any concerns about our products,
you can contact us on
**ProductSafety@springernature.com**

In case Publisher is established outside the EU,
the EU authorized representative is:
**Springer Nature Customer Service Center GmbH**
**Europaplatz 3, 69115 Heidelberg, Germany**

Printed by Libri Plureos GmbH
in Hamburg, Germany